Butterflies
Will Burn

Butterflies Will Burn

Prosecuting Sodomites in Early Modern Spain and Mexico

Federico Garza Carvajal

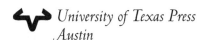 University of Texas Press
Austin

Library of Congress Cataloging-in-Publication Data
Garza Carvajal, Federico.
    Butterflies will burn : prosecuting sodomites in early modern
Spain and Mexico / Federico Garza Carvajal.
        p.   cm.
Revised and updated edition. Originally published in 2000, by
the University of Amsterdam, under title: Vir : perceptions of
manliness in Andalucía and México 1561–1699.
Includes bibliographical references and index.

    ISBN 978-0-292-70221-9 (pbk. : alk. paper)

    1. Men—Spain—Andalusia—History.   2. Men—
Spain—Andalusia—History.   3. Masculinity—Mexico—
History.   4. Masculinity—Mexico—History.   5. Trials
(Sodomy)—Spain—Andalusia—History.   6. Trials
(Sodomy)—Mexico—History   7. Sex role. I. Title:
Prosecuting sodomites in early modern Spain and Mexico.
II.   Garza Carvajal, Federico. Vir.   III. Title.
    HQ1090.7.S7G37   2003
    305.31'0946'8—dc21

                                                      2003007724

For~
    my parents, María P. Carvajal[†] and Federico G. Garza

For~
    Javier del Río

Tierra-Piedra-Adoquín.
Textura-Variado.
Firmeza-Solidez.
Caliente.

Sentido del tacto, muy variado.
Ves lo que es, lo sientes.
Deja huella, marca.
Te puedes apoyar, es estable.
Se proyectan las cosas, las sombras.
La tierra gira y da vueltas, y vueltas, y vueltas . . .

JOSÉ IGNACIO LUCIO PÉREZ,
Notes for *Portarretrato Ocre 1/2*

CONTENTS

LIST OF ILLUSTRATIONS

NOTES ON TRANSLATION
AND TRANSCRIPTION

I have adopted the following convention for the use of the word "sodomy." When the word is in the context of a theoretical discussion, I use the French *"sodomie."* When the word is linked to a Spanish archival source, or when the discussion that follows seems to flow from such a source, I use *"sodomía"* or *"sodomías."* On the other hand, when the word forms part of the ordinary text, I use "sodomy."

Likewise, I have adopted a number of historically traditional conventions for the Spanish transcriptions. Unless noted otherwise, I transcribed and translated all the contents of the archival documents that make up this study. When I quoted directly from an archival source, I use the original Spanish name or spelling. When a word forms part of the ordinary text, I employed modern-day Spanish rules of grammar. As a matter of my own proper style, I did not translate Spanish proper names or names of places into the English.

ABBREVIATIONS

AGI   Archivo General de Indias, Seville

AGN   Archivo General de la Nación, Mexico City

AGS   Archivo General de Simancas

AHN   Archivo Histórico Nacional, Madrid

AMS   Archivo Municipal de Sevilla

ARCV   Archivo Real Chancillería, Valladolid

BCV   Bibliothèque de la Casa de Velázquez, Madrid

BFT   Biblioteca de la Facultad de Teología, Burgos

BLAC   Benson Latin American Collection, University of Texas at Austin

BN   Biblioteca Nacional de Madrid

BNS   Bibliotheek Nederlands Scheepvartmuseum, Amsterdam

BR   Bibliotheek Rosenthaliana, Universiteit van Amsterdam

BRAH   Biblioteca de la Real Academia de la Historia, Madrid

BUG   Biblioteca de la Universidad de Granada

BUS   Biblioteca de la Universidad de Salamanca

CEDLA   Centre for Latin American Research and Documentation, Amsterdam

PKB   PreuBischer Kulturbesitz Bibliothek, Ibero-Amerikanisches Institut, Berlin

ACKNOWLEDGMENTS

I extend my heartfelt gratitude to Theresa May, editor-in-chief of the University of Texas Press. Her keen insight and perseverance have enabled me to publish this book.

The original book, titled *VIR: Perceptions of Manliness in Andalucía and México, 1561–1699*, received staunch and unwavering support from Leo Noordegraaf and Arij Ouweneel, history professors at the Universiteit van Amsterdam. Leo read the initial proposal and the subsequent chapter drafts with interest and wholeheartedly understood my claim to write a different sort of history. He also provided me with all the necessary papers to placate the university and governmental bureaucracies in the Netherlands. Subsequently, Leo secured the funding for the initial publication of this work.

Arij, for his part, accommodated my stay at the UvA's Centre for Latin American Research and Documentation (CEDLA). Over the last years, he read through even the most mundane folios I presented him with—always eagerly and in a timely way. His ability and desire to venture beyond demarcated epochs and entrenched academic paradigms or disciplines have enriched the scope of my writing. In both Leo and Arij, I have found two astute mentors and two good friends.

For the current edition, I have completely rewritten the prologue, chapters 1 and 2, the epilogue, and the appendices. Chapters 3 and 4 were also partially revised. Mary Elizabeth Perry, David William Foster, William B. Taylor, Ramón A. Gutiérrez, Pete Sigal, James N. Green, and two anonymous readers generously provided me with useful tips for the revisions and publication in the United States.

Additional advice for this revised edition also transcended academic disciplines. This was evident in the kind words of encouragement expressed to me by Rebeca Siegel, Asunción Lavrín, Emilie L. Bergmann, Paul Julian Smith, Anthony J. Cascardi, Norma Alarcón, Margaret Chowning, Nicholas Spadaccini, Gregory S. Hutcheson, Alain Saint-Saëns, Serge Gruzinski, Pamela Voekel, Eric Zinner, Nikki Craske, Moshé Sluhovsky, Luis Marentes, Elisa Servín, Verónica Grossi, Eduardo

Archetti, David Montejano, Susan Deans-Smith, Solange Alberro, Sandra Lauderdale Graham, Mari Carmen Ramírez, Rita Cano Alcalá, Raúl Villa, Jeffrey Merrick, Teófilo Ruiz, Jesús Escobar, Jodi Bilinkoff, Carolyn Boyd, Josiah Blackmore, Barbara Weissberger, Richard Kagan, David Nirenberg, John D'Emilio, David Higgs, Pilar Cuder Domínguez, Pablo E. Pérez-Mallaína, Pedro Pérez Herrero, Carlos Baztán LaCasa, and Eduardo Suárez, the chief editor at Laertes who published the Spanish edition of this book.

My gratitude also extends to those who read, critiqued, or edited portions or all of the original manuscript: Geert Banck, Harm Den Boer, Brucht Pranger, Mattijs Van de Port, María José Ramírez Ramírez, Gery Nijenhuis, Theo van der Meer, Alan Bray, Kees Smit Sibinga, Margot Morshuis, Florine Boucher, Rob Aitken, Alfredo Leewis, Rebeca Siegel, Susan Eckstein, Standish Meacham, Santiago Hernández, Rafael Carrasco, Andrés Moreno Mengíbar, Jorge González Aragón, Ana Morales, Koldo J. Garai, Jaime del Val, and Javier del Río.

I'm especially indebted to Rosemary Wetherold, who meticulously edited this current edition. Her penchant for clarity undoubtedly enhanced its contents. Additionally, Lynne Chapman at the University of Texas Press has worked diligently to ensure the manuscript's timely publication.

The staff at CEDLA, in particular, María José Ramírez Ramírez, Jolanda Van de Boom, Hanna Berretty, Marinella Wallis, Graça de Oliveira, Patricia Dekker, and Kees den Boer attended to my endless requests with admirable expertise. Aliet Soeteman and Louise Hesp, administrative assistants at the University of Amsterdam's Faculty of the Humanities, most graciously drafted all the correspondence required by the university. I am also indebted to Lars and Bruce Hamilton Maddox; the latter is a keen philanthropist and benefactor of the original version.

The work on this manuscript began back in the early 1990s while I pursued graduate studies at the University of Texas at Austin. Laura Gutiérrez Witt, head librarian at the Benson Latin American Collection, tutored me in the art of seventeenth-century Spanish paleography. In the summer of 1991, Antonio Bolós Márquez and I took refuge from the hot Texas sun in the BLAC's Rare Books Reading Room, and we transcribed the first of the many *procesos* that have informed this study. Dennis Varela and Felipe Campos, information technology specialists at UT's College of Education, formatted the early versions of this study and succinctly resolved any computer glitches.

Upon my arrival in Amsterdam, Auke Jacobs instructed me in sixteenth-century paleography, and in the process he transcribed the 1561 *proceso* against Cristóbal and the 1562 trial of Antón de Fuentes. Cristina Gómez Gonzalo, an archivist residing in Valladolid, transcribed the court summation related to Catalina de Belunza.

María Antonia Colomar at the Archivo General de Indias in Seville identified and later put at my disposal the sodomy *procesos* already catalogued by staff archivists. Chelo Díez Ortega, María Eugenia Martín Razo, and Concha Alvarez Merino labored enthusiastically to identify other sources on *sodomie* in Andalucía and in Castilla y León. Over the past years, they have tended to all my solicitations. María Teresa Conde Carmona and Jesús Camargo Mendoza at the AGI taught me how to access the archival documents electronically. Pilar de la Fuente and Isabel Aguire at the Archivo General de Simancas, María Teresa López at the Archivo Real Chancillería in Valladolid, and Fray Candido Rubio at the Biblioteca de la Facultad de Teología in Burgos all unselfishly allowed me access to their archival holdings.

María Auxiliadora Castillo and José Luis Rodríguez at the Librería Roldana in Seville secured a number of rare books for me. Their literary breadth of knowledge is evident in the works cited. Lastly, His Excellency, Señor Duque de Segorbe, the secretary general of the Fundación Casa Ducal de Medinaceli in Seville, kindly agreed to the reproduction of Ribera's artwork.

Over the years, a number of warmhearted friends have opened up their households and hosted me as their guest. German Lizt Arzubide and Luis Mario Schneider—ardent *estridentistas*—kindly greeted my stays in Coyoacán and Mexico. Jean E. Jarosek, Jack van Est, and Katy and George Hughes have hosted my subsequent visits to Austin. In Bilbao, known now more for its Guggenheim rather than for its drab terrorism, José Lucio and Miren Begoña Arceo exposed me to the multidimensional cultural richness of the Spanish Basque state. Chelo and Jesús Díez Ortega provided me with lodging in Valladolid and fondly shared with me the delectable joys of early modern cuisine in today's Castilla y León.

I have dedicated this book to my parents, María P. and Federico, who confronted their lifetime together with sustained courage and vigor. They always shared their dedication, affection, and sense of tolerance with me and my siblings, Omar and Verónica. Regrettably in September 1999, my mother died, stricken by cancer, shortly after the initial completion of this manuscript. The fulfillment of this study drew much from the strength of my family and from the unwavering friendship of Javier, who fondly and patiently wished to understand how to confront the difficulties we met along the way.

Butterflies Will Burn is my tribute to all of them.

Ghent, July 2002

Butterflies
Will Burn

PROLOGUE

VARIED TEXTURES

Madam, language is the instrument of empire.

> Response of humanist Antonio de Nebrija upon presenting his
> Spanish grammar book in 1492 to Queen Isabel, who had asked
> what use she, who spoke Spanish already, could have for such
> a work; quoted by A. Pagden in *Spanish Imperialism and the Political
> Imagination*

LIKE MANY of his fellow contemporaries in early seventeenth-
century Seville, Fray Pedro de León believed that sodomy
constituted a sin and a crime *contra natura,* one that had been
imported from abroad and then spread like some contagious, pestilential plague—*"la lacra,"* as he often stated.[1]
In fact, wrote de León, the Lord Mayor of His Majesty's
Prison in Seville had the "brilliant foresight to imprison the sodomites
apart from the other prisoners for fear of their contamination."[2] "Very
dangerous," thought de León, "to allow two boys to lie together in bed."[3]
But the pestilential vice respected no boundaries.

One day Cristóbal Chabes, another friar who labored in the same
prison, witnessed how "an old man named Villarreal inserted a nautical
cable in the form of a robust man's member—measuring at least a third
part of a yard in length—inside his arse," thereby "reproducing the same
effect that sodomites do to other men."[4]

The prison authorities promptly accused the "filthy and dishonest"
Villarreal of having committed the "sin of pollution with himself" and
sentenced him to a public flogging. Subsequently, the unfortunate Villarreal died, not because he had indulged himself with the cable but after
the authorities flogged him to death as punishment for his depravity. As
Villarreal slowly perished, remarked de León, he "vomited his intestines
as he lay in the stench of his dregs as an example of the amount of filth
present in this wretched and pestilential vice."[5] Fray de León, renowned
for his peppery sermons in Seville, forewarned others who rollicked in
same-sex play.

Sodomites are like butterflies, professed de León. "Butterflies," tempted by the allure of a burning flame, "fly back and forth, each time getting closer and closer to the open fire." At first flight, a butterfly "flutters close to the flames and burns only a wing." But the temptation and the seductive allure of the glowing flames are too great. The butterfly "flutters yet closer and burns another little piece of its wing until eventually it is fully burned." Sodomites "who did not amend themselves, driven by the sin, just like butterflies eventually will end up in the fire and burn," assured de León.[6]

The textualization of sodomy as a sin and a crime against nature, a sort of contagious pestilential plague often imputed to be imported from abroad, and the perceptions and depictions of sodomites as vile, contemptible, even effeminate men—all constituted discourses of Spanish manliness. Early modern theologians, historiographers, and literary writers—otherwise known as *los moralistas* in the vernacular—fabricated these discourses with the intent of fomenting the politics of empire in Spain–New Spain.

In *Butterflies Will Burn*, I have attempted to interrogate the specific ideas uttered by a particular group of privileged men and women to buttress their discursive depictions of early modern Spanish manliness and, by extension, sodomy. Although a glimpse of sodomitical cultures will be garnered as this work unfolds, the focus of this study remains on those discourses that reflected Spain's perceptions of manliness and not necessarily on the historical reality of sodomites.[7] In fact, sodomy prosecutions in early modern Spain–New Spain reveal more about the "discursive acts of constructing and representing" and rather less about the "constructed or represented."[8]

Specifically, I have focused on the descriptions of sodomy that emanated from Andalusia, center of Spain's colonial undertaking, and New Spain, its first and largest viceroyalty. The archival documents and other literary production consulted for this study—described below in greater detail—cover the period between 1561, the year of the earliest sodomy prosecutions during Spain's emerging colonialist epoch, and 1699, the year that marked the death of Habsburg rule in Spain–New Spain. A number of questions are central to this study.

Why did the Spanish courts prosecute sodomites in Spain–New Spain during the early modern period, and what sort of discourses justified these prosecutions? Can one establish a link between perceptions of sodomy and notions of Spanish manliness? Did perceptions of manliness indeed intertwine themselves with Spain's imperialist-colonialist politics?

Finally, can one establish that textual perceptions of *sodomie*, of sodomites, differed in content or even changed in context in the peninsula and in the viceroyalty? In my effort to sketch an ideological portrait for my study of early modern Spanish perceptions of manliness and of sodomy, I have resorted to a kaleidoscopic mélange of epistemologies.

Postmodernism

First, I positioned my study of early modern Spanish manliness squarely within the field of postmodern theorizing and theorists—namely, Derrida, Spivak, and Ahmad—as well as historians White, Ankersmit, Hunt, and Jenkins. I also obtained the use of postcolonial criticism and its discursive protestations against major knowledges, and on behalf of minor knowledges, identified as "quintessentially political and oppositional" by Seth, Gandhi, and Dutton. For them, the paradigm of postcolonialism remains "a space for critical dissent and dissection rather than an authoritative voice of what it was to be colonialism . . . one that points not towards a new knowledge, but rather towards an examination and critique of coercive knowledge systems concomitantly, in a committed pursuit and recovery of those ways of knowing which have been occluded— or, in Foucault's vernacular, 'subjugated'—by the epistemic accidents of history."[9]

All these writers have provided us with rich imaginaries for thinking in emancipatory ways. "I am convinced," wrote Ankersmit, "that underneath the postmodernist fat the thin man really is there and that we ought to listen to him since he can tell us a lot about the historical text that we do not yet know and that the proper historian never bothered to tell us."[10] Postmodern ways of thinking have indeed signaled the end for the often more privileged metanarrative history and proper history.[11]

Metanarrative history is the consideration of the past in terms that assign objective significance to what are actually contingent events. It does this by identifying their place and function within a general schema of development. The past is used to advance a specific point of view, for example, early modern Spanish imperialism. Proper history means the disinterested study of the past for its own sake, on its own terms, as objectively and impartially as possible. It regards itself unproblematically and thus as being nonideological and nonpositioned.[12]

However, proper or traditional history, as a style of writing, is merely an ideological defense of a particularly narrow-minded professional code, for it is just as politically positioned as any other: history is always for someone. The idea of writing an objective, neutral, disinterested text, where explaining and describing something is done from a position that ostensibly isn't a position at all, is a naive one. For all these reasons, meta-narrative and traditional histories are both myopic and moribund.[13] Therefore, *Butterflies Will Burn* is conceived as an unabashedly subjective and quintessentially political interpretation of sodomy prosecutions in early modern Spain—New Spain.

Artificial Positions

Politically constructed categories such as the perfect early modern Spanish Vir (or Man), manliness, sodomy, or sodomites, as well as the representations of those histories have "no meaningful existence and truth independent of the historian" or any other representer. Representers of history attach "meaning and coherence" to their representations as they "work with gathered data and render it intelligible to themselves" and to their prospective audiences.[14]

"Description," wrote Ahmad, "is never ideologically or cognitively neutral." When one describes, one specifies a "locus of meaning," one "constructs an object of knowledge," and one "produces a knowledge that will be bound by that act of descriptive construction."[15] Derrida, pointing to the artificiality of all positions, wrote: "actuality is indeed made; it is important to know what it is made of, but it is even more necessary to recognize that it is made."[16] The past as history always has been and always will be necessarily configured, troped, emplotted, read, mythologized, and ideologized in ways to suit ourselves.[17]

White reminds one that there is "an inexpungeable relativity to every representation of historical phenomena" such that when it comes to apprehending the historical record, there are no grounds in the historical record itself for preferring one way of constructing its meaning over another.[18] Indeed, according to Ouweneel, one can only begin to "understand" the past, that is, in the form of writing or representing history, if one "can understand the present: not the whole of present-day society, but one's own position," or if one can understand, in the words of Spivak, one's "positionality or subjectivity" in that society.[19] Consequently, the historian's positionality and the subjectivity of a historical object of study indubitably contribute to one's own singular interpretation of a given epoch or figure.[20]

Nietzsche's argument that the real world has now been recognized as a fable means that it always has been and always will be the narrated and interpreted. For Ankersmit, the narrative text refers, but not to a reality outside itself, and the criteria of truth and falsity do not apply to historical representations. If one recontextualizes Marx or Nietzsche, truth emerges as nothing more than a collective lie manifested by the very sort of repression it generates and perpetuates.[21] All discourse is bound to self-referential simulacra. Like the writing of history, the idea of sodomy perceived as a crime and a sin *contra natura* was not given but actively produced; it was interpreted by a range of hierarchical and selective processes—facetious or artificial procedures—fictional devices that were subservient to various powers and interests.

The Imperial Sphere

It is clear that the past doesn't exist historically outside of historians' textual, constructive appropriations, so that history, being made by them, has no independence to resist their interpretative will. In *Butterflies Will Burn*, I have pretended to do no otherwise. How then have I set out to represent all these competing ideologies?

In early modern Spain–New Spain, attempts at cultural domination, as a specific practice of ruling, functioned as a major aspect of imperialism. Perceptions of manliness in the early modern period reflected how the textual constructs of gender within the rubric of Spanish imperialist-colonialist history engaged and propelled each other's discursive forms. Within an ever changing imperialist-colonialist formation, both Spain and New Spain nurtured the multiple attributes indicative of early modern Spanish manliness.[22] Discourses, however, should not be understood solely in terms of dominance, for the other "obliquely leaves its trace" in any text and thus makes it difficult to define the margin by using a dichotomy of center and rim.[23]

Throughout Chapter 1, I expand on my use of postmodernist theory and the writing of history. In an effort to avoid reductionist notions often associated with "the analytics of textual reading," I have attempted to identify the "determinate set of mediations" that connected the textual outputs of the early modern moralists with "other kinds of productions and political processes"—a central concern of western Marxist cultural historiography with respect to issues of empire and colony.[24]

Accordingly, I have reappropriated the notion of a national bourgeoisie, a determinate ideological form of cultural production defined as both repressive and bourgeois.[25] In Spain the ascendancy of an embryonic national bourgeois state and its form of cultural imperialism began to coalesce at the beginning of the sixteenth century, well into the reign of Isabel and Fernando. Spanish contemporary political theorists had already begun to speak of Spain as a universal or world monarchy to champion Christendom over Protestantism and defend Europe from the threat of the "despotic" Ottoman Empire.[26]

As the early modern period aged, Spain–New Spain functioned as a single colonial space and not as discrete entities, culturally independent of each other. Thus, I have situated my discussion of sodomy prosecutions within the imperial sphere—and not within the more discrete charm of gender or nation—as the most useful category of analysis. I have sought not to *ghettoize* the historicity of early modern Spanish sodomy prosecutions as yet another nauseating dosage of "gay, queer identified, transgender,"[27] or whatever today's *être en vogue* signifier inimical to historical inquiry. Although gender should function as a mode of interrogating one's efforts at historical reconstruction, an exclusive focus on gender itself "can never be adequate for a feminist historiography," because other categories of analysis skew that experience.[28]

Additionally, categories such as the perfect early modern Spanish Man, the sodomite, or the ubiquitous effeminate sodomite in New Spain coexisted in a perpetual state of redefinition. These discursive motifs, far from being a generalized colonial condition, emerged as a specific practice of Spanish imperial rule in its attempt to textualize "just causes" of cultural domination. Ever changing "political and economic imperatives of colonial rule constantly rearticulated their specificity."[29]

Over the course of the early modern period, the types of discourses of manliness and of sodomy evident in the archival and literary documents have come to symbolize Spain's attempt at a cultural reconfiguration of its gushing borders. Early modern Spanish *moralistas* aptly utilized descriptions of sodomy as one central aspect in the colonizing discourses of imperial Spain. A brief history of how these descriptions emerged and changed is presented in Chapter 1.

By assembling a "monstrous machinery of descriptions"—of bodies, of desires, of politics, of sexualities—the early modern moralists attempted in their discourses to "classify and ideologically master colonial subjects."[30] In this process, perceptions of manliness became a language fictionalized to narrate the various tropes subsequently associated with the early modern Spanish sodomite. The moralists' textualization of sodomy as a crime and a sin *contra natura* constituted a particular sort of ideology.

Early modern moralists had sought to "reinvent their core at the expense of marginal others."[31] Derrida's ideas of identity and difference informed my attempt to posit that early modern Spain needed to constitute the sodomite and New Spain both as its other, thereby constituting itself, its own subject position.[32] Foucault's epistemological juxtaposition of archaeology and discourse—not just things said but also as practice or something formed in language[33]—shaped my interrogation of early modern perceptions of manliness, of sodomites in Spain, and of the variations of those definitions pertinent to New Spain.

My critical reading of Spain's imperialist-colonialist discourses related to notions about manliness and *sodomie* presented in Chapter 2 supports this idea of constituting identity through difference and the representation of an inferiorized other.[34] Narrowing the focus to perceptions of manliness, as a discourse, helped illustrate how this initial practice generated other discourses linking sodomy perceptions with xenophobia, religion, or catastrophic occurrences in the peninsula and with anthropophagy, human sacrifices, or effeminacy in New Spain.[35]

The textual descriptions of sodomy discussed in this study will reveal how the multiple scaffolds of manliness erected by Spain changed in context as the moralists and other writers sought to fabricate just causes for its colonial undertaking in New Spain.

Prosecuting Sodomites

At least two types of tribunals—secular and ecclesiastical—prosecuted sodomites between the latter part of the fifteenth and the seventeenth century in Spain–New Spain.

Roughly sketched then, the Spanish Inquisition held jurisdiction over sodomy cases in the kingdom of Aragon that included the tribunals of Valencia, Barcelona, Zaragoza, and Palma de Mallorca. Carrasco, García Carcel, Bennassar, Monter, Rossello, and Bover Pujol, among others, have aptly presented their findings of these tribunals.[36]

Secular tribunals prosecuted sodomites in Madrid, Valladolid, Seville, Cádiz, and Granada—important metropolises in the kingdom of Castilla y León. Over the course of the early modern period, both secular and ecclesiastical courts held jurisdiction over sodomy cases and other "sexual crimes" prosecuted in the Audiencias (tribunals) of New Spain.[37]

In all these tribunals, the sodomy cases—second only to heresy prosecutions—constituted an average of 5 percent of the total number of cases prosecuted by these courts. The inquests conducted in Andalusia and in

New Spain resulted in the burning of some seventy-five men and the interrogation of some five hundred other individuals within a period of 130 years. However, in Castilla y León, the secular courts burned close to 100 percent of all accused sodomites, whereas about 38 percent of accused heretics were executed.[38]

Although the total number of sodomy cases and burnings may seem marginal or even minute compared with the number of prosecutions for heresy, this fact alone does not render them of "marginal importance" or warrant their exclusion by historians or "respectable historiography."[39] One does well to point to the exorbitant costs involved in garroting[40] and burning sodomites or to a possible assimilation of the "perfect man" imago by sodomites as possible explanations for this dearth. Nonetheless, early modern sodomy prosecutions demonstrated a direct correlation between Spain's imperial politics and its perceptions of manliness.

I have concentrated my research, in part, on the discourses evident in some three hundred cases prosecuted by the secular criminal High Courts in Seville, Cádiz, Granada, and Mexico City between 1561 and 1699 as well as those prosecuted by the Audiencia de la Casa de la Contratación (House of Trade Tribunal) located in Andalusia.

Almost all of the sodomy cases prosecuted by the House of Trade Tribunal initially occurred on board ships to or from the Indies or in the harbors that functioned as ports of call. The lawyers for the defense in the vast majority of these cases appealed the various sentences to the Casa's land tribunal located in Seville and later relocated in Cádiz.

The Catholic monarchs Isabel and Fernando created the Casa de la Contratación in 1503 to regulate colonial commerce and shipping between the peninsula and the Indies.[41] In 1511 the Casa de la Contratación acquired juridical powers, in the form of a tribunal, to prosecute both civil and criminal crimes committed on board Spanish ships en route to and from the Indies. By 1524 the Audiencia de la Casa de la Contratación fell under the appellate jurisdiction of the Council of the Indies, and thus a final appeal in both civil and criminal crimes rested with this tribunal.[42]

In Chapter 3, my discussion of some 175 sodomy cases consulted and prosecuted in Andalusia will highlight xenophobic politics and the codification of sodomy as a crime and a sin as the pertinent contexts for early modern issues of manliness.

The sodomy cases prosecuted in the peninsula typified the issues crucial to the moralists' depiction of Vir, a sacrilege that included the codification of *sodomie* as both a crime against the monarchy and a sin against God; the repetitive depictions of how sodomites violated the image of the new Spanish Man; perpetuating the xenophobic belief that only other nationals were naturally susceptible to sodomitical practices; an incessant preoccupation with quantifying the physical aspects of sodomy; and, finally, the use of science to dignify and buttress this discursive dogma.

The Mexico City sodomy cases tried by His Majesty's Criminal Court alluded to in Chapter 4, some 125 in total prosecuted between 1657 and 1658, revealed the way in which colonial politics tainted issues of gender identities in terms of class and ethnicity, thereby producing different or contradictory perceptions about sodomites in the capital city and viceroyalty of New Spain.

Although systematic, the Spanish peninsular courts had not actively pursued the prosecution of sodomites, as did the Mexican High Court in the mid-seventeenth century. In the peninsula, individuals most commonly denounced sodomites. This, and not any form of orchestrated efforts on the part of the courts, set the repressive juridical apparatus in motion. But in Mexico City between 1657 and 1658 the Mexican High Court unleashed an unprecedented prosecution of sodomites that culminated in the arrest and the interrogation of at least 125 of its metropolitan citizens.

In mid-seventeenth-century Mexico City, colonial authorities confronted a new and endemic cultural phenomenon—"effeminate sodomites" or "men who walked, talked, and dressed as women"—a discursive description lavishly embellished in comparison with its use to describe sodomites in the Spanish peninsula. After the initial contact between Spaniards and Indios, colonial officials and chroniclers began to describe an entire people as sodomites, a notion often associated with anthropophagy, human sacrifices, and anything diabolical. Colonial officials also likened sodomy to a "sort of cancer, one that contaminated and spread its diabolical infestation," perpetuated by effeminate sodomites.

Unfortunately, no *procesos*[43] for the Mexican sodomy cases prior to 1699 could be found. One can perhaps attribute this to a *motín* (uprising) that occurred in Mexico City in 1692. The uprising subsequently led to the burning of the viceroy's palace, home to the archives of the viceroyalty. Thus, "very little remains of criminal proceedings before the eighteenth century."[44]

The findings presented here related to the 1657–1658 Mexican sodomy cases emanate, in part, from the surviving court summaries and lists of indices of the accused, which included data on ethnicity, age, and class. Further descriptions of sodomy and sodomites offered by chroniclers, the clergy, viceroys, and lord mayors of Mexico City further complemented the court summaries and indices. Sodomy *procesos* reappeared in Mexico in conjunction with those cases prosecuted between 1750 and 1850.[45]

Collectively, the cases prosecuted in Andalusia and in Mexico, in conjunction with the other sodomy cases prosecuted in Spain, beginning at the twilight of the fifteenth century and continuing up until the end of the seventeenth century, represented a rupture with the tolerance afforded the practice of sodomy in previous centuries. Perceptions of sodomy, however, changed in context as early modern moralists sought to fabricate just causes for their colonial undertaking in New Spain.

Over the course of the early modern period and up until 1699, the types of discourses evident in the archival and literary documents have come to symbolize Spain's attempt at a cultural reconfiguration of itself. Siegel identified this phenomenon as a sort of "collective imperial identity crisis" brought about by reconquest, discovery, and dissemination of cultures, in a constant attempt to colonize others.

For those in positions of power, their discursive descriptions buttressed and perpetuated their privileged status whether represented in terms of ethnic, gender, or religious diatribes. These privileged protagonists and their malediction had sought to "reinvent their core at the expense of marginal others." Although the subaltern, such as sodomites, might have exploited their sexual genre "to subvert the social order, to validate their way of life, and to configure collective identities with access to discursive power," they also "subscribed to notions of the hegemonic—access to imperial and religious forms of power—in early modern society,"[46] and in the process they affirmed the official discourse about Spanish manliness.

Sources and Saucy Tales

The archival documents consulted for this study cover the period between 1561 and 1699. Many of the archival descriptions of sodomy will appear here, in print, for the first time since their initial recording in the early modern period. The documents include some three hundred *procesos*, or the recorded legal proceedings by a scrivener of sodomy trials prosecuted by the Andalusian and Mexican secular Royal Courts. These manuscripts are kept in dark boxes, stored within the confines of archives in Austin (Texas), Mexico City, Seville, Granada, Valladolid, Simancas, Madrid, and Burgos.

A *proceso* varied in length from some one hundred to five hundred folios in total and consisted of the telling denunciations of the accused, the graphic charges put forth by the prosecuting attorneys, the arguments for and by the defense, confessions by the accused and accounts by eyewitnesses, lengthy descriptions of the tortures inflicted upon the accused, sentences or appeals, and, finally, the justifications and descriptions of the sentences carried out by the different tribunals.

Although written by scriveners supposedly attached to the dominant culture(s), the *procesos*, albeit "indirect," not only reveal Spain's attempt to "comprehend the other by reducing it to self" [47] but also afford a glimpse into how individuals, on both sides of the Atlantic, contested and mediated the imposition of gendered constructs. Although one may label a source as not "objective," this does not negate its usefulness.[48] Even "meager, scattered and obscure documentation can be put to good use," and the result of not doing so is a refusal to "analyse and interpret" data.[49]

Other documents consulted consisted of various court summary reports of these trials; royal edicts; ecclesiastical bulls, sermons, and position papers; correspondence between colonial officials; memoirs or manuscripts written by mariners, soldiers, and the clergy; inventories of personal possessions owned by the accused; and bills of costs for the torture, strangulation, and burning of sodomites. In addition to the archival material, I have also combed through the literary production of theologians, casuists, and other writers of the early modern period—the intelligentsia in positions of power and influence, those court and ecclesiastical favorites who directly participated in shaping Spanish imperial politics and who textualized *sodomie* as *el pecado y crimen contra natura*.

Published Latin-Spanish-English dictionaries of the period and their wonderful conservation of the vernacular complemented these sources. My search for archival documents on sodomy specific to early modern Andalusia and Mexico by no means implies an exhaustive perusal of the archives of such material. However, at the time of writing, I have included those known references to the sodomy archival documents catalogued by researchers and archivists alike in the respective archival sites identified both in the Spanish peninsula and in America Septentrionalis.

The texts reappropriated for my history about manliness, as a specific form of discourse, did not constitute a particular genre of master texts. Nor did the *procesos*, which do comprise a significant amount of the archival material presented here, enjoy any privilege over the sermons, vignettes, or other writings of the early modern period.

The focus on the history of change in the socially constructed meanings of sodomy attempts to provide a broader understanding of how some aspects of the dominant and the subaltern responded to perceptions of sodomy.[50] Thus, cultural formations such as *sodomitas, putos, cavalgar por el culo, Negros, Mulatos, las Indias,* or *América* are not always enclosed in quotation marks or italicized, and they are not represented here to titillate or disturb the reader. Rather, these terms are utilized in the hope of explaining their raw and textually violent use in the early modern period.

My discussion of the sodomy discourses, my descriptions of the physical examination of bodies for "scientific proof of the sin and crime" *contra natura,*[51] or my allusions to the purported sexual habits and acts of individuals might strike some as much too perverse in nature, highly erotic, or, to others, perhaps even pornographic—a saucy tale rather than a historical narrative.

"Really," wrote Pérez-Mallaína in reference to the descriptions of sodomy contained in a sixteenth-century *proceso,* "the dauntless testimonies and the audacious adventures contained therein appeared to have been taken from a pornographic novel, so much so that one could laugh at its contents, were it not for the cruel destiny of its protagonists." In his *Hombres del Océano,* Pérez-Mallaína decided to protect the reader from representations of sodomies depicted in the *procesos,* for he deemed these descriptions to be much too graphic for a postcolonial audience. He sifted through the language contained in the documents and reproduced the "least lewd and brazen descriptions of sodomy, thereby, not offending too much the sensibilities of the reader."[52] Really? Lewd? Offending sensibilities? Pérez-Mallaína's need to sieve the sources reminds one of a similar problem faced by van de Port in his study of the relationship between war and unreason in today's Yugoslavia.

Van de Port's discussion of positivism pointed to how "social scientists in their need to classify, to control, to purify are taught the ideal of measurement, if not in the strictly quantitative sense, then metaphorically." Although van de Port found "nothing wrong with elucidating a subject by ordering material, classifying and structuring mechanisms indispensable to language users and any textualised representation of reality," he nonetheless took umbrage at academe's "passion for tidying up" or sanitizing sources, a process "aimed more at types and degrees of ordering" rather than at providing one with ways of structuring material as a more "valid procedure" of analytical interpretation. When one attempts to "tidy up" or to sanitize sources, "things," argued van de Port, "inevitably get left out," which in turn inevitably gives rise to "reductionist views" of analytical inquiry.[53]

Consequently, more traditional historians like Pérez-Mallaína risk overlooking important things that have been left out and could prove crucial to cultural analyses, overshadowed by one's own sheer fear of venturing beyond traditional conventions of historical inquiry. Rather, in the process of not directly engaging the totality of one's sources, there is a danger of missing the more global implications represented by the regrettably violent discourses about *sodomie* and the prosecution of sodomites in Spain—New Spain.

Given these ideological positions on whether or not to sanitize sources and on the function of language as discourse, I have resisted the temptation to tidy up the rhetoric contained in the archival sources, for that would be tantamount to a historical complicity in perpetuating the notion of *sodomie,* of sodomites as *contra natura.*

It would be as if the early modern moralists, in pure sadistic form, had succeeded in their efforts to dupe an entire subject population into believing and accepting their repetitive unutterably vile, nefarious, and repugnant characteristics of the sin against nature. Nonetheless, I have not sought to portray sex for sex's sake, with no references whatsoever to a larger global aesthetics or historicity other than to simply offer the reader raw descriptions of naked bodies and assorted acts, aimed specifically to shock, as is often the case in postcolonial studies of gender, artistic installations, or photo exhibitions in Western homopolitan centers.

So-called sodomies in early modern Spain—New Spain never constituted anything *contra natura.* If one had to label anything at all related to sodomy as "unnatural," I would point to the moralists' attempts to differentiate between distinct types of men purely to champion Spain's politics of empire. The manifestation of political power as reflected by, say, the spectacle of burning sodomites at the stake becomes even more complex and blurred, for that same might veered beyond the scaffold and directly onto the pages of the literature produced by moralists and other writers alike.[54]

The physical violence inflicted upon the sodomites by their superiors, by the courts, by the doctors, or by their own peers; the textual violence of a repetitive and graphic vernacular employed by the moralists to depict *sodomie* as *contra natura;* the violation of the self inflicted by cruel, sadistic theater of tortures; the garroting and burning of *sodomitas;* and the unceasing self-gratifying attempts by moralists to define in the most perverse and vile terms the abominable nature of a different erotic zone— all reflected a discourse dominated not by a moral order but rather by a complete lack of one.

CHAPTER I

A TOTAL MAN AND A TOTAL WOMAN

Textual Effigies and the
New Postcolonial Historian

ENTENDER EL AMOR

Sal de ti mismo, explora el abismo
que al fondo se enciende una luz
esa mirada perdida en la nada
buscando lo mismo que tú
aprender algo en la vida
entender a tope el amor
descubrir como es el mundo
inventar una ilusión.

Mónica Naranjo, *Palabra de mujer*

IN 1626, as Alonso Díaz Ramírez de Guzmán, a Spanish ensign, sat on a stone cliff in front of a palace in Genoa, a "gallant and well-dressed Italian soldier" sporting a grand wig of many locks, approached him and asked, "Sire, are you a Spaniard?" To which Alonso responded, "Yes." "In that case," mused the Italian soldier, "your lordship must be quite haughty and arrogant, like most Spaniards, although you are not the proud heroes you tend to boast about." "I," retorted Alonso, look upon Spaniards as "quite manly in every respect." "And I," insisted the Italian soldier, "take them all for great lumps of turd." Alonso stood up and cautioned the well-dressed gallant, "Do not, sire, utter such words, for the worst Spaniard is better than the best Italian." [1] The two men drew their swords and began to swashbuckle. The Italian soldier then fell to the ground as "many others, their swords drawn" came to his defense, and Alonso fled.

A couple of years earlier, Alonso, an ardent defender of early modern Spanish bravado, left his native San Sebastián and made his way south to the harbors of Andalusia, lured there by the excitement of "commerce and galleons." Like so many young men before him, Alonso became a grummet. In 1602 he boarded one of those galleons and set sail for the Indias. Alonso Díaz arrived first in Cartagena de Indias, before embarking for Colombia, Panama, Peru, Chile, and Mexico. Along the way, Alonso secured "three slaves—one black, the other, a different color; and one Negra, who sautéed his meals."[2]

In the course of his stay in the Indias, Alonso garnered a number of mercantile and military appointments, having distinguished himself for his business acumen and his sense of bravery. When a group of Araucano Indios in Valdivia, a port in Chile just southeast of Santiago, killed his company's ensign and deprived the company of its standard, Díaz and the other soldiers set off in pursuit of the Indios and the company's banner. When Alonso, in triumphant form and "with particular valor," reached the cacique who had usurped the company's standard, Díaz snatched it from him and killed the Indio. The retrieval of the company's flag, itself tantamount to honor and empire, earned Díaz the military rank of ensign.[3]

Alonso Díaz—a chivalrous defender of empire—indeed represented many of the ideal attributes of the "new, perfect Spanish Vir," or Man. In this chapter, I expand on my use of postmodernist theory and the analytics of textual reading. In doing so, I will attempt to identify the political imperatives that produced discourses about manliness, sodomy, and sodomites in early modern Spain–New Spain.

Fabricating the Perfect Spanish Vir

During the last quarter of the fifteenth century, privilege, based on the "natural hierarchies" of race, class, and religion, extended to the monarchy, to well-positioned theologians, to casuists, magistrates, scriveners, historiographers, in short—the Spanish intelligentsia, who were also referred to as los moralistas and directly participated in the imperial expansion. The literati—men, mostly, in positions of political and economic power—nurtured the textual construct of a new and perfect Spanish Man.

Declarations issued by these writers about manliness formed an "important part of the ideological armature of what has some claims to being the first European nation state." Spain's principal "ideological concern became its self-appointed role as the guardian of universal Christendom and to act in accordance with Christian ethico-political principles" enacted by the theologians and jurists.[4] Although these politicos of privilege and power functioned within the upper realms of the Spanish monarchy and the Catholic Church, I do not imply nor do I believe that this particular class of men constituted a monolith.

Rather, I have grouped their ideological writings together to isolate their discourses about empire, Vir, and *sodomie*. A more detailed account of their epistemological Vir and its relationship to sodomy is further elaborated in Chapter 2. Here, I wish briefly to emphasize that *los moralistas* unveiled their discursive fantasies of the new Spanish Man, a concept riddled with sexist, religiously intolerant, and xenophobic visions of power in an effort to buttress Spain's imperial politics aimed to defeat the likes of Moors, Jews, sodomites, and Indios.

Back in 1487, Alonso de Cartagena, bishop of Burgos, had already described specific manly customs with respect to law, women, friendship, war, and love.[5] When I speak of Man in early modern Spain–New Spain, I refer to what theologians of the Thomistic Scholastic termed as Vir. These theologians defined man, "by nature," as a disciple on Earth or a collaborator of God—an idea irefully promulgated by the present-day Opus Dei.[6] Man, according to the scholastic, constituted a continuous process of creation, for it is in him, in his seed, in his semen, that the potential for new and future beings is harbored.

This theological hallucination, lauded by historiographers and literary writers alike, also portrayed the labor of Woman in the procreation process to a naturally purely passive state—comparable to that of a vase, one that sat empty until water was poured in. Naturally then, these theologians believed that the predetermined function of the sexual act was always oriented toward procreation for the continuation of new beings.[7]

The new Spanish Man also possessed impeccable customs and displayed a sense of "gallantry, honor, veneration and worship for his Prince." A "passionate man beyond reproach" always dignified his manner of dress and, as a purveyor of "heroic virtues, religious fervor, and piety," knew always how to repent. Virtues like "humility, charitableness, and a capacity for suffering" were additional characteristics of the ideal Christian man that permeated the mystical poet Antonio Panés' *Calidades del varón perfecto* and *El cavallero perfecto*, written by Salas Barbadillo at the end of the sixteenth century.[8] *Los moralistas* had helped foster these fantastic attributes of the perfect Spanish Man, and Alonso Díaz had readily internalized them.

Caught in the Act

The genteel and gallant Alonso Díaz, who was always well dressed, had studied Latin early in life and could also read and write both Spanish and *vascuence*.[9] Our resolute and chivalrous fellow not only possessed an accentuated bravado but also displayed his own healthy brand of xenophobia and Catholic zeal.[10] At one point in his life, lost somewhere in the Andes, "tired, barefoot, his feet injured," Alonso "stood next to a tree and cried for the first time in his life." As he stood next to the tree, he "prayed and invoked his salvation in the name of the most holy Virgin Mary and Joseph, her husband." On the following morning, the "heavens above opened up when he saw two Christian men" come before him, one of whom eventually took Díaz to his wife's estate for lodging and repose.[11]

The couple, who had a "Mestiza for a daughter," or the offspring of "a Spaniard and an India," offered the daughter's hand in matrimony to the ensign. But Alonso refused to marry the wealthy merchant's daughter, for in his words, that "poor girl was just too black and too ugly, just like some devils"; in short, she was "contrary to his liking." Instead, Alonso preferred women with "pretty faces."[12] Indeed, our learned fellow Alonso Díaz embodied many attributes of the *caballero perfecto*—a discursive daydream disseminated by early modern moralists.

Unfortunately, Alonso's otherwise brilliant career began to display shades of tarnish. As he journeyed throughout the Indias, the ensign had already endured at least four platonic relationships with different women and had admittedly killed more than fifteen men, including his only brother, all in defense of his "manly honor" or in defense of the "Spanish nation." The ensign's shenanigans finally caught up with him. In Chile, as in Peru, Alonso had enjoyed an infamous reputation as a reckless, brawling gambler. In 1620, while he was in Peru, local officials arrested him and charged him with murder. Alonso, finding himself in quite a bind, summoned his confessor and simply revealed himself to the priest.

In his defense, Alonso ingeniously argued that a secular court could not pass sentence in his case, for he professed to be "a nun," moreover a "virgin," actually named Catalina de Erauso, and as such, his case fell under ecclesiastical and not secular jurisdiction. Apparently convinced of his story, the secular officials relegated the case to the appropriate ecclesiastical authorities.[13] Thereafter, in the "most discrete manner," the confessor, with the assistance of some *comadres,* confirmed Alonso's original *sexo* and Catalina's virginity.

After these requisite examinations, Agustín de Carvajal, bishop of Cuzco, concurred with Alonso's story and upheld the ensign's appeal. Notwithstanding, the ecclesiastical officials also confirmed that Catalina had served as a novice in a Basque convent but had never actually taken her vows as a nun. The bishop likewise confirmed the number of years that Alonso had served "his King and the various valiant deeds he had performed on numerous occasions as well as the number of honorable distinctions" he had received as an ensign. Despite the numerous decorations, the bishop of Cuzco required Catalina to again "dress in a nun's habit," much to Alonso's dismay, and "ordered her return to Spain."[14] Catalina, "dressed as a nun," later disembarked in Cádiz, before the curious gaze of a "multitude of people" drawn there once her story had become public lore.[15]

Months later when the Italian soldier had approached him, Alonso Díaz, dressed in splendid princely regalia, was sitting outside a friend's palace in Genoa, en route to Rome, where he intended to relate his story to Pope Urbano VIII. Previously, Alonso had met King Felipe IV in Madrid, who had rewarded the ensign yet again, this time with a "pension for life" and the "license to dress like a man." In this way, Catalina de Erauso succeeded in evading the ire of the early modern secular courts, and even Inquisitorial tribunals, despite their propensity to eagerly discipline and punish any type of sexual defiance during this epoch.

Erauso did not represent the likes of a bearded lady, the sort painted by Ribera for all to gawk at (Fig. 1.1).[16] Alonso Díaz exploited these notions of man and nature as one possible justification for his alternative gender.[17] Not only had Erauso emulated the perfect Man; she also embodied the early modern Spanish depictions of the perfect Woman. Catalina, the virtuous woman, a virgin, and her devotion to Catholicism constituted, in the eyes of moralists, a woman beyond reproach. Although Catalina de Erauso renounced her identity as woman and other more traditional forms of sexuality, Alonso Díaz supported the gender prescription of virgin for unmarried women.[18]

Virginity, a supposed state of purity, facilitated a closer relationship to God, and this implied an even greater status for early modern Spanish women. Notions of delicacy, tenderness, and, above all, obedience to man—in short, effeminacy—characterized the ideal portrait of an early modern Spanish woman. Catalina, the chaste virgin, a devout Catholic, obedient to man, who thought and acted like one, indeed merited great admiration from the early modern moralists. In his *El cortesano,* Baltasar de Castiglione, a favorite of Carlos V, depicted the ideal woman as a natural appendix of man (Fig. 1.2).

The Spanish courts had been especially severe with so-called sodomites and other individuals who overstepped neatly defined gender borders or subscribed to other forms of sexual transgressions. But the courts did not prosecute Alonso/Catalina; in fact, quite the opposite. Alonso/Catalina garnered further acceptance and more fame after his/her "com-

1.1. La mujer barbuda, 1631, oil on canvas, Jusepe
de Ribera, Museo Hospital de Tavera, Toledo.
Reproduced with the permission of Director
Excelentísmo Señor Ignacio de Medina y Fernández
de Córdoba, Duque de Segorbe.

ing out of the closet."[19] Why didn't the courts prosecute the gallant
Alonso? Was it because Catalina de Erauso assumed the identity of a man,
but not just that of any man?

In my effort to trace the epistemological history of manliness depicted in the "autobiographical writings" of Catalina de Erauso, I have
juxtaposed her manuscripts with those of the learned fellows referred to
above.[20] These texts, in combination with a vast array of archival docu-

1.2. **Notions of a perfect early modern Man.** The front cover of Castiglione's *El cortesano,* a favorite of Carlos V. Biblioteca Nacional de Madrid.

ments identified in the prologue, will help to explain how Catalina/Alonso and these learned fellows circumvented the rigidity of early modern gender codes to legitimize the existence of Alonso Díaz and to deny that same legitimization to sodomites of any *sexo.* I have attempted to underscore their possible reasons for having justified or even tolerated some ruptures of gender roles, especially when these ruptures, as in the case of Alonso Díaz, reified notions of the new Spanish Man. I should like to propose that the textual comments attributed to Catalina de Erauso and any other perceptions of Spanish manliness or of sodomy are best understood within the context of an expanding discourse in support of empire, both in the peninsula and in the Indias.

A Universal Monarchy

During the sixteenth and seventeenth centuries, the Spanish monarchy constituted the largest single political entity in Europe. Until the War of

Succession, it controlled more than two thirds of Italy and the whole of Central and South America. With the accession of Carlos V in 1516, Spain acquired a "distinct ideological identity." The Habsburg monarchy began to depict itself as "a self-assured champion (and exporter) of Christian cultural values, the secular arm of the papacy, and the sole guardian of political stability within Europe" (see Fig. 1.3).[21]

Contemporaries referred to the territories over which the Habsburgs ruled as an empire. After 1556 the Spanish monarchy became a "conglomerate of six semi-discrete parts": Castilla y León (which encompassed Andalusia), Aragon, Italy, the Netherlands, Portugal (1580–1640), and the Indias. Spanish and non-Spanish political theorists alike perceived the

1.3. **Map of Spain.** J. Speed, "Spaine newly described, with many adictions, both in the attires of the people and the setuations of their cheifest Cityes" (1625). In *A Prospect of the Most Famous Parts of the World* (London: printed by M.F. for W. Humble, 1646). Reproduced with the permission of the Archivo General de Indias, Seville.

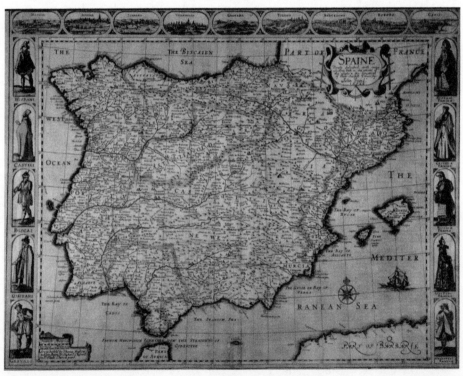

relationship between the kingdom of Aragon and Castilla y León as a component part of what by the early sixteenth century they termed Hispania.[22] Humanists during the reign of Carlos V, like Ginés de Sepúlveda, or early modern political theorists, like the Italian-born Tommaso Campanella, vigorously supported a universal sovereignty or a world empire.[23]

In Italy the notion of a Spanish "universal empire" was discussed as a political solution to impending threats from abroad. The Italian states, in particular those in the south, seemed vulnerable to the aspirations of the Ottoman Empire. The threats posed by the Ottomans on the one hand and Protestantism on the other prompted Campanella to champion a "universal—and by this he understood truly worldwide—Spanish Monarchy," or "Empire." Campanella urged the Castilian crown to exploit its imperial and papal powers, for he considered them as crucial for the implementation of "cultural manipulation and political control." [24]

The true empire should be "a single community, with a single currency," and "the King of Spain had to," as Campanella put it, *Hispanizare* (Hispanize) his subjects. The political *fray* believed that the crown "under the pretext of honor" should have forced Neapolitan barons to be fully Hispanized by compelling them to "imitate the habits, customs, and manners of Spain." The Turks, civil disorder, economic decay, and luxury—referred to as the *vulgo*—had all turned the mind of the people, in the eyes of Campanella. This "mutation of the state" was described by Campanella as "the radical and complete transformation of systems of knowledge and religion," and therefore the world "needed" Spain at the forefront to fulfill God's will and to protect the faith. Furthermore, language, as Antonio de Nebrija reminded Queen Isabel, would "of course function as the prime instrument of Empire." [25] Thus, a new type of Spanish Man, a vision inextricably bound to imperialist ambitions, was required to affront such *vulgo*.

It was within this context of empire that the early modern writers methodically crafted the discourses of a new Spanish Vir to champion a universal monarchy.

The Discrete Charm of Imperialism

In my attempt to historicize perceptions of early modern Spanish manliness and of sodomy, I have chosen to focus on Spanish imperialism and not on nationalism or gender as the primary category of analysis. Although "nation" functions globally as a component of identity, historical focuses on nationalisms have "frequently suppressed questions of gender and class," [26] not to mention overlooking differences of religion and ethnicity—categories that overlapped with early modern Spanish imperialism. Given the overlap among these categories, it made greater sense to analyze my interrogation of manliness from a "global social analytic" and to focus on an imperialist world system that defines social as "the intersection of the political, the economic and the ideological." [27]

My historical account of the many ways in which the early modern moralists "constructed knowledge" about sodomy in Spain–New Spain exposes links between perceptions of manliness and the power-knowledge nexus of imperialism-colonialism. [28] In *Orientalism*, Said has suggested that, under political and economic imperatives, late eighteenth-century European imperialism fabricated certain knowledge about the Orient, itself constituted for the exercise of imperial power. This knowledge produced what would henceforth become the Orient, and that phenomenon remains fundamental to understanding one discursive aspect of colonial rule. For the purpose of elucidating how *sodomie* evolved as one discursive aspect of Spanish colonial rule, I have appropriated Said's definition of "Orientalism" as a style of thought based upon an "ontological and epistemological distinction." [29]

Despite Ahmad's criticisms of Orientalism and his arguments for more historical accounts of imperial social formations and their transformations as the basis for understanding their historicity, Said has expanded our understanding of how colonial rule employed discursive descriptions to help cement its ideological perspectives. [30] I suggest that the discursive aspect of imperial power also applies to early modern Spanish imperialism.

Take for example, the rupture in discourses concerning sexualities that began roughly in conjunction with the proclamation of the 1497 sodomy *Pragmática*. In making this proclamation, the moralists repudiated Moorish Spain and instead emphasized the cultural value of a post-Columbian Spain—distinctions made as a discursive practice or function that appears to be an "ideological corollary of colonialism." [31] The moralists' discourses of sodomy had provided the Spanish crown with yet another "just cause" for cultural domination.

The discourses of manliness contained in the memoirs of Catalina de Erauso, in moralists' texts, or in the *procesos* of sodomy trials have made it possible to investigate any links between the politics of the Spanish Empire and perceptions of Vir. Well-articulated hierarchies based on class, ethnicity, religion, and gender formation determined and in some instances "overdetermined" both the politics and the ramifications of early modern manliness.[32] Within the context of the expanding empire, moralists employed a "set of discursive and institutional arrangements" to constitute a "sex/gender system," or a way of negotiating back and forth between "chromosomal sex and social gender."[33]

My focus on Spain's imperial sphere is meant to look beyond bipolar oppositions such as Spain versus New Spain or heterosexual in juxtaposition to homosexual, each constructed as discrete cultural monoliths whereby all that is constituted as exotic or genderlike *other* becomes homogenized into a "singular cultural formation." The upshot of valorizing Spain, New Spain, or sodomites along such lines freezes or dehistoricizes the global sphere within which struggles between the peninsula and the viceroyalty actually took place. When one emphasizes these politically homogenized formations and all their classes, religions, and ethnicities, they assume a singularized oppositionality, or a site—idealized, simultaneously—of "alterity and authenticity."[34]

It follows then that neither the colonizers nor the colonized constituted homogeneous groups in the early modern period. Instead, early modern peninsular cultures and the cultures of New Spain should be explained "in relation to one another, and as constitutive of each other" in particular moments of communication and contact.[35]

Perceptions of manliness in the early modern period reflected how the textual constructs of gender within the rubric of Spanish imperialist-colonialist history engaged and propelled each other's discursive forms. Within an ever changing imperialist-colonialist formation, both Spain and New Spain nurtured the multiple attributes indicative of early modern Spanish manliness.[36] Although all these categories may initially appear to have represented natural differences based on national origin, one cannot assume that Vir, Spain, and the sodomite constituted "fixed or self-evident categories."[37]

These historically constructed categories coexisted in a perpetual state of redefinition. Ever changing "political and economic imperatives of colonial rule constantly rearticulated their specificity." Thus, discursive motifs such as the "manly Spaniard" or the "effeminate sodomite" emerged as one of Spain's culminating attempts to textualize just causes of cultural domination. Therefore, these cultural formations should be interpreted in relation to "specific practices of ruling, rather than as a function of a generalized colonial condition."[38]

The manly Spaniard and the effeminate sodomite exposed issues particular to Spain, issues that were termed just causes as Spain's colonial apparatus sought to impose its cultural domination in Spain–New Spain. For early modern Spain, this meant fortifying its construct of Vir in combination with its need to discipline a multilingual, multicultural, supranational labor force—tradesmen for the most part, in the cases consulted for this study.

Beyond Gender

Historians writing about the early modern period cannot hope to further enrich our knowledge of gender specifications in Spain–New Spain on the basis of a bipolar opposition between colonizer and colonized or by situating their work solely within the category of gender. The insistent emphasis on either the bipolar opposition or the discrete category of study valorizes and privileges the categories of nation or gender over other categories of historical analysis.

Recent feminist scholarship has ventured beyond an exclusive analysis of any given sex-gender system to interrogate other issues and categories rather than simply focusing on the history of women and sexuality. This new scholarship has defined gender—itself skewed by class, ethnicity, and religion overlaps—as a "useful category of analysis" for explaining the many ways in which (colonial) societies constructed and represented relations of power.[39] Sangari, Vaid, Bem, and Butler, among others, have proposed that Western societies and cultures, throughout different modernizing epochs, have gendered all aspects of reality.

Thus, gender should function as a mode of interrogating one's efforts at historical reconstruction. However, because other categories of analysis skew the experience of gender, an exclusive focus on gender itself "can never be adequate for a feminist historiography."[40] Alonso Díaz' diatribes about Italians, Indios, and Negras, juxtaposed with his representations of the honorable Spanish man, provide an example of the way in which the ideology of gender intersected with the categories of ethnicity and xenophobia.

Gender formations should not then be "understood in stable or abiding terms"[41] either within or between the borders of nations. Although patriarchy may be universal, its specific structures and embodied effects are certainly not.[42] This insight has challenged the "assumption inherited from nineteenth-century bourgeois feminism that women are naturally or essentially united by their common subordination."[43] The prosecution of sodomites, witnessed in most parts of early modern Europe, also functioned differently across space and time.

A Retrospective of Queer Historiography

With a couple of noted exceptions, some of the recently written so-called gay or queer historiography has remained stagnant within the sex-gender paradigm and has positioned the homopolitan cultures of, say, England, the Netherlands, and France in a demarcated First World and simultaneously located or frozen its brother cultures of Spain, Italy, and Mexico in another world.[44] In his comparative analysis of eighteenth- and nineteenth-century "gender and the homosexual role in modern Western culture," the American-based historian Trumbach concluded:

> It is now clear that Western homosexual behaviour has always operated within the terms of two world-wide patterns. Adult men, who married women, had sexual relations with males, who in some cultures were adolescent boys, and who, in others, were adult men who had permanently adopted a transvestite role, situated somewhere between the other two genders. The active adult male partner in these acts maintained his dominant gender status; adolescent boys left behind their passivity at manhood; and only the transvestite male undertook a permanent new gender role as a result of his sexual conduct. Homosexual behaviour in the West was always enacted within an illicit subculture, both before and after 1700. It can also be shown that the appearance of the adult effeminate male as the dominant actor in the subculture occurred only after 1700. It is only after that year that the use of the model of the gay minority, with its subculture and its roles, becomes appropriated in the study of Western societies. It is [my] insistent argument that the minority model was fully established by 1750, at least in north-western Europe, that is, in the Netherlands, France, and England.[45]

To suggest that all "Western homosexual behaviour has always" been or was always this or that, both before and after this or that year, is to argue, in effect, that *sodomies* originating within social spaces identified as those outside northwestern Europe are not true Western *sodomies.* In this scenario, the birth of the modern Western homosexual, as the categorical site of opposition, with its indelible mark of constitution and difference as its metatext, devours cultural heterogeneities into a single metaphor.[46]

Trumbach also affirmed that "the appearance of the adult effeminate

male as the dominant actor in the subculture occurred only after 1700";
in short, "the model of the gay minority . . . was fully established by 1750,
at least in north-western Europe." Furthermore, "in 1750 there was for
women who sexually desired women not yet any role parallel to the new
role for male sodomites." Trumbach's assessment of "Western homosexual behaviour" reduces all homopolitan cultures to an ideal type and im-
plicitly fully expects one to narrate early modern *sodomies* commensurate
with that privileged type. The ideal type of sodomitical formations as-
sumes that gender sexualities or the category of nation are themselves
"trans-historical, supra-national, or self-identical categories."[47]

Bhabha suggests that no "privileged narrative of the nation" nor any
"single model could prove adequate" when one attempts to reconstruct
the nation's "myriad and contradictory historical forms."[48] The same
thought should apply to narrations of (homo)sexualities. Moreover, a
number of other characteristics could account for differences in Western
sodomitical formations. Mechanisms of social control such as the punishment meted out by Spanish courts could have also contributed to a
distinct form of sodomitical culture in early modern Spain—New Spain.
Not only did Trumbach freeze early modern *sodomies* within a First World
sphere, but his ethno-sexocentric model conflated the histories of both
female and male sodomites.

Trumbach further inflated the histories of northwestern European
countries by adding that "from the documentation it is apparent that by
the nineteenth century the modern Western system of sexuality and its
related gender roles were fully in force in the United States as well as
in the most modernising societies of that day, the Netherlands and England."[49] Furthermore, "at the end of the eighteenth century it is apparent that Italy, and probably most of southern and central Europe as well,
had not adopted the new system."[50] Perhaps this was the case. However,
shouldn't one instead ask how, if at all, did *sodomies* in southern Europe
differ from their counterparts in the north? And what, if anything, accounts for the similarities or differences?

To do so is to avoid the conflation of European cultures at any historical juncture and to reject the notion of a privileged narrative of sexuality emanating from any one culture. If, as Bhabha has suggested, one
should not advocate a privileged narrative of the nation, then, by extension, one should debunk a privileged narration of homosexuality. "We
cannot," as Weeks argues, "understand homosexuality just by studying
homosexuality alone," but instead one should go "beyond the confines of

homosexuality in particular or sexuality in general" to seek a broader understanding of gender and its intersection with other categories of historical analysis.[51]

The use of gender as a category for cultural analysis can create a number of interpretative obstacles, given the propensity of this category to generate "distinctions and abstractions."[52] If one attempts to resist homogenizing interpretations of *sodomies*, sodomy prosecutions in Spain–New Spain should be analyzed in relation to one another and not within the context of English or Dutch early modern histories. By doing so, one can compare and contrast the peculiar sodomitical formations of Spain–New Spain with sodomy prosecutions within other European imperial orbits and establish whether or not *sodomies* functioned differently across time and space.

Halperin, in his work on the history of homosexuality, described sexuality as "culturally variable rather than a timeless, immutable essence." He too rejected the notion that the sexual nomenclatures of the contemporary West functioned as "transcultural, and trans-historical terms, equally applicable to every culture and period." For Halperin, the forms of what might appear to be similar sexual practices in different countries of the West "did not travel well from one historical moment to another."[53]

However, Halperin also acknowledged that "the distinction between homosexuality and heterosexuality, far from being a fixed and immutable form of some universal syntax of sexual desire, can be understood as a particular conceptual turn in thinking about sex and desire." That occurred in certain sectors of northern and northwestern European society in the eighteenth and nineteenth centuries.[54]

Depicting the "West's" history of sexuality by valorizing "northwestern European" models borders on an ethno-sexocentrism that can sometimes lead to broad generalizations about early modern sodomitical formations. However, as the findings of this study will demonstrate, this "conceptual turn in thinking about sex" is not limited to the "modernising societies of north-western Europe, France, the Netherlands, and certainly England"[55] but was also present in Spain–New Spain—albeit in different forms.

Historicized Man

The prosecution of sodomites in Spain–New Spain reflected "inherently intertwined notions of imperial rule." Perceptions of manliness functioned as one locus within the imperial realm for disseminating power in early modern Spain–New Spain. In this sense, perceptions of manliness—just one dimension of Spanish imperial politics—revealed "the multiple axes along which power was exercised either among or with the colonisers and the colonised as well as between colonisers and colonised." [56]

But the "focus on the imperial social formation points not only to the intersection of the imperial with the hierarchical categories of race, class, religion, gender and sexuality, but also to the essentially disproportionate and contradictory nature of that intersection." [57] In Spain–New Spain, these masked hierarchies overdetermined the gendered notions of manliness. Thus, early modern discourses of manliness functioned as an over-determined context for the concept of effeminacy and revealed one indication of the unevenness in the intersection of metropolitan and colonial contexts.

My discussion of the evolving perceptions of manliness presented in the next three chapters will point to how this uneven and oftentimes contradictory rhetoric manifested itself within the context of Spanish imperial history. Throughout my discussion of Spanish manliness and sodomy prosecutions, I have attempted not to privilege gender or any one of the other categories of historical analysis. In the sodomy cases prosecuted in Andalusia, I shall highlight xenophobic politics and the codification of sodomy as a crime and a sin against nature as the primary contexts for issues of manliness. Early modern moralists described men of other "nationalities" as the complete polar opposite to the idyllic Spanish Vir: "by nature" physically and intellectually inferior, perverted, vile or filthy, lascivious and languorous.

The Mexican sodomy cases prosecuted between 1657 and 1658 instead exposed gender identities in terms of class and ethnicity as the important contexts. The elaboration of the promiscuous sexual appetites of the Indios intersected in complex ways with the elaboration of distinct and self-restrained sexual mores of Spaniards. In an apparent contradiction of rhetoric, early modern moralists nevertheless associated sodomitical practices in the peninsula with the favored manly, or virile, fellows rather than with an effeminate sodomite, the object of colonial derision. The moralists' focus on effeminacy to distinguish the Mexico City sodomite from the sexually virile peninsular sodomite exposed the contradictions of a discourse that attempted to link sodomitical practices with a distinct and distant homopolitan persona defined in terms of "effeminacy and lacking of manly virility." [58]

In seventeenth-century Mexico, colonial officials displayed a particular sense of repulsion for the effeminate sodomite, a phenomenon often infused with images of anthropophagy, human sacrifices, the diabolical, cancer—all characteristics conspicuously absent in textual references to sodomy prosecutions in the peninsula. Whether the colonial authorities described effeminate sodomites in terms of social, economic, or scientific factors such as cancer, widespread disease, and contamination, the emphasis was inevitably on degradation and the diabolical. The popularity of notions of disease, embodied in the concept of effeminate sodomite, does indeed illustrate the essentially interactive process in the deployment of the discursive mechanisms of colonial rule. The disregard of multiple attributes of colonial effeminacy results in neglecting historical analysis of colonial contradictions.[59]

The articulation and rearticulation of sodomy, based on religious or ethnic differences, constantly responded to specific changes in Spain–New Spain that could help explain differences in the perceptions of the peninsular sodomite with respect to his effeminate counterpart in the viceroyalty. Spain fostered the idea of the effeminate sodomite in the Indias primarily in response to its own decaying political and economic domination. Immediately after its occupation of Mexico in the early sixteenth century, notions of effeminacy and passivity had loosely characterized all the inhabitants of the Indias. However, by the mid-seventeenth century, effeminacy evolved from a loosely defined attribute associated with the entire population of New Spain to an attribute associated with the Mexican sodomite.

Colonial stereotypes of effeminacy also evolved in the context of an "ambivalence" that results from the simultaneous identification with and alienation from the colonial other in the formation of the colonial subject.[60] As such, models of the colonial subject based on supposedly universal gender dynamics of identity formation do not offer a satisfactory context for the discursive aspect of colonial effeminacy, given that different historical developments overdetermined this construct.[61] The recurring shifts in the textual constructs of, say, a sodomite or an effeminate one reflected the way in which economic underpinnings undermined the privileges enjoyed by colonial authorities in Spain–New Spain and the political challenge posed by the so-called sodomites.

Unlike the courts that prosecuted sodomy cases in the peninsula, His Majesty's High Court in Mexico City actively pursued and prosecuted effeminate sodomites, men who purportedly "dressed like women" and "wallowed" in the nefarious crime and sin *contra natura*. Although the cross-dressed *mestizas'* form of self-representation, in addition to the many "parties they hosted acting like women," might have appeared as a "challenge to specific colonial policies," one does well to ask whether or not these so-called effeminate sodomites actually subverted gender forms by assuming these new identities.[62] How subversive can one consider cross-dressed *mestizas* or Alonso Díaz, for that matter, to be, when these men actually reinforced Spanish gender forms along ethnic and class distinctions?

Chatterjee and Pandey have labeled these political anomalies and the struggle for legitimacy in one's own culture as the paradox of subalternity.[63] Or, more succinctly, as Sarkar has proposed, the self-perception of effeminacy actually constitutes an expression of hegemonic aspirations.[64] The cross-dressed *mestizas* and Alonso Díaz, then, emerged as products of the contradictions and juxtapositions that characterized Spanish colonial culture.

Writing about sodomy prosecutions in Spain–New Spain from this historicized context allows the possibility of interpreting particular cultural nuances that might have influenced notions of sex and gender evident in the peninsula and in the viceroyalty. In doing so, historians can distance themselves from writing about discrete Western perceptions of sodomy without any reference at all to early modern Spain's suprapolitical project and its relationship to *sodomies.*

A more historicized approach aimed at explaining sodomy prosecutions—their intertwinement situated within an evolving imperial formation in early modern Spain–New Spain—thus implies a closer reading of more traditional interpretations of both Spanish manliness and Mexican sexual norms oftentimes described as mutually exclusive categories of inquiry.[65] Although many studies have broadened our understanding of same-sex sexual norms, some of the recent gender historiography about Spain–New Spain has demonstrated a hesitancy to reconceptualize the definition of early modern manliness within the context of Spain's imperial formation.[66]

The refusal to contextualize issues of gender within the broader category of imperialism-colonialism has resulted in many a "redundant copula."[67] This hesitancy has skewed important contributions to the understanding of sodomy prosecutions in New Spain like Gruzinski's "Las cenizas del deseo," Trexler's *Sex and Conquest,* or Lavrín's work on sexuality because of their predominately "indigenous" or "peninsular" frames of reference.[68] Murray's totalizing narrative, *Latin American Male Homosexualities,* fared considerably worse.[69]

Likewise, Novo's preoccupation with the macabre obfuscated the complexities of the colonial institutions as mechanisms of social control that fueled sodomy prosecutions in New Spain. In his 1960s' *Las locas, el sexo, y los burdeles*, a historicoliterary account of homosexuality in Mexico since the arrival of Hernán Cortés, Novo narrated and in some instances concocted the most sensational aspects of the 1657–1658 sodomy trials in Mexico City. Unfortunately, he ignored any links between the politics of empire and perceptions of manliness.[70]

Back in 1986, Gruzinski used the same archival texts in his seminal article titled "Las cenizas del deseo," the only other publication to date related to sodomy prosecutions in early modern Mexico. However, even Gruzinski's otherwise excellent analysis of these sodomy trials, explained in part as a logical consequence of some neatly described Spanish *mentalité*, overlooks other political factors that might have overdetermined gender formations in Spain–New Spain.

My emphasis on the politics, the textual construction of early modern manliness, and the prosecution of sodomites, as one constitutive principle of imperialism, differs from that of these other works. Unlike these writers, my focal point is on the historical specificity of Spanish manliness rather than on broad historical generalizations about the gendering of the Indias as female and the feminization of the colonized. An adherence to historical specificity allows for a more adequate discussion of the historical events that produced the effeminate sodomite and rejects any line of continuity between *Popol Vuh* and early modern New Spain to help explain away gender formations.

In summation, the focus on Spanish perceptions of manliness, as the site for analyzing the relationship between gender formations and power, has permitted me to attempt a different understanding of how ideology molded these categories in Spain–New Spain. Consequently, I reconceptualize a more traditional historiography by extending the "exclusive national frame of reference to recognise its location in a larger imperial social formation."[71]

Alonso Díaz, a Carefully Concocted Episteme

Colonizers seldom held power unilaterally in colonial Spain or Mexico. The production of colonial knowledge always entailed a "two-way process, mediated out of the contestation and collaboration" between different classes. The appeal of the early modern politics of manliness was symptomatic of the efforts made by the moralists on the one hand and by Alonso Díaz on the other to establish their own hegemony in colonial society.[72]

Alonso Díaz emulated the perfect man in an epoch fraudulently depicted by triumphant histories as Spain's Golden Era, idyllic for some, gilded for others. In what reads more like a propaganda speech for the present-day Partido Nationalista Vasco (PNV) rather than a reference to seventeenth-century Spain, Vallbona wrote:

> Those were days when adventures, wars of conquest, colonization and fame had all been reserved for men. Those who are not familiarized with the world of the Basques are surprised that Catalina lived on the margins of all conventional norms without an encounter with the Inquisition. In order to better understand that impetuous/anxious spirit and her heroics one must take into account her Basque origins. On the one hand, the Basques have distinguished themselves for their individualism, adventurous spirit, valor, and the self-conscience of their strength as an ethnic group. The prestigious role played by the woman in Basque culture is one worth remembering since recent studies have revealed the matriarchal character of said society.[73]

Perhaps, as the xenophobic and extreme-right leader of the PNV, Xabier Arzalluz, often salivates, "all Basques are *genetically* different from other human beings." However, neither Catalina nor Alonso evoked their Basque origins as a precursor to their alternative forms of dressing and living. Catalina de Erauso cherished notions of manly honor, the Spanish nation, and a defense of empire.[74]

Catalina's parents abandoned her at the age of four in a Basque convent, where they fully expected her to undergo her novitiate. Catalina became "displeased with that enclosed life" characteristic of so many nunneries.[75] And so, our future ensign, a native of San Sebastián, fled the convent at the age of fifteen, in part as a result of her discontent and the abuse she suffered at the hands of her aunt, the prioress of the convent. En route to Andalusia, Erauso cut her hair and confected the apparel of a man from the remnants of her forgone habit.

Alonso Díaz spent fifteen of his nineteen years abroad at war in the provinces of Chile, without anyone suspecting or discovering his other identity until his misfortunes in Peru. Because Erauso dressed, acted, and worked like a man, others around him likened the beardless Alonso Díaz to a eunuch. As a soldier in Chile who had fought in many campaigns, the "valiant and honorable ensign had always punctually complied with the orders dictated by any of the four different captains" he had served. Together, the men had "caused great destruction of the enemy in their many battles against the Indios."

In 1624, shortly after arriving in Spain, the thirty-three-year-old Catalina de Erauso informed Felipe IV:

> Although prohibited for a woman to dress in man's apparel, but since this has already occurred, and having worn this apparel for so many years and with so much valor in continuous warfare, it would be just for His Majesty to provide her with, about 500 pesos of rent for life, at the rate of eight reales per peso, a pension dignified of her service to the crown. . . . His Majesty should also have to decide if it best served his interests for her to dress like a woman, however, His Majesty should know that she has no inclination to change or modify her current habit of dress, which is like a man.[76]

Erauso's monetary request amounted to some four thousand reales annually, or the purchasing power to hire between ten and thirteen laborers every day for one year. A hefty sum, no doubt, given that a common laborer in seventeenth-century Mexico earned just a little over one real per day.[77] In her petition to Felipe IV, dated March 1624, Catalina de Erauso indicated that she had departed for Las Indias "nineteen years earlier" and assumed the identity of a Spanish man. She did so "not for an evil purpose," revolution, or indulging in sexual license but only to fulfill her "natural inclination for arms" all "in defense of the Catholic faith and service to His Majesty the King of Spain."[78]

In support of Erauso's petition, Don Luis de Céspedes Xeria, a captain general and the governor of Paraguay, wrote a letter of reference addressed to His Majesty's Council. The captain general had known Alonso Díaz, who "dressed like a man without anybody discovering otherwise" for "more than eighteen years or ever since the time he had joined the ranks of his other soldiers." The honorable ensign had always acted like "a man of very much valor."[79]

Francisco Pérez de Navarrete, a captain of the Spanish Infantry, stated that he had always witnessed "her" act like a "good soldier who always followed orders." "We took him for a man for he always demon-

strated courage," admitted Navarrete. Not until 1623 in Lima had Navarrete seen Antonio in "women's apparel," for then Catalina had unmasked
herself. The upshot of this "very notorious thing," concluded Navarrete,
was that "she became known as *la monja de Chile.*"[80]

Erauso eventually met Felipe IV in August 1625 when she personally
met with him to discuss her petition.[81] Furthermore, on 19 February 1626
the Royal Council of the Indies in Madrid recommended that Felipe IV
grant Catalina de Erauso a yearly pension of "500 pesos at the rate of
eight reales per peso." The ministers also asked the king to rule whether
or not, and in the "best interest of the Crown," Catalina should "change
her habit of dress."[82] The king's royal edict of 23 April 1626 indeed
granted Catalina de Erauso a pension of 500 pesos per year for life and
simply did not stipulate any preference about dress for the ensign.[83]

After meeting Felipe IV, Alonso Díaz left Spain for Rome to meet
Pope Urbano VIII. Alonso embarked on a ship commanded by an entire
lot of French mariners. The crew spent the entire journey conversing with
one another. At one point early in the journey, one French soldier commented that it "behooved the Spanish Monarchy to arrive at a peace settlement with France." Alonso Díaz, the "lone Spaniard amidst so many
Frenchmen" on board the ship "once again demonstrated great courage
having overlooked the notorious danger he had exposed himself to."
Alonso declared, "You have said enough and you have allowed passion
and emotions to overcome your sensibilities,"[84] echoing the second Scholastic's sexualization of reason as a manly attribute and emotion and passion as characteristics of womanly functions.[85]

In Rome, Alonso Díaz dressed in "proper gentleman's apparel," appeared before Pope Urbano VIII, kissed his feet, and briefly related "the
story of her life, her adventures, her sex, and her virginity" to the Holy
Father. However "strange" the related escapades might have seemed to
Urbano, the "affable Pope," nonetheless, granted Catalina de Erauso a
"license that allowed her to continue dressing like a man for life." The
pontiff admonished Alonso to remain "fearful of God and his conscience" and to live a life of "honesty, void of vengeance or injuring
another."[86]

"On 5 June 1626," wrote Pedro Valle Peregrino, "Catalina de Erauso,
while in Rome, came to my house for the first time." Valle Peregrino described Catalina as "large in stature and somewhat bulky for a woman although she had all the appearance of a man." The "flat-chested" ensign
had "dried up her breasts with some, I don't know what kind of remedy,

a sort of jell, given to her by some Italian at a very young age," recalled Valle Peregrino. Catalina had "spread the gel on her breasts," and "although it had caused her great pain," it had not produced "any other harmful effects other than the drying up of the breasts."[87]

His "head held low," the ensign "looked somewhat tattered." Valle Peregrino attributed this condition "more to his life as a valiant soldier rather than to having led the life of a courtesan or experienced the strains of amorous encounters." Valle Peregrino noticed that, although "not ugly, but not beautiful," her face "appeared somewhat badly treated, but not of much age." The ensign sported "short black hair, with a little bit of a foretop, just like a man, in true fashion of the day." Alonso Díaz "dressed like a Spanish gentleman, shiny sword [and all]," revealing his womanly side "only in how she moved her hands, despite their bulky, meaty, and robust appearance." In effect, the ensign "looked more like a eunuch than a woman."[88]

Alonso Díaz spent the next month in Rome as the guest of princes and the most genteel men of Roman society. The Roman Senate named him an honorary citizen of Rome, and they celebrated the ceremony in the Capilla di San Pedro, attended by many cardinals. After the ceremony, at a reception hosted in his honor, Alonso suddenly found himself in the presence of three cardinals.

Cardinal Magallón turned to Alonso and stated, "Your only defect is that you are a Spaniard." "My illustrious Lord," politely offered Alonso, "I believe it is the only good thing I do possess." Catalina de Erauso, alias Alonso Díaz Ramírez de Guzmán, a total Man and a total Woman, had realized the zenith of a soldier's career.

Having left behind the notoriety and commotion he had caused in Rome, Alonso Díaz made his way to Naples before heading back to Spain. One day, as Alonso walked around the quay in Naples, "the laughter and guffaws of two beautiful courtesan dames, who sauntered about in the company of two young men, drew his attention." The dames stared at Alonso. Alonso stared back at the dames, one of whom asked, "Señora Catalina, have you lost the way?" Alonso responded, "Señora *puta*, how would you like one hundred thumps on the scruff of your neck and a hundred slashes to any man who tries to defend you?" The courtesans and the young men all very quietly slipped away.[89]

Alonso Díaz eventually returned to Mexico. On 12 July 1628, Felipe IV instructed the ministers of the Casa de la Contratación in Seville to afford the "Alférez doña Catalina de Erauso" passage to New Spain with-

1.4. **Lithograph of Alférez Alonso/Antonio Díaz, based on Pacheco's painting.** In J. M. Ferrer (ed.), *Historia de la monja alférez, Doña Catalina de Erauso, escrita por ella misma* (Paris: J. Didot, 1829). Biblioteca Nacional de Madrid.

out requesting any information from her whatsoever.[90] In 1630, as the ensign waited to depart for the Indias, "she sat in the Cathedral of Sevilla."[91] Later, Alonso Díaz posed for a portrait painted by Francisco de Pacheco (Fig. 1.4).[92]

Immortalized for centuries to come, on 21 July 1630 Alonso—by then under the new pseudonym of Antonio de Erauso—along with another 160 passengers, set sail for New Spain under the command of General Miguel de Echazarreta.

CHAPTER 2

A BRIEF HISTORY OF EARLY MODERN SPAIN ON *SODOMIE*

La tolerancia, la más benéfica de las virtudes.
La tolerancia, tan escasa entre nosotros.

Francisco Tomás y Valiente, "El crimen y pecado contra natura"

THE EXPULSION of the Moors by Spanish troops from Granada in 1492 initiated a period of somber culture in Spain. "After so much travail, expense, death and bloodshed," wrote King Fernando, "we have won for the glory of God, for the exaltation of our Holy Catholic Faith, and for the honour of the Apostolic See, this Kingdom of Granada, occupied for 780 years by infidels."[1] From that day forward, a new culture would emerge, one in which Catholicism portrayed sexual mores in light of the new religiosity.[2] At the forefront, the Council of Trent—obsessed with sexophobia and the concept of sin—spearheaded a new dogma for the peninsula.[3]

By contrast, Moorish culture in the peninsula had cultivated religious tolerance, great metropolises with intense networks of commerce, an agriculturally advanced countryside, its habitants cosmopolitan, some of whom also possessed grand sexual, homophile tendencies. In some regions of the peninsula, the initiation of young Moorish men into adult life involved sexual relations with the patriarchs. Consequently, many sectors of Moorish culture, both young and old, adhered to the practice of sodomy with some sense of liberty.[4] The infidels simply had to be civilized.

In this chapter, my discussion of the crime and sin *contra natura*, itself a textual fabrication, offers the reader a brief and truthful history of the perfect Spanish Man and of sodomy perceptions—ever changing discourses—written by moralists, casuists, and literary writers within the rubric of Spain's burgeoning imperial formation. The new baroque theological reformation imposed in the peninsula and in New Spain tainted legal-ecclesiastical perceptions of manliness and of sodomy. A misogynist description of the other, xenophobia, and, by the first decades of the sev-

enteenth century, notions of effeminacy all contributed to the textual mutation of the perfect Spanish Man, of sodomy, and of the sodomite.

A Nasty Turn of Events—the Bloody 1497 *Pragmática*

Fernando and Isabel christened a new political-religious era of repression,
one that labeled the Jews a "bloody race" and instructed both Inquisitorial and secular tribunals to simultaneously combat heresy, treason, and
sodomy beginning during the latter part of the fifteenth century. Whereas
in Europe a furor over witchcraft raged, the principal concern of the
Spanish tribunals rested with heretics and the prosecution of Moors,
Jews, and sodomites. The nefarious sin became one of the most horrendous and scandalous crimes to preoccupy the monarchy in sixteenth- and
seventeenth-century Spain.[5] Not surprisingly, on occasions, King Fernando himself had authorized the investigation of suspected sodomites.[6]

In early modern Spain, the prosecution of sodomites and the codification of *sodomie* as a nefarious crime and sin against nature took a nasty
turn in 1497, a marked rupture with the tolerance afforded such practices
in earlier periods in the peninsula.[7] On 22 July 1497 in Medina del Campo,
Isabel and Fernando, their lips still smacking from the sweet taste of reconquest and discovery, proclaimed the first celebrated sodomy *pragmática*
of the early modern period (Fig. 2.1).[8] The 1497 *Pragmática* significantly
aggravated the discourses and the sentences passed against suspected
sodomites. The *Pragmática* concerned itself not so much with the hereto-
fore-articulated social danger that marked the gravity of the sin; rather,
the document addressed the inner guilt or culpability of such an offense
with respect to God. The discursive descriptions of sodomy as a crime
and a sin tacitly recognized it as primarily an offense against God rather
than conceiving it as a danger to the Spanish state.

The "Catholic Monarchs"[9]—a well-deserved title bestowed upon
Isabel and Fernando by Pope Alexander VI in 1494—understood themselves to be sovereigns because "God had wished it so." As such, the sovereigns recognized "no one superior to God," and they argued that the
"crime committed against the natural order caused great infamy on earth
and particular grave offence to the Lord our God."[10] Sodomy, in the
hearts of Isabel and Fernando, led to the "loss of one's virtuous and illustrious pedigree or man's honour." Whoever perpetrated such a crime
and sin not only consented to an "ignoble act" but "ceased to be noble"—
a process that culminated in a "weakened" or "cowardly heart." Furthermore, they proposed that both "secular and ecclesiastical law should join

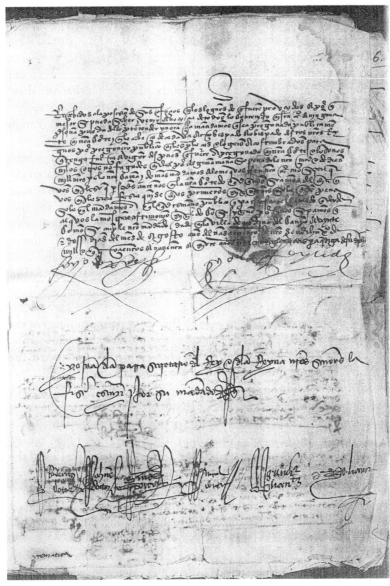

2.1. *Pragmática de los Reyes Católicos acerca de los reos de pecado nefando, Medina del Campo, 22 agosto 1497*, signed "Yo el Rey, Yo la Reyna" (I the King, I the Queen)—the first Spanish anti-sodomy law of the early modern period. Archivo General de Simancas, Cámara de Castilla, leg. 1, no. 4.

forces to punish the nefarious crime, one not worthy of name, destroyer of the natural order, thus punishable by divine justice."[11]

Isabel and Fernando resuscitated perceptions of sodomy that had festered in different parts of the peninsula during other epochs of repression by proposing that sodomy produced in man the fear of torments and punishments that God could inflict upon the place on Earth where these atrocities prevailed. In theory, sodomy laws had existed before 1497.[12] However, in practice, authorities rarely put them to use, as did Fernando and Isabel later in the sixteenth century.

In particular, the Catholic Monarchs drew inspiration from Chapter 21 of the thirteenth-century *Setena Partida*, titled "De los que facen pecado de luxuria contra natura," which defined *sodomítico* as the "sin against nature and natural custom committed by men with each other." The *Partida* traced the evils of the sin to the cities of Sodom and Gommorah, two ancient cities inhabited by "evil people."[13] The *Partida* cautioned "all men to guard themselves against this evil for the sin gives rise to many disastrous calamities on earth such as hunger, pestilence, and torment."[14] In the words of Nietzsche, calamities resurrect the notion that sins have been committed against customs.[15]

The 1497 *Pragmática* concurred with the major points outlined in the *Setena Partida*. A 'Godly fear' had prompted the monarchs to make sodomy laws and sentences even more severe. The monarchs interpreted the penalties stipulated for sodomy in the *Setena Partida* as insufficient to "extirpate the abominable error," and thus they "felt a greater need to be even more accountable to God."[16] Although the *Pragmática* affirmed the death penalty for those condemned sodomites over the age of twenty-five promulgated by the *Partida*, it nonetheless found the penalty insufficient and instituted a new penalty: death by fire. Only fire, as a natural purifier of the maligned, could provide a remedy for sodomy, the unmentionable vice and the abominable crime against nature.[17] At times, the threat of burning a sodomite so terrified the family of the accused that, instead, they themselves administered a pastelike poison to their own relative, an early modern form of euthanasia.[18]

Although the *Pragmática* also granted the Spanish courts the right to confiscate the goods of any accused sodomite, in some instances the courts had to return haphazardly confiscated goods to their rightful owners. Years earlier, Mencía Velázquez, the wife of a convicted sodomite who had his goods confiscated, successfully argued that some of her husband's confiscated goods had actually pertained to her prior to the marriage and as such she rightfully deserved title to possess them. The court acknowledged the separation of goods and ruled in favor of Velázquez.[19]

The *Pragmática* also required the application of systematic torture to any man accused of the nefarious sin, including the nobility and the clergy. During the tenure of the Catholic Monarchs, the courts administered justice differently to nobles and the subaltern.[20] The nobles enjoyed privileges such as special due process and usually found themselves exempted from torture except in the cases of sodomy and heresy. Commonly, nobles paid a monetary fee in exchange for freedom or in very grave cases accepted banishment from the kingdom as punishment for their crimes.[21] In the case brought against the count of Villamediana in 1622 Madrid, a secular court found him and a great number of nobles and other men of humble origin guilty of sodomy. The court executed the men of more humble existence and allowed the nobles the freedom to emigrate to France or Italy.[22]

As in the cases of heresy or treason, the *Pragmática* succeeded in minimizing the evidentiary requirements necessary to justify the condemnation of an accused sodomite. Thus the 1497 *Pragmática* no longer required a sufficient amount of evidence to fully prove the consummation of sodomy. The Catholic Monarchs elevated sodomy to correspond in severity to heresy and treason for "relaxed evidentiary requirements"; the confiscation of goods and the use of torture also figured prominently in the prosecution of those cases.[23]

Finally, in a colossal display of judicious testimony, the Catholic Monarchs did include one last and benevolent clause. The clause stipulated that heirs of accused sodomites should not suffer the infamy of an ancestor. Despite the sodomy laws stipulated by the royal *Pragmática*, other tribunals in Spain issued similar laws or variations of them, and "judicious treatment" became a very relative term during the early modern period.[24]

A wave of sodomy prosecutions would begin after 1497 in the peninsula and in New Spain. The Catholic Monarchs reappropriated the concept of divine law, a construct already elaborated in the *Setena Partida*, to legitimize human rule as one just cause for demonizing sodomy, much to the glee of early modern theologians. They linked sodomy with perceptions of manliness, a category inextricably intertwined with notions of class, religion, xenophobia, and empire. Later in the early modern period, other Spanish monarchs drafted less ambitious and magnanimous sodomy laws.

All the King's Men Except . . .

In 1592, Felipe II opted not to further aggravate the sodomy penalties, although he did relax even further the evidentiary requirements necessary for the prosecution and sentencing of such cases. Like Isabel and Fernando before him, Felipe II also desired to "extirpate the abominable and nefarious sin against nature without allowing sodomites the possibility of avoiding prosecution for lack of evidentiary requirements or because the witnesses did not concur with each other." For Felipe II, "one witness sufficed" to warrant the condemnation of a sodomite. Moreover, if the testimony of two or three witnesses did not concur with each other, even though one of them had participated in the act, the 1592 *Pragmática* nonetheless found the testimony of one "participant" sufficient enough to condemn a sodomite.[25]

In 1530 the Supreme Council of the Inquisition in Aragon had set the precedent for the one witness clause. It ruled that "one witness, albeit an accomplice and a minor of twenty-five years of age, sufficed as proof and evidence of the crime." Only if the witness in question happened to be "the wife of the accused prisoner, could she not possess the required status to testify as a witness."[26]

The Spanish Monarchs did not only resurrect past discourses of sodomy to justify the prosecution of sodomites. They all turned to theologians and other writers alike for additional inspiration for the perfect early modern Spanish Man.

El Varón Divino y Perfecto

Alfonso de Castro, a mid-sixteenth-century Franciscan theologian from Zamora, represented a prevalent theological vision of civil law during the early modern period. Castro considered theologians and secular casuists as amiable partners in the interpretation of laws. Even though Castro conceded the interpretation of human laws to the jurists, he believed that only theologians should dispute the substance of secular laws, for in no instance could human law exist without the recognition of divine law.[27] "The pretensions of the judge," wrote de Beauvoir, "became more arrogant than those of the tyrant; for the tyrant confines himself to being himself, whereas the judge tries to erect his opinions into universal laws. His effort is based upon a lie."[28]

Nonetheless, Castro and other cohort moralists believed in this "universal truth"—that in accordance with the book of Genesis and Scholastic theology, God had labored and created, in six days, everything that existed in the world. Catholic theology defined the creation process as a divine work and as a continuous act. For moralists, the creation process never ceased, its evolution marked by a perpetual continuum or rejuvenation. It was within this context of perpetuity that the idea of Man, as an associate or collaborator of God in the creation and procreation of other beings, emerged.[29]

Thus, Castro and the second Spanish Scholastic, also known as the Thomistic Scholastic, defined the new Vir as a collaborator of God, for in Man, in his seed, in his semen, was harbored the potential for new and future beings. A man was "created in the image of God and deformed only by sin." The moralists described both man and God as passionate, immortal, benevolent, just, truthful, honest, trustworthy, and merciful. The moralists furthered portrayed Vir as "a furious animal, vengeful and lustful, one that needed to be tamed in order to create a perfect animal of Christian virtues," as alluded to in the following aphorisms written by the fathers of the church during the early modern period.

> El hombre es el más noble, y valiente animal de cuantos nuestra madre naturaleza crio: y así se dice animal perfecto, porque le crio Dios a su divino retrato, y figura. (Man is the most noble and valiant animal created by Mother Nature: and so he is said to be a perfect animal, because God created him in his divine image and figure.)

> La dignidad del hombre es muy grande, solo en ser llamado amigo de Dios. (Man's dignity is very great, just by being considered a friend of God.)

> El cuerpo del hombre es el mayor enemigo que tiene, y el mayor traidor que jamás se vio, pues anda buscando la muerte a quien le da de comer. (The body of man is his capital enemy and the worst traitor ever, for death seeks those who wish to feed it.)

> Aunque los hombres puedan estar sin pecado, ninguno hay esté sin el. (Although men can exist without sin, no man exists without it.)[30]

The moralists made use of pessimism, fatalism, and other Christian constructs such as sin, punishment, guilt, or a disdain for the body—all rhetorical devices used to reinforce the image of the perfect gentleman, a recurring theme in their sermons or homilies. As a symbol of honor, strength, and the seducer and owner of his wife, the loyal vassal possessed a virile bravado, one that predisposed him to enlist and fight multiple wars for his prince. A pious gentleman represented the ideal master of his house, one who emulated the king of creation in defense of Catholicism and its venerable customs. This Christo-homocentric fetish of man formed part of Spain's vision for the early modern period—"hombre nuevo, iglesia nueva, sociedad nueva." During the first decades of the sixteenth century, both the crown and the miter made use of the word "new" in their textualized descriptions of man and society.[31]

In addition to the theological textual fantasy of Vir, lawyers and writers alike promulgated other characteristics of manliness. In his 1487 *Doctrinal de los caballeros*, Alonso de Cartagena, then the bishop of Burgos, identified "good customs, respect for the law, women, friendship, war and love" as the "proper attitudes and conduct that all real gentlemen should observe."[32] Cartagena applauded the traditional customs of Castilian society, an old yet stable model of mores that offered society a sense of security that was full of ritualistic and symbolic context.

The aforementioned mood, juxtaposed with the "emptiness and the uncertainty of modernity," held great appeal for Cartagena and his fellow moralists. For them, the perfect Christian gentleman defended venerated religious customs and took refuge in the past to inform his behavior in contemporary society. The old modes of correct behavior of the perfect Christian gentleman affected all levels of the society.[33] The new morality also extended to dress and the characterization of both men and women, according to class, ethnicity, or religious beliefs.[34]

Writers of fiction during the early modern period also mimicked the clichés of the Catholic morality on manliness. Whether dogmatic juridical sentences, sermons in Latin, or the prescribed catechism, they all found their way into the pages of satire or novels. This strict moral dogma transformed itself, in part, because of the fiction or the literary genre of the epoch. The following examples illustrate how images of the perfect Christian gentleman crystallized in different literary genres.

The noble gentleman portrayed by Baltasar de Castiglione, in *El cortesano*, a preferred author of Carlos I, fit the profile of that perfect Christian gentleman, for his "body and soul" emulated "purity of customs."[35] In *El cavallero perfecto*, another eloquent testimonial of the sixteenth century, de Salas Barbadillo depicted man's behavior and life blessed with "Christian zeal and heroic virtues."[36]

De Salas Barbadillo portrayed Don Alonso, the protagonist of the novel, as a gentleman beyond reproach, passionate, yet a man who knew when to repent after having sinned. Don Alonso, the perfect gentleman, defended heroic virtues with his deeds and his spoken words and as such positioned himself as a moral and a political example to his society—in short, as a dignified emulation of the nobles and the perfection of their customs.

For his part, the mystical poet Fray Antonio Panés in his *Calidades del varón perfecto*, dedicated the following allegorical verse to his image of the gallant:

> Arbol el justo a de ser,
> que se arraigue en humildad,
> que crezca con caridad,
> y dure en el padecer.
> (A just man like a tree
> is one rooted in humility,
> one that grows with charitableness
> and endures suffering.)[37]

Even medical doctors soon joined the ranks of theologians in their condemnation of sodomy. Dr. Francisco López de Villalobos proposed a series of punishments, written in verse, in order to remedy their "sufferance." López de Villalobos proposed to "cure" those who indulged in the sin with "hunger, cold, and lashes."[38]

Indeed, in many instances, writers had reappropriated the phrases and the ideas uttered by the fathers of the church as the source of their textual images and constructs.[39] With the perfect gallant in hand, the moralists eventually also saw fit to describe the role of Woman in early modern Spain.

Mujer Sencilla

The moralists also drafted their version of the ideal of woman, an icon cast in the incarnation of the Virgin Mary whose semblance above all embodied "purity, honesty, good will."[40] In part, moralists appropriated their misogynist descriptions based on *Instrucción de la muger christiana*, written by the Valencian pedagogue Louis Vivés in 1523.[41]

Vivés identified "virginity, beauty, abstinence, [and] matrimonial duties" as the pinnacles of women's virtues. He prescribed an entire program of proper behavior and garb for young ladies, virgins, adolescent women, married women, and finally widows. The early modern moralists labeled the transgression of these rigid roles as an ill against the institutions of the family, other social groups, and even Catholicism. Sanctions levied against the transgressors varied from admonishments, corporal punishment, and penitence to instilling sentiments of guilt for every age group.

During the early modern period, a man disposed of different occupational roles—a prince, a military function, an artisan, a humanist, a merchant, or even a clergyman. Women, on the other hand, had fewer options to exercise because Vivés and other moralists continued to relegate them to the roles of "mothers, daughters, widows, virgins or harlots, saints or witches." These identities derived solely from their sexual status and, in many instances, inhibited women from assuming other desired identities.[42]

Saint Thomas of Aquinas had long before planted these seeds of disdain and distrust for women when he advised his brothers to speak to them with "severity" and as little as possible. One could not even trust the most virtuous of women, for, concluded Aquinas, "the greater the virtuosity, the greater their inclination to deceive, for lurking underneath their sweet word hides a virus of great lasciviousness."[43]

The old stereotypes of woman put forward by the fathers of the church combined both the myth of paradise and the concept of original sin, where woman had displayed a fundamental role—an amalgamation of perversity, deceit, and the treason of God's confidence in the first parents. Theologians had constructed a diabolical image of woman for her suspected role in the loss of paradise. After all, as Saint Jerome so eloquently stated, "if woman had caused man's fall in paradise," it should come as no surprise that she could also "seduce those not found in paradise." Furthermore, warned Jerome, "never allow yourself to be alone with a woman"; rather always be in the company of a "witness."[44]

Still later, Saint Thomas of Aquinas, in his *De periculo familiaritatis dominarum, vel mulierum* (The terrible risk of familiarizing with women and its pernicious consequences), argued that "God had created woman more *imperfect* than man and thus obligated her to obey man for he naturally possessed an abundance of sense and reason" (emphasis added).[45]

On the one hand, the moralists recognized the need for women in the procreation process and the continuum of creation. Yet they too recognized her as sometimes cunning, untrustworthy, perhaps even evil, and thus they confined her to the three basic functions described below in order to justify her submission to man. Some of the moralists' aphorisms for women read:

En la vida de la mujer, tres salidas ha de hacer: bautismo, casamiento y sepultura. (Woman has but three functions in life: baptism, marriage, and the grave.)

Al más discreto varón, sola una mujer, le echa a perder. (Only one woman suffices to spoil the most discrete gentleman.)

De la mar la sal, de la mujer mucho mal. (From the sea the salt, from woman much harm.)

Dile que es hermosa, y tornarse ha loca. (Tell her she is beautiful, and mad she becomes.)[46]

The theologians of the baroque defined the labor of women in the procreation process as purely passive. Woman resembled a vase, a mere recipient of man's seed in the procreation process. Castro and his fellow theologians viewed procreation as a natural and a predetermined function of the sexual act between man and woman. The Scholastic defined coitus between man and woman as perfect, independent of whether or not one or the other felt pleasure in the process. The fact that one derived pleasure during the sexual act, though neither necessary nor required for procreation, posed an entirely different dilemma for the Spanish Scholastic. According to the Scholastic, pleasure merely functioned as the stimulus for the realization of procreation. The sexual act between man and woman could have produced satisfaction, and that, defined as either good or bad, depended on the circumstances that had led to the realization of such an act. Consequently, Scholasticism invented its own list of lustful sins.

Having outlined the roles for the perfect man and woman, moralists moreover equipped them with respective sexual functions.

Scholastic Lust

First and foremost, the Spanish Scholastic outlined a hierarchical list of lustful sins developed by Saint Thomas as well as Fray Juan Enríquez, a seventeenth-century moralist.[47] The lustful sins formed part of the original seven capital sins, or the sources from which all other sins originate.[48] The moralists identified the seven capital sins and their contrary virtues as follows:

Pride	Humility
Covetousness	Liberality
Lust	Chastity

Anger	Meekness
Gluttony	Temperance
Envy	Brotherly love
Sloth	Diligence

Despite their notion of procreation as a requisite function of man to further the creation process, the Scholastics developed the hierarchy of lustful sins, for they too realized that man likewise exhibited a sexual appetite. For them, man either dignified his collaboration with God or simply ceded to his own sexual appetite and satisfied an instinct independent of procreation and thus sinned.

The following schematic description cites the most significant sins, from the gravest to the least grave.

Sodomy

Sacrilege with a nun

Sacrilege with a priest

Incest

Adultery

Rape

Prostitution

Simply fornication

The Scholastic understood simple fornication between a man and a woman as the least grave of the lustful sins.[49] It considered simple fornication barely a sin, for it posed no obstacles to procreation, but the Scholastic nevertheless classified fornication as a sin, especially if both individuals could have married prior to the act. Sex for a price did not constitute any graver offense. Both the crown and the miter looked askew at prostitution, perhaps even tolerating it and seldom finding it necessary to prosecute it as a crime. Men in positions of political power protected this profession, for some felt it convenient for women to dedicate themselves to prostitution.[50] In seventeenth-century Spain, prostitution continued to flourish, as it had in the sixteenth century.[51]

Some moralists believed that lustful acts begot others.[52] Lust, in their eyes, was the capital vice that bred many others.[53] From the beginning of the seventeenth century, the moralists based their attempts to close public brothels on this principle of engendering: fornication with whores did not extinguish the flames of passion or greater evils; all to the contrary, it ignited the flames and served to propitiate those desires.[54]

Others argued in favor of the brothel closures, enumerating the extraordinary frequency with which sodomitical acts *contra natura* occurred in these houses of pleasure. The whores, considered skilful masters of the art of hell, had taught the boys to accustom themselves to the nefarious sin: this "vile and tyrannical love so nurtured the condition of those it affected that they eventually became devotees of the act." [55] "Both tamed and wild animals could live the entire year in peace," one aphorism held, but, "as soon as the rutting season began, they tore each other apart." [56]

Theologians considered the rape of a pure virgin by a man as somewhat graver than fornication for the perpetrator who violated the voluntary will of the maiden. In this instance, the moralists perceived the woman as the one wronged or deceived. The Scholastics condemned adulterous relations between men and women as still more serious than rape, for, unlike as with rape, the woman—in this instance labeled the unfaithful one who deceived her husband—besmirched a man's honor but above all violated the sanctity of matrimony.

In 1637 Madrid, a royal scrivener, acting in defense of his honor, performed the function of executioner in his home and killed his wife by garrote, for he suspected her of adultery.[57] Within the sanctity of matrimony, sexual acts—some, not all—prevailed, but beyond these boundaries, married individuals could not engage in any sort of sexual activity that did not lead to procreation.

The moralists defined incest as still more lustful than adultery, having placed a special emphasis on the abuse of the parental role. Contrary to what many anthropologists believe, the moralists did not consider incest as the gravest of the lustful sins in early modern Spain. For the moralists, the sin of sacrilege seemed still graver than incest. Sex with nuns supposed an even graver sacrilege than sexual acts practiced with a priest.

Finally, the moralists defined the *pecado contra natura* as the gravest of the lustful sins, for as a direct offense to God, this sin altered the image of his creation and disturbed the natural order of things. Before the medieval period, theologians had considered sodomy not as a transgression against nature but rather as an impurity.[58] Spain's imperialist ambitions— control of its borders and the acquisition of new territories in the Indias—fortified its desire for a new early modern Vir free of vice.

Sodomía Perfecta

Vir committed the sin against nature by emitting his seed during any sexual act without the possibility of procreation. In its broadest interpretation, the nefarious sin against nature constituted any sodomitical act that jeopardized the economy of creation and impeded the possibility of man's collaborating with God.

In 1550, Antonio Gómez, a casuist from Castile, had argued that man committed the "crime and sin against nature" when he "realized carnal access not intended for natural coitus and the regeneration of its species."[59] This broad definition did not refer only to a purely sexual relationship between persons of the same sex.

The definition also encompassed masturbation and bestiality as sins against nature from a theological perspective. In 1587, secular authorities in Sevilla burned Alonso Pérez and "whipped" the young boy who had ejaculated, or committed the "sin of pollution," with Alonso. The young boy also served a four-year sentence in the galleys.[60]

Furthermore, both the moralists and the secular laws of the early modern period also confirmed sodomy as a crime against the state. In the introduction, or the *Proemio*, of the thirteenth-century *Setena Partida*, the jurist Gregorio López argued that even though in the broadest sense any sin constituted a sin against nature, in the most peculiar sense he considered *sodomie* as the proper sin against nature.

Sodomy became known as *crimen contra naturam, peccatus, crimen nefandum, pecado nefando, crimen cometido contra orden natural, nefando pecado contra natura, el pecado, la sodomía,* or *crimen atrocisimus*. And a sodomite was referred to as *sodomita, sodomista, sodomético, somético, puto, marica, maricón,* or *bujarrón*.[61] "Bujarrón" tended to connote a "pleasure for anal penetration" and a love for young boys.[62]

Vir, of free will, committed *sodomía perfecta* having engaged another Vir in coitus of the ass. A 1544 confessional manual condemned sodomy as an insatiable carnal appetite for "*sexo* outside the ordinary vase." The perpetrator should be condemned without remission for the "abominable handling of the virile member."[63] "If a man had carnal access to another man," argued Gómez, they committed the "abominable and detestable crime of sodomy against nature, the gravest of all crimes, graver still than heresy, and as such the maximum offense to God and nature." In this scenario, Gómez advocated the death penalty and confiscation of all goods for both the "agent and patient."[64]

Conceptualized as a malicious act, the nefarious sin had differed in quality from other transgressions, such as rape or adultery, which also tainted the virtue of man's honor. Despite the established differences between these transgressions that affected the familial order, as in the case of adultery, or the cosmic order, as in the case of sodomy, the courts considered these sins ruptures of a neatly prescribed alliance to the patriarch, on the one hand, and the Holy Father on the other.[65] The early modern moralists believed that blood, or purity thereof, functioned as the common element between man and God and that its fluidity was thwarted by the adulterous act against the honor of the family or interrupted by the sodomitical act.[66]

Yet others committed *sodomía imperfecta* if individuals of the opposite sex enjoyed coitus somewhere other than in "the natural place—*extra vas naturale.*" Man and woman, wrote Fray Bartolomé de Medina, committed sodomy when, during the sexual act, "the woman situated herself in the superior position and the husband in the inferior, a position outside the natural order of things." For Medina, man on his back during intercourse constituted an "anti-natural and disorderly" carnal act.[67]

Man and woman, wrote the moralist López, could also commit the nefarious sin, especially when the sexual act had not lead to procreation.[68] Antonio Gómez had concurred with López: men who committed the nefarious sin with women should also be punished. Gómez cited a case that involved a husband who had attempted to penetrate his wife with an object. She refused and denounced him before Gómez. Because the husband had not achieved his objective, the court condemned him only to lashes and banished him from the province.[69]

Thus, penetration, especially penetration of any ass, and the wasteful spillage of semen dominated notions of early modern sodomy as sin.[70] The Spanish state also defined sodomy as "nefarious, or indignant, lascivious, which cannot be spoken of without embarrassment, a nefarious sin called such for its lasciviousness and its obscenity."[71] In a figurative sense, sodomy became simply known as "the sin." Apparently, no other sin altered the natural order of creation, as did the *peccatus*—considered a direct threat to the image of God. With the consummation of the sodomitical act, the sodomite not only ruptured the notion that man had been conceived in God's image but also rejected a divine invitation to collaborate in the creation.

In the early modern period, lawyers too had defined sodomy as acts that rejected a legal order preordained by God. For the jurists, the concept of nature represented a juridical domain within its species of laws. The lawyers understood *contra natura* as a cosmic experience of sin: the abominable act simply ruined the order of the universe and brought with it tragedy and death as the *Siete partidas* had warned. Sodomy symbolized a grave disorder, for it also rejected a matrimonial alliance.[72]

¿Lesbianas?

The texts mentioned thus far have referred exclusively to Vir, as if sodomy, in the early modern period, represented an exclusive domain of man.[73] But if legal texts during the early modern period had attributed notions of sodomy exclusively to men, theologians in Biblical times had already commented about the possibility of sodomy between women.

One of the earliest descriptions of sodomy as *contra natura* appeared in the New Testament in a letter Saint Paul sent to the Romans in which he referred to sodomy both between men and between women.[74] Lamentably, commented Paul, both men and women had abandoned the "natural use" of their prescribed order when men committed with men, and women with women, the shameful act that was *contra naturaleza*.[75] Back in the thirteenth century, Gregorio López, in his commentary titled "Omes" in the *Setena Partida*, wrote that although the law applied to men, "it included women as well," especially when one woman committed with another "coitus against nature." Thus, concluded López, "feminine sodomy was possible and should be punished."[76]

Despite the possibility of female sodomy, reasoned López, divine or secular law did not castigate coitus between two women. Although he considered "feminine sodomy a grave sin," to him "it could not compare to the atrocious sodomitical vice committed between men, for unlike sodomy between women, sodomy between men perturbed the natural order of things to a far greater extent." Sodomy between women did not alter the economy of the creation, because there was no possibility of coitus involving dissipated semen, and unlike sodomy between men, sodomy between women did not directly offend the image of God.[77] Consequently, argued López, women should have to suffer not the heat of the flames but rather a penalty less severe than death, except when they had employed *"aliquo instrumento virginitas violetur"* with each other.[78]

The Royal Prison in Seville, observed Fray Cristóbal Chabes, in the seventeenth century had "punished many women, for they had wanted to be more manly than nature had intended." In jail, "some women had converted themselves into roosters with the help of a *baldrés* or an instrument crafted from the slothful hide of tanned sheep and shaped into the form of a man's *natura*, which they then attached to themselves with ribbons." These women received "two hundred lashes," and the court "perpetually banned them from the kingdom."[79]

Unlike López, Antonio Gómez, another moralist of the sixteenth century, wrote that if two women committed the crime of sodomy against nature *"mediante aliquo instrumento materiali,"* they should be burned, as dictated in an earlier case he had prosecuted that "involved two nuns."[80] But in the absence of an instrument used for penetration, Gómez argued for a penalty less than death. Apparently, as of 1560, even the Supreme Inquisitorial Tribunal in Madrid knew of no cases that involved sodomy between women without the use of an "instrument," despite accusations to the contrary.[81]

In the first decade of the sixteenth century, Catalina de Belunza suffered the full wrath of the 1497 *Pragmática.* Not only had a secular court confiscated her goods, but it had also submitted her to torture. The attorney general in San Sebastián had accused Catalina and Mariche of "penetrating each other like a man and a woman should, nude, in bed, touching and kissing each other, the one on top of the other's belly or paunch, a crime they had perpetrated on numerous and diverse occasions."[82] Catalina professed her innocence and reiterated her earlier claim that "the court should rule her case null and void, given the incompetence and madness of the attorney general."[83]

In her 1503 appeal before the chancellery in Valladolid, Catalina had not only successfully argued for the reinstatement of her domestic goods but also succeeded in having the lower court's sentence—perpetual banishment from San Sebastián—overturned by the High Court. After all, argued Catalina, "only one witness had testified against her, a woman at that, herself a false and compromised witness, for she also found herself a defendant in the case." The High Court concurred with Catalina and acquitted her of all charges.[84]

Acquittal of "the sin" also worked in favor of *las cañitas* (the little canes), a term of endearment by which neighbors knew Inés de Santa Cruz and Catalina Ledesma in Valladolid. Again, the chancellery in Valladolid absolved Santa Cruz and Ledesma, both described as "whores and sodomites, a profession they executed with the use of cane in the form of a virile member."[85] The case against the sixty-year-old Inés de Santa Cruz and Catalina Ledesma, in her mid-thirties, registered in 1603, represents a rare complete *proceso* that involved sodomy between women in the early modern period still kept in Spanish historical archives.

The moralists' polymythic vision of sodomy and its multiplicity of signifiers meant that, in the rhetoric of the moralists, both man and woman could commit sodomy. Still, many moralists considered sodomy between women, "although a crime," as "inauthentic, imperfect, devoid of scattered or wasted semen," and the courts usually deferred these cases and their sentences to the local bishops.[86] Sometimes, both the courts and the clergy turned a complete blind eye toward other types of gender transgressions in the peninsula.

Magdalena Muñoz—Half Nun, Half Man; Or, Another Saucy Tale

Another saucy tale of the early modern period did not draw the ire of local officials, as illustrated by the situation of a nun named Magdalena Muñoz in 1617. Fray Agustín de Torres described Magdalena as a "manly woman," one who could "hold a sword in one hand" and was "capable of hurling an arquebus with the other."[87]

In 1605, Magdalena, a native of Sabiote, took up residence with a group of nuns in the Coronada convent of Ubeda, located within the jurisdiction of Castile. Shortly thereafter, a group of men from Sabiote approached the prioress and inquired "how she could have allowed a man into the convent." Upon learning of the news, "the nuns, just like women who had little to occupy themselves with, in a fit of frenzy, caused such a turmoil such that it obligated the prioress to examine Magdalena."

During the twelve years that Magdalena labored at the convent, the nuns had on many occasions witnessed to their own satisfaction their sister's gender, although "she had possessed the strength, disposition, and the condition of a man." In 1617, Magdalena herself had summoned Fray Agustín to the convent. As the two sat alone in a room, Magdalena informed the friar that "an accident of nature had converted her into a man." About eight or nine days earlier, the convent had received a bulk of wheat that weighed 100 *fanegas*, or the equivalent of 7,480 kilos.[88]

Magdalena measured, divided, and stored all the wheat in one afternoon. After having toiled that afternoon, Magdalena felt much pain between both her swollen thighs. "Tormented," she understood herself broken after such effort, but she "dared not utter a word for she had not wanted a doctor to see her and render her a broken woman." Three days later, the inflammation had subsided, and in its place a "man's *natura* had sprouted."

Fray Agustín demanded that Magdalena verify the truth, and as she revealed herself, he confirmed "her to be as much a man as the next." In order to avoid another upheaval at the convent, the friar also instructed

Magdalena to request an audience with the Holy See. Magdalena was to inform him that her father had actually forced and threatened her to take her vows as a nun, but that she had never complied with said request.

Fray Agustín then asked the prioress to lock up Magdalena in a cell. He instructed "six nuns, the oldest and most devoutly religious, to enter the cell together, only when they brought Magdalena her meals." The friar then summoned the prior of Baeza to the convent, and together they performed a second examination of Magdalena.

The clerics "saw it" with their "own eyes," and they "felt it" with their own hands. In Magdalena, they had "witnessed and touched a perfect man and his *natura*." A hole, the size of a pine nut, just above the place where "women supposedly have their *sexo*" was all that remained as the only sign of Magdalena's "womanness." Her "new man's *natura* had grown in that same spot."

Magdalena, "a quiet woman" earlier in life, "had said nothing about the small hole"; instead, she had "decided to become a nun." The clerics deduced that the small opening had functioned "like the root or source of a man's urinary tract, its member internally lodged within the walls of the body." Despite her thirty-four years of age, Magdalena's "chest looked as flat as a board." Magdalena had never menstruated. Regularly, "she took to the whip" and "practiced self-flagellation until she bled." She would then "smear the blood on her clothing" and in this way "exhibited her cycles of menstruation" to the other nuns. Magdalena flagellated herself to avoid being known as a *"marimacho,"* or manly woman, by the nuns.

Six days after the growth of her new "member," Magdalena's voice also began to "thicken," and "her upper lip began to darken with hair." Fray Agustín then called upon Magdalena's father and related the story of Magdalena's member to him. The "poor man" thought he "would die of fright." Finally, one night the friar accompanied Magdalena's father to the convent and "dressed Magdalena in a colorful tunic and veil and turned her over to the custody of her father." A "rich man without heirs," the father felt much happiness, for "he now found himself with a very manly son and an eligible bachelor at that."

Magdalena, too, "felt content after what felt like twelve years in a prison." "Liberty for Magdalena," wrote Fray Agustín, "could be sweet, for she now realized herself a manly woman, a naturalness that no other higher being than God could have produced." [89]

Unfortunately, not all those who sought liberty in early modern Spain could readily attain it, because the courts persisted in selectively prosecuting sodomites throughout the peninsula.

The Tales of Fray Pedro de León

In 1981 a manuscript written by Fray Pedro de León, which had remained hidden in the Jesuits' archives in Granada since 1619, finally found its way into the hands of archivists and historians.[90] "I do not offer the manuscript," wrote de León, so that "from it one may draw conclusions." Rather the Jesuit friar, who witnessed Spain at the forefront of Christianity and during its final chapter of expansionism in the early modern period, intended to provide a "glimpse" of Andalusian society (Fig. 2.2).[91]

One of the most interesting sections of his manuscript, entitled "Apéndice de los Ajusticiados," is an appendix of cases adjudicated by the secular High Court in Sevilla. In the "Apéndice," de León recorded the

2.2. **"Vista de Andalucía siglo XVI."** In A. Ortelius, *Theatrvm orbis terrarvm: Opus nunc denuo ab ipso auctore recognitum, multisque locis castigatum, & quamplurimis nouis tabulis atque commentarijs auctum* (Antwerp: In officina Plantiniana, auctoris aere & cura, 1592). Reproduced with the permission of the Archivo General de Indias, Seville.

names of the accused, descriptions of the juridical sentences, and descriptions of the executions he witnessed. He elaborated in great detail on the nature of the crimes committed and the scandalous frequency with which the authorities had invoked the death penalty. But, most important, de León recorded his perceptions of man, of sodomy, and of sodomites.

Between 1578 and 1616, de León had served as chaplain at the Carcel Real de Sevilla—"its numerous cells, galleries, and dungeons depicted as *el miserable.*" The cleric felt "hurt" at the sight of "the lice and the misery" suffered by the prisoners.[92]

Cervantes, whom de León met in Sevilla, described the prison as the place where "all miserable sound makes its bed." The Royal Prison represented a sort of historical realism, one of the principal themes echoed in Cervantes' prologue to *El Quixote.*[93] Mateo Alemán, a *"pícaro"* philosopher of the seventeenth century, considered the prison as "the stopping place for the fool-hearted, for friendships and vengeance, a forced punishment, a slow repentance, a confused republic, a brief ailment, a prolonged death, a port of sighs, a valley of tears, a house of the mad, where one cries out aloud and alone looking after his own madness."[94]

At any one time, the Royal Prison accommodated more than 1800 men and women, some taken there as prisoners from New Spain by officials of the Casa de la Contratación. On any given night and with the consent of the authorities, an additional 150 women spent the night with the prisoners.[95] For Fray Cristóbal de Chabes, another priest who labored with de León, the prison resembled the "worst cage on earth" or a setting that "harbored sickness, pain, torture, vengeance, exploitation," and, in short, "no justice."[96]

Between 1578 and 1616 the secular authorities in Seville sentenced some 309 individuals to death. At least 48 of those 309 victims were burned for sodomy. Additionally, the tribunal of the Casa de la Contratación sentenced another 10 to burn at the stake. Many of the men condemned to death for sodomy verbally related their stories to de León as he sat up with them the night before their executions or as he accompanied them to the *quemadero.* About 15,000 spectators usually attended the public spectacles described by de León. "For the first time in 1578," wrote de León, some eighty years after the celebrated 1497 *Pragmática*, "Sevillian officials had employed fire as an element of the spectacle."

The officials tortured eighteen-year-old Pedro de Multes "with fire": "his hands and arms burned, until he confessed to having committed the crime." A magistrate then condemned him to death. As the young Multes burned, "his many tears and uncontrollable sobs caused much pity among the spectators, who had witnessed the cruelty that induced the young man to shed many tears and display his sentiments."[97]

Despite the tears, de León reminded those congregated that "the gravest sinners are not those burned to death but rather those yet to be arrested."[98] In subsequent sermons, de León expanded on his theories of sodomy.

La Lacra, an Import from Abroad

Unlike his predecessors, de León began to offer other explanations for *la lacra*—an infestation, a disease, a plague—a term he often used when he referred to sodomy. *La lacra* came from abroad, from others, from non-Spaniards, asserted the cleric. Others in the peninsula agreed. "Foreigners," confirmed the sixteenth-century historian Gaspar Escolano, had introduced sodomy into Valencia (Fig. 2.3).[99]

Moreover, moralists claimed a cause-and-effect relationship between calamities, such as hunger or plagues, and the existence of foreign sodomites in those cities or towns.[100] Divine punishment, then, reconciled the city with God by restoring an alliance between the two, a relapse that

2.3. Bartolomew Portugués, or representations of the other. In *Bucaniers of America: Or, a True Account of the Most Remarkable Assaults Committed of late Years upon the coasts of The West Indies, By the Bucaniers of Jamaica and Tortuga, Both English and French* (London: Printed for William Crooke, at the Green Dragon without Temple-bar, 1684). Nettie Lee Benson Latin American Rare Books Collection, University of Texas at Austin.

required the sin to be purged by fire, a symbolic punishment that liberated the maligned imprisoned within the confines of the sodomite.[101]

By the beginning of the sixteenth century, writers frequently associated the sodomite with the condition of the foreigner. Writers had often represented Moriscos (Moors) in literature as consummate practitioners of sodomy.[102] The vast literature of the period also attributed the importation of the sin especially to the influence of the Turks or the Italians.[103]

Mateo Alemán, in his *Guzmán de Alfarache*, wrote that one could find "sodomy, a bestial brutality, in abundance throughout Italy and the Levant." [104] Foreigners composed the majority category of those sodomites condemned in Valencia as well as in Seville. And in the remainder of the peninsula, foreigners, especially the Portuguese, provoked major suspicion and bore the brunt of the repression administered by the Inquisitorial tribunals of the Ancien Régime.[105]

By contrast, in the Dutch republic, observers believed that Spanish diplomats who had gathered in Utrecht for peace talks to end the War of the Spanish Succession had introduced sodomy into the Netherlands in 1713, a vice also considered particularly Catholic and Italian.[106] A Catholic vice? Never, in the eyes of the moralists. But Italian? Certainly. De León, in his sermons and in his writings, would lend prudence to this and other types of Spanish xenophobia.

Big Members—Turks and Moors

In 1616 the Sevillian authorities burned a slave and a Turk named Hamete, also known as Juan and who "should no longer be referred to by his Moorish name, for he died like a Christian." Earlier, Hamete had met a young boy of nine or ten years in the meadows and promised him a number of gifts.

The young boy, "fooled," continued into the meadows with Hamete, and there the "Turk forced himself onto the boy, aggressively attempting to penetrate him." The boy had cried out, "God help me!" Alas, Hamete had not "completed the sodomitical act," save to have "emitted his desire between the boy's little legs." The boy, "crack brained, crying and dripping blood, escaped" and then "appeared before the Lord Mayor." Hamete, upon his apprehension, readily confessed to this and other crimes.

Hamete admitted receiving eight *ducados* from a certain man for each time he penetrated him. This "honorable gentleman" had also asked Hamete to hire "a pair of potent Turks or Moors with big natural members, each paid at the rate of one *real de ocho* for every time they produced the desired effect on him." The secular officials had since burnt the two Turks and had charged the honorable gentleman in absentia for sodomy. The gentleman had long before fled for Italy.[107] Like the gentleman, many other "valiant Spanish boys" customarily sought refuge in Italy.[108]

In the minds of many Spaniards, the Italians reigned as the most notorious sodomites, so much so that one day that same year, when a student went to have his hair cut at a barbershop owned by an Italian, the young man arrived wearing his own "remedy for the cure" of "the sin." Secular authorities in Madrid had just burned another Italian barber for sodomy. When the student entered the barbershop, he took off his "habit or hood and revealed a large basket tightly fitted to his buttocks."

"Why the great basket?" asked the Italian barber. Given that "dangerous times abound" and the "nationality" of the Italian barber, the student felt it "prudent to wear the basket as a preventive measure." The response so offended the barber that a fight ensued between the two and led to the arrest of both men. That afternoon the authorities released the student, who left the commissary "still wearing his defense against the nefarious." [109]

Meanwhile, de León continued to identify other attributes he associated with sodomy.

Don't Dress Like Them, for Butterflies *Will* Burn

The wearing of nontraditional dress and attire, especially new fashion from Italy, or even a young man's "beauty," proposed de León, also predisposed one to the "pestilent vice." In 1585, when secular officials in Seville burned sodomites Salvador Martín, Alonso Sánchez, and Diego Maldonado, a native of Granada and "member of a well-to-do family," de León rationalized that Maldonado, in all probability, had "infected himself with the *lacra* in Italy."

Before his arrest, Maldonado had traveled to Italy to purchase the latest in Italian apparel. Not only should "honorable men flee from these wild beasts," but men should also guard against not resembling the likes of Maldonado and others whose "powdered, painted faces and dress" caused the cleric great consternation.[110] Early modern Vir, in the words of de León, should instead strive to preserve his *"honra de caballero."*[111]

"Some of you do not partake of the vice," cried out de León in one sermon to the men in attendance, but "nonetheless some of you dress as if you do" and thus "you too could be mistaken for one of them." De León believed that "honorable men had no reason to dress, or to wear hosiery or shoes, or curl their hair, in a manner that ventured outside the common, ordinary dress of honorable men." De Leon pleaded, "If you are not one of them, then don't dress like them," for "if you do not sell wine, then do not exhibit a tavern bush on your door."

Young men's dress, especially, should not "attract attention, nor invite comment"; rather it should emulate the "somber common ways of honorable men's sons." "Why do they venture outside the common custom and wear different shoes or curled hair?" pondered the cleric. "Eyes wander" and even "thoughts and discourses go astray at the sight of seeing those men walking with such affected delicacy, such that they resembled whores." When the Jewish people saw John the Baptist in a different habit, the priests asked him, *"Tu quis es?"* Likewise, surmised de León, one could ask of those who wear "rich and splendid dress affected with such daintiness, *'Tu quis es?'"* [112]

Sodomites who "did not amend themselves" and were "driven by 'the sin'" were just like butterflies that, tempted by the light of a fire, "fly back and forth, each time getting closer and closer to the open fire," professed the friar. "Initially," explained de León, the butterfly "burns only a wing." The temptation of the fire is such that it then "burns another little piece of its wing until eventually it is fully burned." Sodomites who "trade in this type of merchandise," foretold de León, "sully their honor and, like the butterflies that eventually ended up in the fire, will burn." [113]

Fancy dress and affected delicacy certainly begot the begotten, as other stories by de León would divulge.

Afternoon Tea in the Meadows

One affluent fellow named Maldonado "had always surrounded himself with spruced up genteel young men, inviting many of them over for afternoon luncheon." Often the men would set off together to an orchard in the meadows of the Sevillian countryside known as the Huerta del Rey, a "popular refuge for those seeking pleasure in the most compromising clandestine social actions of the sixteenth century." [114] On one occasion, Maldonado invited a young boy to the meadows.

The young boy, who suspected Maldonado's bad intentions, alerted the secular authorities about the planned reception. As part of their countersecurity, the authorities went to the meadows and hid among the trees in the orchard. While under a fig tree, eating figs, Maldonado began "uttering tender and amorous words" to the boy. He simply "lost his composure and then attempted to kiss and force himself onto the young boy." When the clever boy cried out, "I'm being forced upon," the authorities jumped out from behind the trees and arrested the fig-eating Maldonado.

In his deposition before the secular authorities, Maldonado readily

denounced many other "young, well-dressed, and beautiful boys" as sodomites. Among these, one in particular captured de León's imagination—
"a very handsome, a very beautiful, and a very well-dressed boy named
Francisco Galindo, who, given his exquisite dress, looked more like a
woman than a man." Women in Sevilla had often murmured to one another that "the attire worn by Galindo had been given to him by those
who used him for their own pleasure."

     In pleasure land, Galindo, the son of a silk vendor, had always as-
sumed the "role of woman or patient, a very coarse thread indeed and
more dangerous than that of silk," unequivocally confirmed de León.
"Instead of learning his father's trade," that of silk weaving, Galindo had
chosen that of a "whore" and had, like other sodomites, "preferred to associate himself with fire," continued de León. "The devil had arrived,"
voiced an alarmed de León from his pulpit. Indeed these demons had
"fanned the flames of sensuality and the pleasures of the flesh that kin-
dled a fire that would eventually consume" such men.[115]

Oh, No! Not the Clergy, Not the Nobles!

The "beautiful Galindo" likewise denounced many other "young gentlemen of Sevilla and some ecclesiastics" as sodomites. However, de León
"purposely" kept these last *procesos* out of public view, for the "ecclesiastics, if found guilty, had their own superiors responsible for said punishment." Often, de León "instructed the young boys not to implicate men
of the religious cloth in their confessions," much to the "gratefulness" of
his "religious superiors and other ecclesiastics."[116] Nonetheless, some of
the most celebrated clergy of the epoch in Seville could not escape prosecution by the secular High Court.

     De León cited the cases of Fray Pascual Jaime and his "accomplice, a
very young and very handsome boy from Vizcaya named Francisco Lega-
zoteca," both burned by the secular High Court in Seville. The burning
of the boy had caused "so much pity and compassion among the crowd,"
for "he wept like a child and cried out that the cleric had bribed him with
garb and splendid apparel" and that he, "like a fool, consented" to the actions of Pascual.

     Pascual Jaime, always "gracefully dressed, curiously enough, wore a
painted face" and seldom went without "the company of well-dressed
young boys with painted faces." Some young boys had presented Pascual
with an uncompromising feat; "he took them home, cleaned them up,
and dressed them in rich splendid dress, all at his own cost." Pascual had

spent forty-eight of his fifty-six years "plagued with the vice." "Be wary," cautioned de León, at the amount of "harm that such a man can cause the Republic."[117]

However, de León succeeded in "hiding from public humiliation the identities of other gentlemen" denounced by Galindo, for, "truthfully speaking, the boy had consented to those acts." The court released "most of these young gentlemen, among the most noble in Seville, including Galindo himself." Inevitably, Galindo "repented, became a priest, and led a most memorable life afterward."[118]

Unfortunately, Galindo's overbearing "prettiness caused him to resume his promiscuous behavior," and subsequently, yet again, he fell victim to the "pestilential vice." Sodomy, "once tasted," observed de León, "became difficult to forsake." In the end, the "beautiful Galindo" also succumbed to the heat of the flames.[119]

Ruffs and Cuffs

Other, less noble individuals enjoyed fewer privileges than those offered to Galindo and his gentleman-friends. The same year as the Galindo case, the High Court accused "Machuco, el Negro," famed for his treatment of "beautiful gallant gentlemen," not of having committed the nefarious sin, but rather of "acting as an *alcahuete* (a pimp of sorts) for the young gentlemen who committed sodomy." Machuco performed "marriages between boys" and "introduced some boys to others by pointing out fellows he knew were also touched by the vice of sodomy." In short, wrote de León, Machuco, el Negro, functioned as a "bloodhound."

On the day of the executions, officials led Machuco and two other boys out of the prison onto an open cart. The prison authorities had dressed Machuco in a "breastplate armor, himself painted on it." Machuco wore a "ruff laced with much silk, his hair curled" and sported a "grand foretop."[120] "Two very beautiful young boys, their faces painted, their forelocks curled, dressed in silk ruffs" stood on either side of Machuco as the procession meandered toward the *quemadero.*

Machuco, "sad and melancholy, grew blacker, as the authorities forced him to join the young boys' hands together just as one does in a marriage" and "just as the Negro had so often performed in Seville." "All of Seville," recalled de León, had turned out and "witnessed the spectacle, for the authorities had never before punished such abominable crimes in this manner."

At the *quemadero,* de León delivered one of his most memorable ser-

mons before the Sevillian aristocracy and other learned men of letters—
"all gentlemen also covered in ruffs, lace, fine linens," and "wearing great
foretops." De León admonished, "Get away from me, those of you who
wear ruffs, cuffs, and foretops, for you smell of cinched wood." Notwithstanding the fashionable advances in European dress, de León and others
condemned the "foretops, the curls, and the silk ruffs." [121]

"No, no," maintained Fray J. Lainez—the ruffs and cuffs did not
constitute "manly dress." Furthermore, "those feminine adornments hin-
dered a man's modesty." [122] In fact, the dress and the adornments that
women wore had long caused concern in the pulpits of the Catholic
Church, because many moralists believed that particular garb and accou-
trements incited lustful sins. [123]

De León forewarned the stupefied nobles who witnessed how the
"wearing of fine linens, ruffs, cuffs, and great locks of hair hanging from
the forehead defamed those burned at the stake." "The common people,"
on the other hand, present at the spectacle "rejoiced" upon hearing de
León's attack on the splendid dress of the aristocracy (Fig. 2.4).

From that day forward, "a reformation ensued and the aristocracy
abandoned this type of garb." Some of the most "honorable gentlemen"
of Seville called upon Fray de León at his home, "forever grateful" to
him for his ruffs-and-cuffs sermon. When others met him on the street,
they laughed and said, "My lord, may God bless you." "Brilliant discourse, Fray," flattered the Lord Mayor of Sevilla. "You should be made
bishop." [124]

In addition to proper dress and adornments, de León pinpointed
other signs readily identifiable in sodomites.

Those Sodomites—They Could Even Sniff Each Other Out

Young and old men alike, cautioned the friar, should have learned to recognize these "signals." Good men should "never allow their hand to be
held by a less than honorable man," explained de León. The "lovers of the
bestial vice," assured the cleric, "knew each other's identity by their tac-
tile signals and by certain other signals they made to each other."

"Upon touching hands with men," the sodomites instantly "knew
who pertained to their fabric and who did not," and they quickly ascer-
tained "if they could dare" to go ahead with their vile proposals. The
sodomites could "smell each other" at a distance. They recognized each
other's "sentiments," by observing "the way they walked" or "other movements of the body," as if uttered by "spoken words." Sodomites immediately recognized each other by "eyesight." "If an honorable boy ever

2.4. **Philip IV and a page in "ruffs and cuffs."** *Felipe IV y el enano Miguel Soplillo,* 1620–1621, Rodrigo de Villandrando. Reproduced courtesy of the Museo Nacional del Prado, Madrid.

recognized these signals," recommended de León, the boy should "bombard" the sodomite and "violently frighten him away."[125]

At the beginning of the sixteenth century, Spain's borders, whether represented in new types of dress, ideas, or commerce, were gushing wide open. De León and writers alike attempted to contain this unraveling, having likened sodomy with notions of effeminacy—a far cry from the rhetoric employed earlier by the moralists concerning the crime and sin *contra natura*.

María, Marica, Maricón

Notions of effeminacy in association with a man's proper dress and perceptions of sodomy would gradually gain notoriety in the peninsula and reach a high-pitched level of hysteria in mid-seventeenth-century Mexico City.

When Sevillian officials burned a cook named Domingo Palacios and a gardener named Juan Bueno in 1593, de León explained that an innkeeper had ousted Domingo from his quarters because he looked like a *maricón* (effeminate man or coward) or a *marica* (queer, from the Latin *mulier*).[126] The philological origins of the effeminate or effeminacy date back to the early fifteenth century.[127] Notions of effeminacy in early modern Spain encompassed at least four different meanings (Fig. 2.5).

In the first instance, effeminacy was attributed to someone "inclined to pleasure" or "lustful, or dissolute."[128] In 1437, Santillana described an "effeminate Salomon who, late in life, had submitted himself to the power of woman."[129]

In the second case, effeminacy referred to "a proper characteristic of woman, feminine or something that invoked femininity." Fray Cieza de León, while traveling through the Peruvian countryside in 1533, noticed that "many husbands remained home weaving and performing other effeminate or feminine labors."[130] Don Quixote asked, "What do you want, Sancho?" as he emulated "Sancho's effeminate and hurtful tone of voice."[131] In *Filomena*, Lope de Vega also employed this notion of effeminacy when he depicted Diana "as tall and as one who possessed a well-proportioned body lacking a feminine face."[132]

In the third case, effeminacy meant "weakness, delicateness, or blandness." In 1566, Bartolomé de las Casas described "the inhabitants of occident as more effeminate, bland, and weak-hearted" than their counterparts in the peninsula.[133] When a soldier brought his sergeant some water while the entire company of men suffered a great thirst in the Libyan

en la voz Perla. Del polvo de las perlas ò *margaritas*, con azúcar, se hacen tabletas para confortar el corazón.

MARGARITAS. Llaman en los Puertos de Galicia unos caracolillos pequeños, que arroja el mar à las orillas. Lat. *Cochleæ marinus minutissimus.*

MARGARITAS. En la Náutica son los botónes de baivèn o piola, que se dan à los bastardos de los racamentos por la cara de proa, y con los chicótes se hace una curiosa labór. Vocab. marit. de Sev. Lat. *Funibus appositus globulus in navi.*

MARGEN. f. f. La extremidad y orilla de algunas cosas: como la margen del rio. Viene del Latino *Margo*, *nis*. Lat. *Crepido. Labrum*. BETISS. Guichard. lib. 1. pl. 33. No queriendo aceptar el empeño de un combate, à que fueron provocados à la *margen* del Pó. PINEL, Retr. lib. 1. cap. 3. Los dos rios tienen sus *márgenes* adornadas de jardines de varias flores y frutas.

MARGEN. En el papél y los libros, se llama aquella porcion que se dexa en blanco à una parte, ò à entrambas, o por cortesía ò por conveniencia. Lat. *Margo*. SART. P. Suar. lib. 3. cap. 18. Pues atreviendose por tantas partes à la *margen*, en ninguna ha ofendido lo escrito.

Andarse por las *márgenes*. Phrase metaphórica, que significa no ir en derechúra à lo principal del intento. Lat. *Circumire. In reclam viam minimè ingredi.* ABARC. Annal. Interregno 2. cap. 1. num. 8. Los quales empezaron la guerra, y para no *andarse por las márgenes*, el Gobernador del Reino..... oficio al Infante sus fuerzas.

MARGENAR. v. a. Lo mismo que Marginar. GIL GONZ. Theatr. de Avil. lib. 2. cap. 17. Dice el que *margenó* sus obras, que oyo decir al Obispo de Burgos (que estando un dia este Doctor delante del Rey Don Juan y sus Pages que le servian, dixo al Rey, &c. JACINT. POL. pl. 17.

 La que emendó lo acertado,
 y margenó lo perfecto.

MARGINAL. adj. de una term. Lo que está ò pertenece al margen: como Nota marginál. Lat. *Marginalis*. GIL GONZ. Theatr. de Avil. lib. 2. cap. 17. Y dice la nota *marginál*, que fueron excelentes sabios.

MARGINAR. v. a. Annotar ò apuntar alguna cosa al margen de un libro ò escrito. Es formado del nombre Margen. Lat. *Notam, vel signum margini apponere. Marginare.*

MARGINADO, DA. part. pass. del verbo Marginar. Lo assi señalado con notas ò apuntamientos en el margen. Lat. *Ad marginem notatus. Marginatus.*

MARGOMAR. v. a. Lo mismo que Bordar. Es voz antiquada. Lat. *Plumare.* MEN. Coron. Copl. 7. Fizo una tela è *margomó*, siquier debuxó en ella toda la historia suya è del falso Tereo.

MARHOJO. f. m. Lo mismo que Malhojo. Trahen esta voz Nebrixa y Covarr.
 Tom. IV.

MARIA. Nombre Dulcíssimo de la Madre de Dios y Señora nuestra.

MARIA. Llaman à la vela blanca, y mayór que las demás, que se pone en el superior lugar del Tenebrário, y no se apaga: y por su candór y mantener su luz siempre, le han dado este nombre. Lat. *Cereus albus medius in tenebrario.*

Arbol de *Maria*. Es un arbol de la India, parecido al pino; pero la hoja se parece à la del algarrobo, y el fruto es redondo, como la manzána, con sus pepitas como ella. Hiriendo los Indios su tronco, en los tiempos del mayor calor, arroja por las incisiones una resina líquida, pero crassa, y que tira al olór del limón, la qual recogen en unos vasos como cocos, que forman à este efecto de una especie de cera negra, que crian en aquellas partes unas abéjas del mismo colór: y esta resina es la que se llama balsamo ò azéite de Maria. Este nombre parece se le dieron al arbol, por haberse descubierto los primeros, y reconocido sus propriedades, en la Villa de Maria, una de las de la Provincia de Cartagéna, adonde se crian en gran abundancia y en la Isla de Tolú Lat. *Arbor indicus sic dictus.*

MARIAL. adj. de una term. Lo que pertenece à Maria Santissima Nuestra Señora. Y substantivado se toma regularmente por el libro que contiene las alabanzas y elogio de Nuestra Señora. Lat. *Marialis, e.* NIEREMB. Var. ilust. Vid. del P. Geron. de Florencia. El afecto grande que la tenia le movió à no querer imprimir otra cosa, sino lo que toca à sus alabanzas, como lo hizo en los dos tomos de su *Marial*, que tambien han parecido.

MARIANO. adj. Lo que pertenece à Maria Santissima Señora nuestra. Lat. *Ad Sacratissimam Virginem Mariam pertinens.* CORN. Chron. tom. 3. lib. 3. cap. 8. Reservando la Providencia Divina la gloria deste triumpho para Scoto, à quien eligió para Doctor *Mariáno*, y Alexandro nuevo, que con la espáda sutilíssima de su ingénio, cortasse los enmarañados hilos deste nudo Gordio.

MARICA. f. f. Lo mismo que Hurráca.

MARICA. Se llama el hombre afeminado y de pocos brios, que se dexa supeditar y manejar, aun de los que son inferiores. Lat. *Vir mulier.* FIGUER. Passag. Aliv. 8. Corrompíame el todo la sangre vèr las calcillas por otro nombre atacadas, de que se adornan: no las desampara tal *marica* destos ni un instante. TORR. Trad. de Oven. tom. 1. pl. 27.

 Tu eres Marica el marido
 y tu marido el marica.

MARICA. Se llama tambien el espárrago mui delgado y de poca substáncia. Lat. *Asparagus gracilis.*

MARICON. f. m. El hombre afeminado y cobarde, y lo mismo que Marica. Lat. *Vir mulier.* QUEV. Tacañ. cap. 23. Y porque no le tengan por *Maricon*, abaxe esse cuello y agovie de espaldas.

 Rrr 2   MA

2.5. *María*, *marica*, *maricón*: defining effeminacy and sodomites. In *Diccionario de la lengua Castellana en que se explica el verdadero sentido de las voces, su naturaleza y calidad, con las phrases o modos de hablar, los proverbios o refranes, y otras cosas convenientes al uso de la lengua*, vol. 4 (Madrid: En la Imprenta de la Real Academia Española por la viuda de Francisco del Hierro, 1732–1737).

Desert, the sergeant refused the water and reproached the subordinate, stating, "I am not more effeminate than my soldiers."[134]

The fourth meaning of effeminacy related specifically to men who were sodomites. It implied the "loss of virile characteristics in one's aspect, dress, and manners; decadence, degradation, or corruption."[135] In 1513, Alfonso Herrera proposed "that not all roosters made good *machos*." He argued, "Some, by nature, are effeminate."[136] De las Casas, in his 1566 *Apologética*, described the men of the Indias as tremendously "vile, weak, and effeminate—susceptible to all nefarious vices." Furthermore, he wrote, "these effeminate men congregate in public and infamous places to effect the nefarious vice just like whores." The men that "wore the apparel of women also labored alongside them and performed feminine tasks." The others in the town "adored and revered these effeminate men."[137]

Mateo Alemán, in his 1597 literary work, *Guzmán de Alfarache*, referred to men who "liked to paint their faces." He wrote that "apart from the actions of effeminate *maricas*, those actions too lent themselves to rumors and suspicions of men committing vile things, for they smeared themselves with adornments solely permitted to women."[138] The thought of "rewarding an effeminate man, who spoke, dressed, and adorned himself as a woman, infuriated" Lope de Vega, as he wrote in *Hermosa Angélica*, published in 1602.[139]

In 1603, Quevedo, echoing the words of his contemporary Pedro de León, wrote that Tacano had "lowered his ruff" so that no one would mistake him for a *"maricón."*[140] Again in 1609, Quevedo reminded his readers in *España defendida* that he "most lamented the manner in which men imitated women in their splendid dress and effeminacy."[141] In one of the earliest publications of the Spanish language, Covarrubias, in his 1611 *Tesoro de la Lengua Castellana*, defined an effeminate man as "a womanly man inclined to occupy himself with all their duties and to speak their vernacular in a delicate tone."[142]

Notions of the "effeminate sodomite" in the Spanish peninsula and in New Spain are present in the literature and in the sermons of some moralists throughout the sixteenth century—despite the contrary opinion held by McIntosh, Bray, and Trumbach. They have argued that the "effeminate sodomite" did not emerge in Europe until the end of the seventeenth century, and even then it did not necessarily refer to a man who maintained amorous relations with another man.[143]

Although effeminacy comprised one aspect of Spanish perceptions of sodomy, it did not constitute the predominant discourse associated with sodomy prosecutions during the early modern period in the peninsula. The cases prosecuted by the High Courts in Seville and Granada and those prosecuted by the Casa de la Contratación in Seville, for the most part, support the findings of Carrasco, Bennassar, and García Carcel.[144]

Reflections of an Epoch and Its Tribunals

At least two types of tribunals, secular and ecclesiastical, prosecuted sodomites between the fifteenth and the eighteenth centuries in Spain and in New Spain. In Castilla y León, which included the courts of Granada and Seville, secular tribunals prosecuted sodomites, while in Aragon, which included the tribunals of Valencia, Barcelona, Zaragoza, and Palma de Mallorca, sodomy prosecutions fell under the jurisdiction of the Inquisitorial tribunal.[145] Over the course of the colonial period, both secular and ecclesiastical courts held jurisdiction over sodomy cases in the tribunals of New Spain. The multiplicity of jurisdictions often became blurred and varied from one historical moment to another.

Carrasco and García Carcel have documented the following information. Between 1540 and 1700 the Inquisitorial tribunal prosecuted 380 sodomy cases in Valencia, another 791 in Zaragoza, and 453 in Barcelona. In Valencia the tribunal sentenced 37 men to burn between 1566 and 1775, the vast majority between 1616 and 1630 right in the midst of the Counter Reformation.[146] The tribunals did not condemn any sodomites to burn at the stake after 1630; instead they condemned sodomites to the gallows or administered lashes or perpetual banishment from the kingdom. In Castile this shift occurred from the last decade of the seventeenth century.

In contrast, the High Courts in Granada and Seville, along with the tribunal of the Casa de la Contratación prosecuted 175 sodomy cases between 1560 and 1699 in which they sentenced some 50 sodomites to burn at the stake. These cases, in addition to the 125 prosecuted by the High Court in 1657–1658 in Mexico City, represent the scope of this present study.

During the latter part of the seventeenth century, *contra natura* was no longer "a contemptible act in and of itself but became the external sign of an interior disorder."[147] Moralists no longer conceptualized sodomy as a "taboo" but rather as an error in judgment. They began to understand the lustful sins less as threats to a system of religious beliefs and more as the beginning of a new social ethics. The emerging ethics began to describe the sodomite as in a state of servitude, as one who had "aban-

doned himself" and whose desires overwhelmed his reason—a servant of
the flesh or passions. The moralists converted the sodomite into "a disorder, a figure without reason, a threat to the state.[148] Gone were the diabolical images of sodomy understood solely as an act saturated with satanic overtones.

Even so, the strict norms of the Catholic Church often collided with
subaltern yearnings for greater tolerance than that predicated by the ecclesiastical mob.[149] Alfonso Gil, a Portuguese laborer who became "inebriated while working in the countryside," informed his fellow companions that he thought it "not a sin to do it to a man." His companions
disagreed, for they considered "it a bad thing and a grave concern for the
Inquisition." "In my breeches," boasted Gil, "now that's an Inquisition!"
When Alonso appeared before the Inquisitorial tribunal, he explained
that he had uttered those words because he had "drunk too much in the
hot sun." The tribunal in Granada sentenced him to attend one mass and
banished him from the province for one year.[150]

The subaltern rebelled against the Thomist notion of sin and sexuality. It triumphed in a purely hedonistic sentiment, and a libertinism re-
emerged to oppose the acerbic mode of Catholic repressive discourses.[151]
Isabel and Fernando's vision of a restrained society—a defender of the
Catholic faith, a champion of empire—had crumbled. Seventeenth-
century Spain had transformed its borders, having become sensitized to
issues of identity, religious, ethnic, and gender differences.

The Spain of Felipe IV, a highly stratified and status-conscious society, also found itself haunted by the specter of economic and political de-
cline.[152] Significant currents had swept across early modern Spain. After
the Council of Trent, dissolved in 1563, Spain emerged as a bastion of
Catholic conservatism against the stream of Protestant Reformation, the
enemy without, and the anxieties about *limpieza de sangre*, seen as the enemy
within. A return to Scholasticism and the emergence of an iron doctrinal
zeal, sternly fixated on the suppression of heresy and sexual desires, had
momentarily ruled the day.[153] And so tribunals prosecuted the "infamous
infernal trio composed of heretics, witches, and sodomites" because they
lived depraved lives—a sign of an erroneous faith.[154]

Other historical factors influenced the evolution of a new sense of the
Spanish self. The attempted colonization of New Spain facilitated the
emergence of a new wealth-accumulating individualism, which no doubt
offered the prospect of an enhanced social status, one not inherited by
religion or accident of birth. The seventeenth century ushered in the con-

solidation of a property-owning bourgeoisie at the expense of the aristocracy. The growth of private reading had represented a relative democra-
tization of knowledge.[155] Still, Spain evolved as a society grounded in the
historical and "theatrical images it made of itself."[156] The degree of art
and artifice used to fashion and promote a struggling empire was to become a symptomatic rather than a causative historical factor in the continuing prosecution of sodomites.[157]

During the latter part of the seventeenth century, sodomy had evolved
to represent simultaneously not only a despicable act but also an external
sign of an internal moral disorder. Sodomy, in the new ethical sense, became known as a perversion.[158] The sodomy *Pragmáticas* all remained in
effect in the peninsula and in New Spain up until the institutionalization
of the penal codes in the nineteenth century. By then, sodomy became a
"symbol of a way of being, a spirit, licentiousness, an imagination of passions, a natural determinism."[159] But already during the eighteenth century, the peninsular courts no longer burned sodomites. Tomás y Valiente
interpreted the new benevolence as the effect of a decaying political system and not the cause for the change.[160] This change, as the following
chapters will help illustrate, had little to do with the progress of Spanish
humanism and tolerance.

CHAPTER 3

MARINER, WOULD YOU SCRATCH MY LEGS?

Sodomy Prosecutions in Andalusia, and the Ensign Who Liked His Kisses with a Bit of Tongue

De los sodomitas . . . no sólo no sabemos de ellos pero ni querrí-
amos saber que supiesen de nosotros; que en ellos peligrarían nues-
tras asentaderas y los diablos por eso traemos colas porque como
estan aca habemos menester mosqueador de los rabos.

Francisco de Quevedo, El sueño del infierno

I N 1698, Magistrate Villarán pronounced both Bartholomé, a mariner from Sicily, and Giovanni Mule, a native of Palermo, guilty
of having committed the "nefarious sin of sodomy" on board
Nuestra Señora del Carmen, an admiral's ship docked in the harbor
complex of Cádiz while waiting to set sail for the Indies. Three
years later, after a lengthy appeal process before the Royal Council of the Indies in Madrid, Bartholomé Varres Cavallero, who was twenty-
six years old, "with minute diffidence came out of the Royal Jail in Cádiz
mounted on an old beast of burden, dressed in a white tunic and hood,
his feet and hands tied." About his neck "hung a crucifix of God our
Lord." Giovanni Mule, who was about the age of fourteen and had been
rebaptized by the Spaniards as Juan Mule, was "nude from the waist upward, his hands and feet also tied," and "rode on a young beast of burden" just behind Bartholomé (Fig. 3.1).[1]

The procession meandered through the Cadizcan countryside "without having passed in front of a church or any other sacred place until it
arrived at a site known as *el Salado.*" There, Giovanni, who had been "sentenced to public humiliation," was placed "within site of the execution"
by Juan Antonio, the executioner. Juan Antonio then "tied Bartholomé to
a pole erected in the ground and after half an hour administered *garrote* in
such a manner [that the mariner] died a natural death." Bartholomé "remained in this state within public view for more than half an hour" after
the strangulation.

3.1. Shirtless to the stake. Drawing by Christoph Weiditz, 1529. Biblioteca Nacional de Madrid.

Afterward the executioner "covered the entire cadaver with many portions of logs and faggots." Juan Antonio lit the fire, and the "cadaver burnt into ashes all within the eyesight of Juan Mule, whom the executioner *passed over the flames* and [thereafter] banished him permanently from this kingdom."[2]

The Tribunals in Andalusia

The findings presented in this chapter on early modern Spanish perceptions of sodomy emanate from some 175 cases, or *procesos*, prosecuted by secular tribunals in Andalusia. After studying the *procesos* of the sodomy cases prosecuted by the High Courts in Seville and Granada and the Casa de la Contratación tribunal in Andalusia, I have attempted to explain whether or not Spain's imperialist-colonialist politics "altered and exploited" the nation's perceptions of manliness and of sodomites. Further, did these categories emerge as products of "ruptures in the political economy of colonialism"?[3]

In Seville and Granada, the two Royal High Courts customarily prosecuted the sodomy cases, although an Inquisitorial tribunal existed in Seville. Convicted sodomites could have their cases retried before the Royal Chancellery in Granada, the highest-ranking criminal court in Andalusia. The final avenue of appeal rested with His Majesty's Royal Council—the highest appellate court in Spain.[4] In addition to the two High Courts in the Seville-Granada metroplex, a third tribunal—the Audiencia de la Casa de la Contratación—founded in Seville and later relocated to Cádiz, also prosecuted sodomy cases.

Fernando and Isabel established the Casa de la Contratación in 1503 to regulate colonial commerce and shipping between the peninsula and the Indias.[5] In 1511 the Casa de la Contratación acquired juridical powers, in the form of an *audiencia*. The new status permitted the Casa to prosecute both civil and criminal crimes, like sodomy, committed in the harbors of Andalusia or on board the ships en route to and from the Indias.[6] The Casa's tribunal consisted of a sole *letrado* with a formal degree in law, a public prosecutor, two scribes, and other pertinent officials. By 1524 the Audiencia de la Casa de la Contratación fell under the appellate jurisdiction of the Royal Council of the Indies, and thus a final appeal against torture and death sentences rested with this tribunal.[7]

Ships traveling to and from the Indias also functioned as tribunals. On board the captain general's ship, the *Capitana*,[8] the tribunal consisted of the captain general, who assumed the duties of chief magistrate and sole judge; a court assistant; a scrivener; and other assistants or counselors.[9] The captain general could initiate an investigation, summon the testimony of witnesses, preside over the torture sentences, pass sentence, and finally carry out the death penalty. A convicted sodomite could appeal a guilty verdict issued on board the ships to the Casa's tribunal on land and finally to His Majesty's Royal Council in Madrid.

Unlike sodomy cases prosecuted in the Inquisitorial tribunals, those prosecuted in the secular courts did not proceed in secrecy. The accused knew the identity of his or her accuser(s) and their witnesses. And like the Inquisitorial tribunals, secular tribunals allowed the accused to draft a list of enemies and witnesses for court testimonies. Lastly, tribunals customarily provided the accused with an officially appointed lawyer.[10]

When the accused failed to make adequate confessions, the tribunals invoked the use of torture sessions to procure the desired evidence. The most widely used forms of torture were the rack, the gallows, the pendulum, the hoist, and water torture. In the event of a guilty verdict, as stipulated by the sodomy *Pragmáticas,* the courts resorted to the garroting and the burning of sodomites as the requisite sentences for this crime.[11]

The earliest documented executions of sodomites in early modern Spain occurred during the decade of the 1560s in Andalusia, Castilla y León, Aragon, and Mallorca.[12] In addition to the successful prosecution of the Bartholomé-Mule case, the Audiencia de la Casa de la Contratación prosecuted at least 15 sodomy cases and sentenced 7 men to burn between 1560 and 1699. The High Courts in Sevilla and Granada prosecuted some 147 cases. They sentenced "several women" accused of sodomy to lashes, exiled one man for sodomizing himself with a cable, sent another to "the steps and the string,"[13] and burned some 65 sodomites between 1578 and 1616.[14] In Aragon, by contrast, the Inquisition prosecuted some 1,623 sodomites between 1540 and 1700.[15]

In all these tribunals, the sodomy cases—second only to heresy prosecutions—constituted an average of 5 percent of the total number of cases prosecuted by these courts. Although the number of Andalusian cases may seem marginal or even minute relative to the number of sodomy prosecutions in Aragon, the courts in Andalusia or in Castilla y León burned almost 100 percent of all convicted sodomites, whereas about 38 percent of convicted heretics were put to death.[16]

To Burn a Sodomite

Pérez-Mallaína has attributed the relatively small number of sodomy prosecutions in Andalusia to a fear of burning. The risk of ending up burned at the stake, according to Pérez-Mallaína, must have encouraged some form of discretion among sodomites. For even in cases where power holders discovered sodomitical relationships, the partners had been carrying them on in secrecy for months, and only unforeseen circumstances had brought them to light.[17] Other factors could also account for this dearth of sodomy prosecutions in Andalusia.

From the testimony presented in the Andalusian sodomy trials, one can argue that many sodomites indeed assimilated, perhaps even self-imposed, the imago of the perfect Spanish Man. Some sodomites would later make use of the moralists' textual jargon pertinent to Vir in an effort to plead their innocence and portray them as honorable men incapable of offending God. In a strange sort of way, this self-imposed facade of manliness assumed by practicing sodomites actually subverted gender roles in Spain. By exhibiting many of the manly characteristics sketched by the moralists, men, in the cold light of day, passed themselves off as

chivalrous defenders of the new morality. Under the cover of night, however, they indulged in other necessities. Paradoxically, this type of subversion both accepts and rejects early modern notions of Spanish Vir.

A more material explanation might have greater significance in explaining the relatively small number of sodomy prosecutions in Andalusia—the trial fees, which sometimes led to graft, and the high cost of
burning a sodomite. In the Bartholomé-Mule case, the solicitor general
submitted a copy of the "costs incurred for the execution" to the lord
ministers of the Royal and Supreme Councils of the Indies. The list of
costs transcribed below totaled "809 reales *de plata*," a substantial amount
of money, for which the solicitor general sought total "reimbursement." [18]

> A Bill of costs and expenses associated with the execution of the
> death by fire sentence submitted by Minister of Justice Andrés
> Muñoz Obregón to the Ministers of the Royal and Supreme
> Council of the Indies for reimbursement Cádiz 18 January 1671.
> Costs incurred to bring an executioner from the city of Jerez to
> Cádiz and other costs associated with the execution of the sen-
> tence passed by the Ministers of the Council and War Ministry
> of the Indies against Bartholomé Varres and cohorts administered
> by D. Manuel de Helguero, His Majesty's Solicitor General of
> the Royal Fleet.
>
> Three ministers from the Ministry of Royal Justice traveled to
> Xerez to hire an executioner—boat fare to the port—three
> silver reales   003
>
> For three horses to travel to the port of Xerez—each horse
> four reales   012
>
> Eight horses for the return of the three ministers, the execu-
> tioner and four guards from Xerez to the port—each four
> reales   032
>
> Meals and beds on that night in the port—forty reales   040
>
> For the boat taken to this city, fares to embark and
> disembark—ten reales   010
>
> For the return of the executioner to Xerez with the four
> guards and the three of us from this city we incurred the costs
> itemized above for a total of one hundred and nine reales   109

For the breakfast of four guards and the executioner, lunch, dinner and beds—each eight reales totaling one hundred and twenty   120

The costs for the execution—sixteen quintals[19] of firewood— each two silver pesos totaling thirty-two   032

Liquid naphtha—six reales   006

For the horses that transported the firewood to *el Salado*— four silver pesos   004

For twelve pieces of kindling wood—six silver pesos   006

For a pike and some hooks—ten silver pesos   010

For two nooses made of esparto, two water carriers, two beast halters and a ball of rope required by the executioner—eight reales   008

For a quarter of timber for the construction of the gallows and a carpenter—sixteen reales   016

For the salaries of the four guards from Xerez—one hundred and twenty eight reales   128

For six days pay for the executioner—four *ducados* or one hundred and forty one reales   141

For the salaries of the three ministers sent to Xerez to hire the executioner one hundred and twenty reales   120
                                                                                         809

For a total of eight hundred and nine reales of ancient silver or one hundred one reales silver distributed by me to the persons mentioned in the bill of cost sworn to God and to the Sword: Cádiz eighteenth January seventeen hundred and one = Andrés Muñoz Obregón, scrivener[20]

The costs involved in burning a sodomite, some 809 reales, in the case of Bartholomé, roughly equaled one fifth of the yearly pension granted to Alonso Díaz, or the purchasing power needed to hire three laborers every day for about nine months in early modern Mexico City.[21]

The *procesos* and the other archival material consulted for this study of sodomy prosecutions have enabled me to forge a more succinct focus of analysis and interpretation "from the history of imperialism/colonialism to the more specific relationship of that history to sexuality and issues of gender." [22] This narrowed focus of analysis has resulted in the present interpretation of how the textual representations of sodomites evident in the court *procesos* further nurtured representations of manliness, of *sodomie,* and of sodomites in the peninsula. But the *procesos* likewise provided a glimpse of the ways in which accused sodomites mediated and contested the power of the courts.

The inherent relationships among imperial politics, manliness, Catholicism, and xenophobia all skewed perceptions of sodomy as an illegitimate form of Spanish early modern bourgeois respectability. [23]

Horrified, the Witnesses Wished to See No More

The Bartholomé-Mule case typified the various juridical-ecclesiastical discourses about *sodomie* and *sodomitas.* The early modern moralists shrouded these perceptions in religious, xenophobic, or anti-*natura* tropes in their attempts to codify sodomy as a crime and a sin in Spain. The Bartholomé-Mule sodomy case also helped to expose the contradictions inherent in these sexual discourses and the abuse of power relations of the Spanish baroque.

In a letter to Carlos II, Martín de Aranguren y Zavala, the major general of the fleet, sought confirmation for the execution. "Respectfully, my lord," argued the major general, "the enormity of this horrific, detestable, and grave crime in the eyes of the God our lord dignified an exemplary and prompt punishment." The major general sensed "a great need in this city and harbor of Your Majesty's kingdom to demonstrate the exemplary consequences" that awaited those who committed "this atrocious crime or other grave sins of the same species on land or during navigation" but who had "escaped punishment for lack of evidentiary requirements." [24] "The aforementioned mariners," concluded the major general, "with little fear of God and their own consciences failed in their obligations, having committed the atrocious, abominable crime and heinous sin." [25]

His Majesty's attorney general concurred with the major general's request for the confirmation of the executions. In the attorney general's opinion, Bartholomé and Mule had committed "a crime so horrendous, so hideous and abominable, so nefarious, that one finds no voices in any tribunal in this kingdom that can explain such treachery." Both men, argued the attorney general, "had exercised a very sordid and repulsive crime according to the depositions given by the witnesses." [26]

The witnesses had "found the boy's entire backside soaked, filthy, and replete with the viscous smell and the feel of the semen Bartholomé had poured and scattered." The witnesses had stood by the boy "horrified," and some had even "turned their faces not wanting to see any more." [27] "We stood there astonished," recalled one sailor, "having witnessed such a ghastly sight and the sin of sodomy." [28] "Frightful," stated another, "given the scandalous nature of this sin and as such, a grave offense to God." [29] Thus, the attorney general surmised: "Given the abominable and treacherous crime, its commission indubitably proven, with the depositions of six witnesses, the execution should proceed at the place the deformity occurred and as an example to the plethora of other nationals who congregate in those harbors drawn there by commerce and galleons." [30]

"Furthermore," wrote the attorney general, "the stay of execution has impeded the departure of Major General Aranguren from Cádiz to La Havana." "Indeed, my lord," wrote Juan de Helguero—the solicitor general of the Spanish fleet, which was docked in Cádiz—"many people of different nationalities witnessed, in full view, Bartholomé's cadaver burned and reduced to ashes, [and] I trust this shall serve as an exemplary punishment to them all." [31]

The Council of the Indies upheld Bartholomé's sentence of execution issued by the Audiencia de la Casa de la Contratación, much to the satisfaction of Alverto de Ysasi, the tribunal's lord magistrate, who assured the ministers in Madrid that he would "effect an expeditious resolution in this case," for, he continued, "there are many prisoners in this prison of different nations inclined toward this species of crime, and given their inferior fabric [in which] they entomb themselves at night in the subterranean dungeons, one should dread the abominable consequences of such congregations." [32]

A Disturbing Panorama on the Horizon

For the prosecutors of the 1698 Bartholomé-Mule case, Seville, particularly its cultural composition, caused them great distress. The Guadalquivir River linked Seville with the Andalusian side of the Atlantic, and that fluvial context conferred upon the metropolis its status as one of Spain's premier ports and provided the early modern Spanish fleet with unrestricted access to the Sevillian harbor. [33] At the end of the fifteenth century, the inhabitants of Seville numbered about 40,000. By the end of the sixteenth century, the number of inhabitants had swelled to more than 150,000 (Fig. 3.2). [34]

The alcazar in Seville provided a respite for the nobility, as did the

3.2. **"Sevilla siglo XVI."** In G. Braun and F. Hogenberg, *Civitates orbis terrarvm*, 3 vols. (Coloniae Agrippinae: Apud G. Kempensem sumptibus auctorum, 1572–1618). Reproduced with the permission of the Archivo General de Indias, Seville.

towering cathedral and the multitude of monasteries for ecclesiastics. During the early modern period, Seville was an important economic, agricultural, and artistic center. It remained the largest city in Andalusia and one of the largest metropolises in the peninsula, indeed in Europe. Wheat, vineyards, olive oil, and salted fish all circulated in abundance.

Since the Middle Ages, Genovese bankers had resided in Seville, and by the early modern period they had become the most important source of finance for the trade with the Indies. The opening of the Strait of Gibraltar as a maritime route in the medieval period had given rise to trade with Italy and Flanders, as well as with Africa and the European continent. The admirals of the Spanish fleet organized the defense of Gibraltar from Seville. In the early modern period, Andalusia had become a significant stimulus for western European cultural expansion. Other industries flourished. Cervantes, Alemán, Quevedo, Lope de Vega, Delicado, and Pacheco all contributed to the evolution of letters and art in Andalusia.[35]

The mariners who congregated in Seville and formed a pluralist cultural mélange hailed from Galicia or Cantabria in the north of the peninsula. They arrived from Catalonia and other parts of the eastern shores of the Mediterranean. The came from as far away as the Low Countries, France, Portugal, Sicily, Genoa, Turkey, or the Greek islands. Many of the mariners set up their new households in the neighborhood of Triana, along the east bank of the Guadalquivir River. By the end of the seventeenth century, Triana, home to many immigrants drawn there by the prospects of wealth, had become one of the most populated neighborhoods in Seville.

Mateo Alemán, a writer born in mid-sixteenth-century Seville, described the metropolis "as one well equipped for the success of any estate," a metropolis where one could "sell and buy any type of merchandise." In an allusion to the multicultural dimension of its population, Alemán portrayed Seville as one common nation, or an "unabashed meadow, an open countryside, one difficult to escape, an endless globe, a mother of orphans and a cape of sinners, where everything is a necessity, yet possessed by nobody." [36]

Seville's multilingual labor force, the raw material for the voyages, alongside its network of commercial trade routes for distributing goods and its ability to finance these undertakings—all facilitated the expansion of the Indies fleet. Although Seville functioned as the administrative and commercial center for the Indies colonial enterprise, it formed part of a vast harbor complex that extended south to Sanlúcar de Barrameda and the port of Santa María, and as far as the Gulf of Cádiz. Most Spanish ships that set sail for the island of San Juan de Ulua, east of Veracruz in New Spain, did so from these ports.

Neither the larger merchant ships nor the war galleons could navigate up the Guadalquivir River and into Seville. Instead they cast anchor some eight *leguas,* or forty-four kilometers away from Seville.[37] The total trip along the Guadalquivir was about fifteen *leguas,* or eighty-nine kilometers. Unlike the more advanced ports in Santander, Málaga, Antwerp, and London, Seville had not equipped its port with cranes and dockyards; thus it could not accommodate heavy commercial traffic.[38] The advances in the technologies of ships and harbors, however, did not wholly solve the problem of privacy and space on board many ships.

Cruel and Indifferent Spaces

The sixteenth century was an age of small ships—some 300 tons in weight and 15 meters in length. Over the course of the sixteenth century, an above-average ship of about 550 tons measured 25 meters in length (Fig. 3.3). Symbolically though, the ship itself as metaphor epitomized the height of early modernity. The ship as metaphor represented a piece of land belonging to the empire, and within its hull and decks it transported to the Indias an ethos that Spain deemed appropriate for export—its form of civilization, its technological advances, its new Vir, and its Catholic dogma.[39]

In 1571, Captain General Cristóbal de Erauso ordered officers to place Moisés Maldonado, a mariner accused of blasphemy, in the ship's dungeon. Maldonado would have preferred to "wear iron shackles, the type used in an ordinary prison," rather than to have been "confined in the ship's dungeon," especially when life on board the ship already represented a "sufficient punishment of sorts."

3.3. **Space on board a seventeenth-century ship.** *Architectura Navalis* (1629). Biblioteca Nacional, Madrid.

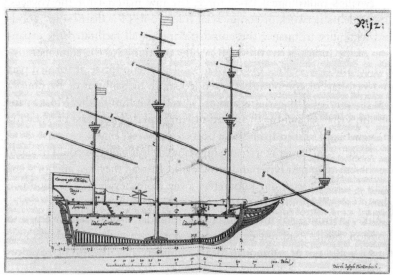

Fray de la Torre, one of the missionaries who accompanied Bartolomé de las Casas to the Indies in the mid-sixteenth century, described their ship as a "very confined prison, so powerful that no one could flee or escape despite the absence of shackles or chains." The "cruel and indifferent space treated both prisoners and passengers alike," lamented de la Torre.[40]

Maldonado also detested his confinement in the ship's dungeon for other reasons. The mariner preferred to live life at sea on deck, where many and distinct diversions took place. Maldonado had pleaded with the captain, "Do you take me for a heretic or some dishonest man such that I cannot even go on deck where all the passengers sleep and fornicate?" Maldonado demanded, "Allow us to live our own lives."

In any event, concluded the mariner, "the female passengers on board the ship fornicated from fore to stern . . . let us fuck wherever one finds the space to do so."[41] Although fewer in number, women throughout the early modern period did travel to the Indias as passengers, crew, or "mistresses of the captain generals."[42]

But, for the common mariner, the ship provided little privacy. To put it in a different perspective, a captain, a master, a pilot, thirty-five mariners, six gunners, fifteen grummets, and five pages composed the crew of a 250-ton ship.[43] The average number of mariners on a galleon was seventy-nine, and another forty-three on the merchant ships.[44] A ship's crew of seventy men occupied about 150 to 180 square meters of living space, or about the size offered by a two-story canal apartment with a small garden in the center of early twenty-first-century Amsterdam. Live animals such as horses, pigs, sheep, goats, and fowl also traveled on board the ships.

An English mariner on his way to the Indies described how one day, as the ship he traveled on was navigating its way through a violent rainstorm, the passengers could not contain their laughter when they witnessed several dizzy pigs, unable to withstand the constant rocking of the ship, vomit all over the ship's deck. Other animals and insects— mainly rats, ticks, fleas, and roaches—also accompanied most vessels. A crew could have killed up to a thousand rats at a time.[45]

The mariners also endured shortages of drinking water in an extremely hot environment, because the ships sailed primarily in the summer. Sometimes they substituted wine in lieu of water. They ate mainly biscuits and cheese and, whenever they could get them, salted meats and fresh fish.[46]

Some mariners ate, sat, slept, and played dice and cards on their *cajas.*

A mariner's *caja,* filled with clothing and personal belongings, was his most treasured possession. The officers of course slept below deck in private quarters. Others slept next to the glory hole.[47]

On the main deck, open to the delight of the stars and a cool breeze at night, the mariners formed cubicles called *ranchos* with the chests of four or five other *camaradas.* The comrades sat in their semiprivate quarters and sometimes sang or told and read stories aloud to each other, although many were illiterate.[48]

A survey of the Mexican Inquisition's inspection reports of ships arriving in New Spain between 1572 and 1600 noted that books were brought on board 326 of the 330 ships inspected.[49] The most widely read genre was books of devotion, such as prayer books, the lives of saints, and histories of the popes. Tales of chivalry in novel or verse form followed closely behind the pious texts.

Romantic novels, books of ballads, and history books completed the group of favorite genres. Three particular historical moments captured the imagination of the mariners and others traveling on board the ships: the splendor of the Roman Empire, the reconquest of the Iberian Peninsula from the Arabs, and the conquest of the Americas.

Two texts from Mateo Alemán's *Guzmán de Alfarache*—Part 1, published in 1599—had found their way on board a ship as early as 1600. The following table quotes the names of books and authors recorded on the Mexican Inquisitorial most-read list.

The ten most widely listed books found on ships sailing to Las Indias between 1572 and 1600 are as follows:[50]

1. *Libro de la oración y meditación y otras obras,* by Fray Luis de Granada
2. *Flossanctorum,* by Alonso de Villegas
3. *Orlando Furioso,* by Ludovico Ariosto
4. *Historia Pontifical,* by Gonzalo de Illesca
5. *Amadis de Gaula* (Anónimo)
6. *La araucana,* by Alonso de Ercilla
7. *Oratorios y consuelos espiritual* (Anónimo)
8. *Repertorio de Chaves,* by Alonso de Chaves
9. *La Diana,* by Jorge de Montemayor
10. *El cancionero de Guzmán* (Anónimo)

Pages and Pages on Board the Ships

A schematic hierarchy of officers and crew staffed many of the Spanish galleons. Many nobles considered a career at sea to be dishonorable; they feared it would diminish their social status. Thus, few nobles rose to the rank of admiral or captain general. Instead noble gentlemen and rich merchants owned the ships, but so did those of more humble lineage, such as pilots or even mariners. The pages, grummets, and lower-ranked officers, such as the pursers or boatswains who provided the manual labor on board the ships, came from the less noble sectors of society.

Pages and grummets formed the first tier of mariners on the hierarchical ladder (Fig. 3.4). They fluctuated in ages between eight and seventeen, with an average age of fifteen. The pages served their masters, while others, as our *procesos* have indicated, served everybody on board the ships. These young boys eventually learned the trade of mariner, and as apprentices they measured the time on board and performed all the menial tasks. The grummets, young sailors between seventeen and twenty years of age, climbed the yards and retrieved the sails, loaded and unloaded the ships, procured fresh water, and gathered wood.

At the age of twenty, a grummet became a mariner. The older mariners between twenty-eight and thirty-five years of age often mistreated the grummets and at times used them as punching bags. The older mariners set up and maintained both the standing and the running riggings.

3.4. **Grummet and page at work.** Drawing by Christoph Weiditz, 1529. Biblioteca Nacional de Madrid.

They trimmed sheets and took the helm when necessary. They assisted the gun crews in battle. The gunners in turn possessed the skills necessary to fire the guns.[51]

Petty officers included carpenters, caulkers, and scriveners. Large fleets also employed a barber-surgeon and a chaplain. The next tier of officers included the purser, who was responsible for the dispensary, and the boatswain or warrant officer, who, assisted by his mate, was responsible for handling the crew and maintaining the ship.

The upper echelon of power on the ship rested with the pilot, a purely nautical function and the most specialized of the crew; the master of the ship, or the economic administrator who usually owned a share of the ship's stock; and the captain, the chief military officer. But the highest military ranks on the high seas consisted of admirals, captains general, and masters-at-arms—all officers who commanded the warships and fleets of the armada.[52]

Dress also distinguished the officers from the mariners. Officers wore a *jubón*, a waist-length coat over the shirt. *Calzas,* or silk knee-length pants, worn with hose complemented the officers' *jubón.* The mariners wore shirts, or *zaraguelles,* along with broad breeches, called *calzones* and made of French linen or cotton, from the waist to the ankles. Both officers and mariners wore blue wool capes, or *capotes.* Mariners sported red wool bonnets, and the officers opted for silk or suede bonnets.[53]

The first generation of lesser-skilled mariners sailing to and from the Indias probably came from the countryside, as many *procesos* have indicated. Urban laborers performed the more technical marine jobs.

One captain complained about the inadequate origins of his soldiers and mariners. His crew consisted almost entirely of tailors, shoemakers, and servants. *Negros* and *mulatos,* some of them freed slaves, occupied most of the posts as pages and grummets. Some two thirds of the entire population of mariners were illiterate.[54] About 90 percent of the Spanish mariners hailed from Andalusia, and the other 10 percent from Cantabria.[55]

This disproportionate ratio of mariners within the peninsula, and the high number of foreign mariners working on board the Spanish ships, exacerbated a link between xenophobia and the practice of sodomy.

Sodomie and Xenophobia

As the early modern period progressed, the sodomy cases prosecuted on board ships and in the harbors of Andalusia became lengthier, and they took longer to resolve. One aspect was constant in all these cases—the belief that sodomy was an exclusive practice of the other—those from abroad, from other nations.

In 1573, Juan García accused the honorable gentleman Nicolás Cardona, a Sevillian, of having attempted to commit sodomy with a young page. General Cardona was in command of the Spanish fleet of Tierra Firme in 1569, and in 1571 King Felipe II named him admiral of the *Armada de la Guarda de la Carrera de las Indias,* or second in command of that fleet.

However, the captain general of the same fleet found Cardona guilty of sodomy, condemned him to torture by water and rack, and had him imprisoned in Santo Domingo. Cardona contested his sentence, and in 1573 the royal tribunal in Santo Domingo absolved him and sentenced the young page to one hundred lashes for perjury.[56]

The captain general, a native of Cantabria, had opposed Cardona's royal appointment and consequently refused to invest him with new powers. He had hoped that the king would have instead named one of his cohorts from the northern provinces in Spain and not an Andalusian "as the new second in command." The majority of the mariners that made up the armada, wrote the captain general to His Majesty, were "Vizcaínos, Guipuzcoanos, and Asturianos," and they had "rendered many years of service to the king since the inception of the fleet."

Thus, reasoned the captain general, they had hoped that the king would have bestowed the post on "one of them." In the end, the captain general succumbed to the king's orders and named Cardona as admiral of the fleet in 1571. The ships' crews, moreover, included a high proportion of foreign mariners.

When Columbus reached Spain with a large number of Genoese, the Franciscans on the island complained about an invasion. In 1526 the crown limited the number of foreign-born crew members on board Spanish ships to 20 percent of the total. Nevertheless, more than 50 percent of Magellan's expedition came from a variety of countries in western Europe. In one instance, the Council of the Indies advised a captain general that foreigners could constitute no more than one third of the entire crew on an armada.[57]

By 1568 the Casa de la Contratación had prohibited foreign boatswains on the ships and had limited the number of foreigners to six per ship, for fear of mutiny. In reality, the official figures show that one in every five mariners came from outside the peninsula.

Portuguese were about 50 percent of foreign crew members, followed by Italians, Flemish, and Germans. Fewer English and French made up the crews of the armadas. At least one third of the gunners, who were skilled workers, came from Flanders, Italy, or Germany. Of all the officers on board the ships, only masters and pilots could be nationalized.[58]

Over the course of the early modern period, the Casa's tribunal prosecuted officers—such as a general of the armada, a master, a boatswain, an ensign, and a purser—for sodomy. However, the majority of those prosecuted for and accused of having engaged in sodomitical behavior represented the lower tiers of the ship's labor force and foreigners. One of the earliest sodomy prosecutions by the Casa implicated a Sicilian master named Salomon Antón and a Genoese grummet. Both were accused of committing the nefarious sin during Magellan's expedition around the world. In 1519, on board the *Victoria*, Captain Magellan had the Sicilian master burned at sea off the coast of Santa Lucia in Brazil.

The following year, António Varesa, the Genoese grummet implicated in the case, drowned in those same Brazilian waters just off the coast. A group of mariners had apparently thrown him overboard under suspicious circumstances.[59] Juan Bautista Finocho, a mariner on the galleon *San Tadeo*, was also burned in the harbor of La Havana in July 1575.[60]

In 1565, after the captain's ship *San Pelayo* had disembarked some soldiers in Florida to help dissuade the French Huguenots, it navigated toward Hispaniola. On board, thirty foreigners, mostly from the Levant and Flanders, made up its crew. The captain was holding three prisoners on board: two Frenchmen for having claimed to be Catalans, and a master from Italy who was accused of sodomy. As the ship made its way toward Hispaniola in the Caribbean to avert an impending storm, the three prisoners, led by the accused sodomite, convinced the "other foreigners" on board the ship to imprison the Spaniards.

The foreigners overpowered the twenty Spaniards on board and assumed control of the captaincy. However, the successful mutineers argued among themselves, and the mutiny crumbled. Some of the mutineers wanted to navigate the ship to France, others to England, while yet others simply wanted to use it to plunder other Spanish ships full of bullion. Various fights and killings ensued. The ship en route to France instead ended up marooned in Denmark. The Italian sodomite had saved himself from the torture and the stake that awaited him on the peninsula. However, he had not avoided an assassination attempt perpetrated by one of his fellow mutineers, and he died at the hands of his executioner.[61]

This case was partly responsible for the 1568 decree that prohibited foreign masters on Spanish ships, limited the number of foreign mariners on board, and required the issuance of permits or licenses to the foreign mariners before they were allowed to work on the ships.[62] In theory, that would have accounted for about 12 percent of any crew during the early modern period.

In practice, however, official figures provided by the Casa indicate that at least 20 percent of any given crew continued to come from abroad. This could account for the fact that some Portuguese, Italians, and Flemish attempted to pass themselves off as Galicians, while Greeks and Hungarians claimed to be Basques and the French attempted to pass as Catalans.[63]

Not all accused sodomites received a royal appointment and support in their struggles for survival. The younger pages and grummets, especially, suffered humiliating experiences at the hands of the older officers. Often, younger mariners, who practiced their own forms of sexual play with each other, caused particular ire among the officers, who severely punished these practices. I would suggest that court magistrates and ship officers alike tended to punish more severely men of similar age accused of having committed sodomy.

Crown officials of lower rank also resorted to accusations of sodomy, as in the case of the honorable gentleman General Cardona, for political or economic blackmail, and such accusations continued to gain currency throughout the early modern period. Monies functioned as a powerful incentive in the prosecution of sodomy trials. Along the way, many ship officers instituted their own schedules of fees for tortures and other miscellaneous court tasks. They wrote new sodomy laws independent of those prescribed by the royal *Pragmáticas* and applied them disparately. The officers improvised tortures and death sentences in conformity with their own sadistic tendencies.

A close reading of the *procesos* moreover discloses the existence of at least two vernaculars—one used by court officials, the other by the subaltern—in the early modern period with reference to the singular phenomenon of *sodomie*, or, in simpler terms, *cabalgando por el culo*. The use of these vernaculars varied as a function of class, ethnicity, and religion.

Cristóbal with Gaspar

On 1 June 1560 a Spanish fleet, spearheaded by the captain's ship *Nuestra Señora de los Clarines el Cornio*, sailed en route to Spain from San Juan de Ulua in the Indies. Pedro de las Ruelas, the captain general and a knight of the

Order of Santiago, accused "Gaspar of having committed the nefarious sin against nature with Cristóbal." The admiral on board his own ship, *El Corchapín,* ordered Gaspar Hernández, "a Portuguese grummet," and Cristóbal Gutiérrez, "a fourteen-year-old page from Triana," to appear before him so that he could "inform himself of a certain crime committed on board the ship." [64]

"Last Friday night, at around eleven o'clock," replied Cristóbal, he had "fallen asleep in between Juan of Triana and Gaspar on the forecastle deck of the ship." As he slept between the two sailors, he "awoke and found his breeches untied and lowered." Having noticed this, Cristóbal, "horrified," got up and "supported" them up again, as he "continuously made the sign of the cross," for Cristóbal recalled "that on two or three other nights" he had also found his breeches "lowered," having had to "support them" on each occasion. Notwithstanding, Cristóbal "tucked his shirt into the supported breeches" and again situated himself "in between Juan and Gaspar." [65]

Before Cristóbal fell asleep, he witnessed how "Gaspar came closer to him as if to sleep with him and do it to him," and again the grummet had attempted to "untie the breeches and truss" Cristóbal's shirt. Cristóbal turned to Gaspar and shouted, "You rogue, I will tell the ship's master about your habits." Gaspar replied, "You wish me ill and intend to cause me harm." Cristóbal had wanted to inform the admiral and the pilot so that they could cast Gaspar "alive into the sea." Instead he related his story to his cousin Martín, who in turn, on the following morning, informed the ship's master, a mate, and the pilot about the incident. [66]

The captain general centered his interrogation of Gaspar, aged twenty-one, primarily on several essential points. Had the young grummet "ever committed the nefarious sin against nature?" asked the captain general, or had the mariner "ever penetrated [Cristóbal] in the cunt"? Had Gaspar "untied Cristóbal's breeches?" and "how many other times before" had the grummet "intended to commit the aforementioned sin against nature?" [67] Had Gaspar placed his "armed natural member in between the page's buttocks, wanting to fuck him in the cunt"? Had Cristóbal touched, "with his hand," Gaspar's "exposed and erect member"? Had the grummet "practiced the profession of *puto* for a long time with Cristóbal as well as with other persons"? And had he ever "kissed Cristóbal on the mouth"?

"Only under the cover of the blankets," admitted the young Cristóbal, had "Gaspar kissed him on the mouth." [68] "Never!" responded Gaspar. Gaspar had known Cristóbal for about one month and admitted only to having slept with Cristóbal "many times both on the forecastle deck and in the stern" and insisted that perhaps "between dreams" he might have "placed his leg over" the younger page.[69]

Efficacious Tortures

Given Gaspar's age and status as a minor, the captain general appointed a soldier, Guillermo de Cuellar, "to serve as his guardian or advocate in the case." Cuellar accepted the charge and immediately "posted a surety of twelve *ducados* of gold bond for His Majesty's coffers"—something not stipulated by any of the royal sodomy *Pragmáticas* during the early modern period. However, true to the dictates of said *Pragmáticas*, the captain general sentenced Gaspar to "torture and tortures" so that he would "declare the truth" about whether or not he had committed "the sin to Cristóbal."[70]

Cuellar, in defense of Gaspar, "implored his lordship to suspend the torture sentence until a lawyer could offer such consent and advice, for the captain general, albeit a knight, was not lawyer."[71] Despite the arguments presented by Cuellar, the captain general "proceeded with the torture session and admonished Gaspar to state the truth."[72]

In the presence of Cuellar, the ship's scrivener "warned Gaspar," stating that, "should the grummet suffer the dislocation of an arm, leg, or other member or should death occur during the torture," the young Gaspar "could not fault his lordship." Cuellar advised Gaspar "never to declare a thing." Then Nicolas, a Frenchman, "tied Gaspar's arms together, placed him on a ladder, and gave him eighteen turnabouts of the ropes."

The captain general instructed Nicolas to inflict yet another turn about of the ropes and ordered him also to tie Gaspar's muscles and legs to the ladder. Once tied, "Nicolas again began to squeeze" the young grummet. However, despite the continuing "straightening of the ropes," Gaspar did not confess anything. Consequently, the captain general ordered Gaspar "to be given water," not to quench his thirst but rather as another method of torture.[73]

Nicolas "placed a handkerchief over Gaspar's face and tucked part of it into his mouth and then began to pour in a pitcher of water." This technique produced a sense of drowning. The captain general insisted upon more jugs of water until Gaspar had consumed "a total of seven pitchers," but still the torture yielded no confession. The captain general had Gaspar removed from the ladder, ordered him taken to the ship's deck, and there placed him on a pulley.

Cuellar intervened and beseeched the captain general to "suspend the torture on the pulley for at least twenty-four hours." The inflicted ropes and water torture had already "broken Gaspar," pleaded Cuellar, "and his intestines could fall out." At the very least, declared the guardian, "his lordship should consult a man of science." The captain general magnanimously agreed and resumed the tortures three days later.[74]

The "ugly enormity" of the crime, reasoned the captain general, warranted the torture on the pulley that hung from the ship's yard.[75] Nicolas "took Gaspar's hands, placed them behind his back, and neatly tied the wrists together with a piece of linen cloth." Other seamen on board "weaved a cordage made of hemp through the pulley and used it to hoist Gaspar upward toward the height of the pulley."

From *El Corchapín*, anchored some distance away, Sebastian and the other mariners on board witnessed the torture of Gaspar. "We could very well see Gaspar and the torture," stated Domingo and Corzo, because the "the pulley hoisted Gaspar upward and lifted him up high" into the air.[76]

Gaspar hung in that state until his executioners released the cordage, and the young grummet, with his hands tied to the end of the rope, fell suspended in midair in an early modern version of a bungee jump. The captain general ordered the mariners to "hoist him up again and again" until Gaspar finally agreed to "tell the truth."[77]

Gaspar eventually swore, "before God," that "Cristóbal had asked to be fucked in the cunt, once in the harbor of Puerto Rico and another two or three times on board the ship, where Cristóbal himself had taken Gaspar's "rod in his hands" and had "inserted it into his own cunt. Furthermore, continued Gaspar, "Cristóbal had fucked him in the cunt three times."[78]

The younger Cristóbal withstood only "two turnabouts of the ropes"[79] until he too admitted his complicity with Gaspar. However, Cristóbal changed his version of the events three times, "for fear of the torture" and "the embarrassment" he felt at "the number of times" he had committed "the sin with Gaspar." Cristóbal had not, despite the grummet's allegations, penetrated Gaspar.[80]

After the young page confessed under the duress of the torture, Ludovico, a mariner on board *El Corchapín*, "overheard Cristóbal relate his story to a group of sailors" and later the young page "attempted suicide by jumping into the sea." Domingo added, "Cristóbal jumped into the sea for fear of the torture he had received."

According to Pablo Antonio, "Cristóbal said they had squeezed him with the ropes"; thus he had "jumped into the sea and swam from the captaincy [*Nuestra Señora de los Clarines*] to *El Corchapín* because they had given him very cruel torture" and "confessed to what was not true for fear of more torture." Juan Corzo also "saw the rope markings and scars on Cristóbal's arms" and stated that the seamen publicly commented how both Gaspar and Cristóbal "had received very grave tortures."[81]

Tortures or not, the captain general had obtained two confessions, and based on these findings he announced his sentences.

A Yawl of Naphtha

The captain general found Gaspar guilty of committing sodomy, condemned him to burn, and had all his goods confiscated.[82] Gaspar's goods consisted of "his salary, two blue breeches, one shirt, and some shoes." The young grummet bequeathed his "two cots to Cristóbal's cousin, Martín," and the "ship's master defrayed the costs of the trial from Gaspar's salary," a pecuniary penalty not alluded to by the royal sodomy *Pragmáticas.*[83]

The sergeants at arms then led Gaspar from *Nuestra Señora de los Clarines* onto a yawl, under the guard of sentinels and accompanied by the crier, who publicly declared Gaspar's crime and sin.[84] The other mariners situated him within site of the rack, where, upon arriving, Gaspar cried out that he had "fucked Cristóbal in the cunt, not three times but seven or eight times!" Furthermore, "Cristóbal had rejoiced when and consented to" each time Gaspar had penetrated the page.

Then a "black grummet executed the strangulation on the rack until Gaspar died naturally." Afterward he "placed Gaspar on a board in the yawl of naphtha" and set it on fire, and "it burned for more than half an hour."[85] One week later, the captain general sentenced Cristóbal to a similar punishment.[86] However, Cristóbal's guardian quickly came to his defense and "petitioned the right to appeal the sentence before any of His Majesty's judges."[87]

In Defense of Cristóbal

Cristóbal named Juan Bautista as his new guardian charged with presenting his appeal in Madrid.[88] In his first letter to the magistrates of the Casa de la Contratación, Juan Bautista presented a list of "wrongful nullities" that should exonerate Cristóbal and argued that "the death sentence issued by the captain general should be revoked because a trial of law had not rendered the decision." Also, Bautista argued that "Cristóbal, a boy under the age of fourteen, should not have stood trial under Spanish law or received torture, for he required the assistance of a guardian ad litem."[89] Thus, the torture of a minor nullified the trial. Furthermore, Cristóbal had not received a copy of the circumstantial proof presented against him, nor did he possess the competence with which to defend himself against those charges.[90]

Because the captain general had failed to grant Cristóbal such assurances, Bautista argued for the dismissal of a "null and void case." The captain general had simply "proceeded quite recklessly." In cases of "life or death," the courts could not proceed without the "advice of a lawyer, a natural right of the defense." Although the incidents took place at sea, pleaded Bautista, the captain general could have waited to argue his case in a peninsular court. For these reasons, the case against Gaspar "should have been nullified."

The appeal had come too late for Gaspar. Bautista also questioned the validity of confessions obtained under the fear and duress of torture. Away from tortures, Cristóbal denied having committed the aforementioned crime. Bautista found it likely that Cristóbal had not committed the crime, "for he had voluntarily denounced Gaspar." In any event, argued the guardian, "Gaspar's confession lacked the sufficient amount of evidentiary requirements in conformity with the laws of the kingdom to prosecute Cristóbal." Finally, Bautista employed other arguments in his defense of the young Cristóbal. He described Cristóbal as "a minor of good customs and good fame, one never accused of such a crime."[91]

"Given Cristóbal's appearance," reasoned the mariner Ludovico, "he must be eleven or twelve years old." Ludovico knew "Cristóbal as a good and publicly timid boy." Sebastian added that Cristóbal was "a quiet boy of good customs with a reputation on board the ship of being incapable of committing crimes."[92] All these sailors, with the exception of Sebastian, knew how to sign their names.[93]

Three neighbors from Triana testified before the Casa's Audiencia in defense of Cristóbal. One of the neighbors, Catalina Bernal, lay in bed close to death; thus she testified in her house before the scrivener.[94] Bernal said that Cristóbal was about twelve years old, "because since his birth they [Cristóbal and his parents] had lived next door to her." The three neighbors "knew both him and his mother very well" and had "always known Cristóbal, the boy, as a quiet, good, well-indoctrinated son of very good honorable parents and the grandson of good grandparents unaccustomed to committing the crime." The three neighbors did not know how to sign their names.[95]

On 26 March 1561, Hernando Maldonado, the forty-year-old magistrate in charge of the Casa prison in Seville, echoed the sentiments of the three neighbors. He stated that, "after the incarceration of Cristóbal, six Frenchmen held prisoner fled and the door of the prison remained open until the next morning." The remaining prisoners and Cristóbal "beckoned the magistrate to come see the open door and told him that the Frenchmen had fled." Maldonado also reported, "On another occasion, three other men imprisoned for thievery fled though a hole." When the escapees made their way through the "patio of the Casa, Cristóbal and Juan Vázquez, another prisoner, both cried out, saying that some prisoners intended to flee." Alerted, Maldonado "came out and reapprehended the prisoners."

Later, Vázquez told Maldonado that "Cristóbal had first seen the escapees and had then informed him so they could together cry out for help, for Cristóbal, only a boy, feared the Frenchmen would kill him." The French escapees had "wanted to take him with them." Cristóbal told San Martín and Batea that "he was not guilty and he did not want to flee but to be set free by the courts." Other prisoners described him as "simple, innocent, and covetous and one who many times over said and did things just like a boy of little prudence."[96]

Cristóbal, according to San Martín, "stated that he would not flee even if the door remained open." Magistrate Maldonado concurred with the other prisoners. He too described Cristóbal as "a simple boy with little understanding."[97] The magistrates of the Casa de la Contratación spared Cristóbal's life and instead sentenced him to "permanent banishment from the kingdom on 9 August 1561" (Fig. 3.5). On 25 August 1561 the Royal Council of the Indies in Madrid upheld the sentence.[98]

Vigilante Voyeurs

Sometimes things just kept repeating themselves. In September 1603 the ministers of the Casa de la Contratación officially instructed their prison officials to remove a *mulato* named Gerónimo Ponce from his cell and to hold him alone in separate quarters because he had committed the "nefarious sin" with his cellmate, another *mulato*. Ponce was brought from La Havana, where authorities had accused him of having committed the nefarious sin, to the Casa's jail in Seville, where he was charged with the same crime.[99]

Manuel Hernández, the prison jailer, informed Minister Bustamante that "around midnight last night, Captain Melchor López Tinoco and

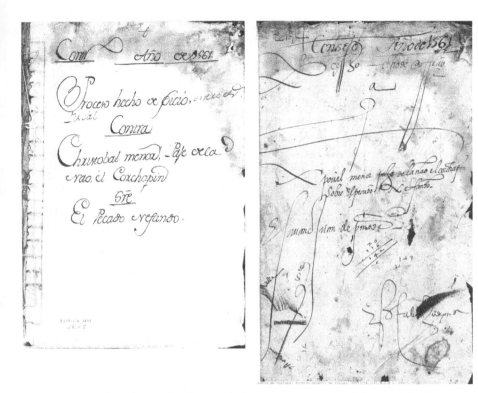

3.5. **Appeal trial records of Cristóbal,** *paje menor,* **1561; Justicia, 1181, N2, R5.** *(A, facing page)* "En el pleito . . . fallamos"; final sentence—permanent banishment from the kingdom. *(B, above left)* "Año de 1561, Proceso hecho de oficio entre el fiscal contra Christobal menor paje de la nao el Corchapin s[ob]re el pecado nefando"; frontispiece. Reproduced with the permission of the Archivo General de Indias, Seville. *(C, above right)* "Año de 1561"; back of the frontispiece.

Pedro Sánchez, two other prisoners, summoned him to the prison and asked him to separate the two *putos"* in the adjoining quarters. Tinoco and Sánchez had witnessed "Juan Ponce and Domingo López, a *morisco,* both without breeches, and on the floor lying together in one of the rooms situated on the second story of the prison." [100]

By the time Hernández entered those same quarters to investigate the charges, he found Ponce alone in the upper cot and Domingo in the lower cot. The jailer ordered Ponce out of the quarters and placed him in another room, pending further instructions from the ministers. "Why do

you set me apart?" asked Ponce. "For *puto* and for having penetrated Domingo," replied the jailer. "Look, sire," said Ponce, "for the love of God,
I'm about to be set free, and although I trussed his legs backwards, I did
no such thing."[101]

Sometime before midnight, Domingo himself had allegedly informed
Tinoco that a "stiff" Ponce had "made love to him." After dinner, as Ti-
noco entertained himself playing dice with Captain Francisco de Meza,
Domingo again approached him and boasted, "That *mulato* loves me."
Ponce, in the presence of the other prisoners, had then instructed Do-
mingo to go sleep upstairs.[102]

After the two *mulatos* had disappeared, Tinoco stated, "My dear men,
we shouldn't consent to this type of *bellaquería*—we shouldn't have allowed Domingo to go upstairs and we should inform the jailer." Tinoco
complained to the jailer, "What a good thing we have going on here. Such
people should not be allowed to be present in the company of honorable
men." The jailer reassured the prisoners, "Let the *putos* go upstairs. They
will burn."[103]

The three *voyeurs*—Pedro Sánchez, Francisco de Meza, and Captain
Tinoco—had, on that given night, decided to keep watch over the *mulatos,* each taking turns to go upstairs, peeping through a hole in the door,
and watching for any movement in the cell. Finally, Tinoco had seen
"Ponce's leg over Domingo's body." He rushed downstairs to summon
Pedro and Francisco. The three vigilantes, barefoot so as not to be detected, proceeded with great caution upstairs to certify the unfolding
events. Pedro held a lit candle as Tinoco grabbed a stick in one hand and
a knife in the other.[104]

Once upstairs, the vigilantes "busted into the quarters and saw Domingo on the floor, lying facedown on his stomach, his breeches lowered
and his shirt trussed." Next to him lay Ponce, "pretending to be asleep
and covering his eyes with his arms." Tinoco cried out to Domingo,
"Mad dog! Take your blanket and go downstairs."[105]

Kill the Mad Dog!

Once downstairs, the three vigilantes held Domingo captive in the servants' quarters. "Tell us what happened or we will kill you here with
blows," warned the others. "I haven't done anything bad," claimed Domingo. "Ponce placed his legs over me and touched my muscles and body,
and I told him to stay away," added Domingo. "You dog," remarked
Tinoco, "that is not the truth. Say it or I will have to kill you with [this]
knife."

"Kill the dog!" declared Pedro, as he threatened Domingo with the stick. "If you don't tell us the truth, we will have to kill and burn you. Say it, you dog. We all saw it!" threatened Tinoco. "I have already stated the truth," reiterated Domingo.[106]

Ponce then entered the servants' quarters under the pretext of having to "piss" and asked, "What is this, Señor Pedro?" "You dog, you and your filthiness" came the favorite response. "What is the meaning of this, Captain Tinoco?" insisted Ponce. Tinoco loudly cried out, "You are both dogs, for I have seen you both, with my own eyes, consummate your filthy misdeeds." "What misdeeds?" asked Ponce. "Did you not penetrate Domingo?" asked Tinoco. "Through where?" retorted Ponce. "Through the anus!" replied Tinoco.[107]

"It's certain that Ponce placed his leg over me," interjected Domingo. "Look," pleaded Ponce, "don't denounce me, my honorable man. For the love of God, promise me, for I am about to be freed from prison." A tireless Tinoco observed, "You dog, how dare you plead for a helping hand!" As he exited the quarters, he confidently affirmed that Ponce and Domingo would burn, "for we shouldn't have to sleep with this."[108]

Anecdotes of Love

Domingo's master had brought Domingo to the prison that morning with the intention of selling him. As the master asked for more fetters, he publicly announced to the other prisoners that "his slave had all the misgivings of the world, and far from lacking another, he was also a *puto*."[109] Domingo López, a twenty-year-old slave, appeared before the Casa's magistrates and in the presence of his guardian ad litem confirmed that his master had earlier deposited him in the tribunal's prison. The magistrates asked Domingo whether his master had described Domingo as a *puto* to the other prisoners.

Domingo replied that his master had stated that he "lacked *only* this misdeed."[110] One of the magistrates asked whether a "stiff" Ponce had caressed Domingo's face and throat with his hand and made love to him, "having said he had gone without for fifteen days." According to Domingo, Ponce had, in fact, "placed his hand on Domingo's face and throat, uttering words of endearment, and stated that he had not done it with anybody in two days."[111]

The magistrates also learned that when Domingo went upstairs to retire on the given night in question, he saw how Ponce had arranged both beds side by side. "Come here and scratch my backside," requested Ponce. As Domingo commenced the scratching, Domingo began to touch him.

"Why don't you remove your breeches?" requested Ponce. "What for?" asked Domingo. Ponce again "began to touch the slave, put his hand into Domingo's codpiece, [and] touched his flesh and his muscles," and when the *mulato* proceeded to "feel his member," Domingo had not consented and "had turned his body away."[112]

Still later, Ponce succeeded in persuading Domingo to remove his breeches and sleep without them. Domingo, fatigued due to a hip injury inflicted by his master, simply took off all his clothes and placed them over his body as he lay on his side. Ponce remained asleep and neither placed his legs over him or did any other thing, according to Domingo.[113]

The illustrious magistrate admonished Ponce to declare the truth and warned him that if "during the torture he should die, break a leg or an arm, or should one of his eyes pop out," he himself and not they deserved all the blame. "I don't know what else to say," declared Domingo. The magistrates summoned Francisco Velásquez, the city's executioner, and ordered him to denude Domingo. As the men erected the necessary apparatus for the requisite torture in this type of case and removed the shackles from Domingo's ankles, the young boy said that he wanted to tell the truth.

Domingo admitted that after "he had removed his breeches and lay face down, Ponce had trussed his shirt and climbed on top of him." Domingo had wanted to cry out, but Ponce threatened him, saying "Quiet, or I'll choke you." The slave remained still as Ponce, "holding on to Domingo's shoulders, forcibly attempted to insert his member into his cunt." Ponce succeeded inserting "only the head," for his "fat member did not fit" Domingo. Once the *mulato* finished, Domingo found "his cunt wet with Ponce's semen." Confession in hand, the magistrates had the rack removed from the quarters and suspended the torture session. Domingo, described by the scrivener as a "tad shade" (light-skinned) *mulato*, ratified his confession in the presence of his guardian.[114]

The Repeat Offender

Back in 1599, unable to convict Gerónimo Ponce—a free *mulato* from Seville who was also twenty years old—on sodomy charges with a young page, a captain general instead sentenced him to "the steps and the string" (the gallows) for six years without pay.[115] Despite "especially rigorous tortures on the pulley, [on] the rack, and of water" inflicted upon him on board and in the public jail of La Havana, Ponce had resisted and offered no concessions. Unlike the torture of Gaspar on the pulley, the executioner had attached substantial portions of lead to Ponce's feet before hoisting him high in midair. Ponce's lack of expression shocked the mariners who witnessed the torture.

The Casa's porter recalled that Ponce had escaped en route to the Royal Prison upon his return from La Havana. A royal magistrate fined the admiral of the ship for Ponce's escape. Crown officials later reapprehended Ponce and they took him to the Royal Prison in Seville. Still later, officials transferred him to the Casa prison.[116]

In 1607, sometime after Ponce's incarceration in the Royal Prison, secular officials again accused Ponce of sodomy with a boy of eighteen years named Manuel Rodríguez. The other prisoners had often noticed Ponce as he publicly hugged Manuelillo. "Look at those *putos,*" the prisoners muttered to each other. When Ponce and Manuelillo slept together, the other prisoners often "overheard how they both panted—just like when a man and a woman have carnal access with each other." Several prisoners commonly regarded Ponce as a *somético.* Ponce, "possessive and jealous of Manuelillo," always showered him with "many gifts." Francisco Ynfante, "a black *negro* slave," cautioned Ponce about his relationship with Manuelillo.

"Don't do such a thing," advised Francisco. "As it is, you're in here accused of being a *puto.*" Ponce did not heed the advice and retaliated by striking Francisco "on the mouth." A couple of months earlier, the petulant Ponce had also struck Benitillo in the prison courtyard. "Brother, do you strike me because I protect my honor, or do you want me to burn for you?" asked Benitillo, evidently having declined Ponce's advances. "I," concluded Benitillo, "wish not to burn for anyone." [117] But the magistrates did not consider all testimony offered against Ponce and Domingo as acceptable in a court of law.

When Alonso Hernández, a *morisco,* testified against Ponce, the magistrates discounted his testimony after Ponce's advocate argued that *moriscos* did not constitute "legitimate witnesses." Furthermore, argued the guardian, any "sighs" overheard by the prisoners coming from Ponce and Manuelillo could have occurred as a result of the "cold, pain, or sickness" felt by two mariners. The advocate described his clients as "good Christians, fearful of God, honorable and honest men, [and] aficionados of virtuous women." [118]

Despite the arguments presented by the defense, the Royal Court condemned both Ponce and Manuelillo to water and rope torture. Ponce and Manuelillo received some fifteen turnabouts and four jugs of water, but neither confessed to any wrongdoing. That prompted the officials to absolve them both in July 1603. Thereafter, they transferred Ponce to the Casa's prison.[119]

In September that same year, Casa officials accused Ponce of sodomy and submitted him to a series of now familiar questions and tortures. Ponce, for his part, denied ever having placed his hands on Domingo's beard, muscles, or member. He never spoke amorous words to Domingo nor had he caressed his neck. Nor had he stated that he felt "stiff," for he lacked "it." He had not inserted his "fat member" inside Domingo's codpiece or in his cunt. He had not acted as "agent or patient," and he certainly had not "spilled semen in the act."[120]

The magistrates, not yet satisfied with the *mulato*'s revelations, requested the executioner to tie Ponce to the rack. Familiar as he was with the tortures and their sequence of events, Ponce "closed his eyes as if in a fainted state, did not utter a word, made no other movements, [and] withstood a number of turnabouts, until the magistrates suspended the torture."[121] Despite not having confessed to anything, the Casa sentenced Ponce to burn in an apparent violation of sodomy laws.

Ponce's advocate immediately sought to appeal his sentence. The witnesses had not actually seen the act, argued his advocate, and the extraction of Domingo's confession under the duress of torture invalidated the testimony in accordance with additional judicial requirements stipulated by the new *Pragmática*, "a minimum of three witnesses to convict a sodomite," a direct reference to the 1497 *Pragmática*.[122]

On appeal before the Council of the Indies, His Majesty's attorney general nevertheless confirmed the death sentences dictated by the Casa tribunal in what he called a "nefarious and pernicious case." Although Ponce was condemned to strangulation and death by fire in September 1603, the Casa did not execute his sentence until November 1605.[123] No similar verdict could be found for Domingo, for the scrivener did not substantiate the outcome of that case.

Often, accused sodomites suffered merciless episodes of humiliation under the custody of court-appointed officials as these authorities attempted time and again to prove the repulsive state of the crime and sin *contra natura*. If these officials could express the ugliness of such a crime often enough and by using the most disgusting images, perhaps those directly affected by those acts, as well as the other individuals who witnessed them, could in the end accept and perpetuate fantastic versions of Vir.

Ano Horribilis

The Spanish courts, in their attempts to prove the abominable nature of sodomy, sometimes resorted to the use of science to quantify their discursive descriptions. Some courts subjected accused sodomites to humiliating physical examinations. When Fita, the chief surgeon, viewed the external parts of Giovanni Mule's anus, he "realized and saw all its parts lacerated and full of sordid ulcers or callous skin." Fita concluded that since the boy exhibited a "loose" anus, "somebody had, with the boy many times before, committed the sin of sodomy."[124]

Suares, the surgeon's assistant, concurred with Fita, observing that "the boy's backside appeared quite used, loose, and blistered." These markings had occurred, Suares stated, "apparently as the result of the lad's having committed the sin of sodomy and allowing himself to be sodomized numerous times."[125] The chief surgeon himself said to the boy, "This is not your first time, is it?" The boy replied, "It's true."[126]

Despite Fita's initial examination of Giovanni Mule, the magistrate who presided over the case ordered a second examination. "Naturally impossible that the boy committed the sin against nature," reported the second surgeon. "I have seen no signs that demonstrate member penetration."[127] With two contradictory surgeons' reports before him, the magistrate sought "further clarification" and asked two other surgeons "to examine Juan Mule and to ascertain whether or not the unutterable sin against nature had been committed with him."[128]

After these surgeons "very carefully" examined the boy's anus, they found "no initiative or sign with which to presume that someone had, with the boy, executed the sin against nature." Furthermore, they found "no signs that a natural member had penetrated the boy." The boy's anus had revealed "no ulcers, no inflammation, no hemorrhoids, or anything out of the ordinary."[129]

The "contradictions in the surgeons' depositions" prompted the magistrate to demand yet another examination of Giovanni Mule. This time he ordered "all the surgeons to collectively concur and again examine the boy." In June 1698, the chief surgeon Fita and the other surgeons, "with the greatest care for the boy," made the final examination of Mule. "Employing pure anatomical form and with the necessary instruments," Fita and his colleagues "then executed an internal examination" of Mule's anus.[130]

This time around, these men of science detected "a troubling senti-

ment, a scar or corn, both internally and externally, in a state of decay."
The men could not see beyond the "troubled sentiment, for some sort
of inflammation or blockage obstructed their view," but they could not
"probe any further for fear that their instruments would inflict and cause
Juan Mule more damage or result in a new illness." The examiners pondered "whether or not they should proceed with their examination"
in order thus to provide the magistrate with "a much more informed
diagnosis."[131]

The men concurred that they should continue the examination
and "let the instrument pass through the inflamed part." The scrivener
wrote that the instruments apparently "lacerated the blockage." "In their
previous viewing" of Mule, Fita and his colleagues had conducted only
"external and not very extensive observations." In their final examination, the men used a "sagacious workmanship" that allowed them to
perform a more complete examination and to provide revised "final
declarations."[132]

Below Deck with Antón and Alonso

In addition to the hardships already described, mariners also suffered
from the excesses inflicted on them by their immediate superiors. The
abuse of mariners was perpetrated not just by the courts. In fact, many
seamen complained about the way in which ships' officers abused their
positions of power and coerced them into performing sexual favors. Like
crown officials who equated the practice of sodomy with foreigners, some
mariners also associated it with others or believed that those of other nations inherently practiced sodomitical acts. Although the mariners critiqued the power structure presented by the courts and the officers, they
nonetheless also subscribed to official discourses about sodomy (i.e., the
belief that all foreigners practiced sodomy).

In the case of Antón de Fuentes and Alonso Prieto, the pilot took the
ship's master aside on board *Nuestra Señora de los Clarines* and stated, "Know
thou, your lordship, there is a *puto* on board this ship." As the pilot spoke
his words, Alonso, a young page, began to weep.[133] "Why do you weep?"
asked the master. "Be it known to you, your lordship," replied the page,
"that Antón de Fuentes," a *lombardero*,[134] "inserted it in me below deck,
wanting to do it." Antón had pleaded with the young page, "Don't reveal
me and I will give you anything you desire." Alonso sobbed, "Do not
think, my lord, that I wanted to do it with him."[135]

At three o'clock that afternoon, the thirteen-year-old page stood before the captain general and reiterated his recollections of the incidents

on board the ship. Alonso, a native of Cartaya, recalled that as he stood by the open hearth with the other pages, tossing some *migas en una coci-dilla*[136] for the purser, Antón de Fuentes approached the pages with a lit candle in his hand and asked, "Who wants to go below deck with me?" Perico, the purser's page, turned to Alonso and suggested to Alonso, "You go." Antón handed Alonso a lit candle, and they both made their way toward the midship. Once they had descended by way of the hatches through which the mariners lowered bulky goods, Antón asked the pages above to close the trap doors. Antón turned to Alonso and said, "Give me the candle. I will go ahead of you, for I know the way better than you do."[137]

Alonso followed Antón until they reached Antón's large wooden *caja*. Antón handed the candle back to Alonso and asked him to hold open the lid of the chest while he retrieved and untied a bundle of black taffeta. Antón, with the aid of some scissors, cut about three measured rod lengths of the thin black silk, having measured it from the thumb of his right hand up to his breast. He folded the pieces and, with his hand, placed the pieces in his shirt and then returned the bulk of the taffeta to the wooden box.

Antón then took back the candle, and both mariners returned to the hatches along the same path. When they reached the trapdoors, Alonso put the candle out as Antón cried out to the pages because the hatch doors remained closed. The pages did not answer, and so Antón decided to sit and wait on some jars. Alonso also cried out to the pages, but none responded.[138]

What Do You Take Me For—a Moor or a Turk?

As the two waited for the doors to open, Antón turned to Alonso and said, "Sit here and I will look at the *cuchillada* (knife wound) given you. As Alonso placed the ankle of his left foot on a keg, Antón sat next to him and insisted that he "untie his breeches and move toward the light by the hatches." Antón touched Alonso's "spine and his buttocks with his hands and then squeezed *it* between his two hands, wanting to take out the sap." When he had finished, Antón distanced himself from the page without saying anything. He cracked open the trapdoors with his head just as another mariner approached to go below deck. Alonso, meanwhile, remained below deck, repeatedly adjusting his breeches.[139]

A short while later, Antón returned below deck with a lit candle and found Alonso still standing by the hatches. Both men then walked toward the ship's stern. Once there, Antón picked up a riding saddle and placed it over the other saddles there. He placed his hands underneath some chairs and retrieved a piece of a brush made of esparto, ordinarily used to scrub culinary vessels and utensils, which he singed slightly with the candle's lit wick. Antón put the candle out with a piece of wood and cut a piece of the wick with some scissors. He handed the cut piece of wick to Alonso and asked him to place it on top of a fife rail.

"Why don't you slacken your breeches?" asked Antón. When Alonso removed his breeches, Antón made him lie, breast down, on top of some pipes. Antón "trussed" the boy's shirt and took "Alonso's *natura* into his hands as he caressed it tenderly in between his hands." Antón "touched the boy's inner thighs" and then "began to feel his buttocks and his cunt." He "tried to examine the cunt and the thighs with the burned brush as he stuck one finger into Alonso's fundament and pressed the page's member between his hands."

"Do you feel it?" asked Antón. "Yes," replied Alonso. After Antón had "caressed it quite well, repeatedly rubbing and feeling it," the laborer "pulled his own yard out of his codpiece and put it up against Alonso's cunt." When Alonso felt this sensation, he "distanced himself from Antón, took his breeches, raised them, and fled." [140]

Antón pursued Alonso, overtook him, grabbed his hand, and pleaded, "Hush, hush. . . . Don't say anything." When Alonso began to cry out, Antón released him and allowed him to go free. Alonso exited by way of the hatches and set out to find the ship's master, whom he found asleep in his cabin. Alonso did not want to wake the master, so he went to the ship's fore, where the purser offered him something to eat. "I'm not hungry," replied Alonso. The purser said, "Here, take three fish, go scale them, and we will eat them tonight." [141]

As Alonso stood in the fore cleaning the fish, Antón approached him again, with his hands held together and begged, "Hush. For the love of God, don't say anything, and I will please you by giving you anything you desire." But the young page invoked a common saying: "What do you take me for, a Moor or a Turk, a heretic?" I have no reason not to tell my lord the master," Alonso cried loudly. A dejected Antón departed, and Alonso finished salting the fish. Alonso related his story to Melchor de Campos, the ship's master's son, who informed the pilot and the master himself.[142]

An Inadvertent Rub

"But why had the page remained below deck to assist Antón a second time?" asked a curious captain general. The page remained behind a second time because he assumed that "Antón had wanted to see his injured ankle." Anyway, Antón had "never before done or said anything related to it." Alonso said that he simply had "no knowledge of, nor had he ever heard it rumored that Antón had realized carnal access with another boy or man on or off the ship." [143]

On 2 May 1562 in Cádiz, Antón de Fuentes, aged thirty, a native of Barcelona and a mariner for the previous fifteen years, offered his own version of the events. Antón had known Alonso Prieto for "two months or since the time Alonso had boarded the ship." [144] On the day in question, Antón descended below deck to retrieve some black taffeta from a large wooden box because he had intended to sell it.

While below deck, Alonso had begun to wriggle about and complained about a pain he felt in one foot. "Why does it hurt?" asked Antón. Alonso responded that "his inner thighs and buttocks ached because the captain general had given him blows in many parts of his body." [145]

When the two mariners reached the saddles, Alonso mounted a saddle and he showed Antón the backside of his hand. "What have you there?" asked Antón. "It also aches," replied Alonso, "as the page untied and pulled down his breeches."

Antón inspected the page's inner thighs, and he found two dry welts. "Wait, I'll dip them in some hot tallow wax," offered Antón, as he "took a bit of wool from a saddle, dipped it into the candle wax, and anointed Alonso's thighs and welts with the unction of the tallow." Alonso said, "I also have something on my behind." "Show me," replied Antón, as the page turned to show his backside.

Antón "illuminated the boy's posterior with the candle and found the markings of blows or scratches on Alonso's buttocks close to the backbone." Antón said, "Wait, let's anoint them," said Antón as he "took the wool [and] again dipped it into the candle wax," but this time "the dipped wool put the candle out." Antón carefully "anointed the markings," and when he had finished, he "felt Alonso's buttocks with both hands, having asked the page if he felt any pain in any other parts of his body."

Suddenly, according to Antón, "Alonso turned over and said, 'I will tell my lord the master.' Antón responded, 'The devil be, what will you say?'" Alonso, weeping somewhat, jumped up and fled above deck." [146] But for what effect had Antón put his fingers into Alonso's "anus or that part he uses to execute his common necessities?" asked the captain general.

Antón admitted only to having "touched or felt the thighs, but not the *natura,* although he might have inadvertently touched it with his hands as he examined the proximity of the thighs," but he had not "particularly touched the boy nor had he rubbed him" in any way whatsoever.

Moreover, Alonso had voluntarily loosened his breeches. Antón "didn't remember if he had instructed Alonso to do so in order to better view the thighs." Likewise, he "had not put his finger into the fundament nor had he placed his *natura* into Alonso's anus."[147]

Fat *Natura*

During a second interrogation of Alonso, the magistrates insisted on hearing yet more saucy details. "Had Alonso felt or seen Antón's *natura*, his genital member, as the laborer attempted to insert it through Alonso's fundament, and had it caused him any harm?" asked the captain general. Otherwise, "how could the young boy have distinguished the *natura* from another body part?"

"When Antón inserted his finger into my *culo*," clarified Alonso, "he knew fully well that it felt like a finger." But when Antón attempted to insert his "fat *natura*" into Alonso, the young boy had "felt a tightness around the eye of his fundament, caused by the genital member Antón used to piss from." Alonso had not "bled," nor had he suffered any other "harm." In the presence of Antón, the captain general asked Alonso if the laborer "had wanted to have carnal access with him through the fundament from where he realized his necessities?" Alonso reiterated his earlier assertions and affirmed his deposition.[148]

Powders

On 2 May 1562 in Cádiz the captain general condemned Antón to torture and had all of his possessions sequestered. An inventory of Antón's precious box revealed a list of more than 125 items, including expensive textiles, riding saddles, and an extensive wardrobe of fine garments. Three witnesses had testified for the prosecution: the ship's master Alonso de Fuentes; his fifteen-year-old son, Melchor; and the pilot Sebastian Fernández, who all ratified their denouncements of Antón.[149]

Unlike the torture of Gaspar on *El Corchapín*, the executioner placed the nude Antón, his hands tied, on a trow mill.[150] He received nine rotations of the small ropes that had been tied about the brawny part of his arms and his shins. The executioner again repeated the same sequence of the inflicted torture. He had also placed a woolen cloth over Antón's face and poured six jugs of water into his mouth, and thereafter he poured some more water into Antón and added even more small ropes about his muscles. Unlike Gaspar, Antón not only survived the torture but also offered no confession. The officials suspected that Antón had resisted the torture because someone had given him powders.[151]

The investigation took a different turn when the captain general interrogated the cell guard and other prisoners. Nobody had any knowledge of any powders, nor did they know that Antón had been imprisoned for the nefarious sin. In 1562, La Casa de la Contratación in Seville assumed jurisdiction over the case, and Solicitor General Venegas formally charged Antón de Fuentes with "the intent to commit the nefarious sin," and he accused "Alonso Prieto of having permitted the aforementioned to commit the nefarious sin with him"[152] (Fig. 3.6). Once again, the tribunal appointed Juan Bautista, a solicitor of the Casa, to act as Alonso's guardian.[153]

Honorable Men Never Do Such Things

Antón de Fuentes, like many other defendants, attempted to justify his "manliness" by taking refuge in the fact that he was "married with a wife" and had "only touched Alonso because he had wanted to cure his injuries." Antón insisted he had often cured many of the sick mariners on board the ship. "The ship's master Alonso de Campos, his son Melchor, and other persons," claimed Antón, had "induced the page Alonso to denounce him out of the hatred they felt toward him." Antón presented a total of ten witnesses in his defense. In Cádiz on 30 May 1562 the witnesses related their testimonies on board the *Nuestra Señora de los Clarines*.[154]

The witnesses portrayed Antón as "an honorable man of good repute, a very good Christian, one fearful of God and his good conscience." Antón, "quite the lady's man, often attempted conversation with women." About five or six months earlier, he had married María de los Reyes, a resident of Seville. Therefore the witnesses "in fact certainly knew that Antón had not wanted to nor had he committed the crime against nature." Nobody had ever presumed such a thing about him. They related that "the vigorous torture administered by Captain General Pedro Relendes had rendered Antón a maimed man deprived of his left arm."[155] In the early modern period, to survive rigorous tortures was tantamount to proving one's innocence.

These same witnesses vilified Alonso "as a liar and as a young gossipy boy." The page "worked closely with the ship's master and thus greatly respected and feared him." Furthermore, they reported, "the ship's master and Antón didn't get on." On one occasion, "the ship's master had

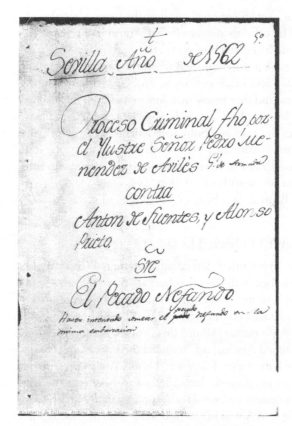

3.6. **Frontispiece of a sodomy trial record.** *Sevilla,
año de 1562, Proceso criminal fecho por el ilustre Señor Pedro
Menendez de Aviles General de Armanda contra Antón de
Fuentes y Alonso Prieto sobre el pecado nefando y haver
intentado cometer el pecado nefando en la misma embarcación,*
Justicia, 855, N11. Reproduced with the permission
of the Archivo General de Indias, Seville.

quarreled with Antón, grabbed his beard, and promised to deny him passage to the Indies." Alonso and Melchor, stated the witnesses, "had col-
luded with the ship's master in an attempt to impede Antón's way to the
Indies." [156]

On 4 July 1562 the Royal Council of the Indies in Madrid issued the
definitive sentence in the case. Bautista had again forcefully argued for the

defense. The council condemned Antón de Fuentes only to "a two-year suspension from the Indies without pay and condemned him to pay all the costs of the case." The ministers "absolved Alonso Prieto of all charges and set him free." [157]

Despite the use of allegations of sodomy as a method of economic or political blackmail, as in the Antón-Alonso case, many pages often complained of the abuse they endured on board the ships traveling to and from Las Indias.

The Handy Boatswain

In April 1566 in the city of Nombre de Dios, Cristóbal de Erauso, the captain general of the Spanish fleet, received notice that Juan Fernández, aged forty and the boatswain on the master ship *San Juan Baptista,* had committed the "crime and sin contrary to nature with many persons." [158] Juan de Sauzedo, a sixteen-year-old page on board the *San Juan Baptista,* appeared before the captain general and stated that "about one month ago, late at night, as he lay asleep underneath the deck of the ship, Juan Fernández had approached him and put his hand inside an opening" in Sauzedo's breeches. Fernández had then "taken the page's rod in his own hand." Sauzedo responded, "Go away. Why do you do such a vile thing?" "Be still," replied Fernández. "I don't want to," replied Sauzedo, as he removed himself from the area. The boatswain had importuned Sauzedo on two other occasions, telling him, "Come lie and sleep next to me." Sauzedo declined the offer: "I don't want to." [159]

Sauzedo recalled that "on one of those three nights, as it rained and all the people on board the ship slept, Fernández had felt his rod as he lay in bed," and the boatswain worked it until the page ejaculated "filthiness." When Sauzedo awoke and witnessed the ejaculated semen, the boatswain reassured him, saying that "he had only pissed" on himself. "Never in his life" had Sauzedo "committed such a thing." [160]

Another page named Pedro Díaz, aged fourteen, came forth and stated that after the master ship had sailed past the Isle of Dominica, as he slept on deck, Fernández had approached him and "touched his rod." Díaz reported that "one dark and rainy night," the boatswain had suggested, "Come lie with me tonight for the love of my bad leg." Díaz acquiesced, and about midnight, as he "lay on his front side" in Fernández' bed, the boatswain "placed his armed rod up against the page's buttocks in an attempt to sodomize him." Díaz did not consent, and he pulled himself away. "Be still," insisted Fernández.

Several other times, Fernández had summoned Díaz to the forecastle deck and asked the page to louse him. Once loused, the boatswain invariably felt Díaz' "rod." Díaz "had not denounced the boatswain earlier for fear of being killed by him." The page also implicated others for having had sex with the boatswain: "Juan de Saucedo, Alonso de Salas Botilla, Lázaro Hernández, [and] Gonzalo and Pedro, both grummets." They were all crew members of the master ship and potential witnesses in the captain general's case against Fernández the boatswain.[161] These pages, along with other mariners, provided the captain general with more of the same type of testimony about Fernández and his shenanigans.

In addition to the pages listed above, other mariners provided the magistrates with additional testimony. About four years earlier, Alonso Suares, a grummet, had sailed to the Indies in the company of Fernández. The boatswain, then a sailor, had put his hand into Suares' breeches. Juan Moreno, a mariner, who sailed on the same ship with Suares, noticed that "Fernández always went around putting his hand into the breeches of some grummets."[162] Miguel Martín, a sixteen-year-old grummet on the current voyage, divulged that on four different occasions the boatswain commanded him "to make his bed and lie with him, for he had a bad leg and suffered from epilepsy."

On one of these occasions, "once the people on board the ship had retired for the night, Fernández touched Miguel's body, his anus, his yard, and his scrotum." Miguel pleaded, "Don't do that," as he abandoned the area "amid the strikes given and the chides uttered by Fernández."[163] The boatswain also asked Gonzalo Fernández, an eighteen-year-old grummet from Oporto, Portugal, to "make his bed and lie with him" because Gonzalo had no clothes with which to cover himself. In bed, Fernández "teased and tempted Gonzalo's rod and groin."[164]

Alonso de Salas Botilla, a fifteen-year-old grummet from Triana in Seville, testified that while on board the master ship in Cádiz fifteen days before it departed for the Indies, Fernández called "at about midnight, while all the people on board the ship slept," and Salas "felt how Fernández had put his hand through a covering in the grummet's breeches, tempting his rod." The grummet lifted his breeches and secured them, tying them with two knots.[165] Salas found himself alone with Fernández on another occasion in the bread room of the ship.

A couple of days earlier, the boatswain, overtaken with curiosity at the sight of Salas' long pubes, had offered "his knife to the grummet and ordered him to cut them." While in the bread room, Fernández asked the grummet, "Did you cut your pubes?" Wanting to look for himself, Fernández "put his hand inside the grummet's breeches, took his rod, felt it with his fingers until it stood erect, and spilled two drops of filthiness." After Salas saw the "nastiness," he "ran out of the bread room and fled."[166]

Further up in the gunroom, Fernández had accosted another boy. "Tell me about your yard," asked the boatswain of Lázaro Hernández, a fifteen-year-old page. "Why do you ask me that? It's not appropriate," replied Lázaro. "Is it much too ask?" mused Fernández.[167]

His Favorite

Fernández had his preferred boy, and the other pages knew this. "Pedro, are you aware that you are the most desired on board this ship by the meanest man in the world?" asked Salas. Salas informed the grummet that some of the pages on board the ship "talked" among themselves about how "Pedro lay next to the boatswain during the entire voyage." "Some pages," continued Salas, had "complained about Fernández' notoriety," for the boatswain had "felt the private parts of every page on board the ship." "The devil be," remarked Pedro, as he informed Salas that he had previously "confessed his suspicions about Fernández to the chaplain."

The ship chaplain instructed Pedro simply "not to travel on the same ship with Fernández." The chaplain had also instructed Lázaro to "leave the master ship" if at all possible, and should the incidents occur again, the page should relate the particulars of the events to "the chaplain or any other priest or clergyman," who in turn would then tell Lázaro what he should do.[168] "Over the last couple of days" and after his consultation with the chaplain, Pedro had refused to obey any of the boatswain's orders, much to the displeasure of Fernández, who "ill treated and beat" the grummet well within the "public view" of the other pages.[169]

The young page had left Villa de Zafra, his native birthplace, about eight to ten years earlier for Seville. He settled in with Juan Ximénez for three years, until he embarked for New Spain as a page. He then boarded another ship and traveled to "the island of Santo Domingo"; from there he returned to Seville and then set sail on the current voyage.[170] Pedro Hernández, the twenty-year-old grummet, often slept with the boatswain in his bed, because Pedro had no clothes with which to cover himself.

Pedro had spent the night with Fernández "between twenty and thirty times" until their arrival in Nombre de Dios. On those nights, "Fernández touched Pedro's body, his rod, his scrotum—all with his hand, and sometimes even kissed him." Some nights Pedro even "found his muscles drenched with the filth that dripped out of his rod or that of Fernández'—the bed stained with filthiness." Fernández promised Pedro, "I will take you to my village, to confer an employment of honor and esteem in arrangement of your marriage." Pedro acknowledged, "I am grateful, and I will accept your promise."[171]

When Pedro overheard "Lázaro, Salas, and Sauzedo," all pages on board the ship, state that "Fernández had forced all three to lie next to him, wanting to fuck them, and made one of them spill filth out of his rod," he denounced the boatswain to the captain general. But "why has it taken you so many days to denounce Fernández?" asked the captain general. Pedro responded that he had not denounced the boatswain until he had "met with his confessor and followed the cleric's advice."[172]

For the Love of My Leg, Cut the Pubes

Years before departing for the Indias, Juan Fernández, the forty-year-old boatswain and pilot, had married Juana Ruiz in Villa de Palos, close to Ayamonte. Fernández would later make use of this fact in his own defense against the accusations brought against him by the seven young mariners.

He had personally known all seven pages for at least seven months.[173] Fernández admitted "that one night Juan de Sauzedo did lie next to him" and that he had seen the page's "breeches open or loosely sewn, his stiff rod and scrotum hanging out" in the open air. The boatswain had only placed "his hands on Sauzedo's wet rod" in his attempt to cover it up.[174]

The boatswain might have done likewise with Pedro's rod, but only "to play with Díaz as boys do until they fall asleep." Fernández acknowledged that he "suffered from a bad leg and received great comfort from the warmth of another person lying next to him." He had, on occasions, asked Lázaro to lie next to him because he received comfort from someone who could subside his malady. The boatswain also "tickled" Lázaro and Miguel Martín, "as boys do." He toyed with their rods and groins, for he fancied himself a "jester" and he liked to watch the pages squirm."[175]

Salas' great pudenda continued to fascinate the obstinate boatswain. The page usually "wore some red breeches opened at the leg," Fernández reported, "and many times you could see his rod." "The other pages," observed the boatswain, "did not have as much pubes" on their pudenda as did Salas. "Why don't you cut it?" asked Fernández, offering the use of "his knife and scissors" to the page.

Fernández said he had often approached Salas to "cover the opening" in his breeches and in the process might have "felt it with his hand." Fernández jested with Gonzalo Hernández, the Portuguese, and also took his rod and scrotum in his hand. The boatswain admitted to having "pulled Gonzalo's long pubes." [176] "Why don't you wash? You are filthy," said Fernández. With that, "some devilish pages and grummets of the ship jumped into the sea to swim." [177]

Unfortunately for Fernández' bad leg, Pedro Hernández did not always adhere to his requests "despite having spent many nights next to him for the aforementioned effect." [178] Pedro had slept in the boatswain's bed from the time the ship sailed from Cadíz to the port city of Nombre de Dios many nights, "for the delightful love Fernandez felt on his leg."

On these nights, Fernández had also tickled Pedro, who laughed as Fernández tempted his rod and scrotum. Sometimes Pedro's member stood erect; however, "Fernández never saw filthiness on Pedro's muscles." The boatswain admitted before the magistrates that he had "promised Pedro," upon their return to Spain, to take him to his village and confer an employment of honor and esteem in arrangement of Pedro's marriage, for the affection he felt toward him. [179]

After the captain general heard the boatswain's confession, Pedro Hernández reappeared before his lordship and modified his earlier confession. Pedro declared that it was true that Juan Fernández, once or twice, had sodomized him "as he lay in bed asleep on his breasts." He also reported that "when he felt Fernández on top, he would try to free himself." [180]

Immediately thereafter, the captain general ordered the arrest of Fernández and Pedro. The boatswain awaited his fate imprisoned, his feet tied to a wooden stock in the captain general's gallery, while Pedro remained captive in the public jail in Nombre de Dios. [181]

On 12 May 1566 the captain general condemned Fernández, for "having committed the sin against nature with Pedro Hernández, a grummet, and with other sailors, on board the master ship." He also condemned Andrés, a Genoese sailor aboard the master ship, for "having intended to commit the nefarious sin" with Fernández while both sat imprisoned in the captain general's gallery. [182]

But if suspicions of powders had clouded the outcome of the Antón-Alonso case, the absence of money tainted the fate of Pedro and the boatswain who suffered from epilepsy.

Money, Money, Money

In June 1566, in the port city of San Cristóbal de la Havana, the captain general asked Juan Fernández and Pedro Hernández to respond to the pending charges levied against them. He ordered the master to relinquish the wages earned by the boatswain and Pedro Hernández to Pablo de Mercado, the master scrivener on board the ship, who was to make use of the monies to feed them and to pay for any other costs of the case.[183]

Both the boatswain and Pedro relied on Francisco de Herrera, a soldier on board the ship, to present their defense.[184] Herrera argued, "Your lordship wrongly inculpated the boatswain and Pedro for having committed the sin against nature, for he lacked the evidence or the proof of the crime's commission." Furthermore, Herrera wrote: "The witnesses are part of the crime and are fearful boys who loathed the boatswain, for he punished their unworthy deeds. The boatswain is a good and virtuous Christian; thus, one cannot fathom or presume him to have committed such a crime. The only circumstantial proof against Pedro is his own confession uttered under the duress or fear of impending torture, and there is no proof of a vile act, although he is weak; he never, of his own free will, consented; quite the contrary, he resisted any advances made by the boatswain." [185]

Herrera requested twelve additional days in which to prepare a more adequate defense. The captain general ordered the scrivener Pablo to grant six pesos of silver to Herrera from the confiscated salaries of Pedro and the boatswain. Meanwhile, Pedro "affirmed" the contents of his second confession, and Herrera requested yet an additional six days in which to finalize his defense.[186] The guardian informed the court he had consulted the services of a lawyer in La Havana with the six pesos granted to him earlier.

The lawyer had charged three pesos and two reales to review the contents of the case and to respond to the charges contained therein. Furthermore, Herrera spent five days in La Havana soliciting a copy of the trial proceedings. That cost him a "lot of monies," for which he sought "more monies" from the proceeds of his clients' salaries.[187]

The captain general "ordered the scrivener to grant Herrera another four pesos of silver, for a total of ten." [188] He also named Vera, a *lizenciado* and a passenger, as his private assessor for the case and asked the scrivener to pay Vera three pesos for his professional services.

By August 1566 the *Nuestra Señora de los Clarines* sat anchored in the port of San Miguel in the Azores, and Vera had still not received any remuneration for his services. Vera approached the captain general and stated that "I have presided over two sentences and expect to advise your lordship on another two." He added that "Fernández' and Hernández' salaries totaled more than one hundred pesos, from which they could pay for my services," and "implored the captain general to have Pablo relinquish the three pesos" owed him.[189]

This time the scrivener also solicited monies for his services in the case, and the captain general granted him twelve pesos for his work on it.[190] Despite the monies paid to these individuals, the case remained in a suspended state until shortly before the master ship arrived in Seville.

Eventually the captain general condemned Fernández and Hernández to "torture on the pulley in the accustomed manner and form," and he "reserved for himself the right" to dictate the "number of times that the aforementioned shall be lifted and suspended in the air for this execution," all "in the name of justice."[191] However, ship officials did not execute the tortures on board the ship prior to their arrival in the metropolis.

Solicitor Gadfly

Back in Seville, the Casa's solicitor general, Venegas—by now well reputed for his defense of torture in sodomy cases—was concerned about the unexecuted sentence. He argued that it was necessary "in the interest of justice to execute the torture on the pulley since the captain general had already sentenced Fernández and Hernández."[192]

In October 1566 the lord ministers of the Casa's tribunal authorized Venegas to proceed with the tortures of the boatswain and the page.[193] Pedro named Gonçalo de Molina as his guardian ad litem, who appealed his case before the Casa's tribunal:[194]

> Sires . . . the torture sentence on the pulley pronounced against Pedro is null, unjust, and grave. Thus, it should be revoked because Pedro is not culpable nor did he commit any crime nor is there good cause to have him imprisoned any more than there is to imprison the other pages and grummets, for each simply said what they knew about the boatswain. If Fernández forced some of them to commit evil and dishonesties, Pedro did not indulge him nor consent to any dishonest acts. Therefore, he should not be imputed or inculpated, for he is a minor. The boatswain punished the pages, and he could summit them to much harm. I appeal to argue the torture sentence before His Majesty and the Council of the Indies.[195]

Venegas insisted "that, despite the appeal, the magistrates should execute the torture sentence and that only monies in moderation should be made available to Molina, because the state should not have to subsidize this proceeding." Molina reminded the court that "he had appealed to argue the torture sentence before His Majesty and that he had requested monies to present that appeal."[196]

In November, Magistrate Salgado ordered Pablo de Mercado, the ship's scrivener, to bring all monies and goods in his possession to the Casa's treasury office and warned that he risked a jail sentence if he failed to comply with the request.[197]

The magistrate dictated that Pablo, the scrivener, must relinquish the silver in his possession to Alonso de Salvatierra, whom the magistrate had further instructed to sell the silver and then give Molina monies so that he could support himself.[198] Evidently the monies never came forth, because the magistrate issued a second admonishment and again ordered Pablo to return the monies in his possession to the Casa's treasury.

Meanwhile Molina asked the ministers "to order Pablo to give him twelve *ducados*" to "at the very least support Pedro, who is poor and dies of hunger."[199] Once again, the magistrate "ordered Pablo to pay Molina the twelve *ducados* and to bring forth all monies in his possession."[200] The Casa's scrivener notified Pablo of this request, because Molina insisted that "Pablo had a certain amount of silver" that "rightfully" belonged to the young page.[201]

The monies never came forth, and on 20 December 1566 the ministers ordered the sergeants at arms to retrieve the monies forcibly from Pablo de Mercado or have him arrested and put in prison.[202] In Madrid, Pedro's guardian argued his appeal before His Majesty and the Council of the Indies.[203]

On 21 November 1566, King Felipe II "revoked the torture sentence and ordered all proceedings and dictates of the case to be given to Pedro Hernández."[204] Even so, the fate of the boatswain remained unresolved.

Great Lumps of Flesh

Further coercion of subordinates and the power struggles between ship officials habitually led to charges of blackmail and accusations of sodomy as a means of deposing or diffusing one's power. In May 1591 on the island and port of San Juan de Ulua, outside Veracruz, Pedro Durán, the sergeant at arms of the fleet docked at the harbor, informed Captain General Antonio Navarro de Prado that "a boy, in the nude, jumped into the sea and swam over to the admiral ship."

When Durán asked Pedro Merino why he had abandoned the master ship, the young boy replied that "Gaspar Caravallo, *mulato,* had kissed him on the mouth four or five times and had wanted to fuck him."[205] Pedro reported that Caravallo had been "tempted" by Pedro's "private parts," including his "cunt." Pedro "feared" Caravallo and believed him to be "a whorish rogue."[206] On one occasion, the purser had "positioned his member" up against Pedro's "posterior vessel, having wanted to insert his member inside" the young page.[207]

As Pedro Merino, who was thirteen or fourteen years old, stood before the captain general, he narrated these and other similar incidents that had taken place on board the *Rodrigo Díaz.* Back in April, Pedro witnessed how Caravallo and Juanes, another page, barred themselves inside a chamber in the ship's stern. Pedro peeped through a hole in the door and saw "Caravallo and Juanes both holding their great lumps of flesh in their hands."[208]

Shortly after Juanes walked out of the chamber, Pedro asked, "What have you done?" Juanes replied that he and the purser had "showed each other their members" in their effort to ascertain "who had the biggest yard." Caravallo, the two concluded, had the "greatest and ugliest member."[209] In fact, Caravallo, according to Juanes, "always showed his private parts to the boys on the ship."[210]

Juanes, a native of Bilbao and an insouciant grummet on board the *Rodrigo Díaz,* lodged with the shipmaster. When he appeared before the captain general to corroborate Pedro's story, he stated that after they had reached the port, Caravallo approached him twice and asked, "*Vizcaíno,* do you want me to fuck you?" To which Juanes replied, "You can do it to the sheep you find on board this ship."[211]

But had the "filthy and dishonest" Portuguese purser "scattered semen," or "did you ever feel wetness?" the captain general asked Pedro. "One day," recalled Pedro, "as he and another page massaged the purser's legs, Caravallo put his hand inside an opening to his breeches, grabbed Pedro's hand, and placed it on his member." Pedro felt how Caravallo's "big member wet his hand." When he "saw the wetness," Pedro "removed and smelled his badly scented hand."[212] As both pages spat into their hands and attempted to wipe them dry, an unabashed Caravallo asked, "Why do you clean your hands?"[213]

Mother of God, Come to My Rescue!

The twenty-seven-year-old literate purser identified himself as "Gaspar de Caraballho," a native of Maezzan and married to a woman who was a resident of Triana. He had known Pedro for a couple of months and denied all the accusations. Nevertheless, the captain general formally charged the "filthy and dishonest Gaspar Caravallo" with attempting to commit the nefarious sin against nature with some pages on board the *Rodrigo Díaz.*[214]

Caravallo responded to the charge by stating that it was "not credible" and therefore he should be absolved and set free. In defense of himself, Caravallo wrote:

> [T]he declarations made by Pedro Merino in this process are not credible. . . . His principal motive was to vilify me; thus your lordship must consider his accusations without merit. . . . [H]e is my capital enemy and his malevolence toward me is the result of my trade as the purser on the ship; as such I order him to perform his duties for the benefit of the ship and I have punished him for his insolence. The pages on board the ship are naive and insolent; they are young boys who have fostered hatred toward me because I have punished them and their negligence. The boys have been persuaded by some persons on board this ship who wish me harm and wish to blemish my honor. I am a good man, a good Christian, fearful of God and his conscience, of good repute and family. Such a person could never be thought to have intended to or even committed such an ugly crime of sodomy. I implore your lordship to absolve me and set me free.[215]

The admiral, then, had an antenna erected on the deck of the ship. Caravallo cried out, "Mother of God, come to my rescue, Mother of God!" The initial hoist lifted his feet "about the lengths of two palm trees above the deck." The admiral again warned him to "state the truth." Caravallo cried out, "Mother of God, you will pay for this!"[216] The lord admiral commenced the torture session:

> The lord admiral ordered Caravallo lowered and he ordered de Agustín de la Cruz *negro* to tie a basket filled with iron to the purser's feet. . . . The lord admiral issued another warning. . . . Caravallo cried out, for he had nothing else to say. . . . Agustín hoisted the body with the attached basket and lifted him very high . . . about the length of two palm trees. . . . [T]he lord admiral ordered him lowered and had another basket of iron tied to Caravallo's feet . . . another warning. . . . [T]he Lord Admiral or-

dered him hoisted up high, about a yard and a half above the deck. . . . I do not deserve this . . . again he cried out. . . . The lord admiral ordered eight balls of iron tied to Caravallo's feet. . . . another warning. . . . Mother of God I don't deserve this I shall be broken! . . . he cried out as foam spewed out of his mouth. . . . The lord admiral had him lowered and had the balls of iron removed . . . and had a piece of lead about the weight of two quintals brought to him. . . . The lord admiral ordered another hoist, but only with the two baskets filled with iron attached to his feet. . . . Caravallo would not respond, as foam spewed out of his mouth and he vomited. . . . The lord admiral ordered him lowered . . . then had the piece of lead attached to his feet . . . another hoist in the air. . . . Caravallo spewed foam out of his mouth . . . apparently suffocating. . . . The lord admiral ordered him lowered, and Caravallo cried out Holy Mother of God! . . . and the admiral admonished Caravallo many times over until he ordered the removal of the baskets of iron and Caravallo vomited and would not utter a word.[217]

After the torture session, the captain general rendered his verdict:

[I condemn Gaspar Caravallo] to prison and [to be] taken out with a halter about his neck, his hands and feet tied, nude from the waist upward exposed on the pillory with a crier proclaiming his crime in a boat around all the boats docked in the harbor of San Juan de Ulua and there give three hundred lashes and he has served for a period of ten years in the galleys of His Majesty Our Lord without compensation and furthermore I condemn him to perpetual banishment from this kingdom and its domains for the duration of his life and I condemn him to pay fifty pesos of common gold half of which will be applied to the coffers of His Majesty Our Lord and the other half given to the Convent of Our Lady of Atocha in Madrid.[218]

Caravallo argued that the captain general had pronounced "an unjust sentence" and he therefore requested permission to appeal his case "before His Majesty Our Lord and his Royal Council of the Indies."[219] In July 1591 the captain general reviewed Caravallo's petition and granted his appeal.[220]

The fleet led by the *Rodrigo Díaz* arrived in Spain sometime before

April 1592. However, His Majesty and the Royal Council never had the privilege to deliberate Caravallo's appeal. Gaspar Caravallo disappeared sometime between his incarceration in the admiral ship's prison cell and the fleet's arrival in the peninsula.

Consequently, His Majesty's solicitor general at the Casa de la Contratación in Seville held the master of the ship, Juan de Lambarri, responsible and in contempt of the law for not having accounted for the whereabouts of Gaspar Caravallo when the fleet docked in the harbor.[221]

Gaspar had understood how power struggles and blackmail, along with a healthy dose of xenophobia, could have deposed him of his rank. This recurring theme would haunt men in positions of power throughout the early modern period. Unlike in the case of General Cardona in Santo Domingo, sometimes not even ties to the nobility could mediate the outcome of an accused sodomite.

Mariner, Would You . . . ?

In October 1606 in La Havana, Xinés Cavallero del Castillo, twenty-three years old and a native of Hellin in Murcia, appeared before the local tribunal. Xinés, an ensign, joined his current regiment as it had meandered through the Andalusian countryside en route to Seville.[222]

Now, on board the *Bartolomé*, a ship sailing back to Spain from the Indies, a group of pages had complained that when the ensign ordered them to remove his cape and stockings, he also asked them to scratch his legs upward from the feet. The ensign, nude in bed, usually took the boys' hands and forcibly placed them on his *natura* and private parts.

On other occasions, Xinés tugged away at the boys' *naturas*. The ensign "kissed some pages on the lips" and usually requested his kisses "with some tongue."[223] Some pages reproached the ensign because "honorable men" did not engage in such acts. "No man should have to suffer nor consent to such indignities" and "I don't want to do that filth," cried out others.[224]

Xinés told a different story. He said that he "feared for the loss of a gold chain and other monies kept in his quarters."[225] After Gerónimo finished "scratching the ensign's legs and also cleaned his toes with a knife," he had exited the quarters on Xinés' orders. The ensign then "hid the gold and again summoned Gerónimo," but the page did not respond and did not return to the quarters on that occasion. Xinés insisted that "the malicious intentions of his enemies had propelled the accusations levied against him." Nevertheless, the ensign "admitted it had been his custom to have his bad and swollen legs scratched every night" by his subordinates on board the ship.[226]

"Lord, have mercy on me," repented Xinés, "for I would never commit such enormity." The ensign rationalized that "the world is full of women," for he, "a sinful man," had himself "spent his fortune as he indulged many of them, in this city and in other places," as future testimony about him and his bon vivant ways would reveal. In fact, continued Xinés, "He had offended God, having often committed many other sins for which he felt much remorse . . . but not the one in question, nor with such persons, nor had he intended it, nor executed it, nor had it ever occurred to him."[227]

Captain Gómez Galiano ordered Xinés, despite his mature appearance, to name a guardian ad litem who could defend his case. The ensign named Juan García Lamea as his advocate, who as he made "the sign of the cross" readily accepted the appointment, having "sworn to argue in defense of his minor's virility before the Lord our God."[228] Gómez Galiano named Gerónimo de Valdés as the prosecuting lawyer representing the crown.

Valdés, in turn, promptly named Sebastian Fernández Cavala as his assistant, "in order to make the necessary inquiries" in the case against the ensign. The "necessary inquiries cost time and money"; thus Valdés "requested fifty pesos from Xinés' coffers" so that he could proceed with the investigation. The captain general granted Valdés' request for monies intended for the reimbursement of the prosecutor and his scrivener.[229]

In November that same year, Gerónimo de Valdés, the prosecutor, formally accused the ensign of "having committed the nefarious sin against nature and having attempted to commit it with many persons in this port." Valdés especially cited the case of Lezmés de Maçuelo, also known as Gerónimo, "a young boy of fifteen or sixteen years with whom the ensign, armed with an ugly diabolical and dishonest vigor, had intended to commit the grave crime."[230]

In his initial reply to the prosecutor's accusations, the advocate García reminded the court that "His Majesty King Felipe III" had appointed Xinés to form part of Captain Amezquita's company. In that same letter, Xinés insisted that he had already "declared the truth in his confession and thus should be liberated." The ensign outlined other factors in his favor. "First and foremost," wrote Xinés, "there existed, for some time now, the great capital hatred and animosity felt toward him by the captain, his young nephew, and the sergeant of his company." Xinés argued that "they had coerced the other boys with wanton promises to testify against him and his honorable life." [231]

"All the witnesses," insisted Xinés, "served either the captain or his nephew." The sergeant, in cahoots with the captain's nephew, aimed solely to strip the ensign of his royal standard and rank. Xinés rejected the testimony offered by Lesmes, the sergeant's servant, for "such a young boy could hardly render a credible accusation." Gómez Galiano sequestered all the witnesses who had testified against the ensign, had them taken to the *Bartolomé*, and ordered both the prosecution and the defense not to talk to them until the young boys had ratified their denunciations. [232]

In fact, Xinés reported, Captain Amezquita and Sergeant Juan Pérez de Andarca, who were uncle and nephew, had cultivated a particular hatred and vendetta toward the ensign. On many occasions, both the captain and the sergeant had spoken ill of Xinés, publicly reproached him, and called him a sodomite with the intent of causing him the gravest possible harm. The captain intended to deprive Xinés of his royal standard and tenure and then to award these spoils to the sergeant. The animosity among the three grew because the ensign had also nurtured this vendetta, publicly stating things about and against the captain. [233]

The defense also claimed that the captain, for his part, had coerced the young boys with threats and promises in exchange for testimony against the ensign. As these young boys awaited their fate, the sergeant, acting on the captain's orders, had them removed from the ship and taken to the captain's house, where they faced threats of bodily harm if they failed to testify against the ensign. Lastly, argued Garça, "Xinés, a very honorable and noble man of good fabric . . . fearful of God, cannot be presumed to have committed this crime." [234]

Later in that November, Sebastian Pérez, Captain Amezquita's young servant, and Lesmes de Maçuelos, the sergeant's servant, both retracted their earlier denunciations of the ensign. Sebastian, "a God-fearing Christian," wished to "unburden his conscience" and stated that "his earlier declarations against the ensign had not occurred." Rather, "the captain and the sergeant had induced and persuaded him to do so." Sebastian had offered the denunciation "because he felt a sense of obligation to the captain and [because] of the fear he felt for himself had he not complied with the wishes of his master." [235]

Likewise, Lesmes admitted that the sergeant had also threatened him and promised him gifts in exchange for his denunciation of the ensign. Lesmes too wished to unburden his conscience. He had scratched Xinés' legs, "but only from the knees downward." Lesmes had also made the other allegations against Xinés because of "fear of the sergeant" and the yearning to acquire "a garment promised to him by the sergeant in exchange for the false testimony."[236]

Despite the two retractions, the ensign's fate remained suspended until May 1607, when his ship, the *Bartolomé*, reached Seville, where the Audiencia de la Casa de la Contratación assumed jurisdiction over the case.[237] Later that month, the lord justices dictated their sentence: "We find that we should condemn and do condemn the ensign to the pulley and water torture . . . having reserved for ourselves the quantity and quality of the aforementioned [torture]."[238]

The solicitor general of the Casa "took offense" at the lord justices' torture sentence and instead argued for the ordinary penalty for the crime. He appealed the case before His Majesty and the Royal Council of the Indies. Francisco Rodríguez, the ensign's newly appointed guardian, also appealed the torture sentence, but for different reasons. Rodríguez presented his appeal on 3 July 1607.[239]

Rodríguez called the sentence "unjust" and argued for its revocation and for the "liberation," as well as for the "absolution" of Xinés. This particular case, reasoned the guardian, "did not correspond to the dictates of the *Nueba Recopilación* of laws pertinent to the nefarious sin" nor did it subscribe to those of the "1596 *Nueba Pragmática*." Xinés' case was not a case of the nefarious sin; thus "these two laws could not apply to its outcome," insisted Rodríguez.[240]

After all, Rodríguez described the ensign as "a man of good breeding [who was] not worthy of such a sentence, for he had served His Majesty on many an occasion and such a thing never once had been uttered or murmured about him." This case had been a total fabrication to strip the ensign of his rank and salary, as Amezquita so aptly achieved. Not only had Amezquita succeeded with the dispossession, but he had also rewarded the spoils to his nephew, the sergeant.[241]

A group of dignitaries offered their support for the ensign in a letter sent to the king. The men—Alberto, the archduke of Austria and duke of Borgoña; the illustrious army general Valther Capata, member of the Royal War Council; and Juan López of the Royal Exchequer—had concurred: "Since the ensign, on various occasions in the past, had well represented the interests of His Majesty, they felt compelled to reinstate his rank and set his salary at ten escudos every month so he may continue serving in the Spanish Infantry."[242]

Notwithstanding the plea made by such a distinguished corps, the Royal Council of the Indies reinstated the torture sentence initially dictated by the Audiencia de la Casa de la Contratación. The lord ministers of the Casa informed the ensign of this final verdict. The ministers warned him to state the truth or risk being sentenced to water and rack torture. The scrivener reminded him that he alone would be responsible for "any broken arms, legs, or death inflicted during the execution of the sentence."[243]

Xinés again declared he had already stated the truth, as reflected in his first confession, and the captain general felt it prudent to suspend the lengthy and vigorous torture. Thereafter, the whereabouts of the ensign disappeared from the historical record.

Peninsular Perceptions

Collectively, the peninsular sodomy cases that make up the core of this study, from the late fifteenth century until the late eighteenth century, have demonstrated the correlations among candid, almost farcical notions of sodomy, xenophobia, and a burgeoning empire. For the most part, the magistrates and the captains general seemed quite intent on proving the physical aspects of the sin and crime against nature as envisioned by moralists. The courts constructed the protagonist exclusively as a juridical subject, and thus the object of the judges' inquiry was to determine the material conditions of the act—had it occurred or not, in which forms, under which conditions and situations, who functioned as agent or patient, and in which positions.

Officials demonstrated an obsessive compulsion in their efforts to quantify sodomy as a horrendous act, looking to the discipline of science in an effort to bolster the rhetoric of the state. More intimate contact like kissing between men, specifically on "the top or the bottom lips," also fascinated many a captain general. Throughout the early modern period, moralists and writers alike continued their attempts to disseminate the xenophobic belief that only other nationals were naturally susceptible to sodomitical practices.

The men and the boys likewise traveling to and from the Indies demonstrated an awareness of sodomitical culture. They uttered different words and expressions when they referred to a "sodomite" or to the "nefarious crime and sin against nature"—the official phrases of the state. In the vernacular of some young mariners, "sodomy" simply meant *cabalgando por el culo*. Although early in the seventeenth century Fray de León and other literary writers began to associate sodomy with effeminacy, the perceptions of the peninsular sodomite tended more toward the virile. In reference to the boatswain Fernández, one page had asked another, "Are you aware that you are the most desired on board this ship by the meanest man in the world"?[244] Ordinary men instead used words such as *"puto"* or *"bellaco"* (rogue) when referring to a sodomite.

"Puto," in the context of these early modern peninsular *procesos,* did not refer to a male prostitute. That reference was particularly used in the Indias, as noted by Gutiérrez.[245] In 1561, Cristóbal had turned to Gaspar and uttered, "You *bellaco,* I will tell the ship's master about your habits."[246] And the captain general of Gaspar asked, "Have you practiced the profession of *puto* for a long time?"[247] One year later, in the Antón-Alonso case, the pilot took the ship's master aside and stated, "Know thou, your lordship, there is a *puto* on board this ship."[248] All stood accused of sodomitical play.

In 1606, as the galleons of an armada stood anchored in San Cristóbal de la Havana, a sergeant informed the captain general that Xinés Cavallero del Castillo, his ensign, was a *puto* and that the "hearsay abounding is that the ensign has committed and commits *the sin* with the young *mancevos"* (emphasis added).[249] As late as 1783, the Real Academia Española in Madrid still defined *"puto"* as "a man who commits the nefarious sin"[250] and *"bellaco"* as "a bad man of vile respect and of a perverse condition."[251]

Specifically, the sixteen cases prosecuted by the Audiencia de la Casa de la Contratación between 1560 and 1698, at the height of the baroque and the Counter Reformation, initially occurred on ships en route either to Spain or to the Indies. At the very least, the cases involved two individuals. The captain general's ship, the *Capitana,* functioned as the initial tribunal for these prosecutions. Interrogations on board ships typically commenced after a captain general received a denunciation from mariners or ship officials.

The interrogations were usually followed by the torture sessions, and in some instances, a given crew hanged the convicted sodomites and then burned them at sea on the admiral's ship. Some men fled and escaped before their scheduled prosecutions, whereas others obtained acquittals. The captains general granted appeals in all the cases that involved minors. With the exception of those individuals burned precipitously at sea, almost all of the accused sodomites routinely appealed their cases. The appointed trustees for the young mariners habitually appealed cases that involved boys younger than fifteen years of age first to the Casa's tribunal in Seville and if necessary before the Royal Council of the Indies.

Accused sodomites personified boys or young men of similar backgrounds and ages, between thirteen and twenty-four. Other cases implicated young men with younger boys under the age of fifteen years. In all cases, the boys and the young men involved engaged in some sort of reciprocal sodomy. That is, they anally penetrated others, as well as allowing others to anally penetrate them. The sodomy cases prosecuted by the Casa, as well as those prosecuted by other tribunals in Andalusia, often revealed how younger boys, in subordinate positions of power, suffered from the abuses inflicted upon them by officials of different ranks both on and off the ships.

With few exceptions, the magistrates tended to absolve the younger boys of any charges levied against them, especially if their counterparts were thirty to forty years old. However, young men in their twenties or thirties usually did not escape the discipline and punishment required by the state for convicted sodomites, notably when those implicated pertained to similar age groups. In many instances, the officials altered, circumvented, or altogether abused established practices of Spanish jurisprudence on board the ships to prove the consummation of the sin.

Despite court-appointed guardians and lawyers, accused sodomites had to pay the court costs out of their measly salaries or from the proceeds of their publicly auctioned goods. In their defense, most men evoked the image of the new Spanish Vir, proposed by the early modern moralists—a chivalrous man, honorable, one who sought a virtuous woman and was a good Christian fearful of God and incapable of committing the nefarious crime and sin against nature—in short, a man of reason.

Significantly, the courts rarely questioned the lifestyles, thoughts, and feeling of these individuals.[252] Nor did Spanish officials actively celebrate orchestrated raids in search of sodomites on board the ships or in the harbors of the Seville-Cádiz-Granada metroplex. Instead, the prosecution of sodomites occurred only after someone had denounced another to the appropriate officials. Only then did the state set its legal apparatus in motion. This was in sharp contrast to the sodomy raids that would be realized by colonial officials in mid-seventeenth-century Mexico City.

CHAPTER 4

COTITA AND THE *ANTIPODAS*

or How a Cadre of Effeminate Sodomites Infested New Spain with an Endemic Cancer Known as the Abominable Sin *contra Natura*

MENTIRA

Mentira lo que dice
Mentira la mentira
Mentira la verdad

Mentira lo que cuece
Bajo la oscuridad
Mentira no se borra
Mentira no se olvida

Todo es mentira en este mundo
Todo es mentira la verdad
¿Por qué será?

Manu Chao, *Clandestino*

WHEN JUAN DE CORREA, aged "over seventy years," appeared before His Majesty's High Court in 1656 Mexico City, the "old *mestizo*" continuously denied ever having committed the nefarious sin against nature. But the lord magistrate persisted in his interrogations of Correa, and the *old man* finally admitted that he had committed the *pecado contra natura* "for more than forty years with many persons," whose names he also revealed. The surgeons of the Mexican High Court, in fact, "proved that Correa had committed sodomy since the age of seven." Correa so "lamented the past." Thus, he "applauded" the fact that "the millennium was soon drawing to an end," because not as many men "took pleasure with him in the present century as they had in the past millennium just before the great inundation of the city." Back then, he still esteemed himself as a "pretty fine young girl." [1]

Decades earlier, Correa had "dressed like a woman along with the other men and boys" he had referred to in his deposition before the High Court. Furthermore, Correa had taught "his skills to the men and the younger boys," because they took "great pleasure committing the nefarious sin among themselves." Correa often hosted parties for his guests at his house and had spent the proceeds of his entire estate on such gatherings. "Although an old man," Correa "still considered himself a beautiful young girl," and he reminded the boys that "one should eat" men just like one "ate a frog": that is, "from the waist downward." [2]

Correa and his comrades no longer ate human meat, but they could surely host a party, much to the chagrin of colonial authorities in Mexico City who with great zeal had sought to exterminate the practices of anthropophagy, human sacrifices, and sodomy in the Indias. The present chapter examines how "just causes" of Spanish imperial rule and perceptions of manliness and of sodomy prompted changes in the textual representations of sodomites in New Spain.

In the Spanish peninsula, moralists defined sodomy as a crime and a sin against God and usually associated its hideous practice with the foreigners. Peninsular moralists and authorities dedicated folio after folio to the physical, raw abominations of the act as they sought to prove its detestable and nefarious nature.

However, over the course of the early modern period in New Spain, colonial officials, jurists, theologians, and other writers associated signifiers like the diabolic, anthropophagy, inebriation, and effeminacy with perceptions of the *pecado nefando*. By insisting on an inherent link between these multiple cultural constructs, historians, chroniclers, and theologians fabricated one more "just cause" for the permanence of colonial rule in the Indias (Fig. 4.1).

As in the peninsula itself, imperialist-colonialist politics would significantly taint and exploit perceptions of manliness and of sodomy in New Spain. Not surprisingly, Spanish writers tended to praise Christian values, whereas chroniclers of indigenous blood extolled the virtues of the pre-Columbian societies. In the midst of these distortions, the sources, especially the reports written by colonial scriveners, offer the reader but a glimpse of how sodomites in the metropolis of Mexico City contested and usurped Spain's early modern *sexo-político* paradigm.

In my attempt to demonstrate how different writers portrayed sodomy and sodomites in New Spain, I have examined the texts of clergy who wandered about the Mexican countryside and relations written by

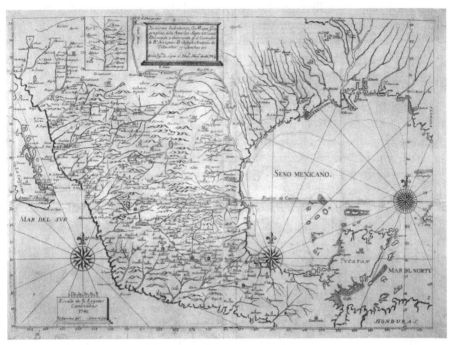

4.1. Mapa de América Septentrional, 1746 (**AGI, Mapas y planos, 161**). Reproduced with the permission of the Archivo General de Indias, Seville.

Hernán Cortés, other conquistadores, and royal historiographers. The authors of these various manuscripts all directly participated in or had some strong affiliation with the discovery, conquest, and colonization of the Indias from 1492 up until the infamous 1657–1658 sodomy prosecutions in Mexico City. The trial records of these prosecutions, post-Columbian manuscripts written by indigenous chroniclers, and the correspondence of colonial officials all complement my reading of the aforementioned texts.

Mi Vida, Mi Amor

Officials of the High Court in the viceroyalty of New Spain proceeded against Correa and successfully prosecuted another 18 men and boys— all accused of having committed the crime and sin of sodomy. The High Court accused and ordered the apprehension of another 103 men in an un-

precedented, brutally repressive pogrom and the active pursuit of sodomites in the metropolis of Mexico City.

The 1657–1658 sodomy prosecutions in Mexico City represent the
only surviving historical accounts of this nature between the time of
the Spanish conquest in 1521 and the late eighteenth century, when the
Mexican Holy Office of the Inquisition assumed jurisdiction over sexual
crimes in New Spain.[3] But in 1657 the colonial authorities had finally un-
covered a web of sodomites in the metropolis—something historiographers had assumed and written about for more than a century and a
half. The incorrigible Correa must have whet some appetites during his
interrogations.

Correa recounted that "he, along with other older men" had often
hosted many a party for "other men and boys." The revelers frequented
a house in the neighborhood of San Juan de la Penitencia, along the
peripheral walls of Mexico City. The men and the boys hosted their
"receptions like women," and they referred to each other as *"niñas."* The
"girls" had each assumed a pseudonym, having appropriated the names
of the "most beautiful women in Mexico City."

The men knew Correa as La Estanpa, the name of a "very graceful
lady who had lived in the city." At the parties, "the men danced and they
presented each to the others as gifts," after which they "committed the
nefarious sin." Correa, "his cape lowered and worn around his waist, sashayed from side to side as he danced with the others," only to stagger and
complain that "he felt overcome by fits of the mother."[4]

"Mi vida, mi amor," uttered those in attendance, as the men and the
boys offered La Estanpa "chocolate to ease his pain" and bathed him
with other "tender expressions of comfort," as well as "endearing, soft,
and amorous" syllogisms.[5]

By the time that colonial authorities heard the aforementioned descriptions of Correa and his comrades implicated in the 1657–1658 sodomy prosecutions in México, perceptions of sodomites already differed
in context and scope from the earlier descriptions in the peninsula. The
seventeenth-century depictions of Mexican sodomites also differed from
the earliest representations of sodomites in the Indias.

Emasculated Aged Meat

Christopher Columbus recorded some of the earliest descriptions of Indios. Subsequent Spanish court-appointed historiographers, chroniclers,
and theologians would later embellish his portraits, even though some of

them had never set foot in the Indias or never had the privilege of actually meeting an Indio in person. In the wake of promulgating their fabricated discourses about *sodomie,* these early modern writers initially described all Indios as sodomites who engaged in anthropophagy and
practiced human sacrifices—a dominant view held by the Spanish intelligentsia throughout Spain's colonial occupation of New Spain.

In a letter to the Catholic monarchs dated 16 October 1492, Columbus described the Indios of Santa María as "somewhat more disposed
to Spanish occupation than their counterparts in San Salvador." "The
women," wrote Columbus "at the very least wore a little piece of cotton,"
albeit "one that barely concealed their *naturas.*" On the island beach of La
Tortuga, Columbus had encountered "two Indios who lacked pieces of
flesh on their bodies," because "the cannibals had bitten them off and
eaten them piece by piece." [6]

In Española, Columbus saw "many naked men carrying bows and
arrows, one of whom looked quite different from the others." This Indio,
in particular, "displayed different actions." Columbus wrote, "He had
painted his entire face with carbon, [and] his very long hair [was] gathered and tied behind his head," on which he wore a hair net "filled with
many *papagayos* plumes." Columbus recalled that such Indios were as "a bit
fatter than those he had seen earlier," and he noted that "they bore no
arms and acted in a cowardly way." "One thousand of them," boasted
Columbus to the monarchs, "could not possibly defeat three of us."

In fact, he found their temperament so "docile" that one could "easily order them around, and compel them to sow crops and undertake
other necessary chores." They should also be forced to "construct villas"
and should be "taught how to dress properly in accordance with our customs," recommended Columbus. These and other Indios like the Caribs
"all had very vile customs," according to Columbus, and among other
customs, "they ate their fellow men." [7]

Columbus not only provided the peninsulars with some of the first
representations of the Indios but also recorded some of the earliest veiled
references that link perceptions of sodomy in the Americas with anthropophagy, docility, and cowardice. In an era when the unspeakable reigned
supreme, descriptions such as "vile customs" sufficed as an adequate signifier to depict the sodomitical appetites of a different other.

Two years later, in 1494, Columbus' physician Diego Alvarez Chanca
sent a letter to Sevillian legislators in which he described their second
voyage to the Indias and in particular elaborated on Columbus' depiction

of the Caribs. "When the Caribs captured boys," wrote Alvarez Chanca, "they cut off the boy's members and removed all their manly organs." These emasculated boys developed feminine characteristics, and "the Caribs used them for the practice of sodomy much like the Arabs enjoyed their young men as eunuchs and *bardajes.*" Once these boys became grown men, "the Caribs killed them and ate them," for they preferred the taste of "aged meat to that of boys or women."[8]

Alvarez Chanca's first reports also suggested links among sodomy, notions of effeminacy, and anthropophagy in the Indias. Alvarez Chanca also became one of the first travelers to the Indias to "confirm that anthropophagy existed among the Indios, albeit a discriminating practice, for they differentiated between the taste of human flesh according to age and sex." Furthermore, he accounted for religious motives and the consumption of human meat among the Indios in the American continent as precursors of sodomitical cultures.[9] Eventually, other fantastic "firsthand" accounts of the Indios and sodomy soon began to circulate in the peninsula.

By the time Pietro Martire d'Anghiera wrote *De orbe novo decades* in 1511 and *Opera legatio babylonica de orbe novo decades octo opus epistolarum* in 1516, the Spanish Monarchs had already accumulated a number of firsthand accounts about the Indios and their sexual habits. D'Anghiera, an Italian physician, arrived in Spain in 1487 and thereafter became a favorite of Isabel's. As the court-appointed councillor of the Indies, the doctor gained personal access to some of the earliest firsthand descriptions of the Indios written by navigators, explorers, and other men traveling throughout America.[10]

Although d'Anghiera never set foot in the Indias, he used these chronicles to produce the first European published texts about the Indios and their cultures. *Opera* and *Decades,* translated into English, Dutch, French, and Italian, set the tone by which subsequent historiographers and theologians, armed with the power of letters, fined-tuned virulent discursive harmonies related to the Indios and their sodomitical cultures.

In *De Orbo Novo,* d'Anghiera narrated a series of events that had taken place during the 1513 explorations of Quarequa in the Isthmus of Panama by Vasco Núñez de Balboa. During these explorations, wrote d'Anghiera, "Vasco Núñez de Balboa came upon a king's house infested with the most abominable and unnatural lechery." Núñez de Balboa had witnessed a "king's brother and other younger, supple men, effeminately dressed in women's apparel" and whom the brother "abused with preposterous" temerity. Not amused, Núñez de Balboa had "commanded forty of them to be fed to his dogs."

When the other islanders realized the severity of the punishment inflicted by the Spaniards upon that "filthy kind of men," the Indios "spontaneously and violently sought out all others they knew to be infected" with this "pestilence." After all, conceded d'Anghiera, these Indios also exhibited a "natural hatred of an unnatural sin." D'Anghiera had not despaired, for "this stinking abomination" had not yet filtered downward to "infect the common man."

In that part of the world, "only the nobles and gentlemen exercised that sort of desire." The Indios knew that "sodomy gravely offended God" and that such vile deeds prompted the "thundering, lightning, and tempests that so often troubled them, or the overflowing waters that drowned their fruits, causing famine and diseases."[11]

Independent of whether or not Indios in the Americas considered sodomy an unnatural sin against God or whether their concept of sin mirrored Spanish Catholic dogma, d'Anghiera's portrait of sodomitical culture among the Indios strongly mimicked the *sexo-político* discourses about sodomy elaborated by the early modern Thomists. The learned doctor transposed the biblical story of Lot and God's angels in Sodom into a collective imagination about Indios who lived on the sandy beaches of sixteenth-century Panama. D'Anghiera's depictions of sodomy as an infectious pestilence that could contaminate a subject population echoed the words of Fray de León and the cleric's own suspicions of a similar plight in the prisons of Seville.

Whether men of letters sailed by sea or by quill, they reinforced historical and literary depictions of so-called sodomites—a xenophobic genre of writing privileged in early modern Spain, especially to buttress notions of empire and to concoct just causes of domination.

Perceptions of sodomy in New Spain would quickly evolve to explain its practice among an entire subject population, one completely consumed by its addiction to the flesh. This precept armed the monarchy with another "just cause" for domination and occupation of the Indies— a theme already proposed at the dawn of the sixteenth century by Hernán Cortés.

All Inebriated Phallic-centric Sodomites

Hernando Cortés had studied Latin for two years in Salamanca before he departed for Santo Domingo, where he set foot in 1504. In his first relation about the Indios of New Spain, actually written by the town council of Veracruz in 1519 but nonetheless attributed to Cortés, he informed Charles V that "the children, men, and women kill and offer sacrifices to their gods." "And Your Majesties," he wrote, "we have come to know, for certain, that they are all sodomites and practice that abominable sin."[12]

The early explorers also recorded having witnessed pictorial or artistic representations of sodomitical practices in New Spain. A genteel Italian man, later simply known as the *conquistador anónimo* who had accompanied Cortés to Mexico, recalled that "particularly in Panuco, the Indios worshipped a man's member," so much so that they had "erected the sculpted phallus in their temples and in the public squares." The sculpted figures had depicted both "men and women in various positions of sodomitical pleasure." The writer described the men of Panuco as "grandiose sodomites, cowards, and often totally inebriated." The anonymous author found that "the multitude of methods employed by the men to satisfy their abominable vice" was "almost too incredible to believe" or even too "unspeakable" to describe.[13]

The Indios "informed" the anonymous writer that the "devil within their idols had possessed them." According to the Indios, "he had instructed them to sacrifice their fellow man, rip out their human hearts and offer the hearts, as well as the blood taken from the tongue, the ears, the legs, and the arms, all to the idols." Among other "notorious facts," the astonished gentleman recalled, "many of them volunteered to be sacrificed, for they actually thought it saved their souls."[14]

"Everybody in New Spain also ate human meat," related the conquistador. The Indios "so esteemed it, above any other type of meat," that they sometimes "simply went to war [and] risked their lives only to kill someone and eat him." At the end of the day, thought the esteemed gentleman, "all the inhabitants of New Spain and those of other adjoining provinces ate human meat, they all commonly practiced sodomy, and they drank in excess." And "like the Moors, these Indios had many wives and moved around like the Arabs."[15]

The excessive consumption of alcohol and the practice of sodomy must have prompted Isabel of Portugal, in the absence of Carlos V, to dictate a royal edict to the magistrates of His Majesty's High Court in Mexico City. Isabel understood that the Indios concocted a "particular type of wine known as pulque," a drinkable substance derived from the agave plant and "fermented with a root" to obtain a greater concentration of alcohol.

Xochitl, a Toltec queen, had first mixed this inebriating cocktail in the Mexican high plateau about 950 A.D.[16] Pulque "ill served God," wrote Isabel, for it caused "inebriation and propelled the Indios to unleash" unwanted practices, such as their "human sacrifices and vices of the flesh," in particular, the "nefarious sin." Thus, in 1529 the Catholic queen ordered the magistrates "to prohibit the planting of the root" or at the very least "to prohibit its use in the fermentation of the wine."[17] Alcohol, however, did not constitute the only problem the colonial authorities faced as they sought to eradicate sodomy from the Americas.

In the mid-sixteenth century, Bernal Díaz del Castillo, a historiographer, had also "seen sodomy scenes carved into the architecture of many buildings."[18] The explorer Fernández de Oviedo also witnessed "sodomitic art depicted in gold jewelry, some weighing around 150 grams."[19] Both the genteel Italian *conquistador anónimo* and Díaz del Castillo described "a great number of statues in a forest-like setting," a sort of contemporary artistic installation "of various sculpted sodomitical positions." The erotic representations, also seen in pottery, included representations of "vulvas, the virile member, coitus, male masturbation, sodomy between men and women, sodomy between men or between women, fellatio, cunnilingus, and sex with animals."[20]

A soldier named Juan de Grijalva had also witnessed the "phallic sculptures as he traveled throughout New Spain. Grijalva had witnessed, among some trees, "a small idol made of gold and another two men carved out of wood, one penetrating the other *a la Sodoma.*" He also saw "another sculpted figure made of baked earth, which depicted a figure with both his hands on his circumcised member, just like almost every Indio in Yucatan." This particular encounter had disgusted the Spaniards, for they "thought it filthy and cruel."

In Nombre de Dios, "as well as in many other places," Grijalva and other explorers had "seen men who dressed and labored like women." They had also come upon both "male and female public bawdy houses."[21] In short, these men had witnessed a pitiful waste of gold and the entire gamut of early modern Spanish sexual impropriety.

By the first quarter of the sixteenth century, chroniclers had etched descriptions of the Indios of New Spain as a phallocentric culture and intertwined perceptions of sodomy with effeminacy, the diabolical, anthropophagy, inebriation, cowardice, and bordellos. The writings of Columbus, Chanca Alvarez, d'Anghiera, Cortés, and the *conquistador anónimo* belong to the earliest collection of writings about the Indios, a genuine tour de force used to depict sodomitical cultures in the Indias that was subsequently cleverly embellished by theologians and historians as just causes for a Spanish Empire.

Filthy Hogs Deserved Domination

Initially, Spain invoked its thirteenth-century *Siete partidas* to legitimize its rights to conquest of the Indias, based solely on the theory of discovery and settlement. In 1493, Pope Alexander VI, a Spaniard by birth, confirmed Spain's moral legitimization of conquest and granted the monarchs the sole legal rights to most of America Septentrionalis based on a temporal rule of the papacy—one that allowed for the conversion of the infidels to Catholicism.[22]

The dispute over Spain's legitimacy over the Indias earnestly began in 1513 when King Fernando asked a commission of theologians and lawyers to discuss the matter. This Spanish view of Indios as unfit men who lacked the ability to reason had presupposed a tragicomic paradox for the enlightened early modern Spanish moralists, because savages could not receive the Christian sacraments. If the Spanish monarchs wished to spread Catholicism throughout their newly discovered territories, they found themselves forced to rule in favor of some form of indigenous consciousness or state of reason. Yet the new rule would have to allow the monarchs access to the land, the wealth, and even power over the Indios.

The commission indeed drafted the first piece of colonial legislation on the matter, titled the Laws of Burgos of 1513, and ruled in favor of Indian consciousness, thus making the Indios apt for conversion to Catholicism. While debating the issue, the commission had qualified Spain's claim over the Indias, a dispute that became the object of a prolonged contention among historiographers, theologians, and other Royal Councils until the end of the eighteenth century.[23]

In 1525 the Council of the Indies commissioned Fray Tomás Ortiz, a Dominican bishop who resided in Tierra Firme, to write about the Caribs—a group of Indios prevalent around the northern coast of South America. Ortiz responded by writing a most scathing critique of Caribs and their cultural attributes. In his report dated that same year, Ortiz emphasized three cultural attributes of the Caribs: they ate human meat, they practiced unnatural sexual acts, and they consumed inebriating drugs. They also "shamelessly walked around naked," and "more so than any other nation" known to Ortiz, the Caribs wallowed in the "bestial vice of sodomy."

The Dominican friar likened the Caribs to mules, somewhat "lazy and stupid." The "mad" Caribs, often "cruel and vindictive," also "lacked reason." Whether depicted as "untrustworthy, thieves, or necromancers," reasoned Ortíz, these "sorcerers" ate "lice, spiders, and worms." These "cowardly filthy hogs," concluded Ortiz, simply "possessed no skills whatsoever" and "lacked the fabric of men." What's worse, wrote Ortiz, the Carib men did not sport "any beards"; instead, they "plucked out whatever hair grew on their entire heads." [24]

That same decade, Gonzalo Fernández de Oviedo, who in 1526 supervised the gold smelting in South American mines, also confirmed the "natural inclinations of the Indios to anthropophagy, sodomy, incest, and suicide." Originally born in Madrid, Fernández de Oviedo, as a young page had served the duke of Villahermosa—himself later burned for sodomy by a court in Madrid.

In 1514, as Fernández de Oviedo roamed around the coast of Tierra Firme, a couple of Indios gave him some gold to smelt. Some of the Indios wore "gold jewelry that depicted one man mounted on top of another in that diabolic and nefarious act of Sodoma," noted the chronicler. One of these pieces of jewelry depicted a "devil made of jewels and gold." Albeit hollow, "the well-carved artifact weighed some twenty pesos of gold." Fernández de Oviedo wrote one of the earliest official histories of America that emphasized the "aberrant nature" of the American Indian's sexuality and brought the issue well within the gaze of the Spanish court. [25]

This conquistador reported having seen a cacique named Behechio in Hispaniola with more than thirty wives "not only for natural use," as most common married men would have. The cacique used his wives "for other bestial and nefarious sins." Cacique Goacanagari also possessed several women whom he "congregated with, just like snakes do," noted Fernández de Oviedo. Apparently, Goacanagari had learned this "abominable audacity from the snakes themselves," but, Fernández de Oviedo continued, "these Indios are much worse, for nature had not provided the snakes any other form to engender." He added, "The Indios of this entire kingdom imitated the nefarious and filthy crimes perpetuated by the infamously vile Goacanagari." [26]

"Common men in New Spain, Santo Domingo, and Tierra Firme," wrote Fernández de Oviedo, "knew many Indios, both men and women, to be sodomites, and they believed sodomy existed quite commonly in these parts." [27] Fernández de Oviedo described the Indios of the northern coasts of South America as "cruel and abominable sodomites who ate human meat and shot poisoned arrows."[28] In "many parts of Tierra Firme, the high priests publicly lived in nefarious concubinage with young boys," something the historian described as a "common practice among the Indios."[29]

The boys "assumed the role of patients for their priests," wrote Fernández de Oviedo. They "wore a type of woman's dress or a shorts-like cotton skirt worn by the Indias to cover themselves from the waist to the knees." The boys also wore "bracelets and other adornments or trinkets traditionally worn by women." These young men "did not bear arms nor performed other manly functions but rather occupied themselves with the daily household trades such as sweeping or washing and other female labors." The women themselves "loathed these *camoyoas*." However, "seldom did the women ever utter a word about these men," Fernández de Oviedo reported, and "when they did speak out, they spoke only to Christians, for they are very submissive to their husbands."[30]

The Indios of Tierra Firme permitted the "patient," or the "man who assumed the position of woman in that bestial and excommunicable act," to wear the apparel of women and to assume their domestic functions. All the men, albeit "unaware of decency or shame," at the very least "covered their *naturas*."[31] In their efforts to justify Spain's imperial politics, Ortiz and Fernández de Oviedo confirmed that sodomites in the Americas looked different and lacked reason. Furthermore, the two authors also linked notions of sodomy with madness, hallucinogenic drugs, incest, suicide, concubinage, and specific gender roles—the patient and the actor—for its consummation.

Both historiographers attributed the "socially accepted *bardajes*" to "most Indios and their cultures." Like d'Anhgiera, Fernández de Oviedo described sodomy as a universal practice, especially among the power-holding Indios, though they too considered "it a sin punishable by the gods." However, sinners never go unpunished, Fernández de Oviedo must have thought when he wrote that "a just God had infected them with syphilis," a disease the Indios "suffered when they committed such vileness as sodomy."[32]

Again, historiographers perpetuated the notion of widespread disease associated directly with the practice of sodomy, while they also began to introduce newer perceptions of sodomy in the colonial context—inebriation, for example, suggested early modern moralists, also led to loss of reason and to fits of lustful behavior. For Fernández de Oviedo, jewelry and men dressed as women also constituted another dimension of the sodomitical genre.[33] Future chroniclers further elaborated stories about the Indios' propensity to dress like women.

Los Amarionados and Other Fantastic Fables

Upon his return to the Spanish court in 1537, another explorer, Alvar Núñez Cabeza de Vaca received great acclaim for his chronicles about the Indios of New Spain, titled *Naufragios y comentarios.* In 1540 the crown named him governor of Río de la Plata as a reward for his service to the empire. Cabeza de Vaca's expedition left Spain in 1527 and arrived in Mexico City in 1536.

Curiously enough, Cabeza de Vaca recorded many instances of cannibalism among the Spaniards as they made their way from the northern part of Mexico into the interior. He did not, however, mention its practice among the Indios he met during his journey. Perhaps other more interesting things had captured his imagination.

As he made his way South along the Texas coast, Cabeza de Vaca wrote:

> [I have witnessed] diabolic practices . . . a man married to another man, *amarionados* or effeminate, impotent men who dressed like women and performed womanly functions, however, they did shoot the bow and arrow and could support heavy loads of weight on their persons. We saw many *amarionados*—most of these taller and more corpulent than the other men were. Many of these effeminate men practiced the sin against nature.[34]

By the mid-sixteenth century, this and many other more fantastic fables about the Indios and their penchant for sodomy in New Spain littered the tales written by historiographers, theologians, and chroniclers. The Aztecs, for example, "ate snakes and lizards." They possessed "no beasts of burden and no ploughs." Instead they used "a long wooden stick to poke through the earth and sow their seeds." They had "spilled great amounts of human blood for the gods as they sacrificed their fellow men, tore out their hearts, and then ate the men." These "heathens acquired property through bartering," and for their currency they used cocoa beans, "kept only for a limited time, for they quickly became rancid and lost their initial value."[35]

Consequently, the Spanish crown legitimized its occupation of the

Indias based primarily on the just cause to reorient "a different culture and its customs, most notably—anthropophagy, human sacrifices, and sodomy." [36] In this sense, "the conquest of Mexico could simply have meant an extension of the Spanish reconquest of the infidels represented then by the Moors." [37] Early modern moralists had long associated the Muslims with sodomy, thus attributing it as a natural phenomenon to others but employing it as a discourse against the Indios. [38]

During the second quarter of the sixteenth century, a second wave of writers began to expand on the earlier perceptions of sodomy in the Indias by suggesting that sodomitical practices caused the spread of diseases such as syphilis and that inebriation did in fact function as a precursor to nefarious vices. These writers also perpetuated the idea of an inherent relationship between sodomitical practices in the Indias and institutionalized effeminacy, in particular in boys dressed like women who performed womanly trades or those who married other men, as yet another dimension of their discursive notions of *sodomie.*

Historiographers also described institutionalized pederasty among the priests and their boy concubines. This group of writers introduced new attributes of sodomitical cultures, such as the wearing of jewelry, as observed by Fernández de Oviedo, or the use of inebriating drugs and the rampant practice of sodomy between men and women. Finally, early modern historiographers directly linked the practice of sodomy in the Indias with the inability to reason and with incest and suicide. These descriptions prompted the colonizers to invoke divine and natural law as justifications for Spain's domination of the Indias.

Divine, Natural Law

Despite Pope Paul II's two bulls in 1537 that granted the Indios of the Americas the status of "reasonable" creatures, court-appointed historiographers, theologians, and other chroniclers continued to debate Spain's legitimate right of domination over the Indias.

Juan Ginés de Sepúlveda, the official historiographer of Charles V, for example, opposed any talk of reason among the Indios. Ginés de Sepúlveda invoked the words of Aristotle's Politics and argued that those of "superior intelligence, by nature, could rule and subjugate others, because nature condemned those of inferior reason to the plight of plebeians." For this reason, Ginés de Sepúlveda thought it better for the Indios to live under the colonial system of servitude, or *encomienda.* [39] Other political theorists phrased it a bit differently.

For Spanish lovers of theology, the sixteenth century had marked the age of its "greatest theologians."[40] Theologians dominated the debate over whether or not the Indios possessed the ability to reason, thereby restraining them from committing the sin against nature. In 1537, Francisco de Vitoria reminded his audience that these issues remained "much too important for lawyers or casuists to determine" their outcome. Vitoria, like many of his counterparts, regarded theology as the mother of sciences, whose domain encompassed everything governed by divine or natural law, rather than human law. As a university professor at Salamanca, Vitoria and two generations of Spanish theologians and jurists became known as the Second Scholastic.

Present-day historiographers Pagden and Lawrance have described Francisco de Vitoria as one of the most influential political theorists in sixteenth-century Catholic Europe and the scholar who resolved, once and for all, Spain's legitimate claim to colonial domination over the Indias. As prime professor of theology at Salamanca, Vitoria delivered a series of relections, or revised readings, to an academic audience. These lectures constituted some of the most influential texts arguing in favor of Spain and empire in 1537, a pivotal year for the defense of the Spanish monarchy and its colonial undertaking.

In his lecture entitled *De los Indios recientemente descubiertos,* Vitoria delivered twenty-four monologues "undertaken not to argue about the truth but to explain it." As a strong defender of the Castilian monarchy, Vitoria turned to his lifelong affinity for divine and natural law as he methodically argued in favor of Spain and empire over the barbarians.[41]

Vitoria argued that the Indios did possess reason and therefore the emperor had no right over them; nonetheless, Vitoria considered "sodomy between men against natural law," something he labeled as "frequent among the Indios," thus justifying war against them. He based his arguments in part on the work of Saint Thomas, who had already considered "vices that contravene human nature, such as anthropophagy, sodomy with animals, or sodomy as execrable." Aquinas considered "eating human meat" to be "inadmissible under any circumstances and as evil as sodomy with animals," which he also "abhorred under any circumstances."[42]

Predating Freud, Vitoria surmised that doctors had "put forth the argument that unbelievers who committed sins against nature, such as idolatry or pederasty or sodomy, all offenses against God, could be forcibly stopped." Vitoria also invoked the work of Aristotle when he professed that "there are some acts we cannot be forced to do, even after the most fearful torture, but ought rather to face death." "Even if everybody agreed it was necessary to fornicate to save one's life, it would not be lawful to do so," explained Vitoria. "No fear, even of death, could excuse an act forbidden in natural law," maintained the theologian.[43]

Vitoria accepted the existence of human sacrifices, anthropophagy, incest, and sodomy—all aberrations against natural and divine law— among the Indios in America, although he himself never traveled beyond Europe. What is more important is that he also accepted the "authority of native rulers" over these very same Indios. He argued that barbarian princes, and not Christian princes, had just cause to "correct crimes against nature." Vitoria concluded that "only non-Christian princes could force their own subjects to give up these rituals or others like them."[44]

On the other hand, Christian princes, said Vitoria, enjoyed "no more power with the authority of the pope than without it." The pope could "punish pagans and barbarians for crimes manifestly against natural law, such as sodomy," but, as Saint Thomas had written, "prelates had received power only over those who have subjected themselves to the faith." Thus, "Christian princes could not wage war on unbelievers on the grounds of their crimes against nature, any more than for other crimes not against nature."[45]

For example, wrote Vitoria, "the monarchy could not use the sin of sodomy, any more than the sin of fornication, as a pretext for its colonial occupation of the Indias." Vitoria considered both fornication and theft to be as unnatural as sodomy. "Barbarians," he said must "oblige themselves not to steal or to practice sodomitical acts." He thought of "murder as a more serious crime" than any merely unnatural sin. Why should it be right to wage war against unbelievers for sins against nature but not for other sins? pondered Vitoria.[46]

Logically then, thought Vitoria, "non-Christian princes would have as much right to declare war on Christians who sinned against nature." Vitoria did not accept the response that "Christians at least held these crimes in abomination as an excuse for intervention," for he thought it "actually worse to commit a sin knowingly than to do it out of ignorance." Christians, he concluded, "had no greater power over unbelievers than they did over other Christians." When a Christian prince, by "just title" became the "prince of pagans," he could compel them "without provocation to accept the Christian law" and could "abolish any of their unlawful and unnatural rituals."[47]

Some theologians believed that "although the barbarians could not be invaded because of their unbelief or their refusal to accept the Christian faith, war could nevertheless be declared on them for their other mortal sins." Some sins, they argued, especially those "against nature, such as cannibalism, incest with mothers and sisters, or sodomy—all offenses against God," were cause for invasion and the barbarians should be compelled to give them up. On the other hand, Christian princes could not compel the barbarians to give up their sins against the law of nature, nor punish them for such sins, because the pope had no jurisdiction over the barbarians.

Likewise, the pope could not make war on Christians based on fornication, robbery, or even sodomy, nor could the pope confiscate their lands and give them to the other princes. If he could, said Vitoria, "since every country is full of sinners, kingdoms could be exchanged every day." Vitoria eventually muddled through his never-ending contradictions and reconciled his discourses related to the legitimacy of Spain's domination of the Indios.

Vitoria addressed the question of the Indios more succinctly in "On the American Indians," which he began by asking if Christian princes could justly convert the barbarians by violence and the sword. He reiterated that only "cannibalism conferred upon the emperor the right of coercion" and then only because Vitoria had already judged "cannibalism as a crime against nature, harmful to one's neighbors and their defense—a legitimate concern to the Spaniards." He went on to outline four grounds on which barbarians could or could not be considered "true masters of themselves." [48]

Vitoria proposed that the emperor could not be regarded as the master of the whole world, and thus the Spaniards could not justify the invasion of the new lands based on that title. Nor did Vitoria consider the pope as "the civil or temporal master of the whole world, in the proper meaning of dominion and civil power." Third, the right of discovery did not guarantee possession of these countries, for the barbarians themselves possessed "true public and private dominion." Although the Spaniards had pressed the barbarians to accept the "faith of Christ" and the barbarians had "refused," this happening "could not justify a just title of dominion." [49]

Furthermore, Christian princes could not, even on the authority of the pope, compel the barbarians to give up their sins against the law of nature, nor could a prince punish them for such sins. [50] Just as Vitoria had so eloquently sketched out the rights of barbarians in the Indias, he also

provided his prince with the "just titles" necessary to ensure Spain's natural and divine right to possess its colonies of Indios.

In the first instance, the Spaniards had the "right to travel, dwell,
and trade in those countries, so long as they did not cause any harm
to the barbarians," and the barbarians in turn "could not deprive the
Spaniards of their right to travel and dwell." The barbarians "could
not prohibit Spaniards from sharing and enjoying things held in common
by both peoples, for example, digging for gold or pearls." Christians also
had the right to preach and announce the gospel in the land of the
barbarians.[51]

Vitoria added that "if the barbarians had converted to Christ, and
their princes tried to call them back to their idolatry by force or fear, the
Spaniards, based on these grounds, could wage war on them and compel
the barbarians to stop committing the wrong." I suppose that meant that
Spain needed only one converted cacique per viceroyalty to legitimize its
"just title" of war against the barbarians. Spain could then "defend the
innocent against the personal tyranny of the barbarians' masters or
against the tyrannical and oppressive laws they professed," such as human
sacrifice, cannibalism, or sodomy.[52]

Vitoria asserted that "in lawful defense of the innocent from unjust
death, the Spaniards could have prohibited the barbarians from practicing any nefarious custom or rite." "Just imagine," pondered Vitoria, "had
all the barbarians recognized the wisdom and humanity of the Spaniards'
administration, and one and all, both masters and subjects, had spontaneously decided to accept the king of Spain as their prince, this could
have happened and could have constituted yet another legitimate title in
natural law."[53]

Vitoria's relections on power and the rights of conquest effectively
anointed Spain's colonialist ambitions and set the agenda for most subsequent discussions of those subjects in Catholic Europe until the late seventeenth century. In Spain, his academic reflections on the legitimization
of the colonization of America became orthodoxy and provided much of
the theoretical underpinnings for an extensive body of ethnographical
writings on the Indios during the subsequent years of the early modern
period.[54]

The Third Coming of Inebriating Perceptions

Notwithstanding the benevolence that Vitoria had bestowed upon the
rights of barbarians in the Indias, theologians and historiographers in the

mid-sixteenth century continued to color their studies with portraits of Indios in fantastic tones. With the exception of the official historiographers for the monarchy, a third coming of writers—those who actually lived and worked in New Spain, published their firsthand histories of America beginning in the mid-sixteenth century. Fray Toribio de Benavente, a Franciscan who later changed his name to Motolinia—"humble one" in Nahuatl—arrived in Mexico in 1524 and led this third wave of historiographers. Motolinia lived in Puebla, Tlaxcala, Texcoco. and Mexico City, and from these places he frequently corresponded with Carlos V.

In 1541, Motolinia informed the emperor of how "mutilations of the teeth, mouth, tongue, ears, and limbs," all executed by the Indios with "maguey thorns," constituted a "standard punishment for their children." A startled "humble one" described New Spain as a "land reminiscent of the inferno." The sight of those Indios unsettled the friar: "[Some of the heathens] cried out at night, while others loudly bellowed out and summoned the devil, others [became] inebriated, others sang and danced with drums and trumpets, especially during the fiesta of their demons." "Incredible," wrote Motolinia, having witnessed "the great quantities of wine each consumed and poured into his body." [55]

First, the Indios "cooked the wine with some roots," probably the same types of roots that Isabel of Portugal had attempted to regulate in 1529. Then, the Indios customarily began "to drink, with great haste, after vespers in groups of ten or fifteen." Those silly men "never stopped pouring the wine until finally, early at night, they began to lose their senses, stumbling, singing, and loudly crying out to the devil." "What a great pity," wrote the humble clergyman, "to have seen men created in the image of God turn themselves into something worse than brutal animals." But the worst of the matter, lamented Motolinia, was that not only did the Indios commit that sin—"no, they committed many other sins." They "drank a certain wine called pulque, to the point of inebriation, followed by sacrifices and the vices of the flesh, especially—the nefarious sin." [56]

Motolinia, among other writers of this period, again demonized all Indios as drunken fools, suggesting that inebriation caused one to fall prey to the flesh pit of sodomy. However, his humble perceptions of Indios and their sodomitical practices must have appeared quite pale to the monarchy by comparison with the more magnanimous discourses preferred by official royal historiographers.

Las Antipodas

When Francisco López de Gómara, former chaplain to Cortés, dedicated his *Historia General de las Indias* to Carlos V in about 1540, he lauded the discovery of the Indias—a New World—as the "greatest thing that occurred after the creation of the earth." It was a New World not because the Spaniards had "newly rediscovered these territories," but rather it was new in the sense that "their things and cultures represented something *entirely different* to ours" (emphasis added).[57] López de Gómara never traveled to the Indias; nonetheless, his vivid imagination allowed him to regurgitate descriptions of otherness spewed before him by Cortés and other conquistadores.

To begin with, López de Gómara detected the existence of "different animals, in general, albeit few in species, as different" in the Indias. Men in the New World, he wrote, "resembled us, except in color." In this narrow sense, had they not "resembled us," one could have "likened them to beasts or monsters and not to a descendant of Adam." However, "one cannot prove their descendancy from Adam and Eve like the rest of men in our hemisphere."[58]

These Indios had no "letters" to speak of, "no currency, no beasts of burden, no wheat, no wine, no iron"—all of which were extremely necessary for the evolution of a "good social order and state of life" that any early modern Spanish man would have desired. No, "despite the hot climate and the lack of wool or linens," López de Gómara saw "no novelty" in the fact that the Indios dressed as nudes.[59]

In fact, Indios who did not know the "true God and lord" reveled in "extremely abominable inhumanness or sins of idolatry, they sacrificed living men, they had an appetite for eating human meat, they conversed with the devil, they practiced polygamy and, of course, sodomy." But the emperor need not despair, because the "lord's mercy had bestowed his benevolence upon the Indios, by now *all* Christians" (emphasis added).

Never, in the history of early modern Europe, had a nation such as the Spanish nation "extended its customs [and] its language" or journeyed such distances by land or by "our ocean," bearing its armament to "discover and conquer." God had, after all, "willed the discovery of the Indias after the reconquest of the Moors," for the Spanish had "always fought against the infidels." Columbus had rightly attributed his find to the monarchy when he inscribed *"Por Castilla y León, Nuevo mundo hallo Colón"* on his coat of arms.[60]

López de Gómara identified the newly discovered infidels as *"antipodas,"* or "men found in the Indias, contrary to us, apparently with their feet held up high and their faces low." He described the people of New Spain as "light chestnut colored, as if suffering from malaria, of medium height, robust and strong, with small beady eyes, bad teeth, [and] widely opened nostrils." They had "very broad foreheads, so broad indeed that if one repeatedly stabbed them with a sword, the sword would break before one could crack the skulls open." These people ate "spiders, ants, worms, salamanders, lizards, snakes, twigs, dirt, [and] the excrement of mules and sheep," and they "proceeded along, in their merry little way, happy, content, singing and dancing." [61]

In New Spain the "men married as many women as they could or wanted." One "cacique named Behechio had more than thirty women at his side." The women all slept with the men "just like chickens do with a rooster." As such, "little or no trust and chastity existed among women." They could purchase "women for the sum of a bow and arrow." And because the men had grown "prone to inebriation," they "frequently mistreated women." [62]

The royal historiographer described the carnivorous "savage cannibals" of Española as *bubosos,* or persons infected with syphilis. Spaniards who slept with the Indias infected themselves with *bubas,* a "highly contagious and painful illness." When some of these soldiers returned to Italy they, in turn, contaminated the Italians, who had then contaminated the French. The French described the illness as the *mal Napolitano,* yet others commonly called it the *mal Francés* or *sarna Española.* The cure also came from the Indias, in the form of a substance derived from a tree named guayacan. [63]

López de Gómara likened the men of New Spain to "deer or snakes, all grandiose sodomites, vagabonds, liars, and ingrates." In Panuco, López de Gómara described "houses of grandiose *putos* where thousands of men publicly congregated at night" evidently to wallow in sin. The "impotent men" or "eunuchs who dressed like women and are not permitted to carry a bow and arrow," López de Gómara wrote, "married other men." [64]

Now, "to talk about *Mejicanos,*" wrote the historiographer, "is to talk in general about all the men of New Spain." In short: "The men very much painted themselves for war and dances. The gentlemen wore a shawl-like garment off their right shoulders, much like *gitanas.* The wealthier men wore many capes to dances[;] otherwise they all walk

around naked. The men married at age twenty and are so very much inclined to carnal acts, both with men and women. The women incidentally
were very proud of their large and long tits, flipping them over their
shoulders and in this way milked the children they carried on their backs
without any remorse or shame." [65]

In his *Eulogy of the Spaniard*, López de Gómara wrote, "Never, my lord,
have others dominated, in armaments and navigation, as we have done in
such a short span of time." The Spaniards had "sermonized the Holy
Scriptures and evangelized the idolaters," and for this accomplishment
"Spain merited admiration in all parts of the world." "God bless the
lord," continued the adulator, because "he gave our men such grace and
the power to eradicate idolatry, human sacrifices, the eating of human
meat, and sodomy—a sin so abhorred and castigated by God." The
Spaniards had taught "these carnal men the art of letters, the use of iron,
and good customs for a better life," for without these things "men fared
no better than animals." [66]

For López de Gómara "this capital worth of man so exceeded that of
the plumes, the pearls, the silver, and the gold, above all, for the Indios
did not even use these precious metals as currency or their proper use."
At the end of the day, the Spaniards' economic worth paled by comparison with "the great quantities of gold and silver owned by the Indios." [67]

Despite the petulant descriptions of Indios and sodomy, sycophants
of the Spanish monarchy and empire still found it necessary to support
Vitoria's just titles of domination well into the sixteenth century.

The Literary Sycophant

Ginés de Sepúlveda, the official chronicler and chaplain for Carlos V in
1536–1556, opted for a much more clever and literary defense of Spain and
empire. In 1547, Ginés de Sepúlveda wrote *Demócrates Segundo o de las justas
causas de la guerra contra los Indios*, a dialogue between himself, as Demócrates,
and Leopoldo, a Lutheran, based in part on the just causes or titles of war
elaborated earlier in the century by Vitoria.

LEOPOLDO: In a just war, Demócrates, you yourself have stated that
just cause is not only necessary but also good intention undertaken in a righteous manner. But this war against the barbarians
is not waged with good intention, for those who wage war simply want to garner large quantities of gold and silver, legitimately
or illegitimately, all against the teachings of San Agustín, who

stated it is not a crime to wage war, but it is a crime to make war for booty. The war waged by the Spaniards is not a just or reasonable war, but rather gravely unjust and cruel for the barbarians.

DEMÓCRATES: Do not believe, Leopoldo, that one who approves of the domain of his prince also approves of the sins committed by his ministers. The first justification of a just war is to repeal force with force when no other option is available. A second justification is the reappropriation of booty or properties unjustly taken. The imposition of punishment to those who have caused a war. Other causes justified wars based on divine and natural law. The destruction of Sodom and Gomorrah was for the good of its inhabitants. This is most applicable to those barbarians vulgarly known as Indios, whose natural condition is such that they should obey others, dominated by arms. This war is just in the opinion of the most eminent philosophers. Before the Christians arrived, the Indios by nature practiced their nefarious sacrifices as part of their religious customs. From us, they received our letters, laws, and morality imbued by Christian religion. They were all barbarians before their domination, educated without any contempt. They were far removed from morality, civil and humane culture, contaminated by said crimes—this provided another justification. After all, God had destroyed those societies who practiced these impious and nefarious crimes and committed all sorts of abominations such as two other things—the cult of idolatry and the celebration of human sacrifices. On the customs and character of the barbarians and the ignorant in Mexico and in New Spain, what can I say now about the impious religion and the contamination of such nefarious people who revere sacrifices and esteem the devil as God, offering him the hearts of humans[?] One thing is to offer the healthy and pious souls of men, but it is quite another to offer human victims, human breasts opened and their hearts torn out, and the meat fed among themselves. Philosophers consider this among the most ferocious and abominable perversities. Those who live without the knowledge of God and religion commit the gravest crime, vile and *contra naturaleza humana.* The most despicable idolatry is that of those who venerate the vilest organs of the human body, those who have as their religion and virtues the pleasures of the body. They are like pigs that always have their gaze fixed on earth, as if they had never looked up toward the sky. Spain had better virtues and was more pious, just, had better letters, laws, and morals, and the Christian religion.[68]

Ginés de Sepúlveda resorted to the Aristotelian notion that nature had predestined some men to be born into servitude and therefore their status as slaves justified their domination. The Indios' religious and sexual promiscuity only helped enhance Spain's right of domination. Not all moralists agreed. Some, in particular Bartolomé de las Casas, vehemently disagreed with the works of Fernández de Oviedo, López de Gómara, and Ginés de Sepúlveda.

Counter-canonical Discourses

Bartolomé de las Casas and his adulation of the Indios set out to offer new readings of old texts. If Ginés de Sepúlveda and many before him represented *sodomie* as *contra natura* in their support of Spain's annihilative politics of empire, de las Casas also carved out for himself an equally absurd and pathetically apologetic doctrine in defense of the Indios.

Bartolomé de las Casas, commonly referred to as the "apostle of the Indios" by postcolonial writers, sailed to Cuba in 1502, picked up a "black" slave boy along the way, and kept him for life before he eventually became bishop of Chiapas.[69] In 1547 de las Casas permanently returned to Valladolid, where he continued to write his *Historia de las Indias*, printed in 1875, and his *Apologética*, finally published in 1909.[70]

In 1542 de las Casas, along with other missionaries and indigenous writers, initiated a literary counteroffensive aimed primarily at the purification of the Indios' sexual habits and a harsh critique launched against the cadre of historiographers who had supported Spanish atrocities in the Indias. He accused the Spaniards of having perpetrated great cruelties against the Indios. The Spaniards, in the words of de las Casas, have "defamed the Indios, having accused them of being infected with sodomy, a great and wicked falsehood." The Indios simply had "no memory of such a filthy vice."

De las Casas argued that the Indios themselves abhorred sodomy and that they themselves considered it an "abominable sin also punishable by death."[71] The apologetic de las Casas wrote that the "people of Española, Cuba, San Juan, and Jamaica customarily did not eat human meat nor indulged in the *pecado contra natura*."[72] De las Casas focused his defense of

Indios on what he perceived as a pre-Columbian rigid "morality and its condemnation of *sodomía*."[73]

In his 1542 *Brevísima relación de la destrucción de las Indias* written for Carlos V, de las Casas flatly rejected as untrue "the unreasonableness of Indios" and adamantly denied their "practice of sodomy." According to de las Casas, fathers abhorred the sin and prohibited their sons from its practice. But if the "boys underwent religious instruction," de las Casas continued, "they had to sleep in the temple and there the older boys corrupted the younger boys," after which families had "great difficulty liberating the young boy from the ill-accustomed vice." For this very reason, fathers seemed "eager to marry their sons, in hopes of separating them from this most vile corruption." Many of the boys "married forcefully against their will," wrote de las Casas, "for they simply married only out of respect for their fathers."[74]

Even in Santo Domingo, affirmed de las Casas, "in the many years he had known the inhabitants, he had never felt, understood, heard, suspected, or known that the Indios committed the nefarious sin." He based his findings on the confession of an old widowed India who had married a Spaniard and lived on the island. "Did sodomy exist among the Indios before the arrival of the Spaniards?" asked de las Casas of the widow. "Absolutely not," she replied, "for if any man had been blemished by it, the women of the village would have eaten him by the mouthful or killed him"—or other words to that effect.[75]

The Indios hung "those men who dressed like women or women who dressed like men if they committed the nefarious sin," but they "burned priests" who had committed a similar offense, wrote Fray Agustín de Vetancurt, who also recorded severe sentences for sodomy before 1519.[76] In another history of the Indias published in 1596, Fray Jerónimo de Mendieta concurred with de las Casas, writing that "among the Indios of New Spain both agent and patient died for it, for they regarded the vice as one against nature." De Mendieta added that "men who dressed like women and women who dressed like men" also received death sentences.[77]

Nevertheless, by the time de las Casas finished writing his *Apologética*, late in the sixteenth century, many Spanish writers had already described the Indios as a people contaminated by the nefarious vice. For de las Casas, this did not constitute a universal truth, as he later sought to prove. Nonetheless, acknowledged de las Casas, "one should not marvel at the fact that in such a large world full of many nations, some of the unfaithful who lacked grace and doctrine practiced sodomy and other vices, but among Christians few if any tolerated such ignominies." De las Casas reminded his readers that he spoke in "universal terms" and that "the majority of the Indios did seem naturally predisposed to acts of goodness, reason, and kindness, more so than other people." [78]

De las Casas portrayed his Indios as "moderate, temperate in their affections, and respectful toward things." They of course observed "abstinence toward the sensuous, vile, and filthy affections." He saw this virtue reflected in how the Indios treated their wives, "whom they had solely for the purpose of perpetuating the human species," for they too esteemed "procreation as a natural process" and felt no desire to "transcend the boundaries of reason." Surely, wrote de las Casas, "all Spaniards had witnessed that in no place had any Indio acted dishonestly, either with their own wives or with other married or single women." Not even in those parts of the Indias where the Indios "dressed denude from head to toe— except for the women who wore a cotton piece on their unmentionable parts." [79]

In a strange sort of way, observed de las Casas, the ability to go "without shoes or, even more importantly, naked, moderated or debilitated the body's desire or inclination for that vice." The learned friar also noticed that "Indias washed frequently with cold water, day and night, as another way to extinguished the flames of the flesh." Collectively, the Indios did not "grovel in laziness—something that did contribute to an indulgence of nefarious vices." [80] Whatever praise he might have reserved for the Indios, Fray Bartolomé wasted none of it on writing about the ills of sodomy.

De las Casas considered the "bestial vice of sodomy as the worst, the most detestable of any human malice and the worst virtue opposed to the quasi-divine heroic virtues of man or the most excellent of all human virtues." But, like many of his contemporaries, de las Casas eventually did provide his readers with examples of sodomy in the Indias. The only exception, conceded de las Casas, existed among the Maya.[81] According to the testimony of some Spaniards, they had "witnessed some young men dressed like women." De las Casas acknowledged that in Cuba also he had seen "only one Indio dressed like a woman," but he "did not know for what reason." [82]

In both the *Apologética* and in his *Historia de las Indias,* Fray Bartolomé confirmed Fernández de Oviedo's observations that religious connotations overdetermined the Indios' perceptions of sodomy. Both historiographers described how parents presented young boys as gifts to their own sons. The "gifts were to be used for sodomitical pleasure until the sons eventually married women." De las Casas and Fernández de Oviedo also witnessed the existence of *bardajes*, or men who dressed and performed the labors of women, especially in Cuba.[83]

Although de las Casas vehemently denied the practice of sodomy among the Indios, in many instances he described its omnipresence in sporadic parts of the Indias. Still, he thought it "a great falseness and pernicious testimony on the part of the Spaniards to state that young boys in the temples committed the nefarious sin with each other." Those writers had committed a "great misdeed," because "if the boys had committed such a sin, their superiors would have burned or strangled them to death."[84]

The Mixes, for example, "cruelly burned their sodomites and celebrated the punishment." The high priests and all other important elders gathered around in one of the temple's rooms, each holding a stake of fire in his hand. Each one applied the stake directly to the denuded body of the delinquent and reprehended him by asking, "Oh, *malvado,* how could you bear to commit such a grandiose sin in the house of our gods?" After being beaten, such delinquents would be taken outside the temple and handed over to boys, who in turn burned them.[85] Again, de las Casas offered explanations for the existence of depravity in the Indias.

If the Indios had eaten human meat or if they indulged in any other contentious vices, they had done so as a result of "bad customs, initiated by particular persons and for particular occasions." As such, these actions could be attributed to "a natural corruption, depravity, some innate sickness or fear of sorcery and other magic spells." The optimistic friar commented, "With God's will, these activities would also cease." After all, rationalized de las Casas, "demons" had "led the Indios astray," and "these wayward men" had been corrupted by "the art of carnal pleasure with each other."[86]

As in the time of antiquity, the Indios indulged in nefarious abuse not out of "the desire or vileness they felt for the vice" but out of "a religious devotion or sacrifices offered to the gods." In Greece the wise men had allowed for themselves the company of one boy. In Rome the "emperor Adriano worshiped Antino like a god," and in France "boys could marry each other without shame or remorse." The "pestilence of Rome" had also corrupted Cartago. But in ancient Spain "thievery and not sodomy had ranked as the most vile of crimes." These "grave and nefarious vices" had overtaken the French, the Scottish, the Athenians, the Greeks, and the Romans, "along with their philosophers, kings, and emperors."[87]

Like the Romans, the Indios might have instituted "infamous public places known as *efebias,* where young lascivious and shameless men resided

and practiced the abominable sin with all those who entered the house."
But the Indios had instituted such places only so that they could later par-
ticipate in the sacrifices to the gods. In Italy, however, they "practiced it
not only in the temples but also in the squares and neighborhoods."[88]

Scriptures had labeled these men as *molles* (literally "soft or weak,"
known also as *effeminatos*) and stipulated their punishment as "death for
their abominable and execrable sacrileges." In New Spain the devil, who
wished to partake in all genres of sins, had induced and taught the Indios
the art of this particular genre practiced by the *molles* and the *effeminatos*
mentioned in Rome.[89]

Tobilla, identified simply as a Spaniard by de las Casas, stated that
"when a certain number of Spaniards came across, in a certain corner of
these provinces, three men dressed like women, they judged them and
found them guilty of committing that corrupted sin simply for wearing
women's apparel." Without any further proof, the Spaniards "unleashed
their dogs on the men [and the dogs] bit them into pieces and ate them
alive as if [the dogs] had been their judges." In de las Casas' estimation,
"the three men quite possibly did not indulge in that but rather wore
women's apparel in order to indicate their defective manliness to others
because their labor included that attributed to women."[90]

In 1623 a friar named Antonio Vázquez de Espinosa also reported
that a "conquistador had burned a number of sodomites" in his relation
on the Indias.[91] De las Casas probably considered the tales written by
Tobilla and Vázquez de Espinosa as isolated incidents. "If more people
suffered from the blemish of this vice and defect," explained the friar,
then "the Spaniards would have suppressed it and Tobilla certainly would
not have gone without writing more about it."[92]

Furthermore, while traveling in Florida, de las Casas witnessed some
"impotent *mariones*, men [who] dressed like women and performed their
skills." The *mariones*, "although quite robust with large bodies and members that enabled them to carry large amounts of weight, did not shoot
a bow and arrow." Although one of these *mariones* had married a "non-
marión," de las Casas did not know whether "religious motives or an error of nature had caused such monstrosity."[93] For all his pretenses and
adoration of the Indios, de las Casas could not help but accentuate other
differences between the Indios and the Spaniards. In particular, he wrote
that the people of these provinces and in all the Indias "sang and danced
differently."[94]

At weddings, funerals, and sacrifices, the people gathered in a plaza
or at a designated home until Indios entered the space, playing their

"trumpets, flutes, and other instruments." Many men and women followed the band, wearing their "most coveted jewelry," and if they were dressed at all, "at least the women wore the best at their disposal," which included "bracelets made of many shells, gold, and other bones." The "denuded ones" wore plumes and painted their bodies red. De las Casas noted that "what we understood as sorcery and witchcraft, they celebrated as a grand gala." [95]

The Indios sang about the "miseries and calamities they had suffered since the arrival of the Spaniards." They sang about the "usurpation of their lands, their women, children, their inherited riches, the ferocity of horses, the cruelty of the dogs, in fact everything sad." At some galas, "troubadours usually followed behind a group of well-armed men who mimicked past battles." Such warriors then "approached the choir of women" present at the happenings and "took with them those they desired for whatever effect and for whatever time necessary without the interference of the appropriate husbands." [96]

When the Indios "tired of singing, dancing, and having cried out about their plight," de las Casas wrote, "they sat down on the floor to eat, where they had previously arranged their poor foods." Despite their attempts to infuse their gatherings with an "aura of splendor," they did not succeed, "because everything the Indios gathered for their galas compared miserably with our very own excesses and magnificent banquets." The poor Indios gathered their "chickens, deer, rabbits, and fish, all cooked or grilled on the open fire," but certainly were not capable of concocting "such exquisite and superfluous delicacies like we do." After the meal, they drank wine made of maize, "potent enough to inebriate," and they drank "until they simply could no longer drink anymore." [97]

Whatever the comparisons, other theologians and indigenous historiographers during the early modern period defended de las Casas and his arguments related to the castigation of sodomy by indigenous cultures in the Americas. Indigenous historiographers resorted to previous perceptions of sodomy in the peninsula as they explained and argued that the indigenous cultures in the Indias had also always abhorred sodomy.

Indigenous Mouthpieces

Indigenous writers eventually also wrote in defense of their cultures and upheld the perceptions of sodomy among the Indios espoused by de las Casas. Fernando de Alva Ixtlilxochitl, born in Teotihuacán and a direct descendant of the Acolhua kings and who in due time became governor of Texcoco, wrote on the Toltec and Chichimec cultures in 1605. As a his-

toriographer of the Toltec and the Chichimec in central Mexico, Alva Ixtlilxochitl reported that "until the arrival of the Spaniards the Chichimec
hanged men who used boys for sodomy, and others simply died for it."
In a curiously similar parallel to sodomy prosecutions in the Spanish peninsula, Alva Ixtlilxochitl insisted that the Chichimec punished in two
ways those who engaged in the nefarious sin.[98]

He who "assumed the function of the woman," wrote Alva Ixtlilxochitl, "had his inner parts removed through his anus as he remained tied
down to a stake, after which some boys poured ashes over the body until
the body was buried under them." They then "covered the entire mound
with many portions of wood and set it on fire." The one who "had functioned as the man" was covered with ashes while he was still alive "until
he died."[99]

The Spaniards also looked to another indigenous form of recorded
history—codices—to reaffirm their perceptions of sodomy among the
Indios. The *Codex Mendoza* of 1548 and *Codex Badianus* of 1552, commissioned by the viceroy of Mexico, Antonio de Mendoza, and written by
indigenous scriveners, did not mention sodomy among the Indios. However, the *Codex Magliabecchi*, written in 1565, in a possible veiled reference to
sodomy, depicted maize as a grain associated with death, rebirth, or illness particularly attributed to sodomitical practices. The *Codex Ramírez* of
1580 on Mexico portrayed sodomy as a "cursed vice."

Codices written before 1492 primarily explained calendar cycles, rituals, and historical sequences of rulers and provided only a glimpse of
morality depicted within the rubric of religious rituals. However, the
codices commissioned by the Spaniards throughout the early modern period strongly depicted notions of immorality in a myriad of discursive
forms—"anthropophagy, human sacrifices, aberrant sexual behavior, and
inebriating drugs."[100]

Colonial missionaries also turned to confessional manuals in their
attempts to substantiate the practice of sodomy among the Indios. The
missionaries prepared the confessional manuals in different languages,
and collectively these books constituted a segment of religious literature
of sinful sexual mores that complemented the other works of theologians
and historiographers. Special sections followed the translations of Christian doctrine, designed to explain the more difficult concepts of the faith
in translation.[101] For the most part, the confessional manuals validated
earlier held conceptions that all Indios practiced sodomy.

The *Confessionario mayor, en lengua Mexicana y Castellana*, written in 1569 and one of the earliest confessional manuals, referred to *"sodomía* between men, between men and women, and between women" in New Spain. Written by Alonso de Molina, a Franciscan friar, the manual invoked the sixth commandment and asked of women in particular "if they had sinned with another woman or had ever committed the sin against nature."[102]

Fray Juan Baptista was a second-generation Franciscan *criollo* and a pupil of Sahagún, who later became Torquemada's instructor. He also associated the urge of sodomitical practices with the drinking of pulque. When Baptista wrote his *Confessionario en lengua Mexicana y Castellana* in 1599, he asked men "if they had sex with themselves or with other men or if they had penetrated their wives outside the conventional vessel." The confessional also preoccupied itself with whether or not "women committed the nefarious sin with other women or with their husbands." Baptista also linked inebriation with sodomy, but only in the case of men.[103]

In 1611, Martin de León, a Dominican friar, indicated in his *Camino al cielo* that "sodomy between young women had become quite widespread in Mexico." He thought it "quite common for young unmarried women to lie one on top of the other and to touch each other, just like man and woman."[104] Bartolomé de Alva's 1634 *Confessionario mayor y menor en lengua Mexicana* addressed sodomy between men as well as bestiality, and like his counterparts, Alva associated inebriation with the practice of sodomy. "When inebriated, lacking reason, did you fall into the abominable sin of sodomy with another man or with an animal?" asked Alva of both men and women. And had husbands, "while inebriated, penetrated their wives in areas not intended for natural coitus?" questioned the manual.[105]

Still later, in 1666, Cristóbal de Aguero, a Dominican, in his *Vocabulario castellano-zapoteco,* also mentioned sodomy between men and between women. Fray Angel Serra, a Franciscan who wrote *Manual de administrar los santos sacramentos* in 1697 for the Charapan Tarascan Indios, devoted a large section of his manual to questions pertinent to "lust, fornication, incest, sodomy, bestiality, and suicide," all within the context of inebriation as the pretext for such vile acts.[106]

The codices and the confessional manuals provided colonial authorities with two distinct methods by which to quantify and monitor sodomitical activity in the Indias. In this way, Spanish officials solicited the help of indigenous historiographers in fabricating and perpetuating peninsular notions of sodomy. Meanwhile, others in the Indias had already begun to dispute de las Casas' benevolence toward the Indios.

The Three Ruffians

López de Gómara, in his 1552 *Eulogy of the Spaniard,* had assured Charles V that, among other things accomplished, the Spaniards had totally eradicated sodomy from the Indias.[107] Notwithstanding such lofty denials of sodomy and sodomites, their sightings kept reappearing during the later part of the sixteenth century.

In 1565, Pedro de Castañeda witnessed "men dressed as women, married to other men who functioned as their wives," among the natives in Sinaloa. He described others in the region as "grandiose sodomites."[108] Juan López de Velasco witnessed a similar situation, which he reported in the *Audiencia of México* of 1574, noting that many natives were much inclined to nefarious vices.[109] Other missionaries who worked in the same region also noted the same.

Fray Bernardino de Ribeiro, otherwise known as Sahagún—he also changed his name to reflect the name of his native village at the time he became a Franciscan—arrived in Mexico in 1529. Shortly thereafter, Sahagún mastered Nahuatl and wrote his *Historia general de las cosas de la Nueva España,* both in his adopted tongue and in Spanish between 1558 and 1565. Far from having presumed a paternalistic defense of the Indios, Sahagún instead reinforced the Spanish repulsive descriptions of sodomites, hermaphrodites, and whores.

In one section of his manuscript titled "On vicious persons such as ruffians and sodomites," Sahagún, revered by many as the quintessential humanist of early modernity, reaffirmed that the "*sodomético,* an abominable patient, nefarious and detestable, deserved to be ridiculed and laughed at by the people." In all his aspects, wrote Sahagún, the *sodomético* presented himself as "womanly or effeminate, in the way he walked, or talked, and for all these reasons he deserved to be burned."[110]

Sahagún detested "the bad odor and the deformity emitted by [the sodomite's] nefarious sin, for it so repulsed men." One wonders how this beloved humanist could have possibly known that sodomitical acts emit any odors at all. Other texts also often associated *coprofilia* and sodomy. The *Codice Florentino* described the sodomite as follows:

> Puto: corrupción, pervertido, excremento, perro de mierda, mierducha, infame, corrupto, vicioso, burlón, escarnecedor, provocador, repugnante, asqueroso. Llena de excrementos el olfato de la gente. Afeminado. Se hace pasar por mujer. Merece ser quemado, merece ser abrasado, merece ser puesto en el fuego. Arde,

es puesto en el fuego. Habla como mujer, se hace pasar por mujer. (Faggot: rotted stench, perverted, excrement, wretched dog,
filthy shit, infamous, corrupt, vicious, mocker, scoffer, provoca-
tive, repugnant, loathsome. Fills the air with smells of excrements.
Effeminate. He passes himself off as a woman. He deserves to be
burnt, he deserves to be scorched, he deserves to be set on fire. He
burns as the fire blazes. He speaks like a woman and dresses like
a woman.)[111]

The moralists had also associated whores, who were tolerated but socially deplored, with scatophagy when they referred to them as *mierduchas*
or *perrillas de mierda*. Sahagún identified the whore, or *puta*, as "a public
woman who sold her body, one who began her art as a young girl and
continued her labor albeit old." She "walked as if inebriated or lost." This
"gallant, well-spruced, unabashed woman sold her body to any man."
Sahagún noted that she was "vicious in her *actu carnal*" and that "a lustful,
filthy, shameless *puta* ambled like a horse" and "painted her face in different colors so much so that she resembled a rose."[112] He reported that
"a *puta* looked at herself in the mirror, she bathed and washed herself carefully, and then [she] refreshed herself so as to appeal to men." She customarily "painted her teeth with some herbs, perfumed herself with some
scents, and wore her hair loose for maximum beauty."[113]

In the end, Sahagún likened her to a "bad, dissolute, and infamous
woman." She "chewed *tzictli* to clean her teeth," and as she "gnawed the
gum and moved her mandible," she "sounded like the snaps of castanets."
Sahagún observed that "the ordinary, gossipy *puta* gads about in the
streets, winking at men with her eyes." This "disquieted and troubled
woman" never stopped looking for vices and good pay from young boys,
whom she often "beguiled." The men of the Indias, observed Sahagún,
instructed their sons "to keep away from food prepared by these bad
women," and the fathers themselves taught their boys "proper behavior in
sleep, eating, drinking, speech, dress, walking, looking, and listening."[114]

Sahagún's disdain for sodomites extended equally to "bad women"
like the hermaphrodite, whom he identified as "a woman of two sexes or
one who has the *natura* of both a man and a woman, a monstrous negli-
gible woman, ignorant of her obligations, who has many woman friends
and servants." According to Sahagún, such a woman "exhibited a genteel
body, talked and walked like a man, and possessed a head full of soft
hair." The hermaphrodite "utilized both *naturas*," which transformed
"her" into an "enemy of men," because she "employed the masculine

sex."[115] Sahagún sketched his decrepit trinity of ruffians—sodomites, hermaphrodites, and whores—as the most maligned sectors of society in New Spain, but other historiographers acquiesced and directly repudiated the discursive aspects of de las Casas' findings of sodomy in the Indias.

They Reeked of Sulfur

Bernal Díaz del Castillo, a historiographer who had traveled with Cortés, wrote about sodomy among the Indios, but not until 1568. His history challenged the more benevolent versions of sodomitical cultures described by de las Casas and his followers. Díaz del Castillo also recorded Cortés' earliest lectures on sexuality to the Indios. When the Spaniards first discovered Yucatán in 1517, a group of Indios "dressed in cotton shirts, their private parts covered only with a small piece of cloth called *mastates*," greeted the interlopers. Díaz del Castillo described these Indios as having "slightly more reason than those they had encountered earlier in Cuba, who walked around with their private parts exposed, except for the women, who wore *naguas*."[116]

As the Spaniards walked around and explored the surroundings in Yucatán, they also "came upon three small houses situated on a small square." The small houses each contained "altars supposedly used by the Indios for the "worshipping of clay idols." Some of the idols resembled the "faces of demons," whereas "others represented tall women or men, and yet others represented some very vile figures or a bulk of Indios participating in acts of *sodomías* and other diabolical gestures." Ten Indios then came out of the houses dressed in "long white tunics" and with "very long hair to the waist or to the feet—hair, drenched in blood, so unkempt and tangled that one could not comb, separate, or cut it." These same Indios had "shredded their ears to pieces, having sacrificed them," and they "reeked of sulfur and gave off another bad odor of dead human meat." These "priests of the idols," known as *papas,* had no wives, and they "practiced the evils of *sodomías*."[117]

The caciques and the *papas,* otherwise called priests by Díaz del Castillo, "had understood our justification for domination when Cortés spoke the most beautiful words of our language" and "urged them to rid themselves of sacrifices and asked them not to eat the human flesh of thy neighbor." He pleaded with them "not to sacrifice men, not to adore idols, not to rob thy neighbor, not to practice *sodomías,* nor the other ugly things the Indios commonly practiced, for the lord our God had willed it so." [118]

"Every day, in our presence," Díaz del Castillo wrote, the Indios "sacrificed four or five Indios whose hearts they offered to their idols," and they "smeared their blood on the walls of the houses used for their worship." Then, according to Díaz del Castillo, they would "cut off the legs, the arms, and the other muscles of men, whom they ate just like a cow obtained at a meat market in our land." The Indios sold the "amputated parts as *menudo* in the *tiangues*," or marketplaces in the town square. The caciques and the *papas* responded that they "disagreed" with Cortés' policy over the idols and the *menudo* sold in *tiangues*, but that they could possibly "resist the practice of the *sodomías*." Cortés had implored the Indios to "cleanse themselves of sodomy," for they had "many young boys who dressed in women's apparel and practiced that vileness." [119]

While traveling through Mexico in 1569, Magistrate Tomás López Mendel also associated sodomy with "the Mexican priests." They engaged in "such abominable lusts and sins," he reported—in fact, they were "too abominable and disgraceful" for him to describe. The priests, speculated the magistrate, had also introduced the "nefarious and widespread customs among the people." [120]

In 1604, Gregorio García, a Dominican friar who resided in Mexico for about twelve years, returned to Spain, where he published his *Origen de los Indios de el nuevo mundo* in 1607. Before the arrival of the Spaniards, assured García, "men in New Spain committed enormous sins, especially that against nature, although repeatedly torched for it and consumed by fire sent from the heavens." And as in the Levant, the Indios of New Spain "punished the sodomites by death," executing the punishment "with great vigor." They "strangled or drowned women who lay with other women," because they considered that practice also to be against nature. In some provinces of New Spain, they "permitted the establishment of public bawdy houses of men for the consumption of this abominable vice." [121] One century after the initial histories on sodomy in the Indias first circulated in the peninsula, García and his compatriots continued to produce incessant and repetitive explanations of sodomitical practices in New Spain.

García explained that the "miserable Indios did so because the devil had tricked them into believing that the gods they adored also practiced sodomy and as such considered it a licit and good custom." He also reported that "some men dressed like women, and if a father had five sons, any one of the five could become a daughter." In such a case, they "dressed him as a woman, instructed him in her labors, and married him just like a girl, even though those in New Spain despised the effeminate or womanly Indios." Such things were reported although "the people had always considered sodomy an abominable, ugly sin, even though some provinces did not punish its infamous sodomites."

García recalled, however, that "bestiality never occurred among the Indios," although it was "practiced by the Jews," and therefore "no law existed against bestiality." [122] Nor had García detected laws against *molicie*, "for they never knew or came to know such sins." Lavrín did not agree:

> Masturbation, always described as an exclusively masculine problem . . . always concerned the church and it targeted the only channel left for the release of masculine sexual urges. . . . [M]asturbation seemed to have been the only choice open to single men . . . and religious authorities closed this option and prohibited "dishonest" body contacts or any form of voyeurism. . . . [I]f during masturbation the person carnally desired another person, a second sin was committed. The sin became graver when another man or a woman was involved in the masturbation act, and it was at its most heinous if the helper incurred pollution himself. On the other hand, actions causing involuntary emissions, such as horse riding, eating in excess, or becoming drunk, did not per se lead to sin, as they were not originally intended to produce emission or pleasure.[123]

Despite García's claims to the contrary, histories of sodomy in the Indias continued unabated well into the seventeenth century.

One Last Fantastic Fable

Juan de Torquemada, a Franciscan, wrote one of the last of the great Spanish discourses about sodomy during the early modern period. His *Monarquía Indiana*, published in 1615, berated "Moctecuhzuma" as "stupid for having thought that whores exercised a worse sin than sodomy, human sacrifices, or eating human meat." [124] One day, when Cortés returned to see Moctecuhzuma, "whose conniving and dissembled happy face hid the pain he actually felt in his heart," the conquistador learned that the Aztec king had ordered "the destruction of a common whorehouse, home to about four hundred women, because their public sins had offended the gods." The gods, reasoned Moctecuhzuma, "had permitted the Christians, who had more power to govern, access into their city." Moctecuhzuma purportedly told Cortés, "I, a man of flesh and bones, exposed to many illnesses and threats, am not so savage or stupid so as not to understand that I possess far less superiority and immortality than do the gods. Regarding the riches of this land—its gold, silver, or stones—do not putrefy yourself, for this is over something that you can have as yours whenever you may please." [125]

Yet Moctecuhzuma "did not consider sodomy, human sacrifices, or the eating of human meat graver or uglier than the trade of the whores." [126] Whatever the rhetoric, whores still had a public function within Aztec cosmology, as depicted by Torquemada's description of the Mexican feast in honor of the *francolín*—a beautiful bird, or godwit—which occurred during the fourteenth month of the Indiano calendar.

During the feast, the Mexicans honored the god Mixcohuatl, and they "sacrificed many young women in memory of love." During this month, known as *quecholli,* the "whores, or public and dishonest women, manifested themselves and offered themselves as sacrifices to the god." The "women known as *maqui,*" according to Torquemada, also "followed the men into war and oftentimes . . . thrust themselves into battle simply to die." These "shameless women," Torquemada wrote, "cursed themselves and other honorable women as they thrust their bodies into death." [127]

The "effeminate and womanly men who dressed in women's apparel" also participated in this feast. The other Indios "detested these men, who painted their bodies and performed the labors of women but who had no contact but with women." [128] Unlike Moctecuhzuma, assured Torquemada, Nezahualcoyotl before him had "abhorred the nefarious vice that other caciques sometimes permitted in their midst." [129]

Nezahualcoyotl had apparently punished "the patient by having him tied to a thick stake in the ground and then had his intestines extracted through the anus." Afterward, the young boys of the village "covered the patient's entire body in ashes, piled wood over the ashes, and lit the fire." The boys also "buried the agent's body in ashes until he died, naturally." Torquemada believed that the Indios in New Spain had "strangled those who committed the nefarious sin," and he insisted that "magistrates rigorously investigated whether or not men committed this crime in the republic and punished them, for they too considered it a bestial vice perpetuated for lack of reason." [130]

Furthermore, the magistrates "strangled men who dressed in women's apparel and likewise women who dressed in men's apparel." If a high priest committed culpable acts of dishonesty with a woman, the community simply banished him from the province and deprived him of his goods. However, if a priest indulged in the nefarious sin, "the community burned, strangled, or killed both participants." The ancient law of God, concluded Torquemada, had prohibited such atrocities among men.[131] Torquemada's crowning work, though, centers around his most fantastic theory on the emergence of sodomy in the Indias.

Although "some Indios in the provinces might have committed the nefarious sin," Torquemada pointed out that nevertheless "laws existed in those provinces that prohibited its practice." Torquemada offered his own theory on how the Indios had "introduced sodomy into these republics": "a demon named Chin had appeared in the form of a young boy and induced all those around him to commit this corrosion just as he had performed it with another demon in the presence of the others." The "Indios did not consider it a sin," Torquemada reported, "for they thought that a god—more properly said, a filthy and vile demon—had actually committed it in their presence." This did not, however, "excuse them from having committed the gravest of all bestial sins that inhibited procreation," Torquemada noted.

Because these men "did not recognize sodomy as a sin, fathers grew accustomed to giving boys as gifts to their sons, so that their sons could keep them and use the boys as women." Indian laws protected this type of relationship. Other boys "could not have access to one's boy concubine," wrote Torquemada, "for that risked punishment equivalent to having violated a matrimonial union." He cautioned, "Do not, my prudent and wise reader, marvel at hearing about such a law, for he who is without God easily falls from grace just like one who travels blindly and falls prey to the devil, an evil and perverse seeker of men, a filthy pervert of customs who sought to pander this type of merchandise among these Indios."

Finally, in his own form of "outing," Torquemada reminded his readers that some "Indios kept boys just like Adrian and his boy-concubine or as in Greece, where every man had access to his boy, even Aristotle, the father of natural philosophy."[132] Not content with a simple elaboration on the emergence of sodomy, Torquemada also provided his readers with his own discourse about *mariones* in the Indias.

Más Mariones

In Florida, "among other barbarities," Torquemada noted "the most abominable one in the world [was that] some men married others as if this established a natural contract, rather than a very grave sin against nature." He noted that the "impotent *mariones* married other men—who could still fornicate with women and bear children." Torquemada did not know for certain if the *mariones* themselves had "caused their own impotency in religious ceremonies or whether an error of nature had caused such monstrosity." [133]

The Spaniards knew that many of those who lived in Santo Domingo "notoriously committed the nefarious sin although those Indios enacted laws that prohibited the bestial vice." Torquemada noted that "the detestable vice had reached such proportions of notoriety among these dirty miry hogs that they solicited each other publicly without remorse and tempted not only men but God's angels on earth, one reason for God's destruction of Sodom." [134]

However, Torquemada pointed out, "the Indios of Vera Paz in Guatemala, in general, did not practice the sin as much as others in and around those provinces." There, he noted, priests "reproached and often argued with the young boys who enjoyed and committed the sin." Time and again, the priests "admonished the boys to renounce the sin, for to relish in such enormity surely meant death." [135]

"One could cry," lamented Torquemada, for "even the wise and gifted Greeks had used their bodies nefariously as sacrifices to render worship to their amorous and vile gods." They had established "gymnasiums as offerings to their filthy gods where they too offered their young boys and converted them into patients of the gods." Torquemada stated that "in these public schools or so-called gymnasiums anyone could take filthy advantage of any of these young boys." The men and boys "denuded their bodies and reveled in the nefarious vices," Torquemada declared. The Greeks "adored these vices and regarded them as godly." Fortunately, wrote Torquemada, "our occidental Indios" also had schools next the their temples, but they used them "to instill in their children and young boys honest and good customs and not the evil abominations taught by ancient Gentiles." [136]

About 130 years after Spain had subjugated the Indias to colonial rule, officials in Mexico could boast of having achieved some successes. Anthropophagy and the scarifying of humans, it seemed, had almost completely ceased among the barbarians. The conversion of the infidels to Catholicism appeared to have reached its pinnacle. And sodomy—well, sodomy still lingered in the minds of some *nefastos.*

Central Market

Cortés described the metropolis of Mexico, or Tenochtitlán: "[as] large as Sevilla or Córdoba, it resembled Venice, its *plaza mayor* two times larger than that of Salamanca, the largest in Spain" (Fig. 4.2). It sat erect in the middle of a lake "adorned with great temples and towers" and exhibited a "large outdoor market full of fish, meat, deer, rabbit, other game, vegetables, fruits, woods, gold glasses, copper artifacts," and other artistic wares such as "clay pottery of better quality than that found in our world." Cortés wrote that "cotton and feathers abounded in such great quantities" that he found it "impossible to fathom." [137]

By the time Gemelli Carreri, a wealthy Italian aristocrat and a doctor of law, first visited the city in 1697, he alluded to its "perfect square plane without any walls or doors," a sort of "tableaux with long, unswerving streets, covered in stones, pointing toward the four cardinal directions" such that one could "almost see the entire city from any direction." [138]

4.2. "Forma y levantado de la ciudad de México," Juan Gómez de Trasmonte, 1628. Nettie Lee Benson Latin American Rare Books Collection, University of Texas at Austin.

People lived comfortably in this "very nice city where one could purchase cacao, flowers, fruits and vegetables of different species all year
round in its central market." About a hundred thousand inhabitants lived
in the city, "the majority *negros* and *mulatos,* who despised the peninsulars
and who one day could very well rebel and wrestle the republic from the
Spaniards."[139]

"Power and wealth rested with twenty-two religious monasteries and
twenty-nine diverse religious orders of friars, all very rich," wrote Gemelli
Carreri, so much so that "Spaniards and other Europeans became part of
the clergy when they could find no other easier way simply to assure
themselves of a steady rent." Given Mexico City's "good edifices and or-
nate churches, one could say it rivaled the best in Italy," the aristocrat observed, "but certainly surpassed it with the beauty of its *damas,* who are
pretty fine and of genteel fabric."[140]

Apparently, Mexico City had harbored not only beautiful women but
also men who wished to pass themselves off as such. In the seventy years
he had resided in the metropolis, Juan Correa, who referred to himself as
a *"linda niña,"* had also noticed the beauty radiated by the *damas* of the city
such that he saw fit to rename himself La Estanpa after one such "fine
lady." The viceroy count of Monterrey had foreshadowed the antics of
La Estanpa in a letter written to Felipe II in 1596.

The Viceroy Count

The viceroy count informed Felipe II that both sodomites and civil servants in New Spain still posed a problem for the colonial state. His
letter to the monarch described "the lack of discipline and the lack of
respect for royal officials by other court officials" within the secular juridical branch of the colonial government in the metropolis of Mexico.
The viceroy count had empathized with the breach of decorum.[141]

"It's understandable and they should be forgiven," the viceroy count
wrote, because the "colonial state poorly paid the civil servants." The colonial "exchequer simply did not have the capital to pay all those associated with the juridical branch of this administration."[142] In folio after folio, the viceroy count made plea after plea to justify higher salaries for
his subordinates and an augmentation of his colonial budget. As part of
this justification for higher salaries, he informed the king that the court
officials merited praise because they had imprisoned and burned "some
delinquents for the nefarious sin and other types of *sodomía.*"[143]

Subsequently, the viceroy count had ordered the apprehension of their
known "accomplices in Guatemala," and he ordered the court officials to

contact their counterparts and compare their findings with "similar cases in Madrid." Unfortunately, the viceroy count did not reveal the number or the circumstances concerning the 1596 burnings in Mexico City. Prior to 1596, the earliest known burning of sodomites by colonial authorities in Mexico City dated back to the 1530s, when secular officials convicted Caltzontzin for "idolatry, sacrifice, and *sodomía*." [144]

Fray Pedro Simón also recorded at least two instances of sodomy prosecutions among the conquistadores. The first case involved three mariners under the services of Nikolaus von Federmann (1501–1542), a German captain in the service of the Welsers, who were bankers to Carlos V. The other incident had involved five Italian mariners during a voyage to Venezuela. [145]

If early modern theologians, historiographers, conquistadores, and other writers had helped etch fantastic notions of sodomy in the minds of learned men in the peninsula, local colonial officials took up the charge well into the seventeenth century. Some sixty years after the viceroy count's letter to Felipe II, it seemed that colonial authorities had still not filled their coffers to the satisfaction of anyone, and the sodomites continued to manifest their presence and to perturb viceroys and dukes alike.

An Endemic Cancer Looms in the Metropolis

In 1658 the new viceroy of New Spain, the duke of Albuquerque, informed Carlos II that the Criminal High Court in the metropolis of Mexico had apprehended about "nineteen prisoners, fourteen of whom" were "sentenced to burn" for having committed the "nefarious sin." "Never in the history of mankind," continued the duke, "have I heard of such complicity." "The idiocies and the circumstances of the nefarious sin" completely overwhelmed the duke, who described them as "incredible and ancient." The duke devoted the first three pages to the sodomy cases, and thereafter, like the viceroy count before him, argued incessantly for the "need to raise the salaries of colonial civil servants." [146]

In addition to his letter, the duke of Albuquerque sent three additional documents to Carlos II. The documents described in greater detail those incidents that fascinated colonial officials pertinent to the 1657–1658 sodomy trials in Mexico City. The first document, a concise letter written by Juan Manuel de Sotomayor, a magistrate of His Majesty's High Court, erroneously depicted biblical tales that he appropriated in order to chastise sodomites and provide graphically diabolical images of them.

At the conclusion of his investigations, Sotomayor confirmed that sodomy, in his words an "endemic cancer," had "extensively contaminated the provinces of New Spain." This "mortal and nefarious vice," he reported, had even "infested and spread among prisoners held captive by the Inquisition in their particular jails," and he noted that ecclesiastical officials had also "begun their own inquiries." Since his arrival in Mexico some twelve years earlier, "not once" had Sotomayor realized the "extent of the contamination." [147]

But Sotomayor consoled Carlos II and himself by recalling, "as some saints had professed, that all sodomites died on the birth of Jesus our Lord." [148] Sotomayor's weary recollection of Catholic indoctrination caused him to conflate the birth of Christ with the biblical tale of Lot and God's angels in Sodom, a city "destroyed by fire and brimstone because of the supposed illicitly sexual activities of its inhabitants." [149]

An eight-folio summary report, which included an appendix about the accused that was written by a scrivener, silhouetted in greater detail the discursive particulars of the 1657–1658 Mexican sodomy cases. [150] The appendix listed in alphabetical order the names, the ethnicities, and the occupations of some 125 individuals either sentenced or under investigation by the High Court. [151]

The scrivener, a permanent member of every tribunal, transcribed in writing, as the legal manuals required, "not only all the defendant's responses and any statements he might make, but also what he might utter during the torture, even his sighs, his cries, his laments and tears." The practice of recording legal proceedings in their entirety supposedly "discouraged irregularities, including the tendency of some examiners to ask leading or suggestive questions." [152]

Technically, as more traditional historians would have one believe, the scrivener should have transcribed everything "uttered" verbatim by the accused, thereby drafting an objective text or factual source. However, a scrivener's filtering of testimony is just as pertinent to how one conceptualizes the writing of history. On numerous occasions, as parts of this study have indicated, the scrivener recorded his own perceptions of individuals or events, thereby substantiating the sodomy discourses fabricated by the crown and the church.

When a scrivener attempted to describe a witness named "Francisca Negra" in a 1602 blasphemy case in Mexico City, he wrote that "she appeared to be about thirty years old, although she did not know her age despite being a Ladina." [153] In the colonial hierarchy of ethnicity, a *ladina* or a *mestiza* descended from one indigenous parent and one Spanish parent. The individual commonly "spoke only Spanish." [154] The scrivener equated ethnicity with a certain level of education and knowledge—the lighter the skin, the brighter the brain.

As the 1657–1658 sodomy tales will illustrate, hierarchies of ethnicity and power overdetermined the outcome of these cases.

Mariquita under the Willows

As Juana de Herrera, a *mestiza*, "washed clothes alongside a wall, outside the city in the neighborhood of San Lazaro" in late September 1657, "two boys in great haste cried out to her" and insisted that she "go see some men playing like dogs." Juana stood up and walked some distance until she reached a group of willow trees. Under one willow, Juana saw "two men, both without their breeches, one on top of the other, committing the nefarious sin." [155]

The "man on top" and the cape he wore concealed the "man on the bottom." Nonetheless, she recognized the "man on top" as "Juan de la Vega, a *mulato* from Mexico City and one she had known for over ten or twenty years." She did not recognize the "man on the bottom," except to say that he "looked like a *mestizo*." Juana "dared not get any closer for fear of getting killed." [156] The frightened *mestiza* returned to retrieve her bundles and dashed off to denounce the two men before Magistrate Sotomayor.

Sotomayor soon learned that Juan de la Vega resided in the barrio of San Pablo, where he let a couple of rooms at the house of Doña Melchora de Estrada. Early that afternoon, Sotomayor had arrived at the house only to discover that Juan de la Vega "had moved on to other quarters." Sotomayor interrogated the other boarders who lodged at the house, one of whom, an Indio named Tomás de Santiago (Fig. 4.3), described Juan de la Vega as an "effeminate *mulato*" who "preferred the nickname Cotita, or the same as *mariquita*," or "effeminate man." What constituted an effeminate man in the estimation of the Indio Tomás?

When Vega walked, stated Tomás, he sashayed his "hips from one side to the other." Cotita "ordinarily wore a *melindre*, a delicate kerchief usually worn on the waist by women, on his forehead." Many "colored ribbons fell out from the openings of both his white jacket sleeves." Not only did Juan de la Vega "sit on the floor in a womanly state," but he also "could also prepare tortillas, *guisaba/sauté*, and washed clothing." When "some young boys called to visit," continued the informant, Cotita individually greeted them as "my soul, my sweetheart, or my love."

4.3. **Representations of early modern Indios in Mexico City.** "Mexico, en Ameriq" (c. 1700), engraved by Pierre Montier. In *Atlas histórico de la ciudad de México,* ed. S. Lombardo de Ruiz and M. de la Torre (Mexico City: Smurfit Cartón y Papel, 1996). Nettie Lee Benson Latin American Rare Books Collection, University of Texas at Austin.

The young men, "so as not to offend" Juan de la Vega, always addressed "her" as Cotita. Initially, Cotita and her guests would sit together on the floor and then later retired to another room where they all "slept together." The Indio Tomás had also slept over on one of those occasions. That night, with the help of "moonlight," he witnessed "how a young *mestizo* boy named Joseph Durán from Puebla de los Angeles and another boy named Gerónimo Calbo from Mexico City committed the nefarious sin." [157]

After the interrogations of Tomás, Sotomayor left Doña Melchora's house in rapid pursuit of Juan de la Vega. Finally, at midnight, Sotomayor located Cotita's new lodgings. Sotomayor and those who accompanied him barged into the room and "surprised Juan de la Vega, Joseph Durán, Gerónimo *'the bald head,'* Miguel Gerónimo Mestizo, and Simón de Chaves Indio, who all clung together naked." On 3 October 1657 the apprehended men appeared before the magistrates of the High Court and initially denied the allegations put forth by Juana de Herrera and Tomás de Santiago.

With the exception of Miguel Gerónimo, the accused sodomites finally succumbed to the probing questions of the magistrates and "admitted having committed the nefarious sin an infinite number of times, with many and different persons." Miguel Gerónimo continued to deny his involvement, even as the other men "revealed the names of their accomplices [and] identified the places, the time, day, month, year, and other circumstances" pertinent to their sin and crime.[158]

Colonial authorities eventually incarcerated an additional eighteen of Cotita's accomplices and issued arrest warrants for another 106 suspected sodomites.

Parties and Pseudonyms

Over the course of the interrogations in the case of Cotita, the individuals queried divulged the particulars of their gatherings. Juan de Correa, "a very fine little girl who since age seven had dressed like a woman," served as the designated courier for many a gathering (Fig. 4.4). As the courier and courtesan, the elderly *mestizo* of seventy years, also known as La Estanpa, informed the other men of "future reunions, their dates and places." The men hosted these gatherings, "just like women, periodically throughout the year in different houses."[159]

The gatherings frequently coincided with Catholic feast days and with the pretext of paying tribute to "Our Lady, the Holy Apostles, or any other ecclesiastical celebrations." Juan Currador, an Indio who also resided in the same barrio of San Pablo, had also hosted many men in his "oratory to celebrate the feast of Saint Nicolas." The many "men congregated in the oratory committed the nefarious sin, danced like women, and cited new dates and places for future gatherings with the pretext of prolonging their nefarious contact." In fact, most of the participants displayed images of the "Virgin Mary and other saints in their private oratories."[160]

Although Miguel Gerónimo denied the denunciations levied against him by Correa and the others, he found it difficult to discredit their testimony. Nonsense, tattled La Estanpa; Miguel Gerónimo had also hosted one of these parties where "they had all committed the nefarious sin." In fact, insisted Correa, the other men "commonly referred to Miguel Gerónimo as La Cangarriana," in reference to his promiscuity, "just like a common whore who lived in the city" known by the same

4.4. **Emulating a beautiful woman.** *Don(Doña) Juan(a) María Romero*, 1794, Ignacio María Barreda. In *Art mexicain du précolombien a nos jours: [catalogue de] l'exposition [au] Musée National d'Art Moderne [Paris]*. Vol. 1. Paris: Les Presses Artistiques, 1952.

pseudonym.[161] Bickering and a biting jealously among the participants who supposedly attended the festive gatherings became evident during the ensuing interrogations.

Su Guapo, Por Puto!

The ensuing denunciations by La Estanpa and Cotita led to the arrest of Nicolas de Pisa, *negro*, also over seventy years old, with whom Correa had jealously quarreled over Nicolás' other *"guapo,"* the name given to "those men with whom they committed these vile acts." Correa also implicated Cristóval de Vitoria, "a Spaniard of over eighty years, missing one eye, half blind of the other, small in stature, bald, and humpbacked." The deformed Vitoria eventually confessed and identified "twenty-three-year-old Gerónimo 'the bald head'" as his *guapo*. Furthermore, declared Vitoria, he had "continuously committed the nefarious sin in this city since the time of the great flood some thirty years ago." He had, however, "lost count of the number of persons he had taught, as had Correa, to commit this harmful sin."[162]

Thus far, colonial officials had interrogated individuals who belonged solely to the laboring classes of the metropolis—identified primarily as *mestizos, negros, mulatos,* and physically deformed Spaniards. The clergy and the aristocracy, two groups that constituted high percentages of sodomy cases prosecuted in the peninsula, remained conspicuously absent from prosecution in the 1657–1658 Mexican cases.

The details offered by accused sodomite Benito de Cuebas, however, suggested that individuals associated with the more accommodated classes in Mexico City possessed a certain knowledge about the particulars of the interrogation and that this certain knowledge might have rendered them immune from prosecution.

The inculpated Benito de Cuebas remained imprisoned eight days before he confessed that "one night before his arrest, as he prayed with his beads, a very handsome and spruce gallant, with a good plight of body, whom he had never before met, called at his quarters and instructed him to flee the city because the colonial authorities had apprehended many of his friends." "But why?" asked the devout Cuebas. "Por putos!" replied the gallant.

The following morning, instead of fleeing the city as instructed by the gallant, Cuebas attended mass at the cathedral, "where he again prayed with his beads in hand and implored the assistance of our lady for his liberation from sin." The beads must have failed Cuebas, for as he exited the cathedral colonial authorities awaited and apprehended him. Cuebas inculpated a number of other less distinguished individuals, some of whom had already fled the city, in what became an active pursuit of sodomites and their property by the colonial authorities.[163]

Diabolical Riffraff

Among the confiscated goods of Miguel de Urbina, "Indio [and] Ladino of good reason," colonial officials "found a statuette of the child Jesus, his face, his back and posterior parts, all burned." Urbina confessed that "one day as he lay in bed with his *india,* just after they had committed a carnal act, he had lamented the absence of the man with whom he commonly communicated with nefariously." Thus, "in a fit of rage, the rabid *indio* took a lit candle in his hand and set fire to the statuette of the holy child" that stood on a small table beside the couple's bed.

The burning of the statuette caused "blotches on the skin, swollen arms, welts, and the same markings as those left on a burned human body." The humanlike welts that "appeared" on the statuette "served notice of God's omnipresence and his disdain for the evils of *sodomía,*" wrote Sotomayor. The torched statuette remained in the "possession of His Excellency, the lord magistrate" of the Mexican High Court.[164]

The viceroy duke Francisco Fernández de la Cueva provided more comforting words to the monarchy. In his letter to Carlos II the viceroy duke confirmed that the "actors and patients, without the need to submit any of them to torture, had confessed the incredibly vile circumstances of their nefarious sins, some having committed it for over forty years." Each of these men had "at least one accomplice or one live witness who testified against him." Two surgeons, of "great and indisputable repute," examined "each of the nineteen sinful bodies." "Indeed," the duke reported, the doctors "had found the bodies quite used and corrupted." However, reassured the duke, his king need not despair for "no men of their fabric nor those of the black cloth found themselves among the convicted, all of whom represented *mestizos, indios, mulatos, negros,* or the riffraff of this empire and city."[165]

Sotomayor's initial interrogations led to the arrest of fifteen men. Despite the pleas of the lawyers for the defense, His Majesty's High Court sentenced fourteen of the fifteen to burn at the stake and confiscated all their goods."[166] In addition to Juan de la Vega, Correa, Miguel Gerónimo, Durán, Chaves, Pisa, Vitoria, Gerónimo Calbo, and Cuebas, the court also convicted Domingo de la Cruz Indio; Matheo Gaspar Indio; Juan Martín Indio; Miguel de Urbina Indio; Juan de Ycita Indio; and Lucas Matheo Mestizo (Fig. 4.5).[167]

Memoria de los à Iusticiados Por auer cometido el pecado
nefando Cuia causa fulmino el S.r L.do Don Ju.o manuel de Sotom.r
Caballero de la orden de Calatraua, del Conseio de Su Mag.d Su alcalde
en esta corte que Sentensio la R.l Sala del crimen en quatro de
este año de mill y seis cientos Zincuenta y ocho. los catorze conuistos y confesos
y otro conuisto que despues estando en la capilla Confeso y auno
dellos por menor de quinze años se sentensio en doscientos acotes y
vendido en minas Por tiempo de Seis años. Cuios nombres son los sig.tes

　　　— Juan de la uega galiano mulato por chonombre
　　　Cotita
　　　— Germo Cauuo mestiso ————
　　　— Joseph Duran mestiso ————
　　　— miguel Germo mestiso. este es el conuisto quicon
　　　feso estando en la capilla —
　　　— Simon de chaues Yndio ————
　　　— Juan uera mestiso ————
　　　— Nicolas pisa negro ————
　　　— domingo de la cruz Yndio ————
　　　— matheo gaspar Yndio ————
　　　— Benito de Cueuas mulato ————
　　　— Xpoual de Vitoria español ————
　　　— Juan martin Yndio ————
　　　— Ju.o mizita Yndio ————
　　　— miguel durbina indio. este quemo la echura de
　　　un santo niño Jesus ————
　　　— Lucas matheo mestiso. el es el menor a q.en se dio
　　　con dos cientos acotes ————

Presos Por este delito en la R.l carzel cuyas causas
Se estan substan siando
　　　— Juan del castillo mestiso ————
　　　— fran melchor indio ————
　　　— Juan de la cruz indio ————
　　　— fran R.o soldado ————
　　　— Simon de morales mulato ————
　　　— Joseph de aumada mestiso ————
　　　— Nicolas mulato mudo ————
　　　— Lorenso R.o castiso guantero ————
　　　— Don ant.o de las casas ————

4.5. **List of the accused in the 1657–1658 Mexico City sodomy trials.** *Memoria de los ajustisiados por haver cometido el pecado nefando, 14 diciembre 1658, México, 38, N 57C.* Reproduced with the permission of the Archivo General de Indias, Seville.

The High Court capitulated to the requests of the defense attorneys and in a display of leniency sentenced Lucas Matheo, a fifteen-year-old boy, to "two hundred lashes and six years of forced mortar labor." Nine other men remained in prison, awaiting the outcome of their cases (Fig. 4.6), and the High Court had summoned another 106 men listed in an appendix of the accused to appear before the tribunal. Sotomayor concluded: "The Tribunal of the Holy Inquisition has interrogated its prisoners and the Ordinary Ecclesiastical had discovered that this mortal, nefarious, and habitual disease had also spread among them . . . may lord our God save your royal Catholic Majesty." [168]

For his part, the scrivener concluded his report by noting: ". . . on that given day in 1658, as the authorities led the fifteen men to the site of execution, Gerónimo spontaneously admitted having committed the *sin contra natura* . . . and . . . they all burned, save one, Lucas Matheo, who received his 200 lashes in the presence of the bonfire." [169]

A Parting Thought

In seventeenth-century Mexico City, the viceroy count, the duke, and their magistrates confronted a "cultural fact"—transvestism, or dressing outside one's prescribed gender role.[170] On the one hand, Cotita and La Estanpa, as modes of self-construction, rejected the cultural representations of manliness based on class, ethnicity, gender, or religion.[171] For them, the borderline between manly and unmanly became permeable and permitted their "border crossings from one category to another." The cross-dressed *mestizas* functioned as marks of "gender undecidability." [172]

From the moment that Columbus and Cortés began to document their perceived differences of Indios, the presence of sodomites, of the transvestite in the Indias, signaled "a category crisis that caused the colonial officials to experience cultural anxiety." The boys and men who dressed like women and performed the labors of women, aptly portrayed by the colonial chroniclers, "embodied symbols of overdetermination and became mechanisms of displacement" for the colonial state. These men and their cultures deconstructed the "binary pole of man-woman" and in the process jeopardized the "national binaries and power relations" of imperial Spain and colonial Mexico.[173]

The auto-emasculation adhered to by a cadre of Mexican sodomites in 1657–1658 facilitated a challenge, albeit limited and contradictory, to the dominance of specific Spanish gender politics. Moreover, the anomalies in gender politics and the cross-dressed *mestizas'* struggle for legitimacy in the metropolis of Mexico also revealed that the self-perception

4.6. Frontispiece of the 1657–1658 Mexico City sodomy trials. *Testimonio de las causas contra los culpados en el pecado nefando, 14 diciembre 1658, México, 38, N 57B.* Reproduced with the permission of the Archivo General de Indias, Seville.

of effeminacy, neatly constructed alongside categories of, say, class or ethnicity, is itself an expression of "hegemonic aspiration" or the "paradox of the subalternity." [174]

Cotita and the *antipodas* both accepted and resisted the Spanish colonial politics of manliness that cast them in the unenviable position of effeminate sodomites—a discourse employed by early modern moralists to buttress Spain's just causes of colonial domination.

EPILOGUE

He Died of a Broken Heart

IN THIS BOOK, I have attempted to demonstrate how the prosecutions of sodomites in Spain/New Spain were intertwined with perceptions of manliness, a historical phenomenon inextricably linked to cultural shifts—religious, political, economic—in the imperial sphere. The first royal sodomy *Pragmática* of the early modern period, issued in 1497, marked a rupture with the libertinism afforded sodomitical practices in the peninsula in previous decades. This decree, in addition to subsequent royal sodomy *Pragmáticas* and other historical occurrences, such as the reconquest of the Spanish peninsula from the infidel Moors, the exile of Jews, and the discovery of America Septentrionalis in 1492—all represented political disruptions that would signal the emergence of Spain's quest for empire.

If the year 1492 had represented the "invention" of "América"—the descriptions of a continent and its inhabitants as defined by Spanish customs and laws—it also marked the start of Europe's attempt to assimilate the "other."[1] In short: the other in one's self; the otherness of groups within the society in which one lives and to which one does not belong; and the other in terms of language and customs. Todorov sensed a correlation between the violent denial of the exterior other in America and the discovery of an inner other within European society and within the European individual.[2]

Columbus initiated the fictionalization of the Indias based on earlier models of the exuberant and the unknown attributed to the other. Mid-sixteenth-century humanists like Campanella, who championed a Spanish universal monarchy to defend Christendom, or Vitoria, who described the Indios as barbarians, provided Spain with many of its underpinnings in support of empire that were termed "just causes" for colonial domination. Other Spanish sycophants like Ginés de Sepúlveda, Bartolomé de las Casas, López de Gómara, or those self-fashioned moralists who associated themselves with the Second Scholastic "loathed the unknown and the culturally different, sometimes described as savage, monstrous, even *contra natura.*" Their writings would spearhead the peninsula's attempt to reconfigure its politics and culture(s).[3]

The perfect Spanish Vir envisioned by the early modern moralists and the sodomite drawn as impotent by many colonial manuscripts functioned in different, often contradictory historical contexts, but also as part of the same historical process—the changes of Spain–New Spain's "global political economy." Contextualizing historical formations like Spanish manliness or sodomites within this global category of analysis has allowed one to go beyond "reductive choices" in political critiques concerned with isolated aspects of social relations.[4]

A contextualized study of the interactions among a manly Spaniard, sodomy, and effeminate sodomites has demonstrated that metropolitan and colonial histories are both often constituted by the history of imperialism. Perceptions of manliness and of sodomites are best understood in relation to one another or as constitutive of each other and not from the framework of discrete national cultures. My focus on notions of manliness as the site for understanding the organization of power in Spain–New Spain attempted a fuller understanding of the "multiplicities of political, economic and ideological domination and subordination in a colonial setting."[5]

The recasting of these political formations within a broader paradigm also refines the historiography on Spain–New Spain by shedding light on their own interaction in an age of imperialism. Imperialist-colonialist politics have demonstrated that perceptions of manliness had as much to do with racial, class, religious, and national differences as with sex difference.[6] In this sense, I have recognized the "imbrication of gender in a variety of different axes of power—to one that does not proceed from a priority given to gender and expanded to include other social relations."[7]

The sodomy narratives discussed in the previous chapters provided some examples of how religion, xenophobia, and ethnicity complicated the politics of imperialism and its intersection with gender perceptions. Whereas my discussion of Bartholomé-Mule highlighted xenophobic politics as an important context for manliness, the Mexican narratives exposed gender identities in terms of the role of class and ethnic identity as the important contexts for understanding manliness.

Perceptions of *sodomie* and of *sodomitas* differed and changed in context both in the peninsula and in the viceroyalty.[8] One commonly held assumption of colonial Latin American society is that postconquest institutions and values crystallized at the end of the sixteenth century and remained stable until the middle of the eighteenth century, a period often referred to as the "mature colonial period" or the "baroque era."[9] However, the institutions of social control and cultural values of colonial

Spanish society both altered significantly throughout the early modern period.

In the peninsula, magistrates and writers alike focused primarily on the sexual object of sodomitical desire—another boy, another man—and on erotic style, repeatedly depicted as penetration of the anus or the wasteful spillage of semen. These focuses were part of the effort to codify sodomitical acts as a sin and crime *contra natura.* These officials associated sodomitical practices as an inherent commodity of foreigners and as something far removed from the chivalrous Spanish Man. Early modern perceptions of manliness, of *sodomie,* and of *sodomitas* had a solid Spanish point of reference.

By the mid-seventeenth century, writers in support of the Spanish Empire fabricated new perceptions of sodomy to reflect Spain's growing colonial ambitions. In New Spain, writers inextricably associated sodomy with notions of anthropophagy, human sacrifices, and effeminacy. Although peninsular writers like De León had also associated sodomy and effeminacy, other moralists nonetheless tended to associate sodomitical practices with the favored manly fellows rather than with the effeminate sodomite—an object of colonial derision. The peninsular focus on effeminacy to distinguish the Mexico City sodomite from the sexually virile peninsular sodomite exposed the contradictions of a discourse that attempted to link sodomitical practices with a distinct homosocial personality defined in terms of "effeminacy and lack of manly virility." [10]

Moreover, the presence of effeminate sodomites in seventeenth-century Mexico City signaled a category crisis and caused colonial officials to experience cultural anxiety. So-called self-identified effeminate sodomites like Cotita and La Estanpa in the metropolis might have represented an attempt at self-reflection, a search for the self outside the prescribed social order—a transgression of hierarchy between the colonial subject and the colonizer. [11] To have perceived oneself from the Spanish perspective of effeminacy implied from the "inception a devaluation" of the periphery from the center. [12] The self-appropriated emasculation represented by Cotita and La Estanpa facilitated a challenge, however limited and contradictory, to the dominance of Spain's colonial politics.

Anomalies in gender politics and Cotita's struggle for legitimacy also revealed what Chatterjee has labeled the "paradox of the subalternity," for the self-perception of effeminacy is itself an expression of "hegemonic aspiration" or "access to imperial and religious forms of power in early modern society." [13] Sodomites on both sides of the Atlantic constantly negotiated and articulated their cultural space. In the process of this articulation, they sometimes incorporated the discourses of the colonizer by appropriation, imitation, acceptance, and negation, oftentimes simultaneously.

Perceptions of the perfect Spanish Man helped mark notions of cowardice and effeminacy—two historical formations of the Second Scholastic, a vision that attributed submissiveness and docility to the Indios, given the relative ease with which the Spaniards conquered extensive territories in the New Spain.[14] The Spaniards' effeminization of the Indios and of sodomites actually "displaced and idealized their subjection" by reducing their relationship with the center to that of a tutor-pupil status.

Indios and effeminate sodomites—by nature analogous to women— inherited their positions of submission because of their own spiritual and manly immaturities.[15] Furthermore, early modern moralists sexualized reason as a manly attribute and relegated emotion and passion as womanly functions, points notably exemplified by the actions of the chivalrous Alonso Díaz/Catalina de Erauso.

After his departure from Spain in the mid-seventeenth century, Díaz again set sail for New Spain, returning as a muleteer and assuming the new pseudonym "Antonio de Erauso," a change granted with the permission of Pope Urbano VIII. In 1645, as Erauso meandered in and around Veracruz, with a "pack of mules and a couple of *negros* transporting textiles to different parts of Mexico," Fray Nicolás de la Rentería spoke with "Don Antonio." To the friar, Antonio de Erauso "appeared to be about fifty years old, with a good plight of a body, olive-skinned and with some little hairs in the form of a moustache." Rentería also reported that Erauso "wore the apparel of men and carried a sword or type of dagger with silver trimming."[16]

Antonio de Erauso eventually fell in love with a young lady he had transported between Veracruz and the metropolis of Mexico. The young lady's parents had entrusted Antonio with her care even though they understood that Erauso "dressed like a man." The passion Antonio fostered for the young girl caused him great distress and almost culminated in a duel with another gallant who eventually married the girl. In his challenge to the gallant, Erauso wrote: "When persons of my fabric call upon others, their noble status assures them the correct treatment, my status has not exceeded the limits required of your lordship, it is inconceivable to prohibit me from calling upon your lordship in your home, furthermore, I am informed that if I walk upon your street you will have me killed. Although I am a woman, my valor impossible for you to conceive, I shall await you, alone, behind San Diego from one until six." [17]

Fortunately for both gallants, a group of influential men impeded the encounter. In 1650 the muleteer from San Sebastián died a quiet death in Cuitlaxtala, and in 1653 "the widow of Bernardo Calderon" commemorated the heroics of Antonio de Erauso in a relation published in Mexico City.

"If with just reason, the eternal memory and the perpetual recollection of the heroics and victories realized by illustrious men in the name of their king and their lord are worthy of remembrance," wrote the widow, one should "marvel at their victories assured by their noble blood and by their natural superiority. [T]hey merit distinctions and their fame soars." The widow concluded, "But for a woman—by nature all so weak and with desperate dispositions—with the appearance of a man, . . . [a woman who had] labored so long and so hard after performing many manly trades, worthy of the most valiant soldier, she not only merits recognition, but, more so, admiration." [18]

The manly Antonio had simply died of a broken heart. Subaltern figures like Antonio de Erauso and Cotita might have contested gender roles in Spain–New Spain, but they nonetheless also affirmed the state's discourses about manliness.

APPENDIX I

NATURA ARMADA

Las declaraciones de Cristóbal Gutiérrez de Triana y Gaspar Hernández, Portuges negro grumete, quemado en la mar el 20 de junio de 1560.

En la mar el golfo del mar oceano yiendo por los reinos de castilla en la nao santa maria el magnifico señor d. Alonzo de las Ruelas almirante ante mi Andres Rodriguez escribano . . . para informase de cierto delito que se ha cometido en la dicha nao por Gaspar portuges grumete hizo la informacion siguiente . . . xbal Gutierrez paje menor de edad de catorce años siendo preguntado por el almirante que es lo que paso y sabe de este caso.

Dixo . . . que la noche pasada que se contaron trienta e vn dias del mes de mayo proximo pasado que fue viernes en la noche que podria ser a las once horas de la noche . . . se echo a dormir en el castillo de proa y estado dormido entre Juan de Triana y Gaspar grumete . . . y estado dormido entre los susodichos recordo con los calçones desamarrados e caydos a baxo e visto esto se espanto . . . y se porsinava porque otras dos o tres noches se los habia hallado de aquella manera y se los torno alzar como sustencia y metio la camisa debaxo de ellos y se torno a hechar a dormir . . . y antes que se tornase a dormir vio como Gaspar le abajaba los calçones y le alzo la camisa y se hacercaba a el . . . y se lo queira hazer . . . y este testigo se bolvio para el y le dixo esas manias que teneis vellaco yo se lo dire al maestre e al piloto.

Preguntado si este vesava en la boca a Gaspar dixo que nunca le veso sino Gaspar vesava muchas veces a este de bajo de la vernia en la boca.

Ante el sn. general y siendo preguntado como se llama dixo que Gaspar natural de villanueva de portiman . . . grumete del navio corchapin . . . preguntado que si conoce a xbal dixo que si de un mes a esta parte poco mas o menos . . . si ha cometido con el [xbal] el pecado contra natura y si lo havia cavalgado alguna vez por el culo . . . dixo que no . . . que si anoche le desato los calçones a xbal paje y cuantas otras vezes se los ha desatado intentando cometer con el el pecado contra natura . . . dixo que anoche el no le desato los calçones ni otra ninguna vez.

Preguntado si anoche le alzo las faldas y le hecho la pierna encima y le alzo la camisa para quererlo cavalgar y le bajo los calçones llendo ar-

[189]

mada su natura dixo que no le desato ni le baxo los calçones mas de que entre suenos le hecho la pierna por encima a xbal . . . preguntado si xbal le tomo a este confesante su natura en la mano fuera de lo los calçones estando arrecho y hecho voces y si le dixo este confesante que callase y no dixese nada dixo que cuando xbal comenzo a hechar voces le dixo calla muchacho y dixo que muchas veces han dormido juntos asi en proa como en popa.

Preguntado si ha mucho tiempo ha de que usa este oficio de puto si con xbal como con otras personas . . . dixo que nunca tal ha hecho con xbal ni con otras personas . . . y que es de edad de veinte y vn andos pocos mas o menos y no firmo porque dixo que no savia excribir.

E despues aviendo visto Gaspar ser menor de veinte y cinco años el sñ. general le mando ser curador a Guillermo de Cuellar . . . y dixo el sñ. general que condenava a Gaspar a tormenta para que diga e declare la verdad de lo que con xbal a echo e cometido en el dicho pecado e si lo a cometido con otras personas y en que partes e lugares . . . y parecio Guillermo de Cuellar . . . e pidio su merced que Gaspar no es persona que tal pecado huvieze acometer con xbal . . . y pide suspenda el negocio asta tanto que tenga letrado que le aconseje . . . porque su merced es cavallero y no letrado y que no se le de tormento alguno a Gaspar . . . porque si algun braço o pierna o costilla se le quebrara de su persona . . . o muriese en el tormento sea a cargo del sñ. general.

El sñ. general dixo que sin embargo se cumpla lo mandado asta que Gaspar diga la verdad . . . e luego fue trayda una escalera y en ella fue puesto Gaspar . . . y Nicolas frances le començo amarrar los braços uno con el otro y dieronsele diez y ocho bueltas y por mi el escribano requeri a Gaspar que dicese la verdad . . . que si en el tormento algun braço o pierna se le quebrase o se le descoyuntase algun miembro o muriese en la tormenta no fuese a cargo del sñ. general . . . e los braços se le amarraron a la escalera e començandole apretar una buelta . . . y yo requeri a Gaspar dixese la verdad . . . Cuellar dixo que nunca tal hiziera y el sñ. general mando amarrar los muslos y las piernas y amarrados le começo Nicolas apretarle . . . fue requerido otra vez . . . Cuellar dixo que nunca tal hiziera y apretados todos los cordeles no confeso nada y el sñ. general le mando dar el agua.

Le fue puesto un pañuelo en el rostro y dentro en la boca y le fuese echado un jarro de agua y luego el sñ. general le mando echar mas jarros de agua y se le charon siete jarrilos de agua por todos y al cada uno de los jarrillos de agua le fue requerido por mi el escribano dixese la verdad . . .

e luego el sñ. general mando quitar a Gaspar de la escalera y que sea llevado encima de la cubierta para darle el tormento de garrucha . . . e Cuellar requerio a su merced que Gaspar esta muy peligroso de mal de muerte
del tormento . . . que su merced de mande suspender el tormento de garrucha asta sean pasadas veinte y cuatro oras . . . y el sñ. general dixo que
porque Gaspar esta mal tratado del tormento le suspende el tormento
asta manana.

E despues en çinco dias . . . el sñ. general mando traer a Gaspar e
mando le sea dado tormento de garrucha . . . e Cuellar dixo que pedia e
requeria a su merced una dos o tres vezes . . . que por quanto la ynfor-
macion contra Gaspar no es bastante para aberle de dar mas tormento . . .
esta quebrado y se le podrian salir las tripas y que su merced es cavallero
y no letrado . . . pide no sele de mas tormento . . . asta que su merced tome
letrado [al margen] auto que sin embargo . . . el sñ. general dixo que man-
dava se le de tormento porque Gaspar no quiere declarar la verdad y ser
el caso ynorme e feo.

E luego . . . le fueron atadas con un pedaço de lienco canamaco las
manos atras muy bien por las muñecas y le ataron un cabo de canamo que
estava pasado por la garrucha la qual estava atada a la entena de la verga
mayor y le començaron a ysar . . . y el sñ. general mando que hiçasen y
estuviendo en lo alto le fue tornado dixese la verdad . . . y el sñ. general
mando lanzar y cayo en seco y luego torno a mandar yzar . . . hasta lo alto
junto a la garrucha y estuviendo alli el sñ. general mando que hiçasen y
estuviendo en lo alto le fue tornado dixese la verdad . . . y el sñ. general
mando largar el cabo el qual cayo en seco y Gaspar dixo baxenme que
yo dixo la verdad y el sñ. general mando a maynar a Gaspar asta lo poner
sentado sobre la jareta de la nao capitana y mando que todas personas
que estavan por alli cerca se apartasen y solamente quedaron Gaspar el sñ.
general y Garcia de Cuellar alguacil real y yo el escribano.

Gaspar dixo que ante dios lo que en el caso pasa es que este confesante entro en el navio corchapin en el puerto de la ciudad de san juan de
puerto rico por grumete y que xbal paje le acometio a que este confesante
lo cabalgase por el culo y que xbal le tomo con su mano la pija a este y se
la metio el propio por su culo ayudandole este y que dentro del puerto de
puerto rico dentro en el navio le cabalgo una bez por el culo este a xbal y
que la noche que el muchacho xbal dize que lo quiso cabalgar por el culo
que es verdad que este le baxo lo calçones y le alzo la camisa arriva por
quererlo cabalgar por el culo pero que no lo hizo y que todo esto sentio
muy bien e lo consentio xbal y que tambien xbal a cabalgado por el culo

a este confesante tres veces pusiendose sobre este . . . Preguntado cuantas veces cabalgo este confesante a xbal por el culo dixo que asta dos o tres veces.

Acabado de confessar Gaspar con el fray Juan nombro por su albazea para que aga bien por su anima a Juan Amador al qual dio derecho en tal caso para que cobre el sueldo que gana e declara que deja en poder de Martin marinero dos capotes y unos calçones de paño azules y una camisa u unos zapatos lo qual manda que Juan Amador lo cobre e lo benda y que juntamente con el sueldo . . . de la mitad de ello agabien y su animo de la otra mitad pague a mi el escribano por el trabajo.

En veinte dias del mes de junio saliendo su merced garrando del puerto de la villa de la playa que es en la isla de la tierra por se azer a la vela mando se execute la sentencia contra Gaspar . . . e se saco a Gaspar de la nao capitana con los soldados de guardia en el batel y se llevo a donde avia ser quemado con pregonero que pregonava su delito y llegando donde le avian de dar garrote al tiempo que se lo quieran dar dixo que mirase en lo que en su confision avia dicho contra xbal . . . el dicho xbal no lo cabalgo mas que lo quiso cabalgar porque burlava con Gaspar y que Gaspar cabalgo por el culo a xbal siete o ocho vezes y . . . dixo que xbal se algava de que Gaspar lo cabalgase por el culo y que lo consentia . . . e luego le fue dado garrote hasta que naturalmente fue muerto por el negro grumete de la nao capitana y despues fue puesto en un batel de alquitran encima de una tabla y le fue pegado fuego y se quemo y tardo en quemarse y arder mas de media hora.

Luego, Juan Bautista curador de xbal dixo que la sentencia pronunciada xontra xbal apelo de ella para ante su majestad e ante quales quier juezes e justicias de su magestad.

Proceso contra Cristoval, grumete de la nao Escorchapin sobre haber cometido el pecado nefando con Gaspar, grumete de la misma nao, 1560–1561, AGI, Justicia, 1181, N2, R5, fols. 2r–19v.

APPENDIX 2

TENTANDO PIJAS Y SIESOS: COMO SE CONFIRMA EL DERRAMAMIENTO DE LA SUCIEDAD

En Sevilla en la casa de la contratación a dos dias de septiembre de mill y seis zientos e tres años los señores presidente e oydores del la real audiencia de la dicha casa dixeron que . . . un mulato llamado Gerónimo Ponce que fue traydo de las yndias a la carcel real por culpado en el pecado nefando a buelto a ynzidir y cometer el dicho pecado con otro mulato cautibo que ansimismo esta preso en la carcel . . . y conbiene se haga averiguacion y castiguen los culpados como la gravedad del delito lo rrequiere . . . y mandaron que a los mulatos los aparten en la dicha carcel.

Confision de Domingo López . . . esclavo de hedad de veinte años . . . preguntado si es verdad que su amo truxo a este a la carcel de esta casa y dixo que este tenia todas las tardad y maldades que podia aver y para que ninguna le faltasse tambien yera puto . . . dixo que es verdad y le parece que su amo solamente dixo que no tenia esta falta.

Si es verdad que este entro en el aposento del servicio y tras del Gerónimo Ponce el qual le puso la mano por el rostro y por la garganta y le hizo el amor diziendole que avia quince dias que no se lo avia a hecho a nadie y que estava arrecho . . . dixo que es verdad que Ponce le llamo que se subiese arriba y este fue arriva con el a su aposento y le dixo Ponce a este que le rascase las espaldas y este se bolbio y le començo a rascalle las espaldas y Ponce le tentava y le dixo como no te quitas los calçones y dixo este que para que se lo avia de quitar y otra vez le torno a tentar metiendole la mano en la bragueta tentandole las carnes por los muslos y le yba a tentar el miembro y este no lo quiso consentir y se bolbio del otro lado.

Avto . . . su señoria mando llamar al verdugo de esta ciudad para que ponga a quistion de tormento a Domingo desnudandole para el dicho efecto . . . estando el sotalcaide quitandole los grillos dixo Domingo que queria dezir la verdad . . . que despues de estar quitados los calçones Ponce se subio enzima de este estando boca avaxo y abiendole alzado la camisa le dixo este que abia de dar bozes y Ponce dixo que callase sino que lo achogaria con lo qual este estubo quedo y Ponce llego a metelle el miembro por el culo y estando este quedo Ponce hizo fuerça por meterselo ajarrando a este de los hombros para el efecto y haziendo fuerça para metello y metio la punta del myembro porque lo demas no le cabia por ser gordo y despues de aver acavado se hallo este moxado el culo de la simyente que le avia echado Ponce y echo esto se recostaron en sus camas . . . y luego yncontinente fue mandado sacar de la sala donde estava el potro de el tormento a Domingo y llevallo a otra sala para que en presençia de su curador se ratificasse en la confision.

> *Causa seguida de oficio de la Casa de la Contratación por el s[eñor] fiscal contra Gerónimo Ponce mulatto y Domingo López sobre haver cometido el pecado nefando de sodomía, Sevilla, 1603, AGI, Escribanía 1075C, N17, fols. 1r–14v.*

Con un dedo puede

Declaracion de Alonso Prieto paje de 13 años . . . E luego torno Anton de Fuentes lombardero con una bela enzendida y se entro debaxo de cubierta donde Alonso estava e despues fue hazia la parte destribor de la urca y Alonso tras el e llegando junto a unas sillas de cavallo Anton tomo una de las sillas en las manos y metio la mano debaxo de las sillas e saco un poco de estropa y la chamusco un poco con la lambre de la vela y luego apagola con una tabla que traya en las manos y luego Anton le dijo a este desatacate y este se desataco los calçones y hizolo echar de pechos sobre unas pipas . . . y le abaxo los calçones y le alço la camisa y le tomo la natura en las manos e se la blandeaba entre las manos e le tentava las berijas e luego le començo a tenar las nalgas y el culo y le començo con la estropilla quemada a vritar el culo y las verijas y le metia un dedo por el culo e se lo estruxava con las manos y le preguntava a este sy lo sentia y este respondio que si y despues de averselo bien sobado y apalpado saco lo suyo de su bragueta e luego se lo ameter en el culo y como este confesante lo sintio que se lo metia desviose del y tomo sus calçones e se los alço y se los ataco yendo huyendo del . . . y llego a el Anton e juntas las manos le dixo calla por amor de dios no digas nada que yo te lo pagare y dare quanto quisieses y este le dixo que es tal me avia [des de hazer] hera por moro o hereje no lo tengo de dejar de dezir a my señor el maestre.

Ratificacion de Alonso Prieto . . . preguntado que en que sintio o vio este confesante que hera la natura e miembro genital de Anton que se lo queria meter por el sieso e si le lastimo . . . dixo que quando llego con el dedo a meterselo por el culo de este sintio bien que era el dedo por quando bolvio con su natura como hera gordo sintio que hera su natura y miembro genital por donde mea porque como le llego a apretar por el ojo del culo y este lo sintio porque quiso thener con el aceso carnal por el sieso donde haze sus necesidades . . . e que nunca le hizo sangre ni lastimo porque este confesante no le dio lugar . . . el señor general mando traer ante si a Anton.

Confesion de Anton de Fuentes . . . Cádiz 2 mayo 1562 . . . natural de Barcelona desde hace 15 años es marinero, de edad de triente años poco mas o menos . . . preguntado a que efecto metio los dedos en el sieso de Alonso por la parte e lugar donde haze sus necesidades . . . dixo que le miro e toco en las verijas y no le toco en la dicha natura como le pudo tocar andando con las manos junto a ello este no le toco particularmente ni le palpo ni sobo . . . dixo que no le puso los dedos en el sieso . . . preguntado que si puso su natura en el sieso de Alonso el qual dixo que me hazeis soy moro o turco y entonces se desvio huyendo . . . dixo que no pasa tal cosa.

Madrid 4 julio 1562 . . . Anton de Fuentes condenado a dos años de suspension de la carrera de las yndias con officio ni sueldo y no lo quebranta so pena de suspension perpetua . . . y a los gastos del proceso . . . Alonso Prieto menor . . . le absolvemos de la acusacion contra el puesta y damosle por libre.

Sevilla, año de 1562, Proceso criminal fecho por el ilustre Señor Pedro Menendez de Aviles General de Armanda contra Anton de Fuentes y Alonso Prieto sobre el pecado nefanda y haver intentado cometer el pecado nefando en la misma embarcacion, AGI, Justicia, 855, NII, n.p.

El mete mano

Declaracion de Pedro Diaz paje . . . dixo que se llego Juan Fernandez piloto y le tomo la pixa con su mano y depues Fernandez le dixo a este pues ven tu aca echate conmigo esta noche por amor de mi pierna que tengo mala y este se echo en la cama . . . y como a la medianoche estando este durmiendo se echo Fernandez sobre este estando echado de pechos y le puso a este su pixa en las nalgas que le queria cavalgar estando arrecho y este no lo consyntio y se yva desbiando del y Fernandez le dezia que estuvese quedo . . . y Fernandez le tomo la pixa estando durmiendo le hizo la puñeta hasta que le hiziere verter suziedad y cuando desperto le dixo que se avia meado e que en su vida le avia sucedido aver hecho tal cosa e que se acuerda que era de noche y estava durmiendo toda la gente y llovio aquella noche . . . y a otro grumete Fernandez le tentava su cuerpo y le tomava con su mano la pixa y los cojones y lo beso algunas vezes y algunas noches se hallo el grumete los muslos llenos de suziedad que avia salido de su pixa o de la de Fernandez . . . y se hallava la cama manchada de la suziedad y en estas noches le dezia que le llevaria a su tierra y le honraria y casaria y este le dezia que ansi lo haria y que se lo agradecia y a oydo dezir a Lazaro y a Salas y a Sauzedo y a Martin pajes que Fernandez los avia hecho echar junto a si y les abia tomado sus pixas y queridoles cabalgar y que hizo al uno dellos salir suziedad de su pixa y estando Salas y Fernandez en la despensa solos le dixo Fernandez si se avia rapado el pendejo porque dias antes le avia dicho que se lo quitase y que el le daria navaje y le metio la mano y le tomo la pixa y le estuvo dando en ella con los dedos hasta que le hizo arrechar y como este vio lo que le hacia se salio de alli y se fue y estandole esta ves dando en la pixa y arrecho le hizo caer dos otroas gotas de suziedad por la pixa.

Juan Fernandez natural de Ayamonte, casado con Juana Ruiz, maestre y piloto en esta carrera de las yndias y que su officio es marinero . . . de cuarenta años . . . conoce a los pajes que testificaban contra el . . . dixo que es verdad que Pedro durmio en su cama muchas noches por amor del provecho que sentia en su pierna y en estas noches le hazia cosquillas e le tentava de la pixa y de los cojones y algunas vezes estava arrecho pero que nunca vio suziedad en los muslos de Pedro . . . dixo que es verdad que Sauzedo se echo junto a el y vio descubierto a Sauzedo los calcones descosydos y la pixa y los cojones de fuera y estando Sauzedo arrecho y el le puso las manos en la dicha pixa y le cubrio luego . . . dixo que es verdad que Lazaro se echo junto a el por el beneficio que recibie de ello . . . e que jugava con el haziendole cosquillas e tomandole la pixa en la mano . . . dixo que es verdad que con Martin se echo ciertas noches una cama y le tentava la pixa e cojones y que . . . es verdad que le tomo tanbien la pixa e los cojones e estiraba del pendejo porque lo thenia largo . . . que como Salas traya unos caragueles roxos abiertos por la pierna se veaya muchas veces la pixa y el llegaba a taparsela y se la tentava con la mano y los otros no trayan tanto pendejo como Salas y que lo demas niega.

Sevilla, año 1566, El fiscal de S[u] M[agestad] con Pedro Fernández grumete S[ob]re que le acusa haver cometido el pecado nefando, AGI, Justicia, 882, N2, fols. 1r–52v.

Ano Horribilis

Cadiz en quatro dias de junio de 1698 . . . D. Juan de Lima alferez de la real armada dijo que la noche veynte y nuebe de mayo siendo como ora de las nuebe y media estando senando llamaron al testigo y haviendo salido hallo que estava Pedro Juan Banjarres marinero quien manifesto al testigo que en vno de los coys havian visto que vn hombre que abordo lla-

man Bartolo el rubio havia cometido el pecado de sodomia con vn muchacho que tambien estava en dicho coy y hizo que buscasen al tal muchacho y luego lo hizo aprehender y llevar al castillo de proa y al dia siguiente vino aborde de dicho navio D. Alejandro Fita zirujano major de la
nao con orden de su senoria para que registrase al muchacho y el testigo
hizo traer y manisfestar para este efecto delante de dicho zirujano major
aque concurrio tambien y se hallo presente D. Miguel Ybanez zirujano
del navio San Ygnacio y entonces el testigo bolvio a amonestar al muchacho dijese la verdad y el muchacho avnque se estubo escusando mucho
tiempo confesso que era verdad que Bartolo la noche del dia veynte y
nuebe lo havia cojido en vno de los dos coys donde estava desnudo acostado y le havia metido el Miembro Mate por el culo y havia estado sobre
el cavalgandolo asta que llegaron vnos marineros de la nao y entre ellos
los dos que havian estado aquella noche en el fogon y tambien manifesto
el muchacho que havian executado con el lo mismo Felipe Esmirla cuio
era el coy en que solia dormir cavalgandolo por detras todas las noches
que dormian juntos y que en vna ocasion le havia cojido Juan Bauptista
Pino en el alojamiento de la nao y tambien lo havia cavalgado.

E luego D. Alejandro Fita zirujano mayor dixo que . . . a bordo de dicho navio el alferez hizo traer el muchacho que es de hedad al parecer
como de catorce anos alto rubio pelada la caveza . . . y como abergonzado
dixo y manifesto era cierto la noche del dia antecedentte estava acostado
desnudo en cueros en vno de dos coys que haviendose dormido le cojio
en el coy Bartolo y le metio el miembro natural por el culo y lo estubo
cavalgando y que vnos de los que acudieron le dio con la mano por que
lo quiso reconoser y no obstante dos le reconosieron pasandole las manos
por la trasera e hizo el testigo desnudar al muchacho haviendole reconosido las partes esternas del ano reconosio que y vio estaban todas Vlse-
radas con vnas Vlseras sordidas y callosas señales de que havian con el
cometido muchas veces el pecado de sodomia por estar todo relajado y
avista de eso el testigo le dijo tu no empiesas aora a que respondio el dicho muchacho que era verdad porque en vna plaza lebante vn alferez lo
havia cavalgado por detras los mas de los dias que alli estubo y tambien
que era verdad lo havia cavalgado tambien algunas noches el cosinero
Phelipe Esmirla en cuyo coy y lo firmo.

Cadiz a seis dias del mes de junio . . . su merced aviendo visto los autos mando que para justificasin deello se haga reconosimiento del muchacho a efecto de que conste ber si con el susod[ic]ho se a cometido o no
el pecado nefando y par d[ic]ho reconozimiento nombra a Diego de Flo-

res maestro scrivano . . . su merced estando en d[ic]ha carsel recivio jura-
mento de Diego de Flores . . . dijo aver visto y reconosido al muchacho y
que al parecer del declarante tiene por naturalmente ynposible el que el
muchacho ayga cometido el pecado contra naturam porque no avisto
señales en que demuestre aver entrado miembro todo . . . Flores de hedad
de sesenta años.

Auto. A dies dias del mes de junio su merced bisto las declaraciones
hechas por Fita, Ybanez y Flores y la contraridad mando para mas aver-
giguacion que D. Octavio de Andrea y D. Pedro Cavanes zirujanos re-
conoscan a Juan Mule si con el sea cometido el pecado contra naturam e
luego su merced en la carcel con asistencia del presente scrivano hizo
sacarlo a d[ic]ha quadra para que hiziesen d[ic]ho reconosimiento y aviendo bisto y mirado con todo cuydado dijeron an bisto con todo cuydado al d[ic]ho muchacho y no hallan yndizio ni señal por donde pre-
suman que con el se halla executado el pecado contra naturam ni señales
de averle entrado miembro natural por que no tiene vlseras ni enflama-
ciones ni callos ni desegualdad . . . son de hedad Andrea que es zirujano
en la Almiranta Real de zinquenta y seis y Pedro Cavanes de trienta y
ocho anos y lo firmaron.

Catorce dias de junio . . . su merced aviendolos visto y la opposicion
que ai en las declarasiones y deposiones de los cirujanos mando que todos concurran con asistencia de el scrivano en la carsel donde buelvan a
hacer el reconozimiento del muchacho como esta prevenido en los autos
respecto de hallarse en esta cuidad Fita e Ybanez de buelta del biaje que
hicieron.

Cadiz a diez y seis dias del mes de junio 1698 . . . declaracion de
D. Alexandro Fita, D. Miguel Suares, Diego de Flores, Octavio de Andrea
y Pedro Cabanes todos cirujanos buelvan juntos a reconoser al d[ic]ho
muchacho . . . y reconosido con todo cuidado al muchacho dijeron Fita
y los demas aver visto y reconocido al muchacho cuia vista han executado
en forma anatomica y con los instrumentos que han sido nesesarios para
el reconosimiento interno en presensia de su merced y de mi el escrivano
y su curador y hallaron vn triste sentimiento en la parte sicatris o callo el
qual estava en una mediocridad de interno a externo y por haver en la
parte interna vna interperna la qual no dio lugar a maior bista por el daño
que se le podia seguir de nueba enfermedad y si se quisiese pasar a maior
dilixensia la dejan de hacer y que convienen todoss en que ha pasado en
aquella parte instrumento contundentte que al parecer ha delaserado la
parte y con declarasion disen los d[ic]hos Flores, Cabanes y Andrea que

el reconosimiento antesedente que hicieron jusgaron de externo y no pasaron a hacer las dilixencias que aora con los hierros e ynstrumentos que eran nesesarios por cuia rason entonses a su parecer no pudieron pasar a declara otra cosa ni ahacer el pronostico interno que aora hasen . . . y lo firmaron todos.

Cádiz año de 1698 causa escriptta de oficio de justicia contra Juan Mole, Bartholomé Barres, Juan Baptista Pino, y Phelip Esmirle, sobre decisse, aver cometido todos, el pecado de sodomía con el dicho Juan Mole, AGI, Escribanía, 1105B, fols. 15r–46v.

COTITA QUE ES LO MISMO QUE MARIQUITA Y SUS LINDAS NIÑAS EN LA CIUDAD DE MÉXICO (1657–1658)

Y de las confesiones de los susodichos resulto el prender a Juan de Correa mestizo viejo de mas de setenta años . . . confeso que havia mas de quarenta años que cometia el pecado nefando declarando muchas personas con quien le havia cometido y se le probo que desde de hedad de siete años le cometio y que se alabava de que el siglo presente estava acabando porque no se olgaven en este como en el pasado que el llamaba que era antes que esta ciudad se ynundase porque entozes el dicho Correa dijo que era linda niña y que andava vestido de muger con otros hombres y que se olgaban cometiendo el pecado nefando y a las personas referidad y a otros mozuelos los enseño con las platicas referidas y gastava su hazienda con ellos y los tenia en su casa diciendoles que aunque hera viejo era mui linda niña y que se havia de comer como la rana de cintura para abajo. Correa de mas de setenta años les llavaba los recaudos de dichas visitas y bailava con los susodichos poniendose por la cintura la capa que traia puesta y quebrandose de cintura y quejandose diciendo que yba malo y que llebava mal de madre a la qual los susodichos le regalaban y davan chocolate diciendoles mi alma mi vida y otros requiebros y al Correa le llamaban la estanpa que era el nombre de una dama muy hermosa que hubo en esta ciudad.

Un dia del siendo por la tarde Juana de Herrera mestiza labandera . . . dixo como el juebes proximo pasado veinte y seis de septiembre estando labando en dicha albarrada que es a la parte de san lazaro fuera de esta dicha ciudad havian llegado a ella vnos muchachos dando la gran priesa y diciendole a vozes que fuese a ver vnos hombres que estavan jugando como perros . . . y vio que estavan dos hombres cometiendo el pecado nefando el uno encima del otro quitados los calzones ambos y el que estava encima tapaba al de debajo con la capa que tenia puesta y la dicha muger dixo que no se atrevio a llegar cerca por que no la matasen y que por este miedo solamente conocio a Juan de la Vega mulato que hera el que estava arriba mulato afeminado que le llamaban Cotita que es los mesmo que mariquita . . . y se quebrava de cintura y traia atado un panito ue llaman melindre que usan las mugeres . . . en las aberturas de las mangas de un jubon blanco que traia puesto traya muchas cintas pendientes y que se sentava en el suelo en un estado como muger y que hacia tortillas y lababa y guisaba y le visitavan unos mozuelos aquienes el susodicho llamaba de mi alma mi corazon y los susodichos se sentavan con el y dormian juntos en un aposento y el dicho Juan de la Vega se ofendia sino le llamaban Cotita.

Cometieron este pecado señaladamente los dia de nuestra senora, de los sanctos apostoles y otras festibidades de la yglesia porque los mas dellos tenian en sus oratorios las ymagenes de nustra senora y demas sanctos referidos y con ocasion de celebrar sus fiestas se conbidavan los unos a los otros y assi se juntavan y cometian el pecado nefando y senalaban las otras casas donde celebrar las fiestas y con este pretexto le yban cometiendo y se llamaban los unos a los otros y estrechavan su correspondencia torpe y nefanda.

Testimonio de las causas contra los culpados en el pecado nefando, 14 diciembre 1658, AGI, México, 38, N57B, fols. 28r–35r.

Carta del alcalde mayor al REY Felipe IV, 19 November 1658

Señor,

Desde que vine a esta ciudad a serbir la plaza de alcalde del crimen que a doce años hetenido noticias de que el pecado nefando tiene mui contaminadas es tas provincias y aunque por lo que toca a mi oficio he procurado atacarle como la prueva destas causas vie ne mas por la providencia de dios que por la diligencia del juez no se ha podido consequir hasta que en veinte y siete de septiembre se me dio noticia de que vna muger avia visto cometer este pecado a vnos hom bres en el campo examine la muger y hize otras diligencias conque aprehendi diez y nueve reos complizes Puse la causa en estado con todos por mi solo con comission que tube para ello de la Real Sala y visitandose se hallaron convictos y confiesos quince reos y en los catorce se executo la pena de fuego y el que quedo fue condenado en pena extraordinaria y con los demas que fueron adecir hasta los diez y nueve se abrio el termino y se van oiendo en justicia y quedan presos nueve cada vno con testigo de vista y otros yndicios—y otros con dos y tres testigos de vista y demas yndicios y an resultado otros cien complices mas que estan llamados aedictos y pregones ninguno con testigo de oidas y todos con testigos de vista y el que menos tiene vn testigo de vista, y entre los referi dosde que se hizo justicia se hallo vn yndio ladino y de buena razon el qual era casado y un dia que se hallo con su muger aviendo tenido con ella acto carnal de rabia que no hubiesa sido con el hombre con quien comunicava nefandamente cogio vna vela y pego fuego aun Sancto nino Jesus que tenia en un altar Junto a su cama al qual se le quemo la cara y las es paldas y sele yncharon los brazos y se le lleno el cuerpo de cardenales y el fuego hizo en el los mismos efectos que si hubiera sido en carne huma na como pareze de los testimonios que remito a VM y porque quando Jesucristo Nuestro Senor nacio murieron todos los someticos como refieren algunos sanctos he tenido por feliz pronostico que quando naze el principe nuestro senor que Dios guarde muchos años aver cogido esta complicidad y comenzado a atacar este canzer que tan cundido y estendido estava en estas provincias pues a resultado desta causa que el tribunal de la Sancta ynquisicion ha echo diligencias con los reos della y el ordinario eclesiastico tiene presos otros esemptos y de su porque asta a estos se avia estendido este achaque tan mortal y nefando y porque VM manda por sus Reales leyes que los juezes se desvelen en el castigo y extirpacin del y por hallarme en la Real Sala el mas antiguo respeto de estar ympedido el que lo es mas que yo y aver actuado esta causa vnica mente me he atrbido a representarlo a VM que mandara lo que fuese servido, Nuestro Senor guarde La Real Catholica persona de VM como la Christiandad hamenester Mexico y noviembre 19 de 1658 D. Juan Manuel de Sotomayor

México 19 de noviembre de 1658, A su Magestad y 18 de junio de 1659 en el navío de las armadas, carta de Don Juan Manuel de Sotomayor alcalde del crimen de aquella ciudad, AGI, México, 38, N57A.

NOTES

Prologue

1. *Compendio de algunas experiencias en los ministerios de que usa la Compañía de Jesus, con que practicamente se muestra con algunos acontecimientos y documentos el buen acierto en ellos, por orden de los superiores, por el Padre Pedro de León de la misma Compañía, 1619,* BUG, caja B76; *Compendio de industrias en los ministerios de la Compañía de Jesus, con que practicamente se muestra el buen acierto en ellos, dispuetos por el Padre Pedro de León de la misma Compañía de Jesus y por orden de los superiores, 1628,* BUS, ms. 573 (3/4/53), tomo 2, ms. 574; P. de León, *Grandeza y miseria en Andalucía: testimonio de una encrucijada histórica, 1578–1616,* ed. P. Herrera Puga. For an earlier analysis of de León's discourses about sodomites, see F. Garza Carvajal, *Vir: Perceptions of Manliness in Andalucía and México (1561–1699).*
2. *Compendio de algunas experiencias,* fol. 255r.
3. Ibid., fol. 223r.
4. *Cristobal de Chabes, Relación de las cosas de la carcel de Sevilla y su trato, N° 60, 1591,* AMS, sec. 2, Señor Conde del Aguila, tomo 3, fol. 49v.
5. *Compendio de algunas experiencias,* fol. 279v.
6. Ibid., fol. 293v.
7. For a discussion about focuses on state constructs rather than on the nature of sodomites, see M. Foucault, *The History of Sexuality,* 3 vols., trans. R. Hurley, and *Discipline and Punish: The Birth of the Prison,* trans. A. Sheridan; G. S. Hutcheson and J. Blackmore, Introduction to J. Blackmore and G. S. Hutcheson (eds.), *Queer Iberia: Sexualities, Cultures, and Crossings from the Middle Ages to the Renaissance,* 1–19; and J. Goldberg, *Sodometries: Renaissance Texts, Modern Sexualities.*
8. C. Brown, "Queer Representation in the *Arçipreste de Talavera,* or the *Maldezir de mugeres* Is a Drag," in Blackmore and Hutcheson, *Queer Iberia,* 74.
9. S. Seth, L. Gandhi, and M. Dutton, "Postcolonial Studies: A Beginning . . . ," *Postcolonial Studies* 1.1 (1998): 7–11; A. Ahmad, "Postcolonialism: What's in a Name?" in R. de la Campa, E. A. Kaplan, and M. Sprinker (eds.), *Late Imperial Culture,* 11–32; B. Moore-Gilbert, *Postcolonial Theory: Contexts, Practices, Politics;* J. M. MacKenzie, *Orientalism: History, Theory, and the Arts.*
10. F. Ankersmit, "Reply to Professor Zagorin," *History and Theory* 29.3 (1990): 96.
11. K. Jenkins, *Why History? Ethics and Postmodernity,* 1–33, 133–160; L. A. Hunt, "Introduction: History, Culture, and the Text," in L. A. Hunt (ed.), *The New Cultural History: Essays (Studies on the History of Society and Culture).* See also L. A. Hunt, ed., *The Invention of Pornography: Obscenity and the Origins of Modernity (1500–1800).*

12. K. Jenkins, *Why History?*, 1–33.
13. Ibid., 1–19.
14. A. Ahmad, *In Theory: Classes, Nations, Literatures,* 99.
15. Ibid., 185.
16. J. Derrida, "The Deconstruction of Actuality," *Radical Philosophy* 68 (1994): 28–41. On reading sources and (re)producing "second-person narratives," see M. Bal, *Quoting Caravaggio: Contemporary Art, Preposterous History,* and M. Callahan, "Mexican Border Troubles: Social War, Settler Colonialism and the Production of Frontier Discourses, 1848–1880," Ph.D. diss., UT Austin (2002), 1–81.
17. Jenkins, *Why History?* 1–33.
18. H. White, "Historical Emplotment and the Problem of Truth," in K. Jenkins (ed.), *The Postmodern History Reader,* 392; H. White, "The History Text as Literary Artefact," *Tropics of Discourse,* 99.
19. White, "Historical Emplotment," 392; G. C. Spivak, "Can the Subaltern Speak?" in P. Williams and L. Chrisman (eds.), *Colonial Discourse and Post-colonial Theory,* 66–111, and in C. Nelson and L. Grossberg (eds.), *Marxism and the Interpretation of Culture,* 271–313. Also see Spivak's discussions about the postmodern condition, identity, writing, and self-representation in "Criticism, Feminism, and the Institution," in S. Harasym (ed.), *The Post-Colonial Critic: Interviews, Strategies, Dialogues,* 17–58. On forms of writing history and the use of different nontraditional paradigms, see A. Ouweneel, "Platgetreden paden: over het erfgoed van de Indianen," *Cuadernos del CEDLA* 4.6 (January 2000): 1–24.
20. A. Ouweneel, *Shadows over Anáhuac: An Ecological Interpretation of Crisis and Development in Central Mexico, 1730–1800,* 27.
21. Nietzsche quoted in V. Descombes, *Modern French Philosophy,* 184; I. Zavala, "La ética de la violencia," quoted in R. Siegel, "La autobiografía colonial: un intento de teorización y un estudio de escritos autobiográficos femeninos Novohispanos," Ph.D. diss., University of Texas at Austin (1997), 1. For a discussion related to discourses and America, see I. Zavala (ed.), *Discursos sobre la "invención" de América.* On the relationships among literature, history, fiction, and truth, see W. D. Mignolo, *The Darker Side of the Renaissance: Literacy, Territoriality, and Colonization,* 1–169.
22. M. Sinha, *Colonial Masculinity: The "Manly Englishman" and the "Effeminate Bengali" in the Late Nineteenth Century,* 4; A. L. Stoler, "Carnal Knowledge and Imperial Power: Gender, Race, and Morality in Colonial Asia," in R. N. Lancaster and M. Di Leonardo (eds.), *The Gender/Sexuality Reader: Culture, History, Political Economy,* 13–36; F. Cooper and A. L. Stoler, "Between Metropole and Colony: Rethinking a Research Agenda," in F. Cooper and A. L. Stoler (eds.), *Tensions of Empire: Colonial Cultures in a Bourgeois World,* 1–58. Starting with the premise that Europe was made by its imperial projects as much as colonial encounters were shaped by events and conflicts in Europe, the authors investigate various ways in which "civilizing missions" in both metropolis and colony provided new sites for clarifying a bourgeois order. They further argue that colonial studies can no longer

be confined to the units of analysis on which they once relied; instead of being studies of "the colonized," they must account for the shifting political terrain on which the very categories of colonized and colonizer have been shaped and patterned at different times.

23. J. Derrida, *Of Grammatology*, trans. G. C. Spivak, vi–vii.

24. A. Ahmad, *In Theory*, 5, 320 n. 5.

25. Ibid., 40; Foucault, *History of Sexuality*.

26. A. Pagden, *Spanish Imperialism*, 1–12; R. E. Tarragó, *The Pageant of Ibero-American Civilization: An Introduction to Its Cultural History*, 1–47. On the imperial condition, see F. Fanon, "Algeria Unveiled," in H. Chevalier (trans.), *A Dying Colonialism*, 21–52; K. de Albuquerque, "On Golliwogs and Flit Pumps: How the Empire Stays with Us in Strange Remembrances," *Jouvert: A Journal of Postcolonial Studies* 2.2 (1998, http://152.1.96.5/jouvert/v2i2/confour.htm): 1–5; and C. Radding, *Wandering Peoples: Colonialism, Ethnic Spaces, and Ecological Frontiers in Northwestern Mexico (1700–1850)*.

27. The scope of queer works is indeed broad. See S. O. Murray (ed.), *Latin American Male Homosexualities*; S. O. Murray and W. Roscoe (eds.), *Islamic Homosexualities*; S. O. Murray, *Oceanic Homosexualities*; and Murray's much awaited and forthcoming *North American Homosexualities*. Other studies include D. Kulick, *Travesti: Sex, Gender, and Culture among Brazilian Transgendered Prostitutes*; A. Prieur, *Mema's House, Mexico City: On Transvestites, Queens, and Machos*; and I. Lumsden, *Machos, Maricones, and Gays: Cuba and Homosexuality*. In a burgeoning market for queer studies, different tones of analysis can be found in R. Parker, *Beneath the Equator: Cultures of Desire, Male Homosexuality, and Emerging Gay Communities in Brazil*, and M. Weismantel, *Cholas and Pishtacos: Stories of Race and Sex in the Andes*. The reader is also referred to the following interview of an American art historian lecturing in Amsterdam. See M. Hemker, "Oppervlakkige openheid is te prefereren boven oppervlakkige koelheid: Jonathan Katz wil homoseksualiteit weer politiek maken," *Folia: Weekblad voor de Universiteit van Amsterdam* 38 (18 June 1999): 11. P. Bustos-Aguilar provides a biting critique of these sorts of works in "Mister Don't Touch the Banana: Notes on the Popularity of the Ethnosexed Body South of the Border," *Critique of Anthropology* 15.2 (1995): 149–170.

28. K. Sangari and S. Vaid, Introduction to K. Sangari and S. Vaid (eds.), *Recasting Women: Essays in Indian Colonial History*, 1–26; S. L. Bem, *The Lenses of Gender: Transforming the Debate on Sexual Inequality*; J. Butler, *Gender Trouble: Feminism and the Subversion of Identity*; C. T. Mohanty, "Under Western Eyes: Feminist Scholarship and Colonial Discourses," in P. Williams and L. Chrisman (eds.), *Colonial Discourse and Post-colonial Theory*, 196–220. J. W. Scott earlier legitimized the category of gender as a respectable focus of analysis; see her "Gender: A Useful Category of Historical Analysis," *American Historical Review* 91 (1986): 1053–1075. See also C. Monsiváis, "Ortodoxia y heterodoxia en las alcobas," *Debate feminista* 6.11 (April 1995): 183–212; and S. M. Socolow, *The Women of Colonial Latin America: New Approaches to the Americas*.

29. C. T. Mohanty, "Cartographies of Struggle," in C. T. Mohanty, A. Russo, and L. Torres (eds.), *Third World Women and the Politics of Feminism*, 14–15; J. Franco, "Beyond Ethnocentrism: Gender, Power, and the Third-World Intelligentsia," in C. Nelson and L. Grossberg (eds.), *Marxism and the Interpretation of Culture*, 503–515; Spivak, "Criticism, Feminism, and the Institution," 17–58.

30. Ahmad, *In Theory*, 99, 185.

31. Siegel, "La autobiografía colonial," 2–15.

32. Derrida, *Of Grammatology*, 141–165.

33. M. Foucault, *The Archaeology of Knowledge*, trans. A. M. Sheridan Smith, 44–55; E. Guerra Manzo, "El problema del poder en la obra de Michel Foucault y Norbert Elias," *Estudios Sociológicos* 17.49 (January–April 1999): 95–120.

34. Ahmad, *In Theory*, 182.

35. On the relationship between famine caused by Muslims and their practice of sodomy in Valencia, see A. Rubio Vela, *Peste negra, crisis, y comportamientos sociales en la España del siglo XIV: la ciudad de Valencia, 1348–1401*, 20–21, and his *Epistolari de la Valencia medieval*.

36. On Spain and its prosecution of sodomy and other sexual transgressions, see R. Carrasco, *Inquisición y represión sexual en Valencia: historia de los sodomitas (1565–1785)*; R. Rosselló i Vaquer and J. Bover Pujol, *El sexe a Mallorca: notes historiques*; R. García Carcel, *Herejía y sociedad en el siglo XVI: la Inquisición en Valencia (1530–1609)*, 288–294; E. W. Monter, "Sodomy: The Fateful Accident," in W. Dynes and S. Donaldson (eds.), *History of Homosexuality in Europe and America*, vol. 5, 276–299; J. Pérez Escohotado, *Sexo e inquisición en España: historia de la España sorprendente*; M. E. Perry, *Gender and Disorder in Early Modern Seville* and *Crime and Society in Early Modern Seville*; J. Contreras, *El Santo Oficio de la Inquisición de Galicia: poder, sociedad, y cultura (1560–1700)*; B. Bennassar, "Le modèle sexuel: l'Inquisition d'Aragon et la répression des pechés abominables," in B. Bennassar (ed.), *L'Inquisition Espagnole (XVe–XIXe siècles)*, 339–369; F. Tomás y Valiente, B. Clavero, A. M. Hespanha, J. L. Bermejo, E. Gacto, and C. Alvarez Alonso, *Sexo barroco y otras transgresiones premodernas*; A. Sarrión Mora, *Sexualidad y confesión: la solicitación ante el Tribunal del Santo Oficio (siglos XVI–XIX)*; F. Vázquez García and A. Moreno Mengíbar, *Sexo y razón: una genealogía de la moral sexual en España (siglos XVI–XX)*; A. García Valdés, *Historia y presente de la homosexualidad: análisis crítico de un fenómeno conflictivo*; and M. E. Perry, *Crime and Society in Early Modern Seville*.

37. S. Alberro (ed.), *El placer de pecar y el afán de normar: ideologías y comportamiento familiares y sexuales en el México colonial*; S. Gruzinski, "Las cenizas del deseo: homosexuales novohispanos a mediados del siglo XVII," in S. Ortega (ed.), *De la santidad a la perversión o de por qué no se cumplía la ley de Dios en la sociedad novohispana*, 255–281; A. Lavrín, "Sexuality in Colonial Mexico," in A. Lavrín (ed.), *Sexuality and Marriage in Colonial Latin America*, 47–95; M. L. Penyak, "Criminal Sexuality in Central Mexico, 1750–1850," Ph.D. diss., University of Connecticut, Storrs, 1993; F. V. Scholes and E. B. Adams (eds.), *Documentos para la historia del México colonial;*

S. Novo, *Las locas, el sexo, y los burdeles;* F. Benítez, *Los demonios en el convento: sexo y religión en la Nueva España;* G. Olivier, "Conquérants et missionnaires face au 'péché abominable,' essai sur l'homosexualité en Mésoameriqué au moment de la conquête espagnole," *Cahiers du Monde Hispanique et Luso-Brésilen* 55 (1990): 19–51; N. Quesada, "Erotismo en la religión azteca," *Revista de la Universidad de México* 28.2 (1974): 6–19; G. Kimball, "Aztec Homosexuality: The Textual Evidence," *Journal of Homosexuality* 26.1 (1993): 7–24; J. Leiva and N. Montoya, *La caña rota: la confesión de un confesor del siglo XVIII;* R. C. Trexler, *Sex and Conquest: Gendered Violence, Political Order, and the European Conquest of the Americas.*

38. Carrasco, *Inquisición y represión sexual,* 65–88.

39. Noordegraaf detected a similar plight in the writing of social history when he professed the need for more of these different sorts of "delectable historiographies." See L. Noordegraaf, "Tot lering en vermaak," in L. Noordegraaf (ed.), *Ideeën en ideologieën: studies over economische en sociale geschiedschrijving in Nederland (1894–1991),* vol. I, 11–14. See also J. Canizares-Esguerra, *How to Write the History of the New World: Historiographies, Epistemologies, and Identities in the Eighteenth-Century Atlantic World.*

40. "Garrote. Se llama también la muerte que se ocasiona de la compresión de las fauces por medio del artificio de un hierro," quoted in *Diccionario de autoridades (Edición Facsímil de 1732),* vol. 2, 29.

41. J. de Veitia Linaje, *Norte de la contratación de las Indias occidentales;* R. Antuñez y Acevedo, *Memorias históricas sobre la legislación y gobierno del comercio de los españoles con sus colonias en las Indias occidentales;* P. Chaunu and H. Chaunu, *Seville et l'Atlantique,* vol. I, 182–184.

42. In Seville the tribunal consisted of a *letrado* (judge) with a formal degree in law, a public prosecutor, two scribes, and other pertinent officials. On board ships, the tribunal consisted of the captain general, who assumed the duties of judge; a court assistant; a scribe; and other assistants or counselors. The sole judge on land or at sea rendered the verdict. Those convicted on board the ships could appeal the guilty verdicts to the tribunal on land. See J. López de Velasco, "De la Casa de la Contratación de Sevilla, y cosas proveidas para la navegación de las Indias," in his *Geografía y descripción universal de las Indias,* 45–47. For a discussion on evidence and narrations, see W. A. Wagenaar, P. J. van Koppen, and H. F. M. Crombag, *Anchored Narratives: The Psychology of Criminal Evidence;* L. Kramer, "Historical Narratives and the Meaning of Nationalism," *Journal of the History of Ideas* 58:3 (July 1997): 525–545; and J. Blackmore, *Manifest Perdition: Shipwreck Narrative and the Disruption of Empire.* On the Spanish colonial legal system, see E. Schafer, *El Consejo Real y Supremo de las Indias: su historia, organización, y labor administrativa hasta la terminación de la casa de Austria;* and M. Góngora, *El estado en el derecho Indiano: época de fundación (1492–1570).* Every ship sailing between Seville and the Indies registered its voyage with the Casa de la Contratación, which kept a record containing a detailed account of the ship, its company, and the contents

of its cargo. The Casa, an administrative agency charged with regulating commerce between the peninsula and the new continent, controlled the fleets, shipments, and personnel involved in trade and colonization. For further discussion, see J. Lynch, *Spain 1516–1598: From Nation to World Empire*, 232–236.

43. The recorded legal proceedings of a given case. They varied in length from one hundred to more than five hundred folios per case.

44. S. Gruzinski, *The Conquest of Mexico: The Incorporation of Indian Societies into the Western World (16th–18th Centuries)*, trans. E. Corrigan, 306.

45. Penyak, "Criminal Sexuality in Central Mexico," 245–301.

46. Siegel, "La autobiografía colonial," 2–31.

47. Ibid.

48. C. Ginzburg, "Morelli, Freud, and Sherlock Holmes: Clues and Scientific Method," *History Workshop Journal* 9 (1980): 5–36.

49. C. Ginzburg, *The Cheese and the Worms: The Cosmos of a Sixteenth-Century Miller*, trans. John and Anne Tedeschi, xvii.

50. Noordegraaf, "Tot lering en vermaak," 11–14.

51. *Cádiz año de 1698 causa escriptta de oficio de justicia contra Juan Mole, Bartholomé Barres, Juan Baptista Pino, y Phelip Esmirle, sobre decisse, aver cometido todos, el pecado de sodomía con el dicho Juan Mole*, AGI, Escribanía, 1105B, fols. 15r–46v.

52. P. E. Pérez-Mallaína, *Los Hombres del Océano*, 174.

53. M. van de Port, *Gypsies, Wars, and Other Instances of the Wild: Civilisation and Its Discontents in a Serbian Town*, 23–28. On the problematization of positivist and heuristic currents in social history, see L. Noordegraaf, "Overmoed uit onbehagen," in Noordegraaf, *Ideeën en ideologieën*, vol. 2, 665–688; and G. C. Spivak, "A Literary Representation of the Subaltern: A Woman's Text from the Third World," in G. C. Spivak (ed.), *In Other Worlds: Essays in Cultural Politics*, 241–268.

54. Foucault, *Discipline and Punish*.

Chapter 1

1. *Vida i sucesos de la Monja Alférez, Alférez Catarina, Doña Catarina de Araujo doncella, natural de S[an] Sebastián, prov[inci]a de Guipúzcoa. Escrita por ella misma en 18 de sept[iembr]e 1646, bolviendo de las Indias a España en el Galeón S[an] Josef, Capitán Andrés Otón, en la flota de N[uev]a España, General Don Juan de Benavides, General de la Armanda Tomás de la Raspuru, que llego a Cádiz en 18 de Noviembre de 1646*, BRAH, Colección Juan Bautista Muñoz, 9/4807, Cap. XX "Parti de Barcelona a Génova," fols. 201r–234v. Erauso, the author, returned to Spain in 1624 and not in 1646, as indicated in the title of the manuscript. The date is later corrected to 1624 in the last chapter of the manuscript (fol. 238v). Erauso supposedly wrote the original manuscript in 1625 and delivered it to Bernardino de Guzmán, an editor in Madrid. The whereabouts of this original manuscript remains unknown. The manuscript consulted for this study is deposited in BRAH. It was copied by Juan Bautista Muñoz on 24 May 1784 from another copy that belonged to Cándido María Trigueros

(1737–1801), a Spanish writer often credited with numerous literary falsifications. On these and other particulars, see R. de Vallbona (ed.), *Vida i sucesos de la Monja Alférez: autobiografía atribuida a Doña Catalina de Erauso*, 1–30; J. M. Ferrer (ed.), *Historia de la monja alférez, Doña Catalina de Erauso, escrita por ella misma*; M. Stepto and G. Stepto (trans.), *Lieutenant Nun: Memoir of a Basque Transvestite in the New World / Catalina de Erauso*; I. Azkune (trans.), *Katalin Erauso*; O. Schepeler (trans.), *Die Nonne-Fahurich, oder Geschichte der Doña Catalina de Erauso von ihr selbst geschrieben*; and S. Velasco, *The Lieutenant Nun Transgenderism, Lesbian Desire, and Catalina de Erauso*.

2. *Vida i sucesos*, BRAH, fols. 208v–209v.

3. Ibid., fols. 202r–203v, 213v.

4. A. Pagden, *Spanish Imperialism and the Political Imagination*, 6.

5. E. Temprano, *El árbol de las pasiones: deseo, pecado, y vidas repetidas*, 47–55.

6. Or is that the Opus Gay?

7. F. Tomás y Valiente, "El crimen y pecado contra natura," in F. Tomás y Valiente, B. Clavero, A. M. Hespanha, J. L. Bermejo, E. Gacto, and C. Alvarez Alonso (eds.), *Sexo barroco y otras transgresiones premodernas*, 33–56.

8. Temprano, *El árbol de las pasiones*, 11–19.

9. *Vida i sucesos*, BRAH, fol. 214v.

10. On chivalry fused with marital, aristocratic, and Christian elements in early modern Europe, see M. Keen, *Chivalry*.

11. *Vida i sucesos*, BRAH, fol. 214v.

12. Ibid., fols. 216r–217v.

13. Ibid., fols. 207r–208v.

14. *Segunda parte de la relación de la Monja Alféres, y dízense en ella cosas admirables, y fidedignas de los valerosos hechos desta mujer, de lo bien que empleó el tiempo en servicio de nuestro Rey y señor*, BLAC, Colección Icazbalceta, no. JGI *Varias relaciones*, 1, 54b.

15. De Vallbona, *Vida i sucesos*, 1–30.

16. Misfits indeed. See I. Burshatin, "Written on the Body: Slave or Hermaphrodite in Sixteenth-Century Spain," in J. Blackmore and G. S. Hutcheson (eds.), *Queer Iberia: Sexualities, Cultures, and Crossings from the Middle Ages to the Renaissance*, 420–453. On visionaries and hermaphrodites, see R. L. Kagan, *Lucrecia's Dreams: Politics and Prophecy in Sixteenth-Century Spain*, and his forthcoming *Inquisitorial Inquiries: The Brief Lives of Secret Jews and Other Heretics*.

17. For a discussion about the limitations of gendered names and language, see M. E. Perry, "From Convent to Battlefield," in Blackmore and Hutcheson, *Queer Iberia*, 394–419.

18. M. E. Perry, "The Manly Woman: A Historical Case Study," *American Behavioral Scientist* 31.1 (1987): 86–100.

19. On queer theories, E. Kosofsky Sedgwick, *Epistemology of the Closet*.

20. R. Siegel, "La autobiografía colonial: un intento de teorización y un estudio de escritos autobiográficos femeninos Novohispanos," Ph.D. diss., University of Texas at Austin (1997), 1–32.

21. Pagden, *Spanish Imperialism*, 1—2.

22. Ibid., 4. For a critique of the term "Spain" as a specious and empty form of liberty, see B. de Spinoza, *A Theologico-political Treatise*, 344.

23. Pagden, *Spanish Imperialism*, 6.

24. Ibid., 6—7.

25. Ibid., 7, 37—63; T. Campanella, *De Monarchia hispanica discursus*; E. Chilmead (trans.), *Thomas Campanella, an Italian friar and second Machiavel, his advice to the King of Spain for attaining the universal monarchy of the world: particularly concerning England, Scotland and Ireland, how to raise division between king and Parliament, to alter the government from a kingdome to a commonwealth, thereby embroiling England in civil war to divert the English from disturbing the Spaniard in bringing the Indian treasure into Spain: also for reducing Holland by procuring war betwixt England, Holland, and other sea-faring countries.*

26. A. Ahmad, *In Theory: Classes, Nations, Literatures*, 159—220; G. C. Spivak, "Reading the Satanic Verses," *Public Culture* 2.1 (1989): 94. On gender and nation, see B. Anderson, *Imagined Communities: Reflections on the Origins and Spread of Nationalism*; A. Parker, M. Russo, D. Sommer, and P. Yaeger (eds.), *Nationalisms and Sexualities*; and G. L. Mosse, *Nationalism and Sexuality: Middle-Class Morality and Sexual Norms in Modern Europe*, 1—22.

27. R. Hennessy, *Materialist Feminism and the Politics of Discourse*.

28. M. Sinha, *Colonial Masculinity: The "Manly Englishman" and the "Effeminate Bengali" in the Late Nineteenth Century*, 13.

29. E. Said, *Orientalism*, 12. See also Said's *Culture and Imperialism* and J. M. MacKenzie, *Orientalism: History, Theory, and the Arts*.

30. Ahmad, *In Theory*, 159—220.

31. Ibid., 179; Said, *Orientalism*, 3.

32. L. Althusser, "Contradiction and Overdetermination," in B. Brewster (trans.), *For Marx*, 87—127; L. Althusser, *Essays in Self-criticism*, trans. G. Lock.

33. E. K. Sedgwick, "Nationalisms and Sexualities in the Age of Wilde," in Parker et al., *Nationalisms and Sexualities*, 239; G. Rubin, "The Traffic in Women: Notes on the Political Economy of Sex," in R. R. Reiter (ed.), *Toward an Anthropology of Women*, 157—210.

34. Ahmad, *In Theory*, 8—9, 33—38.

35. A. Stoler, "Rethinking Colonial Categories: European Communities and the Boundaries of Rule," *Comparative Studies in Society and History* 31.1 (1989): 134—201; "Making Empire Respectable: The Politics of Race and Sexuality in Twentieth Century Colonial Cultures," *American Ethnologist* 16.4 (1989): 634—660; "Carnal Knowledge and Imperial Power: Gender, Race, and Morality in Colonial Asia," in R. N. Lancaster and M. Di Leonardo (eds.), *The Gender/Sexuality Reader: Culture, History, Political Economy*, 13—36.

36. Sinha, *Colonial Masculinity*, 4.

37. Ibid.

38. C. T. Mohanty, "Cartographies of Struggle," in C. T. Mohanty, A. Russo, and L. Torres (eds.), *Third World Women and the Politics of Feminism*, 14—15.

39. J. Scott, "Gender: A Useful Category of Historical Analysis," *American Historical Review* 91 (1986): 1053—1075.

40. Ibid. See also K. Sangari and S. Vaid (eds.), *Recasting Women: Essays in Indian Colonial History;* S. L. Bem, *The Lenses of Gender: Transforming the Debate on Sexual Inequality;* J. Butler, *Gender Trouble: Feminism and the Subversion of Identity;* and C. T. Mohanty, "Under Western Eyes: Feminist Scholarship and Colonial Discourses," in P. Williams and L. Chrisman (eds.), *Colonial Discourse and Post-colonial Theory,* 196—220.

41. Butler, *Gender Trouble,* 1—13.

42. Ibid.

43. A. Parker, M. Russo, D. Sommer, and P. Yaeger, Introduction to *Nationalisms and Sexualities,* ed. Parker et al., 4.

44. Some recent and welcome exceptions to stagnant paradigms include E. L. Bergmann and P. J. Smith (eds.), *¿Entiendes? Queer Readings, Hispanic Writings;* J. Blackmore and G. S. Hutcheson (eds.), *Queer Iberia: Sexualities, Cultures, and Crossings from the Middle Ages to the Renaissance;* D. W. Foster, *Sexual Textualities: Essays on Queer/ing Latin American Writing* and *Gay and Lesbian Themes in Latin American Writing;* D. Eisenberg, Introduction to *Spanish Writers on Lesbian and Gay Themes: A Bio-Critical Sourcebook,* ed. D. W. Foster, 1—21; J. Goldberg (ed.), *Queering the Renaissance;* and A. Saint-Saëns (ed.), *Sex and Love in Golden Age Spain.*

45. R. Trumbach, "Gender and the Homosexual Role in Modern Western Culture: The Eighteenth and Nineteenth Centuries Compared," in D. Altman, C. Vance, M. Vicinus, and J. Weeks (eds.), *Homosexuality, Which Homosexuality?* 151—153. For different and more critical perspectives about early modern Europe, see J. G. Turner (ed.), *Sexuality and Gender in Early Modern Europe,* and L. Fradenburg and C. Freccero (eds.), *Premodern Sexualities.* On England, see J. Weeks, *Sex, Politics, and Society: The Regulation of Sexuality since 1800;* A. Stewart, *Close Readers: Humanism and Sodomy in Early Modern England;* and A. Bray, *Homosexuality in Renaissance England.* On France, M. Rey, "Police et sodomie a Paris au XVIIIe siècle: du péche au desordre," *Revue d'Histoire Moderne et Contemporaine* 29 (1982): 113—124; J. Merrick and M. Sibalis (eds.), *Homosexuality in French History and Culture;* and J. Merrick and B. Ragan (eds.), *Homosexuality in Early Modern France: A Documentary Collection.* On the Netherlands, G. Hekma, "A Female Soul in a Male Body: Sexual Inversion as Gender Inversion in Nineteenth-Century Sexology," in G. Herdt (ed.), *Third Sex, Third Gender: Beyond Sexual Dimorphism in Culture and History,* 213—240; D. J. Noordam, "Sodomy in the Dutch Republic, 1600—1725," in K. Gerard and G. Hekma (eds.), *The Pursuit of Sodomy: Male Homosexuality in Renaissance and Enlightenment Europe,* 207—228; and, lastly, T. van der Meer, "The Prosecution of Sodomites in Eighteenth-Century Amsterdam: Changing Perceptions of Sodomy," in Gerard and Hekma, *Pursuit of Sodomy,* 263—310; "Sodomy and the Pursuit of a Third Sex in the Early Modern Period," in Herdt, *Third Sex, Third Gender,* 137—212; and *Sodoms zaad in Nederland: het ontstaan van homoseksualiteit in de vroegmoderne tijd.* On Spain and Mexico, P. H. Sigal, *From Moon Goddesses to Virgins: The Colonization*

of Yucatecan Maya Sexual Desire and *Infamous Desire;* G. Spurling, "Honor, Sexuality, and the Colonial Church," in L. L. Johnson and S. Lipsett-Rivera (eds.), *The Faces of Honor: Sex, Shame, and Violence in Colonial Latin America,* 45–67; F. Garza Carvajal, *Quemando mariposas: sodomía e imperio en España y México (siglos XVI–XVII);* X. M. Buxán Bran (ed.), *Conciencia de un singular deseo: estudios lesbianos y gays en el estado español;* P. Herrera Puga, *Sociedad y delincuencia en el Siglo de Oro;* C. Espejo Muriel, *El deseo negado: aspectos de la problemática homosexual en la vida monástica (siglos III–VI D.C.);* D. Eisenberg, "Juan Ruiz's Heterosexual Good Love," in Blackmore and Hutcheson, *Queer Iberia,* 250–274; A. Arjona Castro, *La sexualidad en la España musulmana;* F. Núñez Roldán, *El pecado nefando del Obispo de Salamina; un hombre sin concierto en la corte de Felipe II;* and M. A. Nesvig, "The Complicated Terrain of Latin American Homosexuality," *Hispanic American Historical Review* 81.3–4 (August–November 2001): 689–729. On Brazil, see R. Vainfas, *Tropico dos pecados: moral, sexualidade, e Inquisição no Brasil;* and L. R. B. Mott, *O sexo proibido: virgens, gays, e escravos nas garras da Inquisição* and *Homossexuais da Bahia: dicionario biografico (secvlos XVI–XIX).* On masculinities in other parts of Latin America, see E. Archetti, *Masculinities: Football, Polo, and the Tango in Argentina.* Other global approaches to homo histories include R. Bleys, *The Geography of Perversion: Male-to-Male Sexual Behaviour outside the West and the Ethnographic Imagination (1750–1918);* M. Jordan, *The Invention of Sodomy in Christian Theology;* T. W. Laqueur, *Making Sex: Body and Gender from the Greeks to Freud;* G. Ruggiero, *The Boundaries of Eros: Sex, Crime, and Sexuality in Renaissance Venice;* J. N. Green, *Beyond Carnival: Male Homosexuality in Twentieth-Century Brazil;* and J. Quiroga, *Tropics of Desire: Interventions from Queer Latino America.* The following collections of essays all explore normative definitions of sexuality and gender: M. B. Duberman, M. Vicinus, and G. Chauncey, Jr. (eds.), *Hidden from History: Reclaiming the Gay and Lesbian Past;* D. Higgs (ed.), *Queer Sites: Gay Urban Histories since 1600;* J. Goldberg (ed.), *Reclaiming Sodom;* J. Weeks, *Against Nature: Essays on History, Sexuality, and Identity;* and G. W. Bredbeck, *Sodomy and Interpretation: Marlowe to Milton.* The future looks bright as interpreted by S. M. Whitehead, *Men and Masculinities: Key Themes and New Directions;* R. Halpern, *Shakespeare's Perfume: Sodomy and Sublimity in the Sonnets, Wilde, Freud, and Lacan;* and Tom Betteridge (ed.), *Sodomy in Early Modern Europe.*

46. Ahmad, *In Theory,* 95–122, 287–318; J. F. Lyotard, *Toward the Postmodern.*
47. Parker et al., Introduction, 2.
48. E. Balibar, "Racism as Universalism," *New Political Science* 16.17 (1989): 19; H. K. Bhabha (ed.), *Nation and Narration.*
49. Unfortunately, Trumbach's documentation consisted only of secondary sources. However, some of the secondary literature cited did base its findings on archival material.
50. Trumbach, "Gender and the Homosexual Role," 158, 167–168 n. 18.
51. J. Weeks, "Against Nature," in Altman et al., *Homosexuality, Which Homosexuality?,* 199–200.

52. Parker et al., Introduction, 3.
53. D. M. Halperin, *One Hundred Years of Homosexuality and Other Essays on Greek Love*, 43—46.
54. Halperin stipulated, for example, that a "paederast," the "classical Greek adult, married male who periodically" enjoyed penetrating a male adolescent, differed from the "berdache," a "native American (Indian) adult male" who from childhood took on many aspects of a woman and was later "regularly penetrated by the adult males" in New Spain. The berdache, too, differed from the "New Guinea tribesmen and warriors who, from the ages of eight to fifteen were orally inseminated on a daily basis by older youths" who eventually married women.
55. R. Trumbach, "London's Sapphists: From Three Sexes to Four Genders in the Making of Modern Culture," in Herdt, *Third Sex, Third Gender*, 111.
56. Sinha, *Colonial Masculinity*, 17.
57. Ibid., 1—24; G. Viswanathan, "Raymond Williams and British Colonialism," *Yale Journal of Criticism* 4.2 (1991): 47—66.
58. Sinha, *Colonial Masculinity*, 17.
59. Ibid., 19.
60. H. K. Bhabha, "Of Mimicry and Man: The Ambivalence of Colonial Discourse," *October* 28 (1984): 125—133, and "The Other Question: The Stereotype and Colonial Discourse," *Screen* 24.6 (1985): 18—36; R. Hennessy and C. T. Mohanty, "The Construction of Woman in Three Popular Texts of Empire: Toward a Critique of Materialist Feminism," *Textual Practice* 3.3 (1989): 323—359; A. Nandy, *Intimate Enemy: Loss and Recovery of Self Under Colonialism*, 8; L. Phillips, "Lost in Space: Siting/Citing the In-between of Homi Bhabha's *The Location of Culture*," *Jouvert: A Journal of Postcolonial Studies* 2.2 (1998, http://152.1.96.5/jouvert/v2i2/confour.htm): 1—14.
61. Hennessy and Mohanty, "Construction of Woman," 328.
62. Sinha, *Colonial Masculinity*, 7—8.
63. P. Chatterjee and G. Pandey (eds.), *Subaltern Studies 7: Writings on South Asian History and Society*. On political anomalies and the struggle for legitimacy closer to the Mexican frontier, see D. Montejano, *Anglos and Mexicans in the Making of Texas (1836—1986)*.
64. T. Sarkar, "The Hindu Wife and the Hindu Nation: Domesticity and Nationalism in Nineteenth-Century Bengal," *Studies in History* 8.2 (1992): 219—220.
65. Gender parallelism in the imperial order and the legitimizing of power or the relationship between sexual relations and ideology are discussed in I. M. Silverblatt, *Moon, Sun, and Witches: Gender Ideologies and Class in Inca and Colonial Peru*; R. A. Gutiérrez, *When Jesus Came, the Corn Mothers Went Away: Marriage, Sexuality, and Power in New Mexico (1500—1846)*; L. L. Johnson and S. Lipsett-Rivera (eds.), *The Faces of Honor: Sex, Shame, and Violence in Colonial Latin America*; S. M. Socolow, *The Women of Colonial Latin America: New Approaches to the Americas*; S. Molloy and R. McKee Irwin (eds.), *Hispanisms and Homosexualities*; and A. Twinam, *Public Lives, Private*

Secrets: Gender, Honor, Sexuality, and Illegitimacy in Colonial Spanish America. See also R. Adorno, *Guaman Poma: Writing and Resistance in Colonial Peru,* and R. Adorno and K. J. Andrien (eds.), *Transatlantic Encounters: Europeans and Andeans in the Sixteenth Century.*

66. For example, D. Balderston and D. J. Guy (eds.), *Sex and Sexuality in Latin America.*

67. See P. Mason's biting and vitriolic "Sex and Conquest: A Redundant Copula?" *Anthropos* 92 (1997): 577—581, and the response by R. C. Trexler, "Rejoinder to Mason," *Anthropos* 93 (1998): 655—656, followed by P. Mason, "Reply to Trexler," *Anthropos* 94 (1999): 315, and, finally, R. C. Trexler, "Rejoinder to Mason," *Anthropos* 94 (1999): 315—316.

68. S. Gruzinski, "Las cenizas del deseo: homosexuales novohispanos a mediados del siglo XVII," in S. Ortega (ed.), *De la santidad a la perversión o de por qué no se cumplía la ley de Dios en la sociedad novohispana,* 255—281; A. Lavrín, "Introduction" and "Sexuality in Colonial Mexico," in A. Lavrín (ed.), *Sexuality and Marriage in Colonial Latin America,* 1—43, 47—95; R. C. Trexler, *Sex and Conquest: Gendered Violence, Political Order, and the European Conquest of the Americas.*

69. S. O. Murray (ed.), *Latin American Male Homosexualities;* S. O. Murray, *Oceanic Homosexualities.* Murray is equally at home in Islam and elsewhere. See S. O. Murray and W. Roscoe (eds.), *Islamic Homosexualities,* and Murray's forthcoming *North American Homosexualities.*

70. S. Novo, *Las locas, el sexo, y los burdeles.* Novo conflated the histories of secular and ecclesiastical tribunals. Both held prominence in the viceroyalty of New Spain. However, between 1521 and 1698, sodomy records exist only for secular tribunals. This evidently changed because, between 1750 and 1850, only the Mexican Inquisition prosecuted sodomy cases as well as other forms of "sexual crimes." On the Mexican Inquisition and sodomy, see M. L. Penyak, "Criminal Sexuality in Central Mexico, 1750—1850," Ph.D. diss., University of Connecticut, Storrs, 1993. On Novo, see C. Monsiváis, *Amor perdido,* 265—296.

71. Sinha, *Colonial Masculinity,* 3. Gramsci described "subordinate classes" as a culture in juxtaposition to a "dominant class" in power without relegating the former to paternalistic connotations of "inferiority"; see A. Gramsci, *Selections from the Prison Notebooks of Antonio Gramsci.*

72. Sinha, *Colonial Masculinity,* 21—22.

73. De Vallbona, *Vida i sucesos,* 2. This is an interesting quote from a well-researched and well-documented book. Perhaps the fact that the book was published under the auspices of the Basque government's Eusko Jaurlaritza, EMAKUNDE/Instituto Vasco de la Mujer slightly slanted Vallbona's beret; see p. vi.

74. One should not dismiss any historical analysis of Alonso Díaz on the grounds that Catalina de Erauso constituted an exceptional figure of heroic proportions. Examples of microhistories abound. The reader is referred to C. Ginzburg, *The Cheese and the Worms: The Cosmos of a Sixteenth-Century Miller,* trans. John and Anne

Tedeschi; N. Z. Davis, *The Return of Martin Guerre;* and F. Tomizza, *Heavenly Sup-per: The Story of Maria Janis,* trans. A. J. Schutte. Many other women in early mod-ern Spain and in other parts of Europe also lived under the guise or disguise of a man. See G. Mak, "Opgehangen aan woorden: de tweeslachtige memoires van Herculine Barbin," *Lover* 2 (1995): 10 –17; C. R. Boxer, *Mary and Misogyny: Women in Iberian Expansion Overseas (1415 –1815);* M. S. Creighton and L. Norling (eds.), *Iron Men, Wooden Women: Gender and Seafaring in the Atlantic World (1700 –1920);* and R. M. Dekker and L. C. van de Pol, *The Tradition of Female Transvestism in Early Mod-ern Europe.* On the politics of the PNV, see J. Marías, "My Fair Arzallus," *El País Semanal* (19 May 2002): 8.

75. *El Alférez doña Catalina de Erauso ha dado una petición en el consejo, en que refiere ha diez y nuebe años pasó a las provincias del Perú en ábito de barón,* AGI, Sección de Documentos Escogidos, legajo 1, no. 87, 1626 –1630; *Pedimento de Catalina de Erauso para que se le premien los servicios prestados a la corona,* BRAH, Colección Juan Bautista Muñoz, 9/4807, fols. 234r –235v. Other sisters had different motives. See J. Billinkof, *The Avila of Saint Teresa: Religious Reform in a Sixteenth-Century City;* J. E. Traslosheros H., "Los motivos de una monja: Sor Feliciana de San Francisco, Valladolid de Michoacán (1632 –1655)," *Historia Mexicana* 67.4 (1998): 735 –763; E. Arenal and S. Schlau, *Untold Sisters: Hispanic Nuns in Their Own Words;* and F. J. Lorenzo Pinar, *Beatas y mancebas.* On Mexican, Chicana, or Mexican American lesbian identity and literature, see G. Anzaldúa, *Interviews-Entrevistas,* ed. A. L. Keating, and *Borderlands—La frontera: The New Mestiza;* and C. Moraga and G. Anzaldúa (eds.), *This Bridge Called My Back: Writings by Radical Women of Color.* On Spain, see the fol-lowing in P. Cuder Domínguez (ed.), *Exilios femeninos:* P. Cuder Domínguez, In-troducción, 11–12; B. Domínguez García, "La fantasía como exilio interior feme-nino en *Three Times Table* de Sara Maitland," 217–226; and S. Villegas López, "Santidad y exilio: la leyenda dorada de Michèle Roberts," 235–244.

76. *El Alférez doña Catalina,* fols. 8r–10v.

77. A. Ouweneel, *Shadows over Anáhuac: An Ecological Interpretation of Crisis and Development in Central Mexico, 1730 –1800,* 9.

78. *Don Luis de Céspedes Xeria, Gouernador y Capitán General . . . de Paragoay, en las Yndias, por el Rey, nuestro señor, y Capitán de Ynfantería Española . . . certifico y hago fee a Su Majes-tad que conozco a Catalina de Herausso,* AGI, Sección de Documentos Escogidos, legajo 1, no. 87, 1626 –1630, fols. 8r–12v; *Certificación de D[o]n Luis de Cespedes . . . Francisco Pérez de Navarrete . . . Juan Cortes de Monrroy . . . Juan Precio de León,* BRAH, Colección Juan Bautista Muñoz, 9/4807, fols. 235v –243v; *Don Francisco Pérez de Navarrete, Capitán de Ynfantería Española que a sido por Su Majestad y Cavo de Compañías . . . ceritifico que conocí a Catalina de Herausso,* AGI, Sección de Documentos Escogidos, legajo 1, no. 87, 1626 –1630, fols. 8r–12v; *D[o]n Jose de la Higuera y Lara archivero del general de Indias en esta ciudad Pedim[ien]to por el alberez D[oñ]a Catalina de Herauso vecina y natural de la villa de S[an] S[ebastian] provincia de Guipuzcoa,* BRAH, Colección Juan Bautista Muñoz, 9/4807, fol. 234r.

79. *Don Luis de Céspedes Xeria,* fols. 8r–12v.

80. Ibid., fols. 10r–12v.

81. *Pedro de la Valle el peregrino, en su tomo 3° de su viage escrito por él mismo en letras familiares, en lengua italiana a su amigo Mario Schipano, impreso en Bolonia 1677, en la letra ó carta 16 de Roma a 11 de julio de 1626, pág. N° 2 dice lo siguiente,* BRAH, Colección Juan Bautista Muñoz, 9/4807, fols. 232r–233v.

82. *Don Luis de Céspedes Xeria,* fol. 7v.

83. Ibid., fol. 13r; refers also to an edict dated 26 June 1628. See also *Auto, Consejo Real de las Yndias, 19 febrero 1626,* AGI, Sección de Documentos Escogidos, legajo 1, no. 87, 1626–1630.

84. *Vltima y tercera relación, en qve se haze verdadera del resto de la vida de la Monja Alférez, sus memorables virtudes, y exemplar muerte en estos Reynos de la Nueva España,* BLAC, Colección Icazbalceta, no. JGI *Varias relaciones,* 1, 54c. For more about royal favors and perquisites, see A. Feros, *Kingship and Favouritism in the Spain of Philip III (1598–1621).*

85. Siegel, "La autobiografía colonial," 13.

86. *Certificación de D[o]n Luis de Cespedes,* fol. 230r. See also Ferrer, *Historia de la monja alférez,* 116.

87. *Pedro de la Valle el peregrino,* fols. 237r–238v.

88. Ibid.

89. *D[o]n Jose de la Higuera,* fol. 235v.

90. *Don Luis de Céspedes Xeria,* fol. 13r.

91. "Jueves 4 de julio estuvo en la yglesia mayor la monja Alférez . . . fue monja en san sebastián huyóse i pasó a Yndias en hábito de hombre año de 1603 . . . sirvió de soldado veinte años tenida por capón . . . bolvió d España fue a Roma i el Papa Urbano VIII la dispensó i dio licencia para andar en hábito varonil . . . el Rey le dio título de Alférez . . . el Capitán Miguel de Chazarreta la llevó por mozo en años pasados a Yndias i ahora va por General de la flota y la lleva por Alférez." *Pedro de la Valle el peregrino,* fol. 236r.

92. Ferrer, *Historia de la monja alférez,* 120; J. M. Asensio y Toledo, *Francisco Pacheco: sus obras artísticas y literarias, especialmente el libro de descripción de verdaderos retratos de ilustres y memorables varones, que dejó inédito, apuntes que podrán servir de introducción a este libro si alguna vez llega á publicarse.*

Chapter 2

1. Quoted in H. Kamen, *Spain: A Society of Conflict (1469–1714),* 35.

2. A. García Valdés, *Historia y presente de la homosexualidad: análisis crítico de un fenómeno conflictivo,* 37.

3. G. Rousseau preferred the more global term "erotophobia" in reference to similar cultural anxieties in the United States; see "No Sex Please, We're American: Erotophobia, Liberation, and Cultural History," *Arcadia: Zeitschrift für Allgemeine und Vergleichende Literaturwissenschaft* 33 (1988): 12–45.

4. C. Cahen, *Introduction a l'histoire du monde musulman médiéval (VIIe–XVe siècle)*. For sexual life in Spain prior to the early modern period, see A. Arjona Castro, *La sexualidad en la España musulmana;* R. Cansinos Assens (ed.), *El Koran: versión literal e íntegra;* L. Crompton, "Male Love and Islamic Law in Arab Spain," in S. O. Murray and W. Roscoe (eds.), *Islamic Homosexualities: Culture, History, and Literature,* 142–157; W. R. Dynes (ed.), *Encyclopedia of Homosexuality,* 2 vols.; D. Eisenberg, Introduction to *Spanish Writers on Lesbian and Gay Themes: A Bio-Critical Sourcebook,* ed. D. W. Foster, 1–21; J. Eslava Galán, *Historia secreta del sexo en España;* R. Fletcher, *Moorish Spain;* L. P. Harvey, *Islamic Spain (1250–1500);* L. Mirrer, "Representing 'Other' Men: Muslims, Jews, and Masculine Ideals in Medieval Castilian Epic and Ballad," in C. Lees (ed.), *Medieval Masculinities,* 169–186; C. Sánchez-Albornoz, *De la Andalucía islámica a la de hoy;* and A. Huerga, *Historia de los Alumbrados,* vol. 1, and *Los Alumbrados de la alta Andalucía (1575–1590),* vol. 2.

5. F. Tomás y Valiente, *El Derecho penal de la monarquía absoluta (siglos XVI, XVII, XVIII),* 225.

6. See his royal decree against a cleric named Cristóbal González accused of having intended to commit the nefarious sin with an assistant: *Sobre el pecado nefando que trato de cometer un clerigo llamado Cristóbal González con un sacristan,* AGS, Real Cédulas, Cámara de Castilla, no. 25.

7. W. Roscoe and S. O. Murray, Introduction to *Islamic Homosexualities,* ed. Murray and Roscoe, 1–13; Crompton, "Male Love and Islamic Law," 142–157.

8. For perceptions of sodomy that festered in different parts of the peninsula at the end of the Visigothic period, see A. García Valdés, *Historia y presente de la homosexualidad: análisis crítico de un fenómeno conflictivo,* 37–41; J. Boswell, *Christianity, Social Tolerance, and Homosexuality: Gay People in Western Europe from the Beginning of the Christian Era to the Fourteenth Century,* 202–204, 289, 310. In another early, biblical reference to sodomy, Genesis 19 described how, when two angels sent by God to Sodom and Gomorraha, two metropolises renowned for sodomy, Lot provided shelter for them in his house. Before they went to bed, the men of Sodom, both young and old, encircled the house and asked Lot about the men he had sheltered that tonight. "Introduce us to them," begged the men of Sodom. The biblical response to this allusion of sodomitical behavior depicted how God rained fire from the sky and destroyed the metropolises with all their habitants and their vegetation. Quoted in García Valdés, *Historia,* 37, and in Boswell, *Christianity, Social Tolerance, and Homosexuality,* 115–143.

9. Kamen, *Spain,* 35.

10. F. Tomás y Valiente, "El crimen y pecado contra natura," in F. Tomás y Valiente, B. Clavero, A. M. Hespanha, J. L. Bermejo, E. Gacto, and C. Alvarez Alonso, *Sexo barroco y otras transgresiones premodernas,* 41–42. In 1996, Tomás y Valiente, a professor of law at the Universidad Compultense in Madrid and a former member of the Spanish Supreme Court, died in his chair as he sat in his university study, supposedly shot in the head by a member of the Basque terrorist organization ETA.

11. *Pragmática de los Reyes Católicos acerca de los reos de pecado nefando, Medina del Campo, 22 agosto 1497*, AGS, leg. 1, no. 4: "Salud y gracia. Sepades que acatando como Dios nuestro Señor por su infinita clemencia quiso encomendarnos la governacion destos nuestros Reinos e nos facer sus ministros en la execucion de la justicia en todo lo temporal, no reconosciendo en la administracion della otro superior."

12. The reader is referred to the discussion of laws against sodomites and Jews enacted by the *Fuero de Sepúlveda* and the *Fueros Reales*, lib. 4, tít. 9: "De los sodomitas . . . Mandamos que cualesquiera que sean que tal pecado fagan que luego . . . ambos dos sean castigados ante todo el pueblo e despues a tercer dia sean colgados por las piernas fasta que mueran." Quoted in Tomás y Valiente, "Crimen y pecado," 39. See also B. Bennassar, *Inquisición española: poder político y control social*, trans. J. Alfaya, 295–320; A. Mirabet y Mullol, *Homosexualidad hoy: ¿aceptada o todavía condenada?* 143–160.

13. R. J. González-Casanovas, "Male Bonding as Cultural Construction in Alfonso X, Ramon Llull, and Juan Manuel: Homosocial Friendship in Medieval Iberia," in J. Blackmore and G. S. Hutcheson (eds.), *Queer Iberia: Sexualities, Cultures, and Crossings from the Middle Ages to the Renaissance*, 164–169.

14. G. López (ed.), *Las siete partidas del sabio Rey D. Alfonso el nono*, vol. 3, 72–73; Alfonso X el sabio, *Las siete partidas: antología*, comp. F. López Estrada and M. T. López García-Berdoy. From the edition edited by G. López:

> Setena partida, Título XXI, De los que fazen pecado de luxuria contra naturam sodomitico dizen al pecado en que caen los omes yaziendo vnos con otros contra natura, e costubre natural. E porque de tal pecado nacen muchos males en la tierra, do se faze, e es cofa q[ue] pesa mucho a Dios con el. . . . Queremos aqui dezir apartadamente deste . . . e quien lo puede acusar, e ante quien. Et que pena merescen los fazedores e los consentidores. Ley I. Onde tomo este nome el pecado que dize sodomitico, e quantos males vienen del. Sodoma, e Gomorra fueron dos ciudades antiguas pobladad de muy male gente, e tanta fue la maldad de los omes que biuian en ellas, q[ue] porq[ue] vsauan aq[ue]l pecado q[ue] es contra natura, los aborrecio nuestro señor dios, de guisa que sumio ambas las ciudades con toda la gente que hi moraba. . . . E de aq[ue]lla ciudad Sodoma, onde Dios fizo esta maravilla tomo este nombe este pecado que llaman sodomitico. . . . E debese guardar todo ome deste yerro, porque nacen del muchos males, e denuesta, e deffama asi mismo el q[ue] lo faze . . . por tales yerros embia nuestro señor Dios sobre la tierra, hambre, e pestilencia, e tormentos, e otros males muchos que non podria contar. . . . Ley II. Quien puede acusar a los que sazen el pecado sodomitico, e ante quien, e que pena merecen aver los sazedores del, e los consentidores. Cada vno del pueblo puede acusar a los omes que hiziessen pecado contra natura, e este acusamiento puede ser hecho delante del judgador do hiziessen tal yerro. E si le fuere provado deve morir: tambien el que lo haze, como el que lo consiente . . . fueras ende, si alguno dellos lo oviere a

hazer por fuerca, o fuesse menor de catorze años . . . non deve recebir pena, porque los que son forcados no son en culpa, otro si los menores non entienden que es tan gra[ve] yerro como es aquel que hazen. Esa misma pena deve aver todo ome, o toda muger, que yoguiere con bestia, e deven de mas matar la bestia para amortiguuar la remembranca del hecho."

For a discussion about the authenticity of the *Partidas,* see F. Tomás y Valiente, *Manual de Historia del Derecho español,* 237.

15. F. W. Nietzsche, *The Birth of Tragedy and Other Writings,* ed. R. Geuss and ed./trans. R. Speirs. On the exclusion of sodomites and whores from the sacrament of baptism or receiving the Eucharist, see D. S. Bailey, *Homosexuality and the Western Christian Tradition;* C. Espejo Muriel, *El deseo negado: aspectos de la problemática homosexual en la vida monástica (siglos III–VI d.C.),* 151–197.

16. *Pragmática de los Reyes Católicos:*

Titulo XXX, De la sodomía, y bestialidad. Ley I. D. Fernando y Dña Isabel en Medina del Campo a 22 de Agosto de 1497. Pena del delito nefando; y modo de proceder a su averiguacion y castigo. Porque entre los otros pecados y delitos que ofenden a Dios nuestro Señor, e infaman la tierra, especialmente es el crimen cometido contra orden natural; contra el qual las leyes y derechos se deben armar para el castigo deste nefando delito, no digno de nombrar, destruidor de la orden natural, castigado por el juicio Divino; por el qual la nobleza se pierde, y el corazon se acobarda . . . y se indigna a dar a hombre pestilencia y otros tormentos en la tierra . . . y porque las antes de agora no son suficientes para estirpar, y del todo castigar tan abominable delito . . . y en quanto en Nos sera refrenar tan maldita macula y error . . . mandamos, que qualquier persona, de qualquier estado, condición, preeminencia o dignidad que sea, que cometiere el delito nefando contra naturam seyendo en el convencido por aquella manera de prueba, que segun Derecho es bastante para probar el delito de heregia o crimen laesae Majestatis, que sea quemado en llamas de fuego en el lugar, y por la Justicia a quien pertenesciere el conoscimiento y punicion del tal delito . . . y sin otra declaracion alguna, todos sus bienes asi muebles como raices; los quales desde agora confiscamos, y habemos por confiscados y aplicados a nuestra Camara y Fisco . . . y mandamos, que si acaesciere que no se pudiere probar el delito en acto perfecto y acabado, y se probaren y averiguaren actos muy propinquos y cercanos a la conclusion del, en tal manera que no quedase por el tal delinquente de acabar este danado yerro, sea habido por verdadero hechor del delito, y que sea juzgado y sentenciado, y padezca aquella misma pena . . . y que se pueda proceder en el dicho crimen a peticion de parate o de qualquier del pueblo, o por via de pesquisa, o de oficio de Juez: y proceder contra el ue lo cometiere, y en la manera de la probanza, asi para interlocutoria como para difinitiva, y para proceder a tormento y en todo lo otro, mandamos, se guarde la forma y orden que se guarda . . . en los crimenes y delitos de heregia y lae-

sae Majestatis . . . que los que fueren acusados sobre este delito, que lo ho-
biere cometido antes de la publicacion desta Pragmática y no despues, que se
guarden las leyes y Derechos que son hechas antes desta nuestra carta."

For a transcribed version of the *Prágmática*, see *Recopilación de las leyes destos reynos:
hecha por mandado de la Magestad Católica del Rey Don Felipe Segundo Nuestro Señor que se
ha mandado imprimir con las leyes que después de la última impression se han publicado por
la Magestad Católica del Rey Don Felipe Quarto el Grande Nuestro Señor*, lib. 12, tít. 30;
*Novísima recopilación de las leyes de España: dividida en XII libros, en que se reforma la recopi-
lación publicada por el Señor Don Felipe II en el año de 1567, reimpresa últimamente en el
de 1775: y se incorporan las pragmáticas, cédulas, decretos, ordenes y resoluciones reales, y otras
providencias no recopiladas, y expedidas hasta el de 1804 mandada formar por el Señor Don Carlos IV*, 427–429. See also M. J. de Ayala, *Notas a la recopilación de Indias: origen e historia ilustrada de las leyes de Indias*, J. Manzano Manzano (ed.).

17. López, *Siete partidas*, 329–330: "Todo hombre se ha de guardar de este error porque de el nacen muchos males . . . pestilencia y tormentos y otros."

18. *Compendio de algunas experiencias en los ministerios de que usa la Companía de Jesus, con que
practicamente se muestra con algunos acontecimientos y documentos el buen acierto en ellos, por orden de los superiores, por el Padre Pedro de León de la misma Companía*, 1619, BUG, caja B76,
fol. 292v. For a slightly altered version of the same manuscript, see *Compendio de
industrias en los ministerios de la Companía de Jesus, con que practicamente se muestra el buen
acierto en ellos, dispuetos por el Padre Pedro de Leon de la misma Companía de Jesus y por orden
de los superiores*, 1628, BUS, ms. 573 (3/4/53), tomo 2, ms. 574. Herrera Puga nicely
transcribed the original version in P. de León, *Grandeza y miseria en Andalucía: testimonio de una encrucijada histórica, 1578–1616*, ed. P. Herrera Puga.

19. *Petición de Mencía Velázquez cristiana nueva, mujer de Nuño de la Torre, boticario, vecina de la
villa de Arévalo ante el corregidor de dicha villa, por la que reclama la restitución de los bienes que
le fueron confiscados a su marido por cierto delito que cometió, alegando ella, que eran bienes dotales
que llevó a su matrimonio y que estaban comprendidos en la carta de dote otorgada el siete de marzo
de 1479*, ARCV, Pleitos Civiles Quevedo Fenecidos, legajo 315, cajas 1412–1414.

20. For histories about the clergy and their solicitation of men, boys, and others in
early or postmodern times, see J. A. Alejandre, *El veneno de Dios: la Inquisición de
Sevilla ante el delito de solicitación en confesión;* J. Leiva and N. Montoya, *La caña rota: la
confesión de un confesor del siglo XVIII;* A. Sarrión Mora, *Sexualidad y confesión: la solicitación ante el Tribunal del Santo Oficio (siglos XVI–XIX);* P. Rodríguez, *La vida sexual
del clero;* and M. L. Candau Chacón, *Los delitos y las penas en el mundo eclesiástico sevillano del XVIII.*

21. Tomás y Valiente, *Derecho penal*, 319.

22. Marañon, quoted in F. Vázquez García and A. Moreno Mengíbar, *Sexo y razón:
una genealogía de la moral sexual en España (siglos XVI–XX)*, 231: ". . . gran numero de
personas conocidas fueron inculpadas de sodomía desde criados y bufones de las
casas aristocraticas hasta los mismos señores de estas . . . uno de ellos era Don
Juan de Tarsis es la primera vez que el nombre de Villamediana aparece sin una

mujer a su lado. El era jefe de la banda. Los mas humildes fueron condenados a muerte y ejecutados en Madrid . . . a los pecadores encopetados les dejaron huir a Italia y a Francia."

23. Tomás y Valiente, "Crimen y pecado," 43–45.

24. In Aragon the tribunals sentenced minors under the age of twenty-five to death. By 1589 it became customary to apply the death penalty to minors over seventeen years of age. One year earlier, in 1588, a secular court in Seville sentenced Jerónimo, a minor and a slave, and his lady master to burn, having been accused of fornication with each other. That secular court based its decision on Alfonso's *Partida Séptima.* See *Compendio de algunas experiencias,* fol. 285v, and López, *Siete partidas,* partida 7, ley 15, p. 657: "Pero si fuese probado que la mujer casada hiciera adulterios con su siervo, no debe habler la pena sobredicha, mas deben ser quemados ambos por ende."

25. *Novísima recopilación de las leyes,* lib. 12, tít. 30 (ley 2, tít. 221, lib. 8r), 427–429:

> D. Felipe II en Madrid por pragm[ática] de 1592. Prueba privilegiada del delito nefando para la imposición de su pena ordinaria. Por muy justas causas al servicio de Dios . . . y a la buena execución de nuestra Real Justicia, y deseando extirpar de estos reynos el abominable y nefando pecado contra naturam, y que los que lo cometieren, sean castigados . . . sin que se puedan evadir ni excusar de la pena establecida por Derecho, leyes y Pragmáticas destos reynos de no estar suficiente probado el dicho delito por no concurrir en el averiguaciones de testigos contestes por ser de tan gran torpeza y abominación, y de su naturaleza de muy dificultosa probanza; mandamos, que en nuestro Consejo se tratase y confiriese sobre el remedio juridico que se podia proveer, para que los que lo cometiesen fuesen castigados, aunque el dicho delito no fuese probado con testigos, sino por otras formas establecidas y aprobadas en Derecho, de las quales pudiese resultar bastante probanza para poderese imponer en el la pena ordinaria . . . y mandamos, que probandose el pecado por tres testigos singulares mayores aunque cada uno dellos deponga de acto particular y diferente, o por quatro, aunque sean participes del delito, o padezcan otras qualesquier tachas que no sean de enemistad capital, o por los tres destos, aunque padeacan tachas, y hayan sido ansimismo participantes . . . se tenga por bastante probanza; y por ella se juzguen . . . de la misma manera que si fuera probado con testigos contestes, que depongan de un mismo hecho.

26. *Cartas acordadas por el S[eñor] Inq[uisitor] P[residente] y Señores del Supremo de la Inq[uisi]ón para Gobierno en los Tribunales del S[ant]o Off[ici]o,* BN, ms. 848, fols. 77r–77v, 146r–148v.

27. A. de Castro, *De potestate legis poenalis libri duo.* I am grateful to Fray Cándido Rubio, head librarian at the Biblioteca de la Facultad de Teología in Burgos for his warm support, attentive comments, reading, and supervision of the translations from the Latin.

28. S. de Beauvoir, "Must We Burn Sade?" in A. Wainhouse and R. Seaver (comps.), *Marquis de Sade: The 120 Days of Sodom and Other Writings*, 61.

29. Tomás y Valiente, "Crimen y pecado," 34–35.

30. E. Temprano, *El árbol de las pasiones: deseo, pecado, y vidas repetidas*, 53–54.

31. *Fadrique [Biel] de Basilea, doctrinal de los caballeros*, Burgos, 20 June 1487, BN, ms. 6607.

32. Ibid.

33. G. Salcedo de Aguirre, *Pliego de cartas en que ay doze espístolas escritas a personas de diferentes estados y officios*, quoted in Temprano, *Árbol de las pasiones*, 49. The text outlined the adequate manners for the *corregidor*, the soldier, the laborer, the master, the servant, etc.

34. *Pragmática y nueva orden, cerca de los vestidos y trajes assi de hombres como de mujeres*, quoted in Temprano, *Árbol de las pasiones*, 50. Erasmus of Rotterdam had also proposed a series of proper forms of behavior for Christian gentlemen—to renounce the sins of the flesh and avoid fostering a love for things contrary to established dogma. See Erasmus, *El enquiridion o manual del caballero christiano*, D. Alonso (ed.); and B. Bennassar, *L'homme espagnol: attitudes et mentalités du XVIe au XIXe siécle*.

35. B. Castiglione, *El cortesano*, trans. J. Boscán (1534). See also B. Castiglione, *El cortesano: tradvzido de Italiano en nuestro vulgar castellono, por Boscan*.

36. A. J. de Salas Barbadillo, *El caballero perfecto*; P. Marshall (ed.), *Salas Barbadillo*.

37. A. Panés, *Escala mística y estímulo de amor divino*, comp. F. P. Fuster.

38. *Sumario de la medicina*, BN, ms. I-1333, fol. 17r.

39. P. Brown, *The Body and Society: Men, Women, and Sexual Renunciation in Early Christianity*.

40. Temprano, *Árbol de las pasiones*, 59–78.

41. J. L. Vivés, *De institutione feminae christianae: la formación de la mujer cristiana*, trans. J. Beltrán Serra. The original text was published in Zaragoza in 1555. Shortly thereafter, forty editions were published and also translated from the Latin into Spanish, Dutch, Italian, French, and English. Vivés provided the following:

> Instrucción para doncellas: De como se debe criar la doncella, De la doctrina de las doncellas, De que libros debe leer, Del cuidado de la virginidad, De los atavios, afeites y olores, De lo que debe hacer la virgen fuera de casa, Del amor de la virgen, De como ha de buscar esposo. Instruccion para casadas: Que es lo que debe pensar la mujer cuando se casa. De como se ha de comportar con su marido. De los atavios. De como se ha de comportar fuera de casa. Del cuidado de los hijos. De como debe Relaciónarse con el hijo o la hija. Del comportamiento de la madre de familia ya avanzada en edad. Instrucción para las viudas: Del luto o llanto de la viuda. De la continencia y honestidad de la viuda. De como se ha de comportar dentro de casa . . . [y] fuera de casa.

Between the 1940s and the 1950s, during the post-civil-war period in Spain, the Catholic Falange resurrected Vivés' manual and published it under different titles. Yet again, the texts became essential guides that dictated proper behavior, customs, and dress deemed appropriate for the young women of that period. See *La mujer cristiana: de los deberes del marido, pedagogía pueril* and *Formación político-social: primer y segundo curso de bachillerato.* I am indebted to María José Ramírez Ramírez for the use of her copies of *Formación político-social,* texts she read during the 1960s for her social formation classes in a Catholic middle school in Bilbao. The 1960s texts included topics like "La familia, los hijos, el arte de comer, nuestro aspecto personal, la parroquia, el comportamiento en los edificios públicos," etc.

42. Temprano, *Árbol de las pasiones,* 62–63.

43. "Habla poco y con severidad a las mujeres. No se ha de desconfiar menos de las que son mas virtuosas, porque cuanto mayor es la virtud, tanto mayor es la inclinacion, y bajo el encanto de su palabra se esconde el virus de la mayor lascivia." See L. Carbonero y Sol (trans.), *Opúsculos de Santo Tomás de Aquino,* 117–118; F. E. Aragón (trans.), *Conocer por experiencia: un estudio de sus modos y valoración en la Summa Theológica de Tomás de Aquino;* S. Ortega Noriega, "El discurso teológico de Santo Tomás de Aquino sobre el matrimonio, la familia, y los comportamientos sexuales," in S. Alberro (ed.), *El placer de pecar y el afán de normar: ideologías y comportamiento familiares y sexuales en el México colonial,* 17–75; P. Hurteau, "Catholic Moral Discourse on Male Sodomy and Masturbation in the Seventeenth and Eighteenth Centuries," *Journal of the History of Sexuality* 4.1 (1993): 1–32.

44. Carbonero y Sol, *Opúsculos,* 117–118: "Si la mujer pudo vencer al hombre estando en el paraiso, no debe causarnos admiracion que seduzca a los que no estan en el paraiso . . . jamas os detengais con una mujer sola y sin testigo."

45. Ibid.

46. Temprano, *Árbol de las pasiones,* 76–77.

47. J. Enríquez, *Questiones practicas de casos morales por el P. F. Ivan Enriquez del Orden de S. Agustin.*

48. *A Catechism of Christian Doctrine Approved by Archbishops and Bishops of England and Wales and directed to be used in all their Dioceses,* 13.

49. D. Eisenberg, "Juan Ruiz's Heterosexual Good Love," in Blackmore and Hutcheson, *Queer Iberia,* 250–268.

50. In seventeenth-century Salamanca, for example, the local authorities customarily rid the city of prostitutes during Holy Week, for they thought it best not to sin, given the solemnity of the event. Then, on the second Monday after Easter, known as "lunes de aguas," young boys returning from Arrabal carried prostitutes in their arms as they crossed the Tormés River back into Salamanca. Quoted in M. H. Sánchez Ortega, *La mujer y la sexualidad en el antiguo régimen: la perspectiva inquisitorial,* 202, and her earlier "Costumbres y actitudes eróticas en la España de los Austrias," *Historia 16* 124 (1986): 48–58. See also R. Carrasco (ed.), *La Prostitution en Espagne: de l'époque des Rois Catholiques à la IIe République.*

51. Sánchez Ortega, *La mujer y la sexualidad,* 202; M. E. Lacarra, "La evolución de la prostitución en la Castilla del siglo XV y la mancebía de Salamanca en tiempos de Fernando de Rojas," in I. A. Corfis and J. T. Snow (eds.), *Fernando de Rojas and "Celestina": Approaching the Fifth Centenary,* 33–58.

52. Male intimate friendship as a social phenomenon susceptible to sodomy and homoeroticism is nicely sketched by González-Casanovas, "Male Bonding," 157–192.

53. S. de Salazar, *Promptuario de materias morales: en principios, y reglas para examen, y sucinta noticia de los que en breue se dessean exponer para confessores,* 345–346.

54. "... no se remedia ues este mal deseo ... sino antes se enciende mas ... porque menospreciadas las rameras y no haziendo caso de lo que esta en la mano, el animo una vez corrompido con el deleite siempre pasa y pretende cosas peores." Quoted in Ortega, *La mujer y la sexualidad,* 202.

55. Ibid.

56. Ibid.

57. "Madrid, jueves santo de 1637, un escribano real ... habiendo guardado ocasion y dia en que su mujer habia confesado y comulgado le dio garrote en su casa haciendo oficio de verdugo y pidiendole perdon, y esto por muy leves sospechas de que era adultera." Quoted in Tomás y Valiente, *Derecho penal,* 73.

58. Boswell, *Christianity, Social Tolerance, and Homosexuality,* 225–228. On the views of the different schools of philosophy, see Espejo Muriel, *Deseo negado,* 151.

59. A. Gómez, *Ad leges Tauri commentarius: opus elaboratum et perfectum in quo leges LXXXIII ad amussim,* 704–708: "Ley LXX, No. 32–35, Si quis habet accesum ad quamlibet aliam speciem vel materiam non aptam nec determinatam a natura ad coitum et generatinem secundum propriam speciem, committit delictum et crimen contra naturam." (Si alguien realiza un acceso carnal que no esta ordenando al coito natural y a la generación dentro de su especie, comete delito y crimen contra natura.)

60. *Compendio de algunas experiencias,* fol. 254v. On the relationship between pederasty and sodomy, see M. Rey, "Police et sodomie a Paris au XVIIIe siècle: du péche au desordre," *Revue d'Histoire Moderne et Contemporaine* 29 (1982): 113–124.

61. J. Blackmore, "The Poets of Sodom," in Blackmore and Hutcheson, *Queer Iberia,* 195–218.

62. F. de Quevedo y Villegas, "A un bujarrón," in J. M. Blecua (ed.), *Poesía original completa,* 651–652; F. Buendía (ed.), *Obras completas: Don Francisco de Quevedo y Villegas.*

63. P. Ciruelo, *Tratado en el qual se reprueuan todas las supersticiones y hechizerias: muy vtil y necessario a todos los buenos christianos zelosos de su saluacion.*

64. "Si alguien tiene acceso con otro hombre comete el abominable y detestable delito de sodomía contra natura, el cual es mas grave que los demas crimenes, admas del de herejia y tiende a la maxima ofensa de Dios y de toda la naturaleza." Quoted in Tomás y Valiente, "Crimen y pecado," 38–39.

65. Vázquez García and Moreno Mengíbar, *Sexo y razón,* 227.

66. On the convergence of the rupture of alliances against the familial order and God and other discourses about sexuality during the reign of Enrique IV Trastamara, see A. R. Firpo, "Los reyes sexuales: ensayo sobre el discurso sexual

durante el reinado de Enrique IV Trastamara (1454–1474)," *Mélanges de la Casa Veláquez* 20 (1984): 217–226; and G. Torrente Ballester, *Filomeno, a mi pesar: memorias de un señorito descolocado.*

67. Tomás y Valiente, "Crimen y pecado," 40–44.

68. López, *Siete partidas*, 72–73: "Omes, Partida VII, Aunque dice la ley hombres, se incluye tambien a las mujeres tanto cuando una con otra haga contra natura como cuando varon con hembra haga el coito contra natura . . . asi pues el pecado femenino es posible y ha de ser castigado."

69. Tomás y Valiente, "Crimen y pecado," 48.

70. R. Carrasco, *Inquisición y represión sexual en Valencia: historia de los sodomitas (1565–1785)*, 31–32. Sodomy meant three things: in the formal sense, a sin of lust; in a more general sense, a sin against nature, including bestiality; and a trope or metonym depicting the image of fornication through the "filthiest orifice" between men.

71. Ibid., p. 32; *Diccionario de Autoridades (Edición Facsímil de 1732)*, vol. 2, 658b: "Nefando: indigno, torpe, de que no se puede hablar sin empacho . . . Pecado nefando. Se llama el de Sodoma, por su torpeza y obscenidad."

72. Vázquez García and Moreno Mengíbar, *Sexo y razón*, 225.

73. Tomás y Valiente, "Crimen y pecado," 39; Blackmore, "Poets of Sodom," 211–213; M. E. Lacarra, "Parámetros de la representación de la sexualidad femenina en la literatura medieval castellana," in R. Walthaus (ed.), *La mujer en la literatura hispánica de la Edad Media y el Siglo de Oro*, 23–43. For a discussion related to the dearth of sources about female sodomites in Europe, see J. C. Brown, *Immodest Acts: The Life of a Lesbian Nun in Renaissance Italy*, 1–20; J. Bennett, "'Lesbian-Like' and the Social History of Lesbianisms," *Journal of the History of Sexuality* 9.1–2 (January–April 2000): 1–24; and V. Traub, *The Renaissance of Lesbianism in Early Modern England.*

74. M. Jordan, *The Invention of Sodomy in Christian Theology*; J. Richards, *Sex, Dissidence, and Damnation: Minority Groups in the Middle Ages.*

75. "Por esto los entrego Dios a las pasiones vergonzosas pues por una parte sus mujeres cambiaron el uso natural por el que es contra naturaleza . . . tambien los varones abandonando el uso natural de la mujer se abrazaron en la concupiscencia de los unos con los otros, hombres con hombres cometiendo cosas vergonzosas." Quoted in Tomás y Valiente, "Crimen y pecado contra natura," 46–48.

76. López, *Siete partidas*, 21.

77. Tomás y Valiente, "Crimen y pecado," 46–48: "Coito de mujer con mujer no se encuentra castigado por ley divina ni humana . . . aunque este es un pecado grave no es tan grave como el vicio sodomitico de varon con varon . . . mayor es la perturbacion del orden natural en el pecado sodomitico entre varones que entre mujeres."

78. Tomás y Valiente, "Crimen y pecado," 46.

79. *Cristobal de Chabes, Relación de las cosas de la carcel de Sevilla y su trato, N° 60, 1591,* AMS, sec. 2, Señor Conde del Aguila, tomo 3, fols. 39r–52v. For more detailed descriptions of the prison, see *Ensanchez de la segunda parte de las cosas que passan en la carcel reducidoz por Chabes vecino de Sev[ill]a, N° 70, 1592,* AMS, sec. 2, Señor Conde del Aguila, tomo 3, fol. 48v.: ". . . ha avido muchas mugeres, que queriendo ser mas hombres, que lo que la naturaleza les dio se han castigado muchas, que en la carcel se hacian gallos con vn baldres hecho forma de natura de hombre, que atado con sus cintas se lo ponian, y han llevado por esto doscientos azotes, y destierro perpetuo."

80. Tomás y Valiente, "Crimen y pecado," 48.

81. *Cartas acordadas por el S[eñor] Inq[uisidor] P[residente] y señores del supremo de la Inq[uisi]ón para govierno en los tribunales del S[ant]o Of[ici]o,* BN, ms. 848, fol. 77r.

82. *Ejecutoria a pedimiento de Catalina de Belunza, vecina de San Sebastian, año 1503,* ARCV, Registro de Reales Ejecutorias, caja 181, exp. 39, fols. 1r–2r: "Catalina de Belunza y Mariche de Oyarzun usaban en uno como hombre y mujer, echandose en una cama desnudas y retocandose y besandose y cabalgandose la una a la otra, y la otra a la otra, subiendose encima de sus vientres desnudos, pasando y haciendo actos que hombre con mujer deberia hacer carnalmente . . . el cual delito habian hecho y perpetrado muchas y diversas veces."

83. Ibid., fols. 3r–4v:

> El procurador fiscal Juan Sanchez de Sorola pedia las condenase en ellas y las hiciese ejecutar en sus personas y bienes . . . y asimismo pidio que Catalina fuese puesta a cuestion de tormento . . . Catalina fue puesta por dos veces a cuestion de tormento de agua y le fue dado en cierta forma, haciendole sobre ello ciertas amonestaciones y diligencias para que dijese la verdad la cual en los tormentos ni en alguno de ellos no dijo ni confeso cosa alguna antes dijo que era inocente y sin culpa . . . y alego . . . que la acusacion y pesquisa ser ninguno y de ningun efecto en especial porque Juan de Sorola era incapaz e inhabil y persona privada para poner la acusacion porque era hombre mentecato y estaba fuera de su juicio natural segun era notorio.

84. Ibid., fol. 8r: "Lo otro porque habiendo solamente contra ella un testigo y mujer y estando cumplidamente tachada y pareciendo por su dicho y deposicion ser ella participante del dicho pleito."

85. *Criminal contra Inés Santa Cruz y Catalina Ledesma por prostitutas y bujarronas cuya operación ejectuban con una caña en forma de miembro viril, año 1603,* AGS, Cámara de Castilla 2557, Perdones de viernes santo, leg. 9. The history of Santa Cruz and Ledesma is related by the current author in *The Little Canes: Male Fantasies of Carnal Copulation between Inés and Catalina, Two Dykes Roaming the Early Modern Castillian Countryside.*

86. Sánchez Ortega, *La mujer y la sexualidad,* 33.

87. A. de Torres, "Relación de cómo una monja de Úbeda se tornó hombre (1617)," in F. R. Uhagon y Guardamino, Marqués de Laurencin (ed.), *Relaciones históricas*

de los siglos XVI y XVII, 335–337. A surreal counterpart to the plight of Magdalena consists of the travails that occurred to "poor" Fray Diego Núñez, which began as painful bodily functions until one day he peeked into a mirror and found himself sporting a vagina. The case evolved in a 1733 cloister in Amecameca, Mexico, and is wittily recounted in A. Ouweneel, *De vergeten stemmen van Mexico: een reeks ontmoetingen in de acttiende eeuw,* 194–197. On hermaphrodites in early modern Spain, see Vázquez García and Moreno Mengíbar, *Sexo y razón,* 187–284; the authors discuss the discovery of Elena or Eleno de Cespedes' Inquisitorial *proceso* in the early 1970s (p. 191 n. 14). See also I. Burshatin, "Interrogating Hermaphroditism in Sixteenth-Century Spain," in S. Molloy and R. McKee Irwin (eds.), *Hispanisms and Homosexualities,* 3–18; and idem, "Written on the Body: Slave or Hermaphrodite in Sixteenth-Century Spain," in Blackmore and Hutcheson, *Queer Iberia,* 420–453.

88. *carga* = 2 *fanegas;* 1 *carga* = 149.6 kilos. On the conversions of weights and measures, see the tables constructed in A. Ouweneel, *Shadows over Anáhuac: An Ecological Interpretation of Crisis and Development in Central Mexico, 1730–1800,* 371. For an overview of the eighteenth-century Mexican tobacco industry and workers, see S. Deans-Smith, *Bureaucrats, Planters, and Workers: The Making of the Tobacco Monopoly in Bourbon Mexico.*

89. De Torres, "Relación," 337.

90. Fray Pedro de León, born in 1545 in Jeréz de la Frontera, joined the Jesuits in 1567 and died in Seville on 24 September 1632. De León's superiors at the Universidad de Granada stipulated that the manuscript "no se saque de la libreria sin licencia del superior, y que esto sea por dos horas, y se vuelva luego a poner en su lugar," and it was dated "6 mayo de 1619." Another recently discovered manuscript of the early modern period surfaced in the summer of 1977 in the midst of the renovation of the former monastery of the Padres Carmelitas Descalzados de San Lucar de Barrameda in Cádiz, today the parish of Carmen. The masonry laborers found the eighteenth-century manuscript rolled up, inserted in some sugarcane, and hidden in the roof, signed by Fray Francisco González Vázquez, who had lived in Mexico between 1788 and 1822. It contained his memoirs, or confession, of his sexual escapades with some seventy-one young adolescents, mostly boys but also girls. J. Leiva and N. Montoya retell this compelling history in *La caña rota,* op. cit. For a look inside the court, see L. Cabrera de Córdoba, *Relaciones de las cosas sucedidas en la Córte de España, desde 1599 hasta 1614.*

91. *Compendio de algunas experiencias,* fol. 1v.

92. Ibid., fol. 258r.

93. M. de Cervantes Saavedra, *El ingenioso hidalgo don Quixote de la Mancha,* 301.

94. M. Alemán, *Guzmán de Alfarache,* ed. J. M. Micó, vol. 2, 117–128; M. L. Copete, "Criminalidad y espacio carcelario en una cárcel del antiguo régimen: la cárcel real de Sevilla a finales del siglo XVI," *Historia Social* 6 (1989): 105–125.

95. *Ensanchez de la segunda parte,* fol. 53v.

96. Ibid., fols. 49v—53v.

97. *Compendio de algunas experiencias,* fol. 222r.

98. Ibid., fol. 293v.

99. "En fin de dicho mes de julio hablo el demonio como salir de la suya para sacar de quicios al pueblo que quedaba sin cabezas, porque habiendo predicado un maestro Luis Castelloi, de la orden de San Francisco . . . que el vicio de sodomía habia prendido en Valencia, traido por personas extranjeras de allende que a ocasion de mercadear la moraban y que este era el senuelo que llamaba los castigos de Dios que tan espesos llovian sobre nosotros y mas pestilencias, se exasperon las gentes tanto de oir aquel nefando nombre que pusieron faldas en cinta en buscar los culpados y habiendo descubierto cuarto de ellos [la] justicia criminal . . . los mando quemar." Quoted in Tomás y Valiente, "Crimen y pecado," 52—53.

100. Ibid., 53. Wanda echoed a similar sort of "sadomasochism" when she remarked to Severin, "I hope that my whip has cured you, that the treatment, cruel though it was, has proved effective." See L. von Sacher-Masoch, "Venus in Furs," in G. Deleuze (comp.), *Masochism.*

101. Vázquez García and Moreno Mengíbar, *Sexo y razón,* 226 n. 76.

102. B. Vincent and R. Carrasco, "Amor y matrimonio entre los moriscos," in B. Vincent (ed.), *Minorías y marginados en la España del siglo XVI,* 47—71.

103. G. W. Drost, "De Moriscos in de publicaties van Staat en Kerk (1492—1609)," Ph.D. diss., Rijksuniversiteit te Leiden, Netherlands, 1984; A. Mas, *Les turcs dans la littérature espagnole du Siècle d'Or: recherches sur l'evolution d'un thème littéraire;* G. Camamis, *Estudios sobre el cautiverio en el siglo de oro,* trans. M. Guillén.

104. Alemán, *Guzmán de Alfarache,* vol. 1, 125—142.

105. Sánchez Ortega, *La mujer y la sexualidad,* 260—263.

106. T. van der Meer, *Sodoms zaad in Nederland: het ontstaan van homoseksualiteit in de vroegmoderne tijd,* 370.

107. *Compendio de algunas experiencias,* fols. 373r—374r.

108. Ibid., fols. 288r—289v.

109. Ibid., fol. 374r.

110. Ibid., fol. 250r.

111. Ibid., fol. 307r.

112. Ibid., fols. 251v—252r.

113. Ibid., fol. 293v.

114. In his "Hermoso sitio de Sevilla," Morgado described the meadows: "Por lo alto pueden andar toda la cerca mano por mano dos personas. . . . La amenidad y la frescura de la Huerta le habian convertido en el refugio de las clandestinidades sociales mas comprometidas del siglo XVI." Quoted in Herrera Puga, 343—345.

115. *Compendio de algunas experiencias,* fols. 250r—251v.

116. Ibid., fols. 250v–251r. Kamen has argued that the Spanish Inquisition never burned the clergy and therefore acted more benevolently than secular courts in its application of the death penalty. But one can hardly describe the politics of power and the inherent contradictions of religious discourses as benevolence. See Kamen, *Spain*, 35.
117. *Compendio de algunas experiencias*, fols. 287v–290v.
118. Ibid., fol. 251r.
119. Ibid., fols. 255r, 289v.
120. Alemán, *Guzmán de Alfarache*, vol. 1, 140: "Era blanco, rubio, colorado, rizo . . . y traia copete." *"Copete"* is defined as "pelo que se levante encima de la frente mas alto que lo demas" in *Diccionario de Autoridades*, vol. 1, 584.
121. The French and the English also wore elaborate ruffs; however, in Spain the "lace ruff reached its most perfect, uncomfortable, and indulgent form." Between 1560 and 1580, lace became an increasingly important feature of fashionable dress in most European countries. It was representative of a Europe-wide development that gained momentum from the late fifteenth century on, as a result of political and economic changes. The expansion of trade produced new wealth expressed not only in ownership of land but also in cash and in goods—particularly by houses, possession of lavish furnishings, and luxurious dress. The gap between the new bourgeoisie and the poor widened. Lace making, as well as other luxury trade industries, flourished. New ideas, including those of dress, spread relatively quickly across the Continent. The leading courts of Spain, Italy, France, and England drew upon the same raw materials for their clothes: silks, embroideries, and passementerie from Italy and Spain, fine woolens from England, and linen and white work from Flanders. These histories are told in S. Levey, *Lace: A History*; M. Bruggeman, *Brugge en kant: een historische overzicht*; and B. Reade, *Het Spaanse costuum*.
122. P. Boissonnade, *Life and Work in Medieval Europe (Fifth to Fifteenth Centuries)*, trans. E. Power. Quoted in S. de Covarrubias Orozco, *Tesoro de la lengua castellana o española*, vol. 1, 17d: ". . . no es, no, trage de varón el que se vsa; atavío afeminado sí, que le estraña y astiga la modestia." Criticizing the poor state of the Crusade warriors, San Bernardo chastised them: ". . . vosotros haceis todo lo contrario llevais al modo de las damas larga cabellera que os estorba ver lo que teneis alrededor embarazais las piernas con vuestros largos vestidos envolveis vuestras piernas y delicadas manos con grandes velos . . . son estos equipajes de guerra o adornos de mujeres."
123. J. Torres Fontes and R. Bosque Carceller (eds.), *Epistolario del Cardenal Belluga*.
124. *Compendio de algunas experiencias*, fols. 253r–253v.
125. Ibid., fols. 252r–252v.
126. Ibid., fol. 301r: ". . . el primero cocinero y el otro hortelano . . . y a Domingo habian echado de casa porque parecía maricón." "Maricón" is defined as follows: "El hombre afeminado y cobarde, y lo mismo que marica. Lat. Vir mulier.

Marica. Se llama el hombre afeminado y de pocos brillos, que fe dexa fupedi-
tar y manejar, aun de los que son inferiores," in *Diccionario de Autoridades*, vol. 2,
499.

127. See the following, all in Blackmore and Hutcheson, *Queer Iberia:* C. Brown,
"Queer Representation in the *Arçipreste de Talavera*, or the *Maldezir de mugeres* Is
a Drag," 85–89; B. Weissberger, "¡A tierra, puto! Alfonso de Palencia's Discourse of Effeminacy," 291–319. Aggression as another aspect of masculinity-
effeminacy is related in L. Vasvári, "The Semiotics of Phallic Aggression and
Anal Penetration as Male Agonistic Ritual in the *Libro de buen amor*," 130–156;
and for perceptions of effeminacy prior to the early modern period, S. Lipton,
"*Tanquam effeminatum:* Pedro II of Aragon and the Gendering of Heresy in the
Albigensian Crusade," 107–129.

128. *Diccionario de Autoridades*, vol. 1, 104; *Diccionario Histórico de la Lengua Española*,
869–870.

129. A. Gómez Moreno and M. P. A. M. Kerkhof (eds.), *Obras completas: Íñigo López de
Mendoza, Marqués de Santillana;* J. A. de los Ríos (ed.), *Obras de Don Íñigo López de
Mendoza Marqués de Santillana: ahora por vez primera compiladas de los códices originales, é
ilustradas con la vida del autor.* On assuming the female role in a homocentric relationship, see G. S. Hutcheson, "Desperately Seeking Sodom: Queerness in
the Chronicles of Alvaro de Luna," in Blackmore and Hutcheson, *Queer Iberia*,
222–249.

130. P. Cieza de León, *La crónica del Perú*, 57: ". . . muchos de sus maridos están en sus
casas texendo y hilando . . . y haziendo otros oficios afeminados."

131. De Cervantes Saavedra, *El ingenioso hidalgo don Quixote*, 301: "¿Que quieres, Sancho
hermano?, respondio don Quixote, con el mesmo tono afeminado y doliente
que Sancho."

132. In *Filomena*, Lope de Vega wrote, "Era Diana bien hecha y de alto y propor-
cionado cuerpo, no tenía el rostro afeminado, con que pareció luego vn hermano mancebo." See J. Entrambasaguas (ed.), *Obras completas de Lope de Vega.*

133. B. de las Casas, *Apologética historia sumaria: cuanto a las cualidades, dispusición, descripción,
cielo y suelo destas tierras, y condiciones naturales, policías, repúblicas, manera de vivir e costumbres de las gentes destas indias occidentales y meridionales cuyo imperio soberano pertenece a
los reyes de castilla*, vol. 1, ed. E. O'Gorman, 85–87, 401–407, 470–471: ". . . de
los que habitan en la parte hacia el occidente afirma el contrario, diciendo que
son gentes más afeminadas y de más blandos y muelles corazones."

134. "Trayendole vn soldado vn vaso de agua en occasion que todo el exército
padecá gran sed en la Lybia, le derramo, diziendo que no era él más afeminado
que sus soldados." A. de Escalante, *Discurso breve a la Magestad Catolica del Rey nuestro señor don Felipe quarto diuidese en dos partes: en la primera se trata del auxilio y proteccion real en fauor de los pobres en la segunda se trata de la obligación de todos los vassallos al socorro de las necesidades del Patrimonio y Magestad real*, 77.

135. *Diccionario Histórico*, 869–870.

136. A. de Herrera, *Agricultura general, que trata de la labranza del campo, y sus particularidades,* fol. 145v: "Los gallos . . . no son todos buenos para machos, y vnos ay que de su misma naturaleza son afeminados."

137. de las Casas, *Apologética,* vol. 1, 403: "Este fue hombre torpisimo, muelle y afeminado, dado a todos vicios nefandos, según Diodoro." Ibid., vol. 2, 232: "Los afeminados se constituían en públicos o infames lugares para el oficio nefando, como las públicas mujeres." Ibid., 128: "Júntanse y adornanse [los hombres en Asia la Mayor], y cerca deste ejercicio exarden tanto que son quasi como mujeres, afeminados." Ibid., 359: "Vestiéndose vestidos de mujeres . . . íbanse con las mujeres y en oficios y artes mujeriles se ocupaban como ellas . . . a estos tales así afeminados, todos los otros sus vecinos adoran y reverencian." In 1596 the Jesuit de Torres also referred to the "abominable moral talent of effeminate men who dressed in women's clothing," although he did not directly identify sodomy as a characteristic vice of effeminate men; quoted in de Covarrubias Orozco, *Tesoro de la lengua castellana,* 17d. In sixteenth- and seventeenth-century Valencia, for example, cases of cross-dressing fell under the jurisdiction of the criminal tribunals, whereas the Inquisition persecuted sodomites. For more on early modern cross-dressing, see U. K. Heise, "Transvestism and the Stage Controversy in Spain and England (1580–1680)," *Theatre Journal* 44 (1992): 357–374; E. Rhodes, "Skirting the Men: Gender Roles in Sixteenth-Century Pastoral Books," *Journal of Hispanic Philology* 11.2 (winter 1987): 131–149; and C. Bravo-Villasante, *La mujer vestida de hombre en el teatro español (siglos XVI–XVII).*

138. Alemán, *Guzmán de Alfarache,* vol. 1, 245–246: ". . . que pues demas que son actos de afeminados maricas, dan ocasión para que dellos murmuren y se sospeche toda vileza viendolos embarrados y compuestos con las cosas solo a mujeres permitidas."

139. In *Hermosa Angélica,* Lope de Vega asked: "¿Qué furia . . . te incita . . . a dar el premio a un hombre afeminado, con habla, trage y mugeril adorno?" See Entrambasaguas, *Obras completas de Lope de Vega.*

140. F. de Quevedo Villegas, *La vida del Buscón llamado Don Pablos,* in D. Ynduráin (ed.): "Y porque no le tengan por maricon, abaxe effe cuello y agovie de efpaldas." Quoted in de Covarrubias Orozco, *Tesoro de la lengua castellana,* 17d.

141. De Quevedo Villegas, *España defendida,* quoted in de Covarrubias Orozco, *Tesoro de la lengua castellana,* 17d: "Y lo que más es de sentir, es de la manera que los hombres las imitan en las galas y lo afeminado."

142. Ibid.: ". . . el hombre de condición mugeril, inclinado a ocuparse en lo que ellas tratan y hablar en su lenguage y en su tono delicado."

143. M. McIntosh, "The Homosexual Role," *Social Problems* 16.2 (1968): 182–192; A. Bray, *Homosexuality in Renaissance England,* 13; R. Trumbach, "Sodomite Subcultures, Sodomitical Roles, and the Gender Revolution of the Eighteenth Century: The Recent Historiography," in R. P. Maccubbin (ed.), *Unauthorized Sexual Behavior during the Enlightenment, Eighteenth-Century Life* 9.3 (1985): 114–117.

Trumbach noted that the concept of effeminacy at the beginning of the seventeenth century referred to a man debilitated from the excessive carnal access to women.

144. Carrasco, *Inquisición y represión sexual*, 32; R. García Carcel, *Herejía y sociedad en el siglo XVI: la Inquisición en Valencia (1530–1609)*, 288–294; B. Bennassar, "Le modèle sexuel: l'Inquisition d'Aragon et la répression des pechés abominables," in B. Bennassar (ed.), *L'Inquisition Espagnole (XVe–XIXe siècles)*, 343–344.

145. Bennassar, "Le modèle sexuel," 343–344; Tomás y Valiente, "Crimen y pecado," 51. On the revival of the Inquisition by the Catholic Monarchs, see *Cartas acordadas por el S[eñor] Inq[uisidor] P[residente] y señores del supremo de la Inq[uisici]ón para govierno en los tribunales del S[ant]o Of[ici]o*, BN, ms. 848, fol. 77B; S. Haliczer, *Inquisition and Society in the Kingdom of Valencia (1478–1834)*.

146. Carrasco, *Inquisición y represión sexual*, 32.

147. Ibid., 34, 49–50.

148. Vázquez García and Moreno Mengíbar, *Sexo y razón*, 230–232.

149. For other chronicles of counter-reformist Spain at the height of the baroque, see the work of Hernando Pellicer and Jeronimo Barrionuevo, two writers of the seventeenth century in Tomás y Valiente, *Derecho penal*, 229.

150. "1605 . . . en mi braqueta yo tengo la Inquisición . . . comer, beber y fornicar no lo tenia por pecado y que no era pecado . . . era pecado mortal tener el cuenta carnal con una mujer que lo tenia por oficio porque los hombres no debian de andar con otros hombres ni a las bestias." Quoted in Sánchez Ortega, *La mujer y la sexualidad*, 203.

151. M. Foucault, *Historia de la locura en la época clásica*, trans. J. J. Utrilla, 23; Vázquez García and Moreno Mengíbar, *Sexo y razón*, 230–232.

152. J. Brown and J. H. Elliott, *A Palace for a King: The Buen Retiro and the Court of Philip IV*. The king had other worries; see R. Carrasco, "Les pouvoirs et "le pervers": éléments pour une histoire de certains minorités à l'époque de Philippe IV," *Imprévue* (1980–1981): 31–52. See also T. F. Ruiz, *Spanish Society (1400–1600)*, and D. Nirenberg, *Communities of Violence: Persecution of Minorities in the Middle Ages*.

153. B. Parera, "La Escuela Tomista española en el siglo XVII," in *Historia de la teología española: desde fines del siglo XVI hasta la actualidad*, vol. 1, 9–38, and "Los Inicios de la Escolástica Barroca," in *Historia de la teología cristiana: prereforma, reformas, contrareforma*, vol. 2, 596–644; A. Melquiadez, "La teología en el siglo XVI (1470–1580): el ideal de hombre nuevo en nuestros místicos," in *Historia de la teología española: desde fines del siglo XVI hasta la actualidad*, vol. 1, 693–695.

154. Bennassar, "Le modèle sexuel," 343–348.

155. R. J. Pym, "The Subject in Spain's Seventeenth-Century Comedia," *Bulletin of Hispanic Studies* 75 (1998): 290–292 n. 14.

156. Ibid., 276; A. Cascardi, *The Limits of Illusion: A Critical Study of Calderón*, 12.

157. Pym, "Subject in Spain's Seventeenth-Century Comedia," 276.

158. Carrasco, *Inquisición y represión sexual*, 49–50; see the 1758 case of Gesualdo Felices, aristocrat in Valencia, who organized parties for young boys, asking them to spank him and then to engage in further sodomitical play.
159. Vázquez García and Moreno Mengíbar, *Sexo y razón*, 233 n. 90.
160. Tomás y Valiente, *Derecho penal*, 51.

Chapter 3

1. *Cádiz año de 1698 causa escriptta de oficio de justicia contra Juan Mole, Bartholomé Barres, Juan Baptista Pino, y Phelip Esmirle, sobre decisse, aver cometido todos, el pecado de sodomía con el dicho Juan Mole*, AGI, Escribanía, 1105B, fols. 80r–81r; *El fiscal con Bartholomé Barres sobre haver cometido el pecado nefando, 1700, dos autos*, AGI, Escribanía, 960.
2. *Cádiz año de 1698 causa escriptta*, fols. 95r–96r. The scrivener underlined the words "passed over the flames" in the original manuscript.
3. M. Sinha, *Colonial Masculinity: The "Manly Englishman" and the "Effeminate Bengali" in the Late Nineteenth Century*, 9.
4. In northern Castile, the chancellery in Valladolid functioned as the counterpart of its sister court in Granada.
5. J. de Veitia Linaje, *Norte de la contratación de las Indias occidentales;* R. Antuñez y Acevedo, *Memorias históricas sobre la legislación y gobierno del comercio de los españoles con sus colonias en las Indias occidentales;* P. Chaunu and H. Chaunu, *Seville et l'Atlantique*, vol. 1, 182–184; *Compendio de la arte de navegar, de Rodrigo Camoraño, astrólogo y matematico, y cosmógrafo de la Magestad Cathólica de Don Felipe segundo Rey de España, y su catedrático de cosmografía en la casa de la Contratación de las Indias de la ciudad de Sevilla;* J. Pulido Rubio, *El piloto mayor de la Casa de la Contratación de Sevilla: pilotos mayores, catedráticos de Cosmografía y cosmógrafos.*
6. J. López de Velasco, "De la Casa de la Contratación de Sevilla, y cosas proveídas para la navegación de las Indias," in his *Geografía y descripción universal de las Indias*, 45. On royal government in the Indias, see J. M. Ots Capdequí, *El Estado Español en las Indias*, 45–65.
7. López de Velasco, "De la Casa de la Contratación," 45; J. Lynch, *Spain 1516–1598: From Nation to World Empire*, 232–236.
8. For a description of the galleons, see C. R. Phillips, *Six Galleons for the King of Spain: Imperial Defense in the Early Seventeenth Century*. On patterns of immigration, see López de Velasco, "De la Casa de la Contratación," 46; and A. P. Jacobs, "Migraciones laborales entre España y América: la procedencia de marineros en la carrera de Indias (1598–1610)," *Revista de Indias* 193 (1991): 523–543, and his *Los movimientos migratorios entre Castilla e Hispanoamérica durante el reinado de Felipe III (1598–1621).*
9. López de Velasco, "De la Casa de la Contratación," 45.
10. Ibid., 34–35.
11. M. van Harten, *Instruments of Torture: From the Middle Ages to the Age of Enlightenment;* J. L. Bermejo Cabrero, "Tormentos, apremios, cárceles, y patíbulos a finales del

antiguo régimen," *Anuario de Historia del Derecho Español* 56 (1986): 683–727; F. Tomás y Valiente, *La tortura en España: estudios históricos.*

12. B. Bennassar, "Le modèle sexuel: l'Inquisition d'Aragon et la répression des pechés abominables," in B. Bennassar (ed.), *L'Inquisition Espagnole (XVe–XIXe siècles)*, 339–344; R. Rosselló i Vaquer and J. Bover Pujol, *El sexe a Mallorca: notes historiques;* R. Carrasco, *Inquisición y represión sexual en Valencia: historia de los sodomitas (1565–1785)*, 39–41, 50–88, and idem, "Le châtiment de la sodomie sous l'Inquisition (XVIe et XVIIe siècles)," *Mentalités: histoire des cultures et des sociétés* 3 (1989): 53–69; R. García Carcel, *Herejía y sociedad en el siglo XVI: la Inquisición en Valencia (1530–1609)*, 289–291; D. Eisenberg, "Spain," in W. R. Dynes (ed.), *Encyclopedia of Homosexuality*, vol. 2, 1236–1242; A. Redondo (ed.), *Amours légitimes et amours illégitimes en Espagne (XVIe–XVIIe siècles)* and *Relations entre hommes et femmes en Espagne aux XVIe et XVIIe siècles;* F. Vázquez, *Mal menor: políticas y representaciones de la prostitución (siglos XVI–XIV);* A. Saint-Saëns (ed.), *Religion, Body, and Gender in Early Modern Spain;* H. C. Lea, *A History of the Inquisition in Spain*, vol. 4, 361–377; A. Sahuquillo, *Federico García Lorca y la cultura de la homosexualidad: Lorca, Dalí, Cernuda, Gil-Albert, Prados, y la voz silenciada del amor homosexual;* and the following in F. Tomás y Valiente, B. Clavero, A. M. Hespanha, J. L. Bermejo, E. Gacto, and C. Alvarez Alonso (eds.), *Sexo barroco y otras transgresiones premodernas:* F. Tomás y Valiente, "Delincuentes y pecadores," 11–31, and "El crimen y pecado contra natura," 33–55; B. Clavero, "Delito y pecado: noción y escala de transgresiones," 57–89; and J. L. Bermejo Cabrero, "Justicia penal y teatro barroco," 91–108. In Castilla y León, the Chancellery Court in Valladolid prosecuted some twelve cases between 1498 and 1626. See *Ejecutoria del pleito sobre acusar al demandado del pecado nefando el licenciado Zarate y el bachiller Pedro de la Mota, alcaldes de Burgos y el licenciado del Castillo y Diego de Soria, regidores de Burgos que de su oficio procedieron contra Rodrigo de Orozco, vecino de Villaldemiro, año 1498,* ARCV, Registro de Reales Ejecutorias, L 126/13/14; *Ejecutoria a pedimiento de Catalina de Belunza, vecina de San Sebastián, año 1503,* ARCV, Registro de Reales Ejecutorias, caja 181, exp. 39; *Fernán Diañez de Lobon corregidor de la villa de Arévalo con Nuño de la Torre, boticario, cristiaño nuevo, vecino de dicha villa sobre acusarle del delito de sodomía, año 1514,* ARCV, Pleitos Civiles Quevedo Fenecidos, leg. 315, caja 1412–1414, fol. 2r; *Ejecutoria del pleito contra Agustín Corco, Genovés por el pecado nefando, año 1516,* ARCV, Registro de Reales Ejecutorias, caja 312, exp. 30; *Sodomía . . . contra Juan Díaz, Alahama Granada, Francisco de Pinela Logroño, Francisco Ortiz de Legarte, 1531–1534,* AGS, Cámara de Castilla, Memoriales, 203–206, 210, 217–232, 218–291, 221–292, 223–266; *Alonso de Buendia contra Tomás Grueso, intento de sodomía con un hijo de Alonso edad de ocho años, 1572,* AGS, Consejo Real de Castilla, A 205–208; *Proceso del fiscal de S[u] M[ajestad] contra Fernando de Vera, corregidor de Murcia . . . [y] Vera contra Maria Zuniga su mujer por la custodia de su hija, año 1595,* AGS, Consejo Real de Castilla, legs. 387–389; *Criminal contra Inés Santa Cruz y Catalina Ledesma por prostitutas y bujarronas cuya operación ejecutaban con una caña en forma de miembro viril, año 1603,* AGS, Cámara Castilla 2557, leg. 9; *Proceso contra Nicolás de Ibarguen*

por el pecado nefando, año 1616, ARCV, Sala de Vizcaya, legs. 912–1003; and *Proceso contra Francisco de Uribe Aldecoa y Nicolás de Lazagoitia por el pecado nefando, año 1626,* ARCV, Sala de Vizcaya, legs. 1363–1406. The prosecution of sodomy in Castilla y León extended well into the late eighteenth century. See *Manuel Arredondo Carmona, corregidor de Guipuzcoa sobre que se contengan los excesos que cometen los ermitaños de la provincia de Guipuzcoa al solicitar limosnas y cometer actos de sodomía en contravención de la regla de la orden de carmelitas descalzos a la que pertenecen, 1747,* AHN, Consejos Suprimidos, leg. 534, exp. 2; *El fiscal con Francisco Guerrero de Malaga sobre acusarle de abusos deshonestos, 1749,* ARCV, Sala de Vizcaya, legs. 1222–1302; *Sobre la intromision de la Sala de Alcaldes de casa y corte en las causas de comicos especialmente contra Baltasar Diaz, comico y consortes Juan Palanco, corregidor de Madrid, juez protector de comediantes, vecino de Madrid, contra Marcos de Argaiz, alcalde de barrio de Bilbao . . . tres causas contra Nicola Setaro, Italiano, autor de operas . . . Gabriel López, actor y Baltasar Díaz, comico de la Compañía de Eusebio de Ribera, 1773–1778,* AHN, Consejos Suprimidos, leg. 611, exp. 6; *El fiscal con Nicolás Setaro de Napoles sobre acusarle de abusos deshonestos, 1774,* ARCV, Sala de Vizcaya, legs. 1203–1303; *El fiscal con Miguel Rodríguez Serraño, soltero jornalero del campo; Rafael Rubio, casado, albañil y Manuel González, casado esquilador, presos en la carcel de la Real Audiencia Chancilleria sobre acusarles de haber cometido sodomía con Jose de doce años tambien preso en dicha carcel, 1782,* ARCV, Pleitos Criminales, caja 336.1/339.1; and *El fiscal con Juan de Asua de Vizcaya sobre acusarle de abusos deshonestos, 1783,* ARCV, Sala de Vizcaya, legs. 614–701. Also see T. A. Mantecón, "Meaning and Social Context of Crime in Preindustrial Times: Rural Society in the North of Spain, Seventeenth and Eighteenth Centuries," *Crime, History, and Society* 1.2 (1998): 49–73.

13. Popular slang for the gallows, quoted in M. B. Rediker, "Liberty beneath the Jolly Roger: The Lives of Anne Bonny and Mary Read, Pirates," 1–33, and in D. Dugaw, "Female Sailors Bold: Transvestite Heroines and the Markers of Gender and Class," 34–54, both in M. S. Creighton and L. Norling (eds.), *Iron Men, Wooden Women: Gender and Seafaring in the Atlantic World (1700–1920).*

14. *Cristobal de Chabes, Relación de las cosas de la carcel de Sevilla y su trato, N° 60, 1591,* AMS, sec. 2, Señor Conde del Aguila, tomo 3, fols. 39r–52v; *Ensanchez de la segunda parte de las cosas que passan en la carcel reducidoz por Chabes vecino de Sev[ill]a, N° 70, 1592,* AMS, sec. 2, Señor Conde del Aguila, tomo 3, fols. 53r–85v; *Efemérides de Sevilla 1597,* AMS, Sección Especial, Papeles del Señor Conde del Aguila, cuaderno 1, fols. 11r, 32r–33v: ". . . en 29 de dicho ajusticiaron a Don Alonso Henrrigues de Guzmán por el pecado nefando y a un mancebo con quien estando preso lo comettia . . . 1597 . . . en lunes 28 de abril el lic. Pedro Velarde Alcalde del Crimen de la Chansilleria de Granada . . . procedio contra D. Alonso Celles Gixón sobre la muerte de Dña Ines de Guerara su muger defunta y sobre lo demas contenido en su proceso: lo condeno aque fuese llevado por las calles públicas de Sevilla . . . hasta el campo fuera de la puertta de Jerez donde se le diese primero garrote y luego quemado por el pecado nefando . . . y en perdida de todos sus

bienes; yba D. Alonso en mula de silla, vesttido de lutto y con el su paje con quien comettia el delitto con opa blanca en albarda a los quales dos quemaron en el quemadero de la Inquisición en tres deste mes de abril . . . 1600 en 19 de abril quemaron 15 hombres juntos . . . por el pecado nefando." Other histories about sodomy are related in F. de Ariño, *Sucesos de Sevilla de 1592–1604.*

15. E. W. Monter, "Sodomy: The Fateful Accident," in W. Dynes and S. Donaldson (eds.), *History of Homosexuality in Europe and America*, vol. 5, 276–299; García Carcel, *Herejía y sociedad*, 288; B. Bennassar, "Le modèle sexuel," 346; Carrasco, *Inquisición y represión sexual*, 65–88. Periods of greater repression occurred in Valencia between 1530 and 1609, where the Inquisition prosecuted 178 men, and in Zaragoza between 1541 and 1580, where the tribunal prosecuted another 155. The total numbers of prosecutions between 1540 and 1700 were 379 for Valencia, 791 for Zaragoza, and 453 for Barcelona.

16. Carrasco, *Inquisición y represión sexual*, 65–88.

17. P. E. Pérez-Mallaína, *Los Hombres del Océano*, 172. For a hasty translation of Pérez-Mallaína's book, see Pérez-Mallaína, *Spain's Men of the Sea: Daily Life on the Indies Fleets in the Sixteenth Century*, trans. C. R. Phillips. For the life of mariners from a more literary perspective, the reader is referred to the first "queer" novel of the modern period in the Western world: A. Caminha, *Bom-Crioulo.* For an excellent translation of the book into the Spanish, see A. Caminha, *Bom-Crioulo: una obra maestra de la literatura brasileña del siglo XIX*, trans. L. Zapata. R. Howes interrogates Caminha's work in his "Race and Transgressive Sexuality in Adolfo Caminha's *Bom-Crioulo*," *Luso-Brazilian Review* 38.1 (2001): 41–62.

18. *Cádiz año de 1698 causa escriptta*, fols. 101r–101v.

19. One quintal equals a hundredweight. These and other cultural significations are defined in *Diccionario Español e Inglés, conteniente la fignificacion y uso de las voces, con terminos propios a la Marina, a las Artes, Ciencias y Comercio, con la acentuación de la Real Academia de Madrid: nueva edición, revista y corregida defpues de la edición de Joseph Baretti, Secretarie de la Real Correfpondencia de Pintura, Efcultura y Arquitectura*, vol. 1; *Bocabulario de los nombres que usa la gente de mar en todo lo que perteneze a fu arte por el horden alfabetico, 1596*, BRAH, 9/5138, fol. 97r; and *Derofro de mar Mediterraneo, 1614, desde el cabo de Santo Vizente a Cádiz*, BRAH, 9/5138, B 53.

20. *Cádiz año de 1698 causa escriptta*, fols. 98r–100r.

21. A. Ouweneel, *Shadows over Anáhuac: An Ecological Interpretation of Crisis and Development in Central Mexico, 1730–1800*, 7.

22. Sinha, *Colonial Masculinity*, 9.

23. G. L. Mosse, *Nationalism and Sexuality: Middle-Class Morality and Sexual Norms in Modern Europe.*

24. *Cádiz año de 1698 causa escriptta*, fols. 52r–52v.

25. Ibid., fols. 1r–3v.

26. Ibid., fol. 78r.

27. Ibid., fols. 5r–5v.

28. Ibid., fol. 9r.

29. Ibid., fol. 10r.
30. Ibid., fols. 52r–53v.
31. Ibid., fols. 101r–101v.
32. Ibid., fols. 58r–58v.
33. Pérez-Mallaína, *Los Hombres del Océano*, 11.
34. On population and Seville, consult M. A. Ladero Quesada, *Andalucia en torno a 1492: estructuras, valores, sucesos*; F. Morales Padrón, *Historia de Sevilla: la ciudad del quinientos*; A. Domínguez Ortiz, *Orto y ocaso de Sevilla: estudio sobre la prosperidad y decadencia de la ciudad durante los siglos XVI y XVII*; and A. Domínguez Ortiz, *Sociedad y mentalidad en la Sevilla del antiguo regimen*.
35. Pérez-Mallaína, *Los Hombres del Océano*, 12–13.
36. M. Alemán, *Guzmán de Alfarache*, vol. 1, ed. J. M. Micó, 40: "Sevilla era bien acomodada para cualqir granjeria, y tanto se lleve a vender, como se compra, porque hay mercantes para todo. Es partria comun, dehesa franca, nudo ciego, campo abierto, globo sin fin, madre de huerfanos ya capa de pecadores, donde todo es necesidad y ninguno la tiene."
37. Pérez-Mallaína, *Los Hombres del Océano*, 13–19.
38. G. Braun and F. Hogenberg, *Civitates orbis terrarvm*.
39. I owe this point to Ouweneel.
40. Fray T. de la Torre, "Diario del viaje de Salamanca a Ciudad Real, Chiapas (1544–1545)," in J. L. Martínez (comp.), *Pasajeros de Indias: viajes transatlánticos en el siglo XVI*, 248: ". . . el navio es una carcel muy estrecha y muy fuerte de donde nadie puede huir aunque no lleve grillos ni cadenas y tan cruel que no hace diferencia entre los presos igualmente trata y estrecha a todos."
41. *Proceso contra Cristóbal Maldonando en la mar navegando hacia La Havana, 4 octubre de 1572*, AGI, Contratación 58, fol. 58r: "Señor, soy yo algun hereje o algun malhombre que no pueda yo salir a donde otros pasajeros salgan a dormir porque hace calor . . . pues joden ellos, dejenos buscar a nosotros la vida . . . las pasajeras . . . se cabalgan de popa a proa arrimadillas, dejenos a nosotros cabalgar a donde hallaremos."
42. Pérez-Mallaína, *Los Hombres del Océano*, 167–169.
43. *Ordenanzas reales, para la Casa de la Contratación de Seuilla, y para otras cosas de las Indias, y de la nauegación y contratación dellas*.
44. On the annual embarkations from Seville, see P. Chaunu and H. Chaunu, *Seville et l'Atlantique*, vol. 6, 329.
45. M. B. Rediker, *Between the Devil and the Deep Blue Sea: Merchant Seamen, Pirates, and the Anglo-American Maritime World (1700–1750)*.
46. Pérez-Mallaína, *Los Hombres del Océano*, 169.
47. *The Country Life Book of Nautical Terms under Sail*, 2.
48. Pérez-Mallaína, *Los Hombres del Océano*, 158–162.
49. *Libros prohibidos por el Santo Oficio que se entiende habra algunos entre españoles para que los comisarios del distrito los hagan publicar y recoger de las partes a donde no habra llegado el catalogo general, 1587*, AGN, Inquisición, tomo 140, no. 14.

50. Pérez-Mallaína, *Los Hombres del Océano*, 162–166. Prayer books included *Libro de la oración* and *Oratorio espiritual*. In *Flossanctorum*, de Villegas wrote a history of saints, and de Illesca opted for one of popes in *Historia Pontifical*. More literary works included *Orlando Furioso* and *Amadis de Gaula*, two chivalry novels; *La araucana*, an epic military poem; *La Diana*, a pastoral novel; and *El cancionero de Guzmán*, a work about traditions and values. The historical text *Repertorio de Chaves* presented a compilation of medieval and early modern laws. *Flossanctorum, Historia Pontifical,* and *Oratorios y consuelos espiritual* all appeared on the list of material prohibited by the Mexican Inquisition. For further reading, see *Edicto sobre libros prohibidos, 1600,* AGN, Inquisición, tomo 265, no. 2, and tomo 140, nos. 2, 7, and 14; F. Fernández del Castillo, *Libros y libreros en el siglo XVI.*

51. J. de Escalante de Mendoza, *Itinerario de navegación de los mares y tierras occidentales (1575),* 46–50.

52. For a more detailed description of these officers, other mariners, and their vernacular, see Pérez-Mallaína, *Los Hombres del Océano*, 84–128; J. van Beylen, *Zeilvaart Lexicon: Viertaglig Maritiem Woordenboek; Country Life of Nautical Terms;* A. Boudriot, *The Seventy-Four Gun Ship: A Practical Treatise on the Art of Naval Architecture,* trans. D. H. Roberts; H. N. Kamer, *Het VOC Retourschip: een panorama van de 17de- en 18de-eeuwe Nederlandse Scheepsbouw;* and *Diccionario marítimo Inglés-Español redactado por orden del nuestro Señor.* For particulars about other mariners and sodomy, see H. Turley, *Rum, Sodomy, and the Lash: Piracy, Sexuality, and Masculine Identity;* and B. R. Burg, *Sodomy and the Pirate Tradition: English Sea Rovers in the Seventeenth-Century Caribbean.*

53. Pérez-Mallaína, *Los Hombres del Océano*, 153–158.

54. Ibid., 33–60.

55. Ibid., 61. Vizcaínos usually formed the crew for war expeditions, and Andalusians represented the majority of the crew on merchant ships. For a more detailed version of migratory patterns, see Jacobs, *Los movimientos migratorios.*

56. *Testimonio de vista y revista contra Juan García, testigo falso,* AGI, Patronato, 254, N3, General 2, ramo 2, fols. 17r–17v, 19r–20v.

57. *El Consejo de Indias a Sebastián Caboto, Toledo, 12 de noviembre de 1525,* AGI, Indiferente General, 2495: "Señor capitan . . . somos informados como en la Armada va muy poca gente . . . y que los mas de los marineros que lleva son extrangeros de estos reinos . . . y segun que de esto tenemos nos parece que convendria que fuese mas gente . . . y que no fuese mas del tercio de los marineros extranjeros."

58. Pérez-Mallaína, *Los Hombres del Océano*, 45–67.

59. *Relación de las personas que han fallecido en la armada que el emperador nuestro Señor ha enviado al descuubrimiento del especieria de que es capitan general Fernando de Magallanes,* AGI, Patronato, 34, ramo 11, fols. 1r–1v.

60. *Lista de alardes y pagamentos de la gente de mar y guerra de las embarcaciones que componen la armada del lugarteniente general Alvaro Flores, 1565,* AGI, Contaduría, 468, N3; *Gente de mar muerta de galleones, 1565,* AGI, Contaduría, 468, N2, fol. 11r.

61. *Gente de mar muertua de galleones, 1565,* AGI, Justicia, 886 (1565).

62. *Instrucción a los maestres de la Carrera de Indias, Sevilla 26 de marzo de 1568,* AGI, Indiferente General, 2005.

63. Pérez-Mallaína, *Los Hombres del Océano,* 63–68.

64. *Proceso contra Cristoval, grumete de la nao Escorchapin sobre haber cometido el pecado nefando con Gaspar, grumete de la misma nao, 1560–1561,* AGI, Justicia, 1181, N2, R5, fol. 2r.

65. Ibid., fols. 2r–2v.

66. Ibid., fol. 3r.

67. Ibid., fol. 4r.

68. Ibid., fols. 10v–11v.

69. Ibid., fols. 4r–4v.

70. Ibid., fols. 4v–5r.

71. Ibid., fol. 5v.

72. Ibid., fol. 6r.

73. Ibid.

74. Ibid., fols. 6r–7r.

75. Ibid., fols. 7r–7v.

76. Ibid., fols. 44r–48r.

77. Ibid., fols. 7v–8r.

78. Ibid., fols. 8r–9r.

79. Ibid., fol. 10v.

80. Ibid., fol. 15r.

81. Ibid., fols. 44r–48r.

82. Ibid., fol. 18r.

83. Ibid., fol. 20r.

84. Ibid., fol. 18v.

85. Ibid., fol. 19r.

86. Ibid., fol. 21v.

87. Ibid., fol. 22r.

88. Ibid., fol. 23r.

89. "Ad lítem curator. Se llama el que se nombra para defender los pleitos del menor solamente." See *Diccionario Español e Inglés.*

90. *Proceso contra Cristoval,* fols. 24r–25v: "Indicios señal u acción de que se infiere u hace presumir alguna cosa."

91. Ibid., fols. 24r–25v.

92. Ibid., fol. 45r.

93. Ibid.

94. Ibid., fol. 36r.

95. Ibid., fols. 47r–49r.

96. Ibid., fols. 54r–54v.

97. Ibid., fols. 53r–53v.

98. Ibid., fols. 57r–65r.

99. *Causa seguida de oficio de la Casa de la Contratación por el s[eñor] fiscal contra Gerónimo Ponce mulatto y Domingo López sobre haver cometido el pecado nefando de sodomía, Sevilla, 1603,* AGI, Escribanía, 1075C, N17, fol. 1r.
100. Ibid., fols. 1r–2r.
101. Ibid.
102. Ibid, fols. 2r–2v.
103. Ibid.
104. Ibid., fols. 2v–3r.
105. Ibid.
106. Ibid., fols. 3v–6r.
107. Ibid.
108. Ibid.
109. *Sevilla, año 1566, El fiscal de S[u] M[agestad] con Pedro Fernández grumete S[ob]re que le acusa haver cometido el pecado nefando,* AGI, Justicia, 882, N2, fol. 26v: "Luis de la Cueva . . . ser de veinte y un años dijo . . . mochino de ver sus vellaquerias y exzesos siendo ladron y acuchillando a otros hombres . . . estandole desatando las manos para meterlo en la carcel . . . Domingo hincarsse de rodillas llorando diziendo que seria bueno este testigo le pico y enoxado le dijo entra perro ladron putazo . . . miren este puto."
110. *Causa seguida de oficio de la Casa,* fol. 11r.
111. Ibid., fol. 11v.
112. Ibid., fol. 12r.
113. Ibid., fol. 12v.
114. Ibid., fol. 14v.
115. *El fiscal con Gerónimo Ponce sobre el pecado nefando, dos sentencias, año de 1605,* AGI, Sentencias del Consejo, Escribanía, 954. For further descriptions, see M. B. Rediker, "Liberty beneath the Jolly Roger: The Lives of Anne Bonny and Mary Read, Pirates."
116. *Causa seguida de oficio de la Casa,* fols. 24r–28r.
117. Ibid., fols. 31r–33r.
118. Ibid., fols. 38r–63r.
119. Ibid., fols. 72v–75r.
120. Ibid., fol. 22r.
121. Ibid., fol. 19r.
122. Ibid., fols. 70r–83r.
123. Ibid., fols. 88r, 99r, 117r.
124. *El fiscal con Juan Mole, Bartholomé Barres, Juan Bautista Pino, extranjeros, sobre haber cometido el sobre pecado nefando fenecido en 1700,* AGI, Escribanía, 1105B, fol. 16v.
125. Ibid., fol. 18r.
126. Ibid., fol. 16v.
127. Ibid., fols. 25r–25v.
128. Ibid., fols. 25v–27r.

129. Ibid.
130. Ibid., fols. 27v–28r.
131. Ibid.
132. Ibid.
133. *Sevilla, año de 1562, Proceso criminal fecho por el ilustre Señor Pedro Menendez de Aviles General de Armanda contra Antón de Fuentes y Alonso Prieto sobre el pecado nefando y haver intentado cometer el pecado nefando en la misma embarcación,* AGI, Justicia, 855, N11. On 28 July 1562 the tribunal of the Casa de la Contratación transferred this *proceso* to the Council of the Indies in Madrid.
134. A soldier who fired the Lombardy guns. See *Diccionario marítimo Inglés-Español.*
135. *Sevilla, año de 1562, Proceso criminal,* fols. 4r–5r, 10r.
136. *"Migas en una cocidilla"* referred to crumbled bread fried in a pan with oil, salt, red pepper, and sometimes the grease of bacon or ham. See *Diccionario Español e Inglés.*
137. *Sevilla, año de 1562, Proceso criminal,* n.p.
138. Ibid.
139. Ibid.
140. Ibid.
141. Ibid.
142. Ibid.
143. Ibid., fol. 3r.
144. Ibid., fols. 5r–5v.
145. Ibid., fol. 5v.
146. Ibid., fols. 5v–6r.
147. Ibid., fols. 6r–6v.
148. Ibid., fol. 8v.
149. Ibid., fols. 10r–22r. The captain general ordered Miguel de Santa María, the custodian of the sequestered possessions, to pay the following fees from Antón's deposits: 3 *ducados* to Alonso de Segura, the scrivener of the case; 1 *ducado* to Juan de Alva, the royal constable for the imprisonment of the goods; 1 *ducado* to Julián de Guadalajara, the executioner who went to the ship and tortured Antón; 2 *ducados* to Alonso Ortiz, the purser on the ship, who cooked for Antón while he remained imprisoned. Furthermore, the custodian had to pay 10 *ducados* to Juan Martínez, His Majesty's royal scrivener, who took the prisoner from the ship to the Casa's jail in Seville. The total cost came to 17 *ducados,* or 187 reales.
150. Also known as horse or *burro;* a machine on which sawmen saw their boards and timbers; an indented wheel that puts the machine in motion that twists and reels silk. See *Diccionario marítimo Inglés-Español.*
151. *Sevilla, año de 1562, Proceso criminal,* fols. 17v–19v.
152. Ibid.
153. Ibid., fols. 25r–25v.

154. Ibid., fols. 26r–47v.
155. Ibid., fols. 32r–33r.
156. Ibid.
157. Ibid., fol. 62r.
158. *Sevilla, año 1566*, AGI, Justicia, 882, N2, fol. 1r.
159. Ibid., fols. 1r–1v.
160. Ibid., fol. 2r.
161. Ibid., fols. 2r–3v.
162. Ibid., fols. 16r–18r.
163. Ibid., fol. 8v.
164. Ibid., fols. 9r–9v.
165. Ibid., fols. 3v–4r.
166. Ibid., fol. 4r.
167. Ibid., fol. 6v.
168. Ibid., fol. 5v.
169. Ibid., fols. 4v–5r.
170. Ibid.
171. Ibid., fols. 7r–7v.
172. Ibid., fols. 7v–8r.
173. Ibid., fols. 10r–10v.
174. Ibid., fol. 11r.
175. Ibid., fols. 14r–15r.
176. Ibid., fol. 15v.
177. Ibid., fol. 13r.
178. Ibid., fols. 12r–12v.
179. Ibid., fols. 14r–14v.
180. Ibid., fols. 18v–19r.
181. Ibid., fol. 19r.
182. Ibid., fol. 20r.
183. Ibid., fol. 26r.
184. Ibid., fols. 29r–31v.
185. Ibid., fol. 32r.
186. Ibid., fol. 27r.
187. Ibid., fols. 34r–39v.
188. Ibid., fol. 39v.
189. Ibid., fol. 42r.
190. Ibid., fols. 43r–43v.
191. Ibid., fols. 41v–42r.
192. Ibid., fols. 43v–45v.
193. Ibid.
194. Ibid., fols. 45r–45v.
195. Ibid., fols. 47v–48r.

196. Ibid., fols. 48r–48v.
197. Ibid.
198. Ibid., fols. 49r–49v.
199. Ibid., fol. 50r.
200. Ibid., fols. 50v–51r.
201. Ibid., fol. 51v.
202. Ibid.
203. Ibid., fol. 52r.
204. Ibid., fols. 1r–12v.
205. *Proceso contra Gaspar Caravallo Mulato despensero de la nao de Rodrigo Díaz por suzio y des-onesto y aver querido cometer el pecado nefando contra natura con unos pajes del la nao, 1591,* AGI, Contratación, 5730, N8, R4, fols. 1r–2v.
206. Ibid., fols. 2r–2v.
207. Ibid., fol. 3r.
208. Ibid., fols. 22v–23r.
209. Ibid.
210. Ibid., fol. 5v.
211. Ibid., fol. 5r.
212. Ibid., fols. 4r–4v.
213. Ibid., fols. 6v–7r.
214. Ibid., fol. 13r.
215. Ibid., fols. 14r–14v.
216. Ibid., fol. 20v.
217. *Proceso contra Gaspar Caravallo,* fols. 22r–24r.
218. Ibid., fol. 25r.
219. Ibid., fol. 26r.
220. Ibid., fol. 26v.
221. Ibid., fols. 27r–32r.
222. *Proceso criminal fulminado de officio de la Real Justicia contra El alférez Xinés Cavallero del Castillo sobre acusarle que yntento el pecado de sodomía, 1606,* AGI, Contratación, 72, N1, R2, fols. 14v–17r. The tribunal of the Casa de la Contratación also prosecuted the following cases: *El fiscal con Andrés Cupín y otros negros presos en la carcel de Lima sobre haber cometido el pecado nefando, 1590,* AGI, Escribanía, 499B; *El fiscal con Cristo-bal Zamorano y Juan Moreno, su criado, residentes en Panama, sobre pecado nefando, 1621,* AGI, Escribanía, 451A; *El fiscal con Gabriel Ponce de León sobre pecado nefando, Pleitos Audiencia de Santo Domingo, 1648,* AGI, Escribanía, 5B; *El fiscal con Juan Hurtado de Zaldivar sobre pecado nefando, dos sentencias, 1595–1596,* AGI, Escribanía, N953; *El fiscal con Juan Ponce de León y otros vecinos de Huamanga, 1620,* AGI, Escribanía, 504C; *El fiscal con Pedro González, Cristobal Fontanilla y Francisco de Vitoria soldados del presidio de Puerto Rico sobre haber cometido el pecado nefando, Fenecido en 1678,* AGI, Escribanía, 119C; and *El fiscal con Pedro González y otros sobre pecado nefando, dos sentencias, 1678,* AGI, Escribanía, 959.

223. *Proceso criminal fulminado,* fol. 1r.
224. Ibid., fols. 2r–3r.
225. Ibid., fol. 19r.
226. Ibid., fols. 19v–20r.
227. Ibid., fols. 23v–24r.
228. Ibid., fol. 25r.
229. Ibid., fols. 28r–28v.
230. Ibid., fol. 29r.
231. Ibid., fols. 31r–31v.
232. Ibid., fol. 33v.
233. Ibid.
234. Ibid., fol. 54r.
235. Ibid., fol. 88r.
236. Ibid., fol. 89r.
237. Ibid., fols. 159r–159v.
238. Ibid.
239. Ibid., fol. 160v.
240. Ibid.
241. Ibid.
242. Ibid., fol. 165v.
243. Ibid., fol. 181r.
244. *Sevilla, año 1566,* fols. 4v–5r.
245. R. A. Gutiérrez, *When Jesus Came, the Corn Mothers Went Away: Marriage, Sexuality, and Power in New Mexico (1500–1846).*
246. *Proceso contra Cristoval,* fols. 2r–2v.
247. Ibid., fol. 4v.
248. *Sevilla, año de 1562, Proceso criminal,* fol. 10r.
249. *Proceso criminal fulminado,* n.p.
250. "Puto. El hombre que comete el pecado nefando." Quoted in *Diccionario de autoridades,* vol. 3, 443. The original version was published as *Diccionario de la lengua Castellana en que se explica el verdadero sentido de las voces, su naturaleza y calidad, con las phrases o modos de hablar, los proverbios o refranes, y otras cosas convenientes al uso de la lengua,* 6 vols.
251. "Bellaco. El hombre de ruines y malos procederes, y de viles respetos, y condicion perversa y danada." Quoted in *Diccionario de autoridades,* vol. 1, 589.
252. F. Vázquez García and A. Moreno Mengíbar, *Sexo y razón: una genealogía de la moral sexual en España (siglos XVI–XX),* 232.

Chapter 4

1. *Testimonio de las causas contra los culpados en el pecado nefando, 14 diciembre 1658,* AGI, México, 38, N57B, fol. 31r. For a synopsis of this chapter, see F. Garza Carvajal,

"Silk Laced Ruffs and Cuffs: An Inherent Link between *Sodomie* and Notions of Effeminacy in Andalucía and México (1561–1699)."

2. *Testimonio de las Causas,* fol. 31r. Correa's erotic metaphor equated the eating of frog legs, an exquisite delicacy of Spanish / Mexican early modern cuisine, with the consumption of virile members.

3. S. Alberro, *Inquisición y sociedad en México (1571–1700);* S. Gruzinski, "Las cenizas del deseo: homosexuales novohispanos a mediados del siglo XVII," in S. Ortega (ed.), *De la santidad a la perversión o de por qué no se cumplía la ley de Dios en la sociedad novohispana,* 255–281; A. Lavrín, "Sexuality in Colonial Mexico," in A. Lavrín (ed.), *Sexuality and Marriage in Colonial Latin America,* 47–95; M. L. Penyak, "Criminal Sexuality in Central Mexico, 1750–1850," Ph.D. diss., University of Connecticut, Storrs, 1993. On triumphant cantata of Spanish achievement, see J. L. Phelan, *The Millennial Kingdom of the Franciscans in the New World;* and I. Clendinnen, "Disciplining the Indians: Franciscan Ideology and Missionary Violence in Sixteenth-Century Yucatán," *Past and Present* 94 (1982): 27–59, "The Cost of Courage in Aztec Society," *Past and Present* 107 (1985): 45–89, and *Ambivalent Conquests: Maya and Spaniard in Yucatán (1517–1570).* For another perspective about masculinity and power, see S. J. Stern, *The Secret History of Gender: Women, Men, and Power in Late Colonial Mexico,* 167–188.

4. "'Mal de madre,' or hysteric affection, or passion, called also a suffocation of the womb; and vulgarly the fits of the mother; caused by the retention or corruption of the blood and lymphatic vessel," quoted in *Diccionario de autoridades (Edición Facsímil de 1732),* 450. The original dictionary was published as *Diccionario de la lengua Castellana en que se explica el verdadero sentido de las voces, su naturaleza y calidad, con las phrases o modos de hablar, los proverbios o refranes, y otras cosas convenientes al uso de la lengua,* 6 vols.

5. *Testimonio de las causas,* fol. 32r.

6. On La Tortuga, see L. J. Peguero (ed.), *Historia de la conquista, de la isla española de Santo Domingo trasumptada el ano de 1762: traducida de la historia general de las Indias escrita por Antonio de Herrera coronista mayor de Su Magestad, y de las Indias, y de Castilla, y de otros autores que han escrito sobre el particular.*

7. C. Colón, *Textos y documentos completos: relaciones de viajes, cartas, y memoriales,* C. Varela (ed.), 36, 83–85, 114–116. See also the accounts written by Columbus' son F. Colombo, *Historie Del s.d. Fernando Colombo; Nelle quali s'ha particolare, y vera relatione della vita, y de'fatti dell' Ammiraglio d. Christoforo Colombo, suo padre: et dello scoprimento, ch'egi fece dell'Indie Occidentali, dette Mondo Nvovo, hora posseduta del Sereniss Re Catolico nuouamente di lingua spagnuola tradotte nell'Italiana dal s. Alfonso Vlloa, con privilegio,* quoted in F. Guerra, *The Pre-Columbian Mind: A Study into the Aberrant Nature of Sexual Drives, Drugs Affecting Behaviour and the Attitude Towards Life and Death, with a Survey of Psychotherapy in Pre-Columbian America,* 296. On traveling between cultures, see the following by S. Santiago in A. L. Gazzola (ed.), *The Space In-Between: Essays on Latin American Culture:* "Why and for What Purposes Does the European Travel?"

9–24; "The Rhetoric of Verisimilitude," 64–78; and "The Post-Modern Narrator," 133–146.

8. D. Alvarez Chanca, "Carta al cabildo de Sevilla," in M. Fernández de Navarrete (comp.), *Colección de los viages y descubrimientos que hicieron por mar los españoles desde fines del siglo XV, con varios documentos ineditos concernientes a la historia de la marina castellana y de los establecimientos españoles en Indias*, 198–224.

9. Alvarez Chanca, "Carta al cabildo de Sevilla"; Guerra, *Pre-Columbian Mind*, 46.

10. Guerra, *Pre-Columbian Mind*, 48. See also the following works by P. M. d'Anghiera: *The Decades of the newe worlde or west India, Conteynyng the nauigations and conquestes of the Spanyardes, with the particular description of the moste ryche and large landes and Ilandes lately founde in the west Ocean, perteynyng to the inheritaunce of the kinges of Spayne. In the which the diligent reader may not only consyder what commoditie may hereby chaunce to the hole christian world in tyme to come, but also learne many secreates touchynge the lande, the sea, and the starres, very necessarie to be knowe to al such as shal attempte any nauigations, or otherwise haue delite to beholde the strange and woonderful woorkes of God and nature*, trans. R. Eden, 89–90; *Opera: Legatio Babylonica, De orbe novo decades octo, Opus epistolarum (Photomechanischer Nachdruck der Ausg. von 1516 und 1530)*, ed. E. Woldan; and *De Orbo Novo: Historia de l'Indie occidentali*.

11. D'Anghiera, *Decades of the newe worlde; Opera;* and *De Orbo Novo.*

12. H. Cortés, "Prymera Relación," in H. Cortés, *Cartas de relación de la conquista de la Nueva Espana escritas al Emperador Carlos V, y otros documentos relativos a la conquista, años de 1519–1527, Codex Vindobonensis S.N. 1600*, fol. 17v. The transcribed letter can be read in M. Hernández Sánchez-Barba (ed.), *Cartas y otros documentos: Hernán Cortés*, 24. On dress before Cortés, see P. R. Anawalt, *Indian Clothing before Cortés: Mesoamerican Costumes from the Codices*. On Aztec culture, see E. Florescano, *Memory, Myth, and Time in Mexico: From the Aztecs to Independence*, and S. Kellogg, *Law and the Transformation of Aztec Culture (1500–1700)*. On peninsular cultures, see R. Kagan and G. Parker (eds.), *Spain, Europe, and the Atlantic World: Essays in Honour of John H. Elliott*, and D. Brading, *The First America: The Spanish Monarchy, Creole Patriots, and the Liberal State 1492–1867.*

13. El conquistador anónimo, "Relatione di alcune cose della Nuova Spagna, & della gran citta di Temestitan Messico; fatta per uno gentil'homo del signor Fernando Cortese," in J. García Icazbalceta (comp.), *Colección de documentos para la historia de México*, 387.

14. Ibid., 387, 397–398.

15. Ibid.

16. Guerra, *Pre-Columbian Mind*, 9–19.

17. Isabel de Portugal, "Cédula contra el pulque: ques lo propio que Balché," *Anales de Museo Nacional de México* 6.37 (1892). On Spanish preocupations about alcohol use and abuse, see W. B. Taylor, *Drinking, Homicide, and Rebellion in Colonial Mexican Villages*, and S. Corcuera de Mancera, *El fraile, el indio, y el pulque: evangelización y embríaguez en la Nueva España (1523–1548).*

18. B. Díaz del Castillo, *Historia verdadera de la conquista de la Nueva España*, vol. 1, ed. C. Saenz de Santa María, 7. For recent reinterpretation of Spanish-Mexican colonial sources and chronicles, see S. B. Schwartz (ed.), *Victors and Vanquished: Spanish and Nahua Views of the Conquest of Mexico.*

19. G. Fernández de Oviedo, *Historia general y natural de las Indias*, vol. 1, 118–119.

20. Guerra, *Pre-Columbian Mind*, 236, 254–259. For visual and textual representations of pre-Spanish sodomitical acts etched in clay or otherwise, see M. Lucena Salmoral, *America 1492: Portrait of a Continent Five Hundred Years Ago*, 66, 76–77; and C. L. Taylor, "Legends, Syncretism, and Continuing Echoes of Homosexuality from Pre-Columbian and Colonial México," in S. O. Murray (ed.), *Latin American Male Homosexualities*, 80–99.

21. Díaz del Castillo, *Historia verdadera*, 83, 89, 121–122. On phallocentric themes, see E. Monick, *Phallos: Sacred Image of the Masculine.*

22. Guerra, *Pre-Columbian Mind*, 1–2.

23. A. Pagden and J. Lawrance (eds.), *Political Writings: Francisco de Vitoria*, 211.

24. T. Ortíz, "Dixo lo siguiente, acerca de los hombres de Tierra Firme que eran Caribes," in *Historia general de los hechos de los castellanos en las Islas i Tierra Firme del Mar Oceano*, 9 vols., ed. A. de Herrera y Tordesillas, 312; D. Durán, *Historia de las Indias de Nueva España e islas de la Tierra Firme escrita por fray Diego Durán dominico en el siglo XVI*, ed. A. M. Garibay K.

25. Guerra, *Pre-Columbian Mind*, 53.

26. Fernández de Oviedo, *Historia general*, 118–119.

27. G. Fernández de Oviedo, *Sumario de la natural historia de las Indias*, ed. J. Bautista Avalle-Arce, lxxxi, 244.

28. Ibid., 39.

29. Ibid., 12–13.

30. Ibid.

31. Fernández de Oviedo, *Historia general*, vol. 1, 118–119.

32. Ibid., vol. 2, 214.

33. Guerra, *Pre-Columbian Mind*, 56–57.

34. A. Núñez Cabeza de Vaca, *Naufragios y comentarios*, 89, 108.

35. Guerra, *Pre-Columbian Mind*, 9–19.

36. Díaz del Castillo, *Historia verdadera*, 128, 154–155, 213–246, 617–731.

37. Pagden and Lawrance, *Political Writings*, xiii–xxviii, 238.

38. J. Boswell, *Christianity, Social Tolerance, and Homosexuality: Gay People in Western Europe from the Beginning of the Christian Era to the Fourteenth Century*, 350–359.

39. Guerra, *Pre-Columbian Mind*, 2–3.

40. Ibid., 3–5.

41. Pagden and Lawrance, *Political Writings*, xiii–xxviii, 238; F. de Vitoria, *Relecciones del estado, de los indios, y del derecho de la guerra*, 22–26. For further reading, see also *De Indis et de ivre belli: relectiones Francisci de Victoria*, ed. E. Nys.

42. De Vitoria, *Relecciones*; Pagden and Lawrance, *Political Writings*, 211.

43. Ibid.
44. F. de Vitoria, "On Dietary Laws, or Self-Restraint," in Pagden and Lawrance, *Political Writings*, 211–227.
45. Ibid.
46. Ibid.
47. Ibid.
48. F. de Vitoria, "On the American Indians," in Pagden and Lawrance, *Political Writings*, 273–275.
49. Ibid., 252–276.
50. Ibid.
51. Ibid., 277–291.
52. Ibid.
53. Ibid.
54. Pagden and Lawrance, *Political Writings*, xxviii.
55. T. de Benavente (Motolinía), *Historia de los indios de la Nueva España*, ed. G. Bellini, 63–64, 89–97. See esp. p. 64 for a psychedelic description of the "highs" experienced by the Indios after having consumed *teunanacatlth*—literally "meat of God," or mushrooms.
56. Ibid.
57. F. López de Gómara, *Historia general de las Indias*, vol. 1, 5–6, 36.
58. Ibid.
59. Ibid.
60. Ibid.
61. Ibid., 13–16, 50.
62. Ibid., 50.
63. Ibid., 56.
64. Ibid., 13–16, 50.
65. Ibid., vol. 2, 404–405.
66. Ibid., vol. 1, 384–385.
67. Ibid.
68. J. Ginés de Sepúlveda, *Demócrates Segundo o de las justas causas de la guerra contra los indios*, trans. A. Losada, 27–28, 37–59.
69. E. O'Gorman, *La invención de América: el universalismo de la cultura de Occidente*; T. Todorov, *La conquista de América: el problema del otro*, trans. F. B. Burla; S. A. Zavala, *La filosofía política en la conquista de América*.
70. Guerra, *Pre-Columbian Mind*, 67–68.
71. D. Muñoz Carmargo, *Relaciones geográficas de Tlaxcala*, comp. Rene Acuña, 78; R. Acuña (ed.), *Relaciones geográficas del siglo XVI: Tlaxcala*, vol. 1, 200–203.
72. B. de las Casas, *Historia de las Indias*, vol. 2, ed. A. Millares Carlo, 514–518, and vol. 3, 320–323, 326–329. On the mental stability of de las Casas, see R. Menendez Pidal, *El padre las Casas, su doble personalidad*.
73. G. Olivier, "Conquérants et missionnaires face au 'péché abominable,' essai sur

l'homosexualité en Mésoameriqué au moment de la conquête espagnole," *Cahiers du Monde Hispanique et Luso-Brésilen* 55 (1990): 19—51.

74. B. de las Casas, *Apologética historia sumaria: cuanto a las cualidades, dispusición, descripción, cielo y suelo destas tierras, y condiciones naturales, policías, repúblicas, manera de vivir e costumbres de las gentes destas indias occidentales y meridionales cuyo imperio soberano pertenece a los reyes de castilla*, vol. 2, ed. E. O'Gorman, 515.

75. Ibid.

76. A. de Vetancurt, *Teatro mexicano: descripción breve de los svcessos exemplares, históricos, políticos, militares, y religiosos del Nuevo Mundo occidental de las Indias*, 89—91.

77. J. de Mendieta, *Historia eclesiástica indiana*, vol. 1, 83.

78. De las Casas, *Apologética*, vol. 1, 186—187.

79. Ibid.

80. Ibid.

81. B. de las Casas, *Brevisima relación de la destruyción de las Indias*, fol. 5v.

82. De las Casas, *Apologética*, vol. 2, 232—233.

83. Guerra, *Pre-Columbian Mind*, 76.

84. De las Casas, *Apologética*, vol. 2, 24—25.

85. Ibid.

86. Ibid., vol. 1, 470—471.

87. Ibid., vol. 2, 314, 364—365, 625.

88. Ibid., 127.

89. Ibid., 540—541.

90. Ibid.

91. Vázquez de Espinosa, *Compendio y descripción de las Indias Occidentales*, 380, 383.

92. De las Casas, *Apologética*, vol. 2, 540—541.

93. Ibid., 359.

94. De las Casas, *Apologética*, vol. 2, 539—540; Durán, *Historia de las Indias.*

95. Ibid.

96. Ibid.

97. Ibid.

98. A. Chavero (comp.), *Obras históricas de don Fernando de Alva Ixtlilxochitl*, 43—47, 324—325; F. de Alva Ixtlilxochitl, *Obras históricas: incluyen el texto completo de las llamadas relaciones e historia de la nación chichimeca en una nueva versión establecida con el cotejo de los manuscritos mas antiguos que se conocen*, vol. 1.

99. Ibid.

100. Guerra, *Pre-Columbian Mind*, 20, 81—82, 110, 141—142; J. Bierhorst (comp.), *Codex Chimalpopoca: The Text in Nahuatl*; D. Bourne (trans.), *Codex Mendoza, manuscrit azteque.*

101. R. Harrison, *Signs, Songs, and Memory in the Andes: Translating Quechua Language and Culture*, 24—26.

102. A. de Molina, *Confesionario mayor en la lengua mexicana y castellana* (1569), 32—35.

103. J. Bautista, *Confesionario en lengua mexicana y castellana: con muchas advertencias muy nec-*

essarias para los confessores compuesto por el Padre Fray Ioan Baptista de la orden del seraphico Padre Sanct Francisco, 48–51; M. Azoulai, *Les Péchés du Nouveau Monde: les manuels pour la confession des Indiens XVIe–XVIIe siècle.*

104. M. de León, *Camino del cielo en lengva mexicana, con todos los requisitos necessarios para conseguir este fin, co(n) todo lo que vn Xp(r)iano deue creer, saber, y obrar, desde el punto que tiene vso de razon, hasta que muere co(m)puesto por el P. F. Martín de Leó(n)*, 115–117.

105. B. de Alva, *Confessionario mayor, y menor en lengva mexicana (1634)*, ed. B. D. Sell, J. F. Schwaller, and L. A. Homza, 22–25.

106. C. Aguero, *Vocabulario castellano-zapoteco*, 1893.

107. López de Gómara, *Historia general de las Indias*, vol. 1, 384.

108. P. de Castañeda, "The Narrative of the Expedition of Coronado," in F. W. Hodge and T. H. Lewis (eds.), *Spanish Explorers in the Southern United States, 1528–1543: The Narrative of Alvar Núñez Cabeza de Vaca; The Narrative of the Expedition of Hernando de Soto by the Gentleman of Elvas; The Narrative of the Expedition of Coronado*, 273–387.

109. J. López de Velasco, *Geografía y descripción universal de las Indias*, ed. M. Jiménez de la Espada, 185, and *Geografía y descripción universal de las Indias, recopilada por el cosmógrafo-cronista Juan López de Velasco, desde el año de 1571 al de 1574.*

110. B. de Sahagún, *Historia general de las cosas de Nueva España: Primera versión íntegra del text castellano del manuscrito conocido como Códice Florentino*, vol. 1, 383–386. On Sahagún, see J. J. Klor de Alva, H. B. Nicholson, and E. Quiñones Keber (eds.), *The Works of Bernardino de Sahagún: Pioneer Ethnographer of Sixteenth-Century Aztec Mexico.*

111. On the history of *coprofilia* in Mexico, see A. López Austin, *Historia vieja de la mierda* and *Cuerpo humano e ideología: las concepciones de los antiguos nahuas*, vol. 1.

112. De Sahagún, *Historia general*, vol. 2, 607–608.

113. Ibid., vol. 1, 383–386.

114. Ibid.

115. Ibid., vol. 2, 600, 607–608.

116. Díaz del Castillo, *Historia verdadera*, 6–9, 99.

117. Ibid. For different perspectives about sorcery in colonial spaces, see G. Aguirre Beltrán, *Medicina y magia: el proceso de aculturación en la estructura colonial;* and R. Behar, "Sexual Witchcraft, Colonialism, and Women's Powers: Views from the Mexican Inquisition," in A. Lavrín (ed.), *Sexuality and Marriage in Colonial Latin America*, 178–206.

118. Ibid., 96, 113, 117, 163, 165, 177–179, 182.

119. Ibid., 97. On priests and sodomy in eighteenth-century Mexico, see W. B. Taylor, *Magistrates of the Sacred: Priests and Parishioners in Eighteenth-Century Mexico*, 189.

120. T. López Medel, "Relación," in A. M. Tozzer and C. P. Bowditch (eds.), *Landa's Relación de las cosas de Yucatán: A Translation*, 13. For other examples, see T. López Medel, *Colonización de América: informes y testimonios (1549–1572)*, and his *Cartas privadas de emigrantes a Indias (1540–1616)*, ed. Enrique Otte.

121. G. García, *Origen de los Indios del nuevo mundo, e Indias occidentales, averiguado con discurso de opiniones por el padre presentado F. Gregorio García, de la orden de predicadores*, 35; *Origen de los Indios del nuevo mundo*.
122. García, *Origen de los Indios* (1792), III, 115–116, 296–297.
123. Lavrín, "Sexuality in Colonial Mexico," 51–52.
124. J. de Torquemada, *Monarquía Indiana: de los veinte y un libros rituales y monarquía indiana, con el origen y guerras de los indios occidentales, de sus poblazones, descubrimiento, conquista, conversión y otras cosas maravillosas de la mesma tierra*, vol. 6, ed. M. León-Portilla, 402.
125. Moctezuma's discourse to Cortés is quoted in J. Ginés de Sepúlveda, *Historia del Nuevo Mundo*, trans. A. Ramírez de Verger, 149. See also *Juan Ginés de Sepúlveda y su crónica Indiana: en el centenario de su muerte (1573–1973)*.
126. De Torquemada, *Monarquía Indiana*, vol. 2, 169.
127. Ibid., vol. 3, 426–427.
128. Ibid.
129. Ibid., vol. 1, 230, 323, and vol. 3, 125. For a history of Neza, see F. de Alva Ixtlilxochitl, *Nezahualcoyotl Acolmiztli (1402–1472)*, comp. E. O'Gorman; and C. Gibson, *The Aztecs under Spanish Rule: A History of Indians of the Valley of Mexico (1519–1810)*. For the Yucatán, see P. H. Sigal, *From Moon Goddesses to Virgins: The Colonization of Yucatecan Maya Sexual Desire*. On Peru, see *Primera parte de los comentarios reales que tratan del origen de los yncas, reyes que fueron del Peru, de su idolatria, leyes, y gouierno en paz y en guerra de sus vidas y conquistas, y de todo lo que fue aquel Imperio y su Republica, antes que los españoles passaran a el escritas por el Ynca Garcilasso de la Vega*, 603.
130. De Torquemada, *Monarquía Indiana*, vol. 6, 107.
131. Ibid.
132. Ibid., 124–125.
133. Ibid., vol. 3, 124, and vol. 4, 174.
134. Ibid., vol. 4, 125.
135. Ibid., vol. 3, 125–126.
136. Ibid., 275–276.
137. H. Cortés, "Segunda carta de relación," in Cortés, *Cartas de relación*, fol. 32r.
138. G. F. Gemelli Carreri, *Viaje a la Nueva España*, vol. 1, trans. J. M. Agreda y Sánchez, 44–48.
139. Ibid. For other descriptions of New Spain, see T. Gage, *Nueva relación que contiene los viages de Tomas Gage en la Nueva España, sus diversas aventuras, y su vuelta por la provincia de Nicaragua hasta la Habana: con la descripcion de la ciudad de Méjico, tal como estaba otra vez y como se encuentra ahora (1625): unida una descripción exacta de las tierras y provincias que poseen los españoles en toda la América, de la forma de su gobierno eclesiastico y político, de su comercio, de sus costumbres, y las de los criollos, mestizos, mulatos, indios y negroes*, 2 vols., and his original *The English-American, his travail by sea and land: or, A new svrvey of the West-India's, containing a journall of three thousand and three hundred miles within the main land of America With a grammar, or some few rudiments of the Indian tongue, called Poconchi, or Pocoman, By the true and painfull endevours of Thomas Gage*; J. Hortop, *The Rare*

Trauailes of Iob Hortop, an Englishman, who was not heard of in three and twentie yeeres space: Wherin is declared the dangers he escaped in his voiage to Gynnie, where after hee was set on shoare in a wildernes neere to Panico, hee endured much slauerie and bondage in the Spanish Galley and his *The rare travailes of Job Hortop: being a facsimile reprint of the first edition (1591);* T. de la Torre, "Diario del viaje de Salamanca a Ciudad Real, Chiapas, (1544–1545)," in J. L. Martínez (comp.), *Pasajeros de Indias: viajes transatlánticos en el siglo XVI;* and *Bucaniers of America: Or, a True Account of the Most Remarkable Assaults Committed of late Years upon the coasts of The West Indies, By the Bucaniers of Jamaica and Tortuga, Both English and French.*

140. Gemelli Carreri, *Viaje a la Nueva España,* vol. 1, 44–48, and *Giro del mondo del dottor d. Gio: Francesco Gemelli Careri;* "Carta del licenciado Alonso Zuazo al padre Fray Luis de Figueroa, prior de la mejorada, 14 de noviembre de 1521," in García Icazbalceta (comp.), *Colección de documentos para la historia de México,* 358–367; G. Tovar de Teresa, *Pegaso o el mundo barroco novohispano en el siglo XVII;* C. de Sigüenza y Góngora, *Alboroto y motín de México del 8 de junio de 1692,* ed. I. A. Leonard.

141. *Carta del Virrey Conde de Monterrey, 4 noviembre 1596,* AGI, México, 23, N60.

142. Ibid. For more particulars about the viceroy count, see L. Hanke (ed.), *Los Virreyes españoles en America durante el gobierno de la Casa de Austria,* vol. 2, 125–130. Sodomites were not the only problem for colonial officials. For descriptions about multiethnic orgies between men and women, see *Y dijo llamarse Lorensa Francisa y ser doncella . . . 11 de enero de 1687,* AGI, México, 87, R1, N23, fols. 13r–17v.

143. *Carta del Virrey Conde.*

144. F. V. Scholes and E. B. Adams (eds.), *Documentos para la historia del México colonial.*

145. P. Simón, *Primera parte de las noticias historiales de las conquistas de Tierra Firme en las Indias Occidentales.*

146. *Carta del Virrey Duque de Albuquerque, 15 noviembre 1658,* AGI, México, 38, N57. The duke's particulars appear in Hanke, *Los Virreyes españoles,* vol. 4, 155–179.

147. *México 19 de noviembre de 1658, A su Magestad y 18 de junio de 1659 en el navío de las armadas, carta de Don Juan Manuel de Sotomayor alcalde del crimen de aquella ciudad,* AGI, México, 38, N57A. Unfortunately for colonial officials, contamination was not limited to sodomites; see P. Voekel, "Scent and Sensibility: Pungency and Piety in the Making of the Gente Sensata, Mexico, 1640–1850," Ph.D. diss., University of Texas at Austin, 1997. In her subsequent work, *Alone before God: The Religious Origins of Modernity in Mexico,* Voekel focuses on cemetery burials in late eighteenth-century Mexico and challenges the characterization of Catholicism in Mexico as an intractable and monolithic institution that had to be forcibly dragged into the modern world, thus proposing that Mexican liberalism had deeply religious roots.

148. *México 19 de noviembre de 1658.*

149. V. L. Bullough and B. Bullough, *Sin, Sickness, and Sanity: A History of Sexual Attitudes,* 25.

150. *Testimonio de las causas.*

151. *Memoria de los ajustisiados por haver cometido el pecado nefando, 14 diciembre 1658,* AGI, México, 38, N57C.

152. E. Masini, *Sacro arsenale overo prattica dell' officio della santa inquisitione,* 123.

153. *Segundo proceso contra Francisco Hernández mulato esclavo de Pedro López hidalgo curtidor vezino de esta ciudad de México por pacto con el demonio y por blasfemo, 1602,* BLAC, W. B. Stephens Papers, fol. 2r. For a complete transcription of the *proceso,* see Garza Carvajal, "Tattoos, Demons, and the Spectacle of It All. The Second Inquisitorial Trial of Francisco Hernández: 1602–1603." On race and ethnicity, see P. Seed, "Social Dimensions of Race: Mexico City (1753)," *Hispanic American Historical Review* 62.4 (1982): 569–606; E. A. Kuznesof, "Ethnic and Gender Influences on 'Spanish' Creole Society in Colonial Spanish America," *Colonial Latin American Review* 4.1 (1995): 153–175; J. I. Israel, *Race, Class, and Politics in Colonial Mexico, (1610–1670);* and R. Bauer, "Imperial History, Captivity, and Creole Identity in Francisco Núñez de Pineda y Bascuñán's *Cautiverio feliz,*" *Colonial Latin American Review* 7.1 (1998): 59–82. On rethinking colonial categories, gender, and morality in the making of race, see A. L. Stoler, *Carnal Knowledge and Imperial Power: Race and the Intimate in Colonial Rule.*

154. *Diccionario de la lengua castellana,* vol. 4, 864.

155. *Testimonio de las causas,* fols. 29r–30r.

156. Ibid.

157. Ibid.

158. Ibid., fol. 30r.

159. Ibid., fols. 31r–32r.

160. Ibid., fol. 35r.

161. Ibid., fol. 31r.

162. Ibid., fol. 32r.

163. Ibid., fols. 32r–33r.

164. Ibid., fol. 35r. For indigenous visions of a fantastic world, see S. Gruzinski, *Les Hommes-Dieux du Mexique: pouvoir indigène et société coloniale, XVIe–XVIIIe siècles* (English ed., *Man-Gods in the Mexican Highlands, Sixteenth–Eighteenth Centuries*).

165. *Carta del Virrey Conde de Monterrey,* fols. 1r–2v.

166. *México 19 de noviembre de 1658,* fol. 2r.

167. *Memoria de los ajustisiados.*

168. *México 19 de noviembre de 1658,* fol. 2r. On the Spanish Inquisition, see H. C. Lea, *A History of the Inquisition of Spain,* 4 vols. On the Mexican Inquisition, see Alberro, *Inquisición y sociedad en México;* M. Cuevas, *Historia de la iglesia en México,* 5 vols.; J. Toribio Medina, *Historia del Tribunal del Santo Oficio de la Inquisición en México;* and the collection of articles in M. E. Perry and A. J. Cruz, *Cultural Encounters: The Impact of the Inquisition in Spain and the New World.*

169. *Testimonio de las causas,* fol. 34r.

170. M. B. Garber, "The Occidental Tourist: *M. Butterfly* and the Scandal of Transvestism," in A. Parker, M. Russo, D. Sommer, and P. Yaeger (eds.), *Nationalisms and Sexualities,* 121–146; and idem, *Vested Interests: Cross-dressing and Cultural Anxiety.*

Theoretical approaches related to issues of conquest and cultures are coherently discussed in N. M. Farriss, *Maya Society under Colonial Rule: The Collective Enterprise of Survival,* and C. Geertz, *The Interpretation of Cultures.*
171. J. Butler, *Gender Trouble: Feminism and the Subversion of Identity.*
172. Garber, *Vested Interests,* 1–20.
173. Garber, "Occidental Tourist," 125–130. On sodomy and colonial Peru, see P. Cieza de León, *La Chronica del Perv nvevamente escrita, por Pedro de Cieca de Leon, vezino de Seuilla;* G. de la Vega, *Comentarios reales de los Incas,* 3 vols.; *Primera parte de los comentarios reales que tratan del origen de los yncas, reyes que fueron del Peru, de su idolatria, leyes, y gouierno en paz y en guerra de sus vidas y conquistas, y de todo lo que fue aquel Imperio y su Republica, antes que los españoles passaran a el escritas por el Ynca Garcilasso de la Vega;* and J. Anadón, *Garcilaso Inca de la Vega, an American Humanist: A Tribute to José Durand.*
174. P. Chatterjee, *The Nation and Its Fragments: Colonial and Postcolonial Histories.*

Epilogue

1. E. O'Gorman, *La invención de América: el universalismo de la cultura de Occidente.*
2. T. Todorov, *La conquista de América: el problema del otro,* trans. F. B. Burla.
3. R. Siegel, "La autobiografía colonial: un intento de teorización y un estudio de escritos autobiográficos femeninos Novohispanos," Ph.D. diss., University of Texas at Austin, 1997, 8–11. For a discussion related to discourses and America, see I. Zavala (ed.), *Discursos sobre la "invención" de América.* On the relationships among literature, history, fiction, and truth, see W. D. Mignolo, *The Darker Side of the Renaissance: Literacy, Territoriality, and Colonization,* 1–169.
4. M. Sinha, *Colonial Masculinity: The "Manly Englishman" and the "Effeminate Bengali" in the Late Nineteenth Century,* 181–184.
5. Ibid., 3.
6. R. Hennessy, *Materialist Feminism and the Politics of Discourse,* 183–184.
7. For a discussion about boundaries of identity and cultural theory, see R. Radhakrishnan, *Diasporic Mediations: Between Home and Location,* 62–202.
8. J. Deleito y Piñuela, *La mala vida de la España de Felipe IV;* J. Eslava Galán, *Historia secreta del sexo en España.*
9. For example, P. Seed, *To Love, Honor, and Obey in Colonial Mexico: Conflicts over Marriage Choice (1574–1821).*
10. Sinha, *Colonial Masculinity,* 19.
11. "Ambiguity of cultural agency," in the words of R. Siegel, "La autobiografía colonial," 15–18.
12. Ibid., 8–14.
13. P. Chatterjee, *The Nation and Its Fragments: Colonial and Postcolonial Histories;* T. Sarkar, "The Hindu Wife and the Hindu Nation: Domesticity and Nationalism in Nineteenth-Century Bengal," *Studies in History* 8.2 (1992): 219–220; R. Siegel, "La autobiografía colonial," 13.

14. R. Siegel, "La autobiografía colonial," 13. For "reciprocal influences" between European and Andean peoples in the formation of a colonial society in sixteenth-century South America, see the collections of essays in R. Adorno and K. J. Andrien (eds.), *Transatlantic Encounters: Europeans and Andeans in the Sixteenth Century,* and R. Adorno, *Guaman Poma: Writing and Resistance in Colonial Peru.*

15. Siegel, "La autobiografía colonial," 13.

16. *Vida i sucesos de la Monja Alférez, Alférez Catarina, Doña Catarina de Araujo doncella, natural de S[an] Sebastián, prov[inci]a de Guipúzcoa. Escrita por ella misma en 18 de sept[iembr]e 1646, bolviendo de las Indias a España en el Galeón S[an] Josef, Capitán Andrés Otón, en la flota de N[uev]a España, General Don Juan de Benavides, General de la Armanda Tomás de la Raspuru, que llego a Cádiz en 18 de Noviembre de 1646,* BRAH, Colección Juan Bautista Muñoz, 9/4807, fols. 201r–231v.

17. *Relación prodigiosa de las grandes hazañas y valerosos hechos, que vna muger hizo en quarenta años que sirvió a su Magestad en el Reyno de Chile, y en otros del Perú y Nueva España en ávito de soldado. Y los honrosos oficios militares que tubo, sin que fuesse conocida por muger, hasta que le fue fuerza el descubrirse,* BLAC, Colección Icazbalceta, no. JGI, Varias relaciones, 1, 54a, México, Viuda de Bernardo Calderón, 1653.

18. Ibid.

GLOSSARY

abogado — counselor at law; advocate; intercessor or mediator

abominable — abominable; detestable; loathsome; execrable

acargo — charge, office, or job

agente — active; he who penetrates the other

agravios — wrong; an injury

albarán — a writing; sheet of paper; note; acquittance; receipt or pass

albín — bloodstone

alcahuete — pimp of sorts

alcalde — a magistrate of which there are several kinds

alcalde mayor de la justicia — lord chief justice who read an offense in public, at which time sentence was passed upon convicted criminals

alcántara; alcantarilla — bridge; little bridge

alférez — ensign; in chess, a bishop

alguacil — proper name of an officer who apprehends malefactors

alguacil de corte — sergeant at arms; king's messenger

almirante general — admiral or lord high admiral

alojamientos — accommodations

alquitrán — naphtha, a liquid substance flowing out of the earth in some places like melted pitch; used in some places on ships instead of pitch and tar

alzar — to lift; to raise the voice

amainar — to set sail; to take in the sails; as metaphor, to cool, to relent

amarionados — effeminate men; sodomites

amarrar — to make fast; to anchor; to lash or tie

andaluz — Andalusian

ano — the ass or anus

antipoda — the complete opposite of one's own culture

a popa; por la cara de popa — abaft; astern

a proa — afore

apretar los cordeles — to draw ropes tighter, that is, to wind up the rack in order to make a criminal confess; as metaphor, to press a man hard in order to discover a secret, or to do any other thing against his inclination

arrecho — to stand; to be stiff or erect

asesor — assessor; lawyer joined in commission with a judge

asturiano — Asturian

audiencia — the court of judicature

auditor — king's officer or judge, civil or criminal

auto — public act; a decree of a court; all papers relating to a lawsuit

auto de fe — public act of the Inquisition when it brought out its prisoners and read their offenses in public, at which time the sentence was passed

ávido y tenido — covetous; greedy

azotes — strikes with lashes

baldrés — dildo

bardaje — eunuch of sorts who dressed like and performed the labors of a woman

barrio — neighborhood; quarter

batel — ship's small boat; pinnace or yawl

baxel — any sort of ship, especially under three decks; smaller sort

beata — type of religious woman, employing herself in prayer and works for charity; ironically, female hypocrite

bellaco — knave; villain; an arch-wag; rogue; sodomite

bellaquerías — sodomitical play or manners

bernia — coarse type of cloth

bestia de albarda — beast of burden

betún — bitumen, a thick liquid substance

boneta — bonnet

bragueta — codpiece

bubas — syphilis; also known as *mal Napolitano*, *mal Francés*, or *sarna Española bubosos* — persons infected with syphilis

buen aire — fine appearance; gracefulness; elegance

buen bellaco — great knave; ironically, sodomite

buen hombre — good man; ironically, cuckold

buena mujer — good woman; ironically, whore

bujarrón(a) — man who takes pleasure in anal penetration and love for young boys; female sodomite

cabalgar — to mount a horse; to ride

cabalgar por el culo — to penetrate someone through the anus

caballería — military order of knights; cavalry; horse troops

caballero — knight; gentleman; member of the lower nobility, usually propertied

cabeza de proceso — beginning of a process; will; process or trial at law

cabo — rope; end; conclusion; cape; headland

cabo, dar — to throw a rope for another to take hold of

cabo de escuadra — corporal

cacique — title used by the indigenous nobles of Latin America

caja — mariner's private chest, usually filled with clothing and other personal belongings

calabozo — dungeon; bilboes

calçones de lienço — linen breeches

calvo — hairless

calzas — silk knee-length pants

callosas — corn; hard skin

camarada — fellow soldier; companion; bedfellow

camoyaos — young men along the northern coast of South America who dressed like and performed the labors of women

cáñamo — fibrous plant called hemp

capitán de guarnición — governor or commander in chief of a garrison

capitán general — admiral of the fleet; general; captain general

capitana — ship of an admiral or captain general

capitanía — captainship; company of soldiers

capote — blue woolen cape worn by mariners

Casa de la Contratación — House of Trade set up in sixteenth-century Seville to monitor commerce between the peninsula and its colonies

catalán — Catalan; from Catalonia

cayar — to be silent; to hold one's peace; to keep secret

cédula real — royal order

cepo — stocks in which offenders were put

Chancillería — Castilian high courts in Valladolid and Granada; other high courts in Spain were called Audiencias

coger — to gather; to catch; as sea term, to coil a rope

coito — carnal copulation

comadres — women friends of great confidence

contador, teniente de — accountant; auditor; lieutenant; deputy

contramaestre — boatswain; mate of a ship

contramaestre, segundo — boatswain mate

coprofilia — an affinity for excrements and sexual acts

cordage — belonging to a ship

cordelejo, dar — to rack; to vex; to torment

cordeles — ropes; strings. See also *apretar los cordeles*

cotita — short for *mariquita*; nickname and term of endearment; effeminate man; queer

criollo — of pure Spanish descent, born in the Americas

cubierta — any covering; deck of a ship, running the length of the ship

cuchillada — slash; knife wound

culo — breech; fundament

culón — large pair of buttocks; a great breech

curador — governor; guardian; tutor; physician

curaduría — guardianship; tutorship

dama — refined woman

descoyuntarse — to disjoint; to put out of joint

descuidado — neglected; negligence; carelessness

desnudar — to strip naked

desnudo en cueros — naked

destierro perpetuo — perpetual banishment

desvíos — byways; wrong ways

digno — worthy

diligencias — diligence; assiduity

doctrinado — teaching; instruction

doncella — maiden; young woman presumed to be a virgin

ducado; ducat — gold coin equivalent to 440 *maravedís* in the first decade of the seventeenth century

echar grillos — to fetter; to shackle

efebias — male bathhouses

effeminatos — effeminate men

encomienda — colonial system of servitude

entena — yard of a ship to which the sail is made fast

entendimiento — understanding; true explication or sense of the law

escribano — scrivener, notary, secretary, clerk; an officer who, when a criminal is apprehended, draws up his offense, including all the circumstances

escuadra — squadron

escudo — from 1537, a new gold coin equivalent to 10 *reales* or 375 *maravedís*

esmero — care; diligence; attention in doing anything

esparto — a kind of rush or jonquil

estante — large beam; shelf; desk

falda — any garment that hangs down like petticoats; cassock or shirt

fama, buena — good reputation

fiador — he that is bound for another person

fianza — bail; surety

figas; filacigas — ropes made of oakum aboard ships, that is, of old ropes towed out, spun, and twisted again

fiscal — king's solicitor; attorney general; censurer; one who blames

fiscal procurador — king's solicitor general; solicitor of the exchequer

fogón — kitchen of a ship

francolín — beautiful bird; godwit

fray — friar; brother

galera — galley; long wagon

galería de popa — balcony

gallego — Galician

garrote — cudgel

garrote, dar — to strangle; to rack

garrucha — block; pulley

gentil — genteel; nobleman; gentleman

gitanas — wandering gypsies

grumete — a grummet; lowliest type of sailor

guapo — handsome; boyfriend

guayacán — guayacan, a tree; substance from the tree that was used to
   cure syphilis

guipuzcoano — of Guipúzcoa

hazer callos en el vicio — to be hardened in vice

honrado — honorable

indicios — circumstantial proof

inverosímil — that which has not the appearance of truth

izar — to hoist; that is, to hale up anything aboard a ship

jabón — waist-length coat worn by officers

jareta de la nao — nettings on a ship; nets made of small rope

jarro — pot or pitcher

juez del crimen — judge in criminal causes

juicio — prudent; judgment; prudence; wisdom; sentence against a
   criminal

junco — salt-marsh rush; rush junk, a type of boat in the East Indies

junta naval — board

lacra, la — infestation; disease; plague; used to refer to sodomy

ladino — Spanish-speaking Indian and one acclimated to European
   culture

lancha — boat

lanzar — to launch; to dart; to cast as a lance; to turn out; to vomit

legua — league; 8 leagues = 44 kilometers

leña or retama — wood

letrado de ciencia — learned man; lawyer

limpieza de sangre — quest for Spanish racial purity

lizenciado — a licentiate

lombardero — soldier who fired the Lombardy guns

macho — man

maestre — master of a military order

maestro armero — armorer

magui — indigenous female warrior

mal de madre — hysterical affection or passion, also called a suffocation of the womb and, vulgarly, the fits of the mother; caused by retention or corruption of the blood and lymphatic vessel

malvado — wicked one

mancevo — young boy or man

maqui — female warriors

maravedí — a sixteenth-century coin made of silver and copper; 34 *maravedís* = 1 real; 440 *maravedís* = 1 ducat

maría; marica; maricón — effeminate man; coward; woman

marimacho — manly woman; ironically, a dyke

marinero — sailor; mariner; seaman

mariones — effeminate men; sodomites

mariquita. See *cotita*

mastate — small piece of cloth used by American Indians to cover their private parts

matear; matearse — to bring forth; to spring; to shoot

mayor de justicia — lord chief justice

melindre — delicate kerchief usually worn on the waist by women

menosprecio — contempt; spurning; undervaluing

menudo — sautéed dish

merced — term of civility used in Spain to every polite person, as *signoria* is used in Italy *mestiza(o)* — a person of Spanish / European and Indian ancestry

miembro — limb; man's penis

mierducha — whore

migas en una cocidilla — dish of crumbled bread fried in a pan with oil, salt, red pepper, and sometimes the grease of bacon or ham

molicie — masturbation

molledos — brawny parts of the arm

molles — soft weak men

mons veneris — hair on the external part of the pudenda

moralistas, los — theologians of the Thomistic Scholastic

morisca(o) — person of Moorish ancestry; Moslem convert to Christianity

mozo — young servant boy; bachelor

muchacho — boy

mulato — mulatto; Negro; black

naguas — skirts

nao — ship

natura armada — stiff or erect penis

navío almirante — admiral's ship

nefando — heinous; abominable; detestable; not to be named; unutterable

nefario — wicked; villainous

nefasto — sodomite

niñas — girls; term of endearment

Opus Dei — fervent Catholic organization based in Pamplona

paciente — passive one; he who is penetrated

page or *paje* — boy; page

panol del pan — bread room

pañuelo — handkerchief

papagayo — parrot

papas — priests

partes vergonzosas — private parts

patache — advice boat

patrón de bote — boatman or boat's man

pecado contra natura — sin against nature; sodomy

perrillas de mierda — whores

peso — an American silver coin equivalent to 8 reales or 272 *maravedís;* the gold peso = 450 *maravedís*

pícaro — villainous; rascally; knavish; naughty; sexually precocious

pija — penis

piloto — pilot

pipa — tobacco pipe; ironically, penis

plaza — employment; office

plaza mayor — main square

pleito — cause; lawsuit; dispute

posa — buttock

posaderas — ass; buttocks

potro — engine for racking malefactors; buboes

pragmática — royal edict or proclamation

pregonero — crier

presbítero — priest

presidio — garrison or safeguard

presunciones — presumptions; guess; imagination

probatorio testimonio — testimony of proof

procesar — to judge or try a criminal or malefactor

proceso — process or trial at law

provanza — proof

pulque — an alcoholic drink derived from the agave plant and fermented with a root

puto bellaco — grave sodomite; bardash; whore

quadra — room; chamber in a house

quecholli — a particular month

quemadero — stake

ramales — ends of a cord untwisted

ranchos — accommodations; cubicles formed by mariners with their chests

rascar — to scratch; to scrape; to curry

ratificar — to ratify; to confirm

real — a silver coin equivalent to 34 *maravedís*

recibir al prueba — to receive; admit

reconocer — to view; to strip naked; to unclothe

reconocimiento — viewing

relator — relater; reporter; officer in court who acquaints the court with what has been told of the case to be tried

relaxado — loose in the body

remisión — remission; pardon

remitir — to remit; to forgive or pardon [*pleito remitido*] a suit or trial at law returned to the same court from whence it was removed by appeal

remo — oar

remo, echar al — to send to the galleys

reñido — chided; rebuked

reñir — to quarrel or fight

rostro — face to face

rubio — ruddy; fair-haired

salchichas — sausages

sentencia de tormento; sentencia de prueba — opinion; judgment

señales — signs; markings left by a wound

sieso — arse

soga, tener a la garganta una — to have a halter about one's neck

soga o cuerda con que ahorcan los criminales — rope with which criminals are hung

somético — sodomite

sucio — nasty; dirty; filthy

suplicio — punishment

teniente — lieutenant; deputy

tentar — to tempt; to try; to feel

tiangue — market

tormento, dar — to rack

tormento de cuerda — way of racking a man

torpe — base; vile; filthy; dirty

traslado — copy of writing

tribunal — tribunal; judgment seat

tripa ciega — ass gut; rectum

tripas — guts; tripe

tzictli — chewing gum

ulceradas — full of ulcers

ulceras — ulcers

vara — rod; man's penis; wand; twig; stick; yard

vecino — inhabitant; neighbor

verdugo — executioner; hangman

verga — rod; wand; yard; man's penis

vergüenza — pillory

vergüenza, sacar a uno a la — to expose a man as punishment to public
    shame by standing him on the pillory or at the whipping post or
    leading him about with a crier proclaiming his crime

verosímil — likely

vigilante — watchman

vir — in Latin, man

vizcaíno — Biscayan from Biscay

voces, hacer — to cry out; to hollow

vueltas — turning about

vulgo — all things vulgar

zaraguelles — shirts worn by mariners

WORKS CITED

Archival Manuscripts

El Alférez doña Catalina de Erauso ha dado una petición en el consejo, en que refiere ha diez y nuebe años pasó a las provincias del Perú en ábito de barón. AGI, Sección de Documentos Escogidos, leg. 1, no. 87, 1626–1630.

Alonso de Buendia contra Tomás Grueso, intento de sodomía con un hijo de Alonso edad de ocho años, 1572. AGS, Consejo Real de Castilla, A 205–208.

Auto, Consejo Real de las Yndias, 19 febrero 1626. AGI, Sección de Documentos Escogidos, leg. 1, no. 87, 1626–1630.

Bocabulario de los nombres que usa la gente de mar en todo lo que perteneze a fu arte por el horden alfabetico, 1596. BRAH, 9/5138, fol. 97r.

Cádiz año de 1698 causa escriptta de oficio de justicia contra Juan Mole, Bartholomé Barres, Juan Baptista Pino, y Phelip Esmirle, sobre decisse, aver cometido todos, el pecado de sodomía con el dicho Juan Mole. AGI, Escribanía, 1105B.

Carta del Virrey Conde de Monterrey, 4 noviembre 1596. AGI, México, 23, N60.

Carta del Virrey Duque de Albuquerque, 15 noviembre 1658. AGI. México, 38, N57.

Cartas acordadas por el S[eñor] Inq[uisidor] P[residente] y señores del supremo de la Inq[uisi]ón para govierno en los tribunales del S[ant]o Of[ici]o. BN, ms. 848.

Causa seguida de oficio de la Casa de la Contratación por el s[eñor] fiscal contra Gerónimo Ponce mulatto y Domingo López sobre haver cometido el pecado nefando de sodomía, Sevilla, 1603. AGI, Escribanía, 1075C, N17.

Certificación de D[o]n Luis de Cespedes . . . Francisco Pérez de Navarrete . . . Juan Cortes de Monrroy . . . Juan Precio de León. BRAH, 9/4807, fols. 235v–243v.

Compendio de algunas experiencias en los ministerios de que usa la Compañía de Jesus, con que practicamente se muestra con algunos acontecimientos y documentos el buen acierto en ellos, por orden de los superiores, por el Padre Pedro de León de la misma Compañía, 1619. BUG, caja B76.

Compendio de industrias en los ministerios de la Compañía de Jesus, con que practicamente se muestra el buen acierto en ellos, dispuetos por el Padre Pedro de Leon de la misma Compañía de Jesus y por orden de los superiores, 1628. BUS, ms. 573 (3/4/53), tomo 2, ms. 574.

El Consejo de Indias a Sebastián Caboto, Toledo, 12 de noviembre de 1525. AGI, Indiferente General, 2495.

Criminal contra Inés Santa Cruz y Catalina Ledesma por prostitutas y bujarronas cuya operación ejectuban con una caña en forma de miembro viril, año 1603. AGS, Cámara de Castilla 2557, Perdones de viernes santo, leg. 9.

Cristobal de Chabes, Relación de las cosas de la carcel de Sevilla y su trato, Nº 60, 1591. AMS, sec.2, Señor Conde del Aguila, tomo 3, fols. 39r–52v.

Derofro de mar Mediterraneo, 1614, desde el cabo de Santo Vizente a Cádiz. BRAH, 9/5138, B 53.

Don Francisco Pérez de Navarrete, Capitán de Ynfantería Española que a sido por Su Majestad y Cavo de Compañías . . . ceritifico que conocí a Catalina de Herausso. AGI, Sección de Documentos Escogidos, leg. 1, no. 87, 1626–1630, fols. 8r–12v.

D[o]n Jose de la Higuera y Lara archivero del general de Indias en esta cuidad Pedim[ien]to por el alberez D[oñ]a Catalina de Herauso vecina y natural de la villa de S[an] S[ebastian] provincia de Guipuzcoa. BRAH, Colección Juan Bautista Muñoz, 9/4807, fol. 234r.

Don Luis de Céspedes Xeria, Gouernador y Capitán General . . . de Paragoay, en las Yndias, por el Rey, nuestro señor, y Capitán de Ynfantería Española . . . certifico y hago fee a Su Majestad que conozco a Catalina de Herausso. AGI, Sección de Documentos Escogidos, leg. 1, no. 87, 1626–1630, fols. 8r–12v.

Edicto sobre libros prohibidos, 1600. AGN, Inquisición, tomo 265, no. 2, and tomo 140, nos. 2, 7, and 14.

Efemérides de Sevilla 1597. AMS, Sección Especial, Papeles del Señor Conde del Aguila, cuad. 1.

Ejecutoria a pedimiento de Catalina de Belunza, vecina de San Sebastián, año 1503. ARCV, Registro de Reales Ejecutorias, caja 181, exp. 39.

Ejecutoria del pleito contra Agustín Corco, Genovés por el pecado nefando, año 1516. ARCV, Registro de Reales Ejecutorias, caja 312, exp. 30.

Ejecutoria del pleito sobre acusar al demandado del pecado nefando el licenciado Zarate y el bachiller Pedro de la Mota, alcaldes de Burgos y el licenciado del Castillo y Diego de Soria, regidores de Burgos que de su oficio procedieron contra Rodrigo de Orozco, vecino de Villaldemiro, año 1498. ARCV, Registro de Reales Ejecutorias, L 126/13/14.

Ensanchez de la segunda parte de las cosas que passan en la carcel reducidoz por Chabes vecino de Sev[ill]a, N° 70, 1592. AMS, sec. 2, Señor Conde del Aguila, tomo 3, fols. 53r–85v.

Fadrique [Biel] de Basilea, doctrinal de los caballeros. Burgos, 20 June 1487. BN, ms. 6607.

Fernán Diañez de Lobon corregidor de la villa de Arévalo con Nuño de la Torre, boticario, cristiaño nuevo, vecino de dicha villa sobre acusarle del delito de sodomía, año 1514. ARCV. Pleitos Civiles Quevedo Fenecidos, leg. 315, caja 1412–1414.

El fiscal con Andrés Cupín y otros negros presos en la carcel de Lima sobre haber cometido el pecado nefando, 1590. AGI, Escribanía, 499 B.

El fiscal con Bartholomé Barres sobre haver cometido el pecado nefando, 1700, dos autos. AGI, Escribanía, 960.

El fiscal con Cristobal Zamorano y Juan Moreno, su criado, residentes en Panama, sobre pecado nefando, 1621. AGI, Escribanía, 451A.

El fiscal con Francisco Guerrero de Malaga sobre acusarle de abusos deshonestos, 1749. ARCV, Sala de Vizcaya, legs. 1222–1302.

El fiscal con Gabriel Ponce de León sobre pecado nefando, Pleitos Audiencia de Santo Domingo, 1648. AGI, Escribanía, 5B.

El fiscal con Gerónimo Ponce sobre el pecado nefando, dos sentencias, año de 1605. AGI, Sentencias del Consejo, Escribanía, 954.

El fiscal con Juan de Asua de Vizcaya sobre acusarle de abusos deshonestos, 1783. ARCV, Sala de Vizcaya, legs. 614–701.

El fiscal con Juan Hurtado de Zaldivar sobre pecado nefando, dos sentencias, 1595–1596. AGI, Escribanía, N953.

El fiscal con Juan Mole, Bartholomé Barres, Juan Bautista Pino, extranjeros, sobre haber cometido el sobre pecado nefando fenecido en 1700. AGI, Escribanía, 1105B.

El fiscal con Juan Ponce de León y otros vecinos de Huamanga, 1620. AGI, Escribanía, 504C.

El fiscal con Miguel Rodríguez Serraño, soltero jornalero del campo; Rafael Rubio, casado, albañil y Manuel González, casado esquilador, presos en la carcel de la Real Audiencia Chancilleria sobre acusarles de haber cometido sodomía con Jose de doce años tambien preso en dicha carcel, 1782. ARCV, Pleitos Criminales, caja 336.1/339.1.

El fiscal con Nicolás Setaro de Napoles sobre acusarle de abusos deshonestos, 1774. ARCV, Sala de Vizcaya, legs. 1203–1303.

El fiscal con Pedro González, Cristobal Fontanilla y Francisco de Vitoria soldados del presidio de Puerto Rico sobre haber cometido el pecado nefando, Fenecido en 1678. AGI, Escribanía, 119C.

El fiscal con Pedro González y otros sobre pecado nefando, dos sentencias, 1678. AGI, Escribanía, 959.

Gente de mar muerta de galleones, 1565. AGI, Contaduría, 468, N2.

Instrucción a los maestres de la Carrera de Indias, Sevilla 26 de marzo de 1568. AGI, Indiferente General, 2005.

Libros prohibidos por el Santo Oficio que se entiende habra algunos entre españoles para que los comisarios del distrito los hagan publicar y recoger de las partes a donde no habra llegado el catalogo general, 1587. AGN, Inquisición, tomo 140, no. 14.

Lista de alardes y pagamentos de la gente de mar y guerra de las embarcaciones que componen la armada del lugarteniente general Alvaro Flores, 1565. AGI, Contaduría, 468, N3.

Manuel Arredondo Carmona, corregidor de Guipuzcoa sobre que se contengan los excesos que cometen los ermitaños de la provincia de Guipuzcoa al solicitar limosnas y cometer actos de sodomía en contravención de la regla de la orden de carmelitas descalzos a la que pertenecen, 1747. AHN, Consejos Suprimidos, leg. 534, exp. 2.

Mapa de América Septentrional, 1746. AGI, México, Mapas y planos, 161.

Memoria de los ajustisiados por haver cometido el pecado nefando, 14 diciembre 1658. AGI, México, 38, N57C.

México 19 de noviembre de 1658, A su Magestad y 18 de junio de 1659 en el navío de las armadas, carta de Don Juan Manuel de Sotomayor alcalde del crimen de aquella ciudad. AGI, México, 38, N57A.

Ordenanzas Reales, para la Casa de la Contratación de Seuilla, y para otras cosas de las Indias, y de la nauegacion y contratacion de ellas, Valladolid, 1603. AGI, Indiferente General 2003.

Pedimento de Catalina de Erauso para que se le premien los servicios prestados a la corona. BRAH, Colección Juan Bautista Muñoz, 9/4807, fols. 234r–235v.

Pedro de la Valle el peregrino, en su tomo 3° de su viage escrito por él mismo en letras familiares, en lengua italiana a su amigo Mario Schipano, impreso en Bolonia 1677, en la letra ó carta 16 de Roma a 11 de julio de 1626, pág. Nº 2 dice lo siguiente. BRAH, Colección Juan Bautista Muñoz, 9/4807, fols. 232r–233v.

Petición de Mencía Velázquez cristiana nueva, mujer de Nuño de la Torre, boticario, vecina de la villa de Arévalo ante el corregidor de dicha villa, por la que reclama la restitución de los bienes que le fueron confiscados a su marido por cierto delito que cometió, alegando ella, que eran bienes dotales que llevó a su matrimonio y que estaban comprendidos en la carta de dote otorgada el siete de marzo de 1479. ARCV, Pleitos Civiles Quevedo Fenecidos, leg. 315, cajas 1412–1414.

Pragmática de los Reyes Católicos acerca de los reos de pecado nefando, Medina del Campo, 22 agosto 1497. AGS, leg. 1, no. 4.

Proceso contra Cristóbal Maldonando en la mar navegando hacia La Havana, 4 octubre de 1572. AGI, Contratación 58.

Proceso contra Cristoval, grumete de la nao Escorchapin sobre haber cometido el pecado nefando con Gaspar, grumete de la misma nao, 1560–1561. AGI, Justicia, 1181, N2, R5.

Proceso contra Francisco de Uribe Aldecoa y Nicolás de Lazagoitia por el pecado nefando, año 1626. ARCV, Sala de Vizcaya, legs. 1363–1406.

Proceso contra Gaspar Caravallo Mulato despensero de la nao de Rodrigo Díaz por suzio y desonesto y aver querido cometer el pecado nefando contra natura con unos pajes del la nao, 1591. AGI, Contratación, 5730, N8, R4.

Proceso contra Nicolás de Ibarguen por el pecado nefando, año 1616. ARCV, Sala de Vizcaya, legs. 912–1003.

Proceso criminal fulminado de officio de la Real Justicia contra El alférez Xinés Cavallero del Castillo sobre acusarle que yntento el pecado de sodomía, 1606. AGI, Contratación, 72, N1, R2.

Proceso del fiscal de S[u] M[ajestad] contra Fernando de Vera, corregidor de Murcia . . . [y] Vera contra Maria Zuniga su mujer por la custodia de su hija, año 1595. AGS, Consejo Real de Castilla, legs. 387–389.

Relación de las personas que han fallecido en la armada que el emperador nuestro Señor ha enviado al descuubrimiento del especieria de que es capitan general Fernando de Magallanes. AGI, Patronato, 34, ramo 11.

Relación prodigiosa de las grandes hazañas y valerosos hechos, que vna muger hizo en quarenta años que sirvió a su Magestad en el Reyno de Chile, y en otros del Perú y Nueva España en ávito de soldado. Y los honrosos oficios militares que tubo, sin que fuesse conocida por muger, hasta que le fue fuerza el descubrirse. Mexico City: Viuda de Bernardo Caldéron, 1653. BLAC, Colección Icazbalceta, no. JGI, Varias relaciones, 1, 54a.

Segunda parte de la relación de la Monja Alféres, y dízense en ella cosas admirables, y fidedignas de los valerosos hechos desta mujer, de lo bien que empleó el tiempo en servicio de nuestro Rey y señor. Mexico City: Hipólito de Rivera, n.d. BLAC, Colección Icazbalceta, no. JGI Varias relaciones, 1, 54b.

Segundo proceso contra Francisco Hernández mulato esclavo de Pedro López hidalgo curtidor vezino de esta ciudad de México por pacto con el demonio y por blasfemo, 1602. BLAC, W. B. Stephens Papers.

Sevilla, año de 1562, Proceso criminal fecho por el ilustre Señor Pedro Menendez de Aviles General de Armanda contra Antón de Fuentes y Alonso Prieto sobre el pecado nefando y haver intentado cometer el pecado nefando en la misma embarcación. AGI, Justicia, 855, N11.

Sevilla, año 1566, El fiscal de S[u] M[agestad] con Pedro Fernández grumete S[ob]re que le acusa haver cometido el pecado nefando. AGI, Justicia, 882, N2.

Sobre el pecado nefando que trato de cometer un clerigo llamado Cristóbal González con un sacristan. AGS, Real Cédulas, Cámara de Castilla, no. 25.

Sobre la intromision de la Sala de Alcaldes de casa y corte en las causas de comicos especialmente contra Baltasar Diaz, comico y consortes Juan Palanco, corregidor de Madrid, juez protector de comediantes, vecino de Madrid, contra Marcos de Argaiz, alcade de barrio de Bilbao . . . tres causas contra Nicola Setaro, Italiano, autor de operas . . . Garbriel López, actor y Baltasar Díaz, comico de la Companía de Eusebio de Ribera, 1773–1778. AHN, Consejos Suprimidos, leg. 611, exp. 6.

Sodomía . . . contra Juan Díaz, Alahama Granada, Francisco de Pinela Logroño, Francisco Ortiz de Legarte, 1531–1534. AGS, Cámara de Castilla, Memoriales, 203–206, 210, 217–232, 218–291, 221–292, 223–266.

Sumario de la medicina. Salamanca: n.p., 1498. BN, ms. I-1333.

Testimonio de las causas contra los culpados en el pecado nefando, 14 diciembre 1658. AGI, México, 38, N57B.

Testimonio de vista y revista contra Juan Garcia, testigo falso. AGI, Patronato, 254, N3, General 2, ramo 2.

Vida i sucesos de la Monja Alférez, Alférez Catarina, Doña Catarina de Araujo doncella, natural de S[an] Sebastián, prov[inci]a de Guipúzcoa. Escrita por ella misma en 18 de sept[iembr]e 1646, bolviendo de las Indias a España en el Galeón S[an] Josef, Capitán Andrés Otón, en la flota de N[uev]a España, General Don Juan de Benavides, General de la Armanda Tomás de la Raspuru, que llego a Cádiz en 18 de Noviembre de 1646. BRAH, Colección Juan Bautista Muñoz, 9/4807.

Vltima y tercera relación, en qve se haze verdadera del resto de la vida de la Monja Alférez, sus memorables virtudes, y exemplar muerte en estos Reynos de la Nueva España. Mexico City: Hipólito de Rivera, 1653. BLAC, Colección Icazbalceta, no. JGI Varias relaciones, 1, 54c.

Y dijo llamarse Lorensa Francisa y ser doncella . . . 11 de enero de 1687. AGI, México, 87, R1, N23, fols. 13r–17v.

Published Sources and Paintings

Acuña, R., ed. *Relaciones geográficas del siglo XVI: Tlaxcala.* Vol. 1. Mexico City: Universidad Nacional Autónoma de México, 1984.

Aguero, C. *Vocabulario castellano-zapoteco.* Mexico City: Oficina Tipográfica de la Secretaría de Fomento, 1893.

Alemán, M. *Guzmán de Alfarache.* 2 vols. Ed. J. M. Micó. Madrid: Ediciones Cátedra, 1994.

Alfonso X el sabio. *Las siete partidas: antología.* Comp. F. López Estrada and M. T. López García-Berdoy. Madrid: Editorial Castalia, 1992.

de Alva, B. *Confessionario mayor, y menor en lengva mexicana (1634).* Ed. B. D. Sell, J. F. Schwaller, and L. A. Homza. Norman: University of Oklahoma Press, 1999.

de Alva Ixtlilxochitl, F. *Nezahualcoyotl Acolmiztli (1402–1472)*. Comp. E. O'Gorman. Mexico City: Gobierno del Estado de México, 1972.

———. *Obras históricas: incluyen el texto completo de las llamadas relaciones e historia de la nación chichimeca en una nueva versión establecida con el cotejo de los manuscritos mas antiguos que se conocen.* Vol. 1. Mexico City: Universidad Nacional Autónoma de México, Instituto de Investigaciones Históricas, 1985.

Alvarez Chanca, D. "Carta al cabildo de Sevilla." In *Colección de los viages y descubrimientos que hicieron por mar los españoles desde fines del siglo XV, con varios documentos ineditos concernientes a la historia de la marina castellana y de los establecimientos españoles en Indias,* comp. M. Fernández de Navarrete, 198–224. Madrid: Imprenta Real, 1825–1837.

d'Anghiera, P. M. *The Decades of the newe worlde or west India, Conteynyng the nauigations and conquestes of the Spanyardes, with the particular description of the moste ryche and large landes and Ilandes lately founde in the west Ocean, perteynyng to the inheritaunce of the kinges of Spayne. In the which the diligent reader may not only consyder what commoditie may hereby chaunce to the hole christian world in tyme to come, but also learne many secreates touchynge the lande, the sea, and the starres, very necessarie to be knowe to al such as shal attempte any nauigations, or otherwise haue delite to beholde the strange and woonderful woorkes of God and nature.* Trans. R. Eden. London: Rycharde Jug., 1555.

———. *Opera: Legatio Babylonica, De orbe novo decades octo, Opus epistolarum (Photomechanischer Nachdruck der Ausg. von 1516 und 1530).* Ed. E. Woldan. Graz, Austria: Akademische Druck-u. Verlagsanstalt, 1966.

———. *De Orbo Novo: Historia de l'Indie occidentali.* Vinegia, Italy: Octobee, 1534.

Antuñez y Acevedo, R. *Memorias históricas sobre la legislación y gobierno del comercio de los españoles con sus colonias en las Indias occidentales.* Madrid: En la imprenta de Sanchs, 1797.

Aragón, F. E., trans. *Conocer por experiencia: un estudio de sus modos y valoración en la Summa Theológica de Tomás de Aquino.* Madrid: Pontificia Studiorum Universitas A. Thoma Aq. in Urbe, 1992.

de Ariño, F. *Sucesos de Sevilla de 1592–1604.* Seville: Imprenta de D. Rafael Tarascó y Lassa, 1873.

Art mexicain du précolombien a nos jours: [catalogue de] l'exposition [au] Musée National d'Art Moderne [Paris]. Vol. 1. Paris: Les Presses Artistiques, 1952.

Asensio y Toledo, J. M. *Francisco Pacheco: sus obras artísticas y literarias, especialmente el libro de descripción de verdaderos retratos de ilustres y memorables varones, que dejó inédito, apuntes que podrán servir de introducción a este libro si alguna vez llega á publicarse.* Seville: Litografía y librería Española y Extrangera de José Mª Geofrin, 1867.

de Ayala, M. J. *Notas a la recopilación de Indias: origen e historia ilustrada de las leyes de Indias.* Ed. J. Manzano Manzano. Madrid: Ediciones Cultura Hispánica, 1945.

Azkune, I., trans. *Katalin Erauso.* Bilbao: Mensajero D. L., 1976.

Bautista, J. *Confessionario en lengua mexicana y castellana: con muchas advertencias muy necessarias para los confessores compuesto por el Padre Fray Ioan Baptista de la orden del seraphico Padre Sanct Francisco.* Sanctiago Tlatilulco: Por Melchior Ocharte, 1599.

de Benavente (Motolinía), T. *Historia de los indios de la Nueva España*. Ed. G. Bellini. Madrid: Alianza Editorial, 1988.

Bierhorst, J., comp. *Codex Chimalpopoca: The Text in Nahuatl*. Tucson: University of Arizona Press, 1992.

Bourne, D., trans. *Codex Mendoza, manuscrit azteque*. Paris: Seghers, 1978.

Braun, G., and F. Hogenberg. *Civitates orbis terrarvm*. 3 vols. Coloniae Agrippinae: Apud G. Kempensem sumptibus auctorum, 1572–1618.

Bucaniers of America: Or, a True Account of the Most Remarkable Assaults Committed of late Years upon the coasts of The West Indies, By the Bucaniers of Jamaica and Tortuga, Both English and French. London: Printed for William Crooke, at the Green Dragon without Temple-bar, 1684.

Buendía, F., ed. *Obras completas: Don Francisco de Quevedo y Villegas*. Madrid: Aguilar, 1979.

Cabrera de Córdoba, L. *Relaciones de las cosas sucedidas en la Córte de España, desde 1599 hasta 1614*. Madrid: Imprenta de J. Martín Alegría, 1857.

Campanella, T. *De Monarchia hispanica discursus*. Amsterdam: Amstelodomi, 1640.

Carbonero y Sol, L., trans. *Opúsculos de Santo Tomás de Aquino*. Seville: A. Izquierdo, 1862.

"Carta del licenciado Alonso Zuazo al padre Fray Luis de Figueroa, prior de la mejorada, 14 de noviembre de 1521." In *Colección de documentos para la historia de México*, comp. J. García Icazbalceta, 358–367. Mexico City: Editorial Porrua, 1971.

de las Casas, B. *Apologética historia sumaria: cuanto a las cualidades, dispusición, descripción, cielo y suelo destas tierras, y condiciones naturales, policías, repúblicas, manera de vivir e costumbres de las gentes destas indias occidentales y meridionales cuyo imperio soberano pertenece a los reyes de castilla*. 2 vols. Ed. E. O'Gorman. Mexico City: Universidad Nacional Autónoma de México, 1967.

———. *Brevisima relación de la destruyción de las Indias*. Seville: Sebastian Trugillo, 1552.

———. *Historia de las Indias*. 3 vols. Ed. A. Millares Carlo. Mexico City: Fondo de Cultura Económica, 1951.

de Castañeda, P. "The Narrative of the Expedition of Coronado." In *Spanish Explorers in the Southern United States, 1528–1543: The Narrative of Alvar Núñez Cabeza de Vaca; The Narrative of the Expedition of Hernando de Soto by the Gentleman of Elvas; The Narrative of the Expedition of Coronado*, ed. F. W. Hodge and T. H. Lewis, 273–387. New York: Barnes and Noble, 1971.

Castiglione, B. *El cortesano*. Trans. J. Boscán (1534). Madrid: Promoción y Ediciones, 1985.

———. *El cortesano: tradvzido de Italiano en nuestro vulgar castellono, por Boscan*. Valladolid: Por Francisco Fernández de Cordoua, 1569.

de Castro, A. *De potestate legis poenalis libri duo*. Salamanca: Andrés Portonarijs, 1555.

A Catechism of Christian Doctrine Approved by Archbishops and Bishops of England and Wales and directed to be used in all their Dioceses. London: n.p., 1889.

de Cervantes Saavedra, M. *El ingenioso hidalgo don Quixote de la Mancha*. Madrid: Joaquín Ibarra, 1780.

Chavero, A., comp. *Obras históricas de don Fernando de Alva Ixtlilxochitl.* Mexico City: Editora Nacional, 1965.

Chilmead, E., trans. *Thomas Campanella, an Italian friar and second Machiavel, his advice to the King of Spain for attaining the universal monarchy of the world: particularly concerning England, Scotland and Ireland, how to raise division between king and Parliament, to alter the government from a kingdome to a commonwealth, thereby embroiling England in civil war to divert the English from disturbing the Spaniard in bringing the Indian treasure into Spain: also for reducing Holland by procuring war betwixt England, Holland, and other sea-faring countries.* London: Printed for Philemon Stephens, 1660.

Cieza de León, P. *La Chronica del Perv nvevamente escrita, por Pedro de Cieca de Leon, vezino de Seuilla.* Antwerp: En casa de Martin Nucio, 1554.

———. *La crónica del Perú.* Madrid: Artes de la Ilustración, 1922.

Ciruelo, P. *Tratado en el qual se reprueuan todas las supersticiones y hechizerias: muy vtil y necessario a todos los buenos christianos zelosos de su saluacion.* Barcelona: Por Sebastian de Cormellas, 1628.

Colombo, F. *Historie Del s.d. Fernando Colombo; Nelle quali s'ha particolare, & vera relatione della vita, & de'fatti dell' Ammiraglio d. Christoforo Colombo, suo padre: et dello scoprimento, ch'egi fece dell'Indie Occidentali, dette Mondo Nvovo, hora posseduta del Sereniss Re Catolico nuouamente di lingua spagnuola tradotte nell'Italiana dal s. Alfonso Vlloa, con privilegio.* Venetia: Apresso Francesco de' Franceschi Sanese, 1571.

Colón, C. *Textos y documentos completos: relaciones de viajes, cartas y memoriales.* Ed. C. Varela. Madrid: Alianza, 1982.

Compendio de la arte de navegar, de Rodrígo Camoraño, astrólogo y matematico, y cosmógrafo de la Magestad Cathólica de Don Felipe segundo Rey de España, y su catedrático de cosmógrafia en la casa de la Contratación de las Indias de la ciudad de Sevilla. Sevilla: Por Alonso de la Barrera, 1581.

Cortés, H. "Prymera Relación." In *Cartas de relación de la conquista de la Nueva Espana escritas al Emperador Carlos V, y otros documentos relativos a la conquista, años de 1519–1527, Codex Vindobonensis S.N. 1600,* ed. H. Cortés, fol. 17v. Graz, Austria: Akademische Druck-u. Verlagsanstalt, 1960.

———. "Segunda carta de relación." In *Cartas de relación de la conquista de la Nueva Espana escritas al Emperador Carlos V, y otros documentos relativos a la conquista, años de 1519–1527, Codex Vindobonensis S.N. 1600,* ed. H. Cortés, fol. 32r. Graz: Akademische Druck-u. Verlagsanstalt, 1960.

de Covarrubias Orozco, S. *Tesoro de la lengua castellana o española.* Vol. 1. Barcelona: Alta Fulla, 1998.

Díaz del Castillo, B. *Historia verdadera de la conquista de la Nueva España.* Vol. 1. Ed. C. Saenz de Santa María. Madrid: Instituto Gonzalo Fernández de Oviedo, Consejo Superior de Investigaciones Científicas, 1982.

Diccionario de Autoridades (Edición Facsímil de 1732). 3 vols. Madrid: Editorial Gredos, 1990.

Diccionario de la lengua Castellana en que se explica el verdadero sentido de las voces, su naturaleza y calidad, con las phrases o modos de hablar, los proverbios o refranes, y otras cosas convenientes al uso de la lengua. 6 vols. Madrid: En la Imprenta de la Real Academia Española por la viuda de Francisco del Hierro, 1732–1737.

Diccionario Español e Inglés, conteniente la fignificacion y uso de las voces, con terminos propios a la Marina, a las Artes, Ciencias y Comercio, con la acentuación de la Real Academia de Madrid: nueva edición, revista y corregida defpues de la edición de Joseph Baretti, Secretarie de la Real Correfpondencia de Pintura, Efcultura y Arquitectura. Vol. 1.London: A. Cofta de Piestre y Delamolliere, 1786.

Diccionario Histórico de la Lengua Espanola. Madrid: Real Academia Española, 1960.

Diccionario marítimo Inglés-Español redactado por orden del nuestro Señor. Madrid: Imprenta Real, 1831.

Durán, D. *Historia de las Indias de Nueva España e islas de la Tierra Firme escrita por fray Diego Durán dominico en el siglo XVI.* Ed. A. M. Garibay K. Mexico City: Editorial Porrua, 1967.

El conquistador anónimo. "Relatione di alcune cose della Nuova Spagna, & della gran citta di Temestitan Messico; fatta per uno gentil'homo del signor Fernando Cortese." In *Colección de documentos para la historia de México,* comp. J. García Icazbalceta, 387–390. México: Editorial Porrua, 1971.

Enríquez, J. *Questiones practicas de casos morales por el P. F. Ivan Enriquez del Orden de S. Agustin.* Madrid: Por Andrés García de la Iglesia, 1665.

Entrambasaguas, J., ed. *Obras completas de Lope de Vega.* Madrid: Consejo Superior de Investigaciones Científicas, 1965.

Erasmus de Rotterdam. *El enquiridion o manual del caballero christiano.* Ed. D. Alonso. Madrid: S. Aguirre, 1936.

de Escalante, A. *Discurso breve a la Magestad Catolica del Rey nuestro señor don Felipe quarto diuidese en dos partes: en la primera se trata del auxilio y proteccion real en fauor de los pobres en la segunda se trata de la obligación de todos los vassallos al socorro de las necessidades del Patrimonio y Magestad real.* Madrid: Por la viuda de Iuan Sanchez, 1638.

de Escalante de Mendoza, J. *Itinerario de navegación de los mares y tierras occidentales (1575).* Madrid: Museo Naval, 1985.

Fernández de Oviedo, G. *Historia general y natural de las Indias.* 2 vols. Madrid: Ediciones Atlas, 1959.

———. *Sumario de la natural historia de las Indias.* Ed. J. Bautista Avalle-Arce. Salamanca: Ediciones Anaya, 1963.

Ferrer, J. M., ed. *Historia de la monja alférez, Doña Catalina de Erauso, escrita por ella misma.* Paris: J. Didot, 1829.

Formación político-social: primer y segundo curso de bachillerato. Madrid: Editorial Amena, 1966–1967.

Gage, T. *The English-American, his travail by sea and land: or, A new svrvey of the West-India's, containing a journall of three thousand and three hundred miles within the main land of America With a grammar, or some few rudiments of the Indian tongue, called Poconchi, or Pocoman, By the true amd and painfull endevours of Thomas Gage.* London: Printed by R. Cotes, 1648.

———. *Nueva relación que contiene los viages de Tomas Gage en la Nueva España, sus diversas aventuras, y su vuelta por la provincia de Nicaragua hasta la Habana: con la descripcion de la ciudad de Méjico, tal como estaba otra vez y como se encuentra ahora (1625): unida una descripción exacta de las tierras y provincias que poseen los españoles en toda la América, de la forma de su gobierno eclesiastico y político, de su comercio, de sus costumbres, y las de los criollos, mestizos, mulatos, indios, y negroes.* 2 vols. Paris: Librería de Rosa, 1838.

García, G. *Origen de los Indios del nuevo mundo.* Mexico City: Fondo de Cultura Económica, 1981.

———. *Origen de los Indios del nuevo mundo, e Indias occidentales, averiguado con discurso de opiniones por el padre presentado F. Gregorio García, de la orden de predicadores.* Madrid: En la imprenta de Francisco Martínez Abad, 1792.

Gemelli Carreri, G. F. *Giro del mondo del dottor d. Gio: Francesco Gemelli Careri.* Napoli: Guiseppe Rosellí, 1699.

———. *Viaje a la Nueva España.* 2 vols. Trans. J. M. Agreda y Sánchez. Mexico City: Libro-Mex. Editores, 1955.

Ginés de Sepúlveda, J. *Demócrates Segundo o de las justas causas de la guerra contra los indios.* Trans. A. Losada. Madrid: Instituto Francisco de Vitoria, Consejo Superior de Investigaciones Científicas, 1984.

———. *Historia del Nuevo Mundo.* Trans. A. Ramírez de Verger. Madrid: Alianza Editorial, 1987.

Gómez, A. *Ad leges Tauri commentarius: opus elaboratum et perfectum in quo leges LXXXIII ad amussim.* Cologne: Sumptibus Iacobi Crispini, 1628.

Gómez Moreno, A., and M. P. A. M. Kerkhof, eds. *Obras completas: Íñigo López de Mendoza, Marqués de Santillana.* Barcelona: Planeta, 1988.

Hernández Sánchez-Barba, M., ed. *Cartas y otros documentos: Hernan Cortés.* Mexico City: Editorial Porrua, 1963.

de Herrera, A. *Agricultura general, que trata de la labranza del campo, y sus particularidades.* Madrid: n.p., 1790.

Hortop, J. *The Rare Trauailes of Iob Hortop, an Englishman, who was not heard of in three and twentie yeeres space: Wherin is declared the dangers he escaped in his voiage to Gynnie, where after hee was set on shoare in a wildernes neere to Panico, hee endured much slauerie and bondage in the Spanish Galley.* London: W. Wright, 1591.

———. *The rare travailes of Job Hortop: Being a facsimile reprint of the first edition (1591).* Mexico City: G. R. G. Conway, 1928.

Isabel de Portugal. "Cédula contra el pulque: ques lo propio que Balché." *Anales de Museo Nacional de México* 6.37 (1892).

Juan Ginés de Sepúlveda y su crónica Indiana: en el centenario de su muerte (1573–1973). Valladolid, Spain: Seminario Americanista de la Universidad de Valladolid, 1976.

de León, M. *Camino del cielo en lengua mexicana, con todos los requisitos necesarios para conseguir este fin, co(n) todo lo que vn Xp(r)iano deue creer, saber, y obrar, desde el punto que tiene vso de razon, hasta que muere co(m)puesto por el P. F. Martín de Leó(n).* Mexico City: En la Emprenta de Diego López Daualos, 1611.

de León, P. *Grandeza y miseria en Andalucía: testimonio de una encrucijada histórica, 1578–1616.* Ed. P. Herrera Puga. Granada: Facultad de Teología, 1981.

López, G., ed. *Las siete partidas del sabio Rey D. Alfonso el nono.* Vol. 3. Salamanca: En casa de Andrea de Portonarijs impressor de su Magestad, 1555.

López de Gómara, F. *Historia general de las Indias.* 2 vols. Barcelona: Editorial Iberia, 1965.

López de Velasco, J. "De la Casa de la Contratación de Sevilla, y cosas proveidas para la navegación de las Indias." In *Geografía y descripción universal de las Indias,* ed. J. López de Velasco, 45. Madrid: Ediciones Atlas, 1971.

———. *Geografía y descripción universal de las Indias.* Ed. M. Jiménez de la Espada. Madrid: Ediciones Atlas, 1971.

———. *Geografía y descripción universal de las Indias, recopilada por el cosmógrafo-cronista Juan López de Velasco, desde el año de 1571 al de 1574.* Madrid: Establ. tip. de Fortanet, 1894.

López Medel, T. *Cartas privadas de emigrantes a Indias (1540–1616).* Ed. Enrique Otte. Cádiz: n.p., 1988.

———. *Colonización de América: informes y testimonios (1549–1572).* Madrid: Consejo Superior de Investigaciones Científicas, 1990.

———. "Relación." In *Landa's Relación de las cosas de Yucatán: A Translation,* ed. A. M. Tozzer and C. P. Bowditch, 77–121. Cambridge, Mass.: The Museum, 1941.

Marshall, P., ed. *Salas Barbadillo.* Boulder: University of Colorado Press, 1945.

Masini, E. *Sacro arsenale overo prattica dell' officio della santa inquisitione.* Bologna: n.p., 1679.

Mendieta, J. de. *Historia eclesiástica indiana.* Vol. 1. Madrid: Atlas, 1973.

Molina, A. de. *Confesionario mayor en la lengua mexicana y castellana (1569).* Mexico City: Instituto de Investigaciones Bibliográficas, Universidad Nacional, 1975.

La mujer cristiana: de los deberes del marido, pedagogía pueril. Madrid: n.p., 1959.

Muñoz Carmargo, D. *Relaciones geográficas de Tlaxcala.* Comp. Rene Acuña. San Luis Potosí, Mexico: El Colegio de San Luis, Gobierno del Estado de Tlaxcala, 1999.

Novísima recopilación de las leyes de España: dividida en XII libros, en que se reforma la recopilación publicada por el Señor Don Felipe II en el año de 1567, reimpresa últimamente en el de 1775: y se incorporan las pragmáticas, cédulas, decretos, ordenes y resoluciones reales, y otras providencias no recopiladas, y expedidas hasta el de 1804 mandada formar por el Señor Don Carlos IV. Madrid: n.p., 1805–1807.

Núñez, Cabeza de Vaca, A. *Naufragios y comentarios.* Madrid: Historia 16, 1984.

Ordenanzas reales, para la Casa de la Contratación de Seuilla, y para otras cosas de las Indias, y de la nauegación y contratación dellas. Valladolid: Herederos de I.I. de Lequerica, 1604.

Ortíz, T. "Dixo lo siguiente, acerca de los hombres de Tierra Firme que eran Caribes." In *Historia general de los hechos de los castellanos en las Islas i Tierra Firme del Mar Oceano,* 9 vols., ed. A. de Herrera y Tordesillas, 312. Madrid: Imprenta Real, 1601–1615.

Panés, A. *Escala mística y estímulo de amor divino.* Comp. F. P. Fuster. Salamanca: Universidad Pontificia de Salamanca, 1995.

Peguero, L. J., ed. *Historia de la conquista, de la isla española de Santo Domingo trasumptada el ano de 1762: traducida de la historia general de las Indias escrita por Antonio de Herrera coro-*

nista mayor de Su Magestad, y de las Indias, y de Castilla, y de otros autores que han escrito sobre el particular. Santo Domingo: Museo de las Casas Reales, 1975.

Pragmática y nueva orden, cerca de los vestidos y trajes assi de hombres como de mujeres. Madrid: n.p., 1611.

Primera parte de los comentarios reales que tratan del origen de los yncas, reyes que fueron del Peru, de su idolatria, leyes, y gouierno en paz y en guerra de sus vidas y conquistas, y de todo lo que fue aquel Imperio y su Republica, antes que los españoles passaran a el escritas por el Ynca Garcilasso de la Vega. Lisbon: En la officina de Pedro Crasbeeck, 1609.

Pulido Rubio, J. *El piloto mayor de la Casa de la Contratación de Sevilla: pilotos mayores, catedráticos de Cosmografía y cosmógrafos.* Seville: Escuela de Estudios Hispanoamericanos, 1950.

de Quevedo y Villegas, F. "A un bujarrón." In *Poesía original completa,* ed. J. M. Blecua, 651–652. Barcelona: Planeta, 1983.

———. *El sueño del infierno.* In *Los sueños,* 7th ed., ed. F. Indurain. Zaragoza, Spain: Ebro, D.L., 1970.

———. *El sueño del infierno.* In *Los sueños: Sueños y discursos de verdades descubridoras de abusos, vicios y engaños, en todos los oficios y estados del mundo,* ed. I. Arellano and M. C. Pinillos. Barcelona: Planeta–De Agostini, 2001.

———. *La vida del Buscón llamado Don Pablos.* Ed. D. Ynduráin. Madrid: Ediciones Cátedra, 1995.

———. *Las Zahurdas de Plutón (El sueño del infierno).* Ed. A. Mas. Poitiers, France: Imp. Marc Texier, 1955.

Recopilación de las leyes destos reynos: hecha por mandado de la Magestad Católica del Rey Don Felipe Segundo Nuestro Señor que se ha mandado imprimir con las leyes que después de la última impression se han publicado por la Magestad Católica del Rey Don Felipe Quarto el Grande Nuestro Señor. Madrid: Por Catalina de Barrio y Angulo y Diego Diaz de la Carrera, 1640–1641.

Ríos, J. A. de los, ed. *Obras de Don Iñigo López de Mendoza Marqués de Santillana: ahora por vez primera compiladas de los códices originales, é ilustradas con la vida del autor.* Madrid: Imprenta de la calle de S. Vicente baja, a cargo de José Rodríguez, 1852.

Sahagún, B. de. *Historia general de las cosas de Nueva España: primera versión íntegra del text castellano del manuscrito conocido como Códice Florentino.* 2 vols. Ed. A. López Austin and J. García Quintana. Madrid: Alianza Editorial, 1995.

Salas Barbadillo, A. J. de. *El caballero perfecto.* Madrid: n.p., 1620.

Salazar, S. de. *Promptuario de materias morales: en principios, y reglas para examen, y sucinta noticia de los que en breue se dessean exponer para confessores.* Barcelona: Por Antonio Lacaualleria, 1680.

Salcedo de Aguirre, G. *Pliego de cartas en que ay doze epístolas escritas a personas de diferentes estados y officios.* Baeza, Spain: n.p., 1594.

Schepeler, O., trans. *Die Nonne-Faburich, oder Geschichte der Doña Catalina de Erauso von ihr selbst geschrieben.* Aachen and Leipzig: Verlag von J. M. Mayer, 1830.

Sigüenza y Góngora, C. de. *Alboroto y motín de México del 8 de junio de 1692.* Ed. I. A. Leonard. Mexico City: Talleres Gráficos del Museo Nacional de Arqueología, Historia y Etnografía, 1932.

Simón, P. *Primera parte de las noticias historiales de las conquistas de Tierra Firme en las Indias Occidentales.* Cuenca, Spain: D. de la Yglesia, 1627.

Speed, J. "Spaine newly described, with many adictions, both in the attires of the people and the setuations of their cheifest Cityes (1625)." In *A Prospect of the Most Famous Parts of the World.* London: Printed by M. F. for W. Humble, 1646.

Spinoza, B. de. *A Theologico-political Treatise.* New York: Dover, 1975.

Torquemada, J. de. *Monarquía Indiana: de los veinte y un libros rituales y monarquía indiana, con el origen y guerras de los indios occidentales, de sus poblazones, descubrimiento, conquista, conversión y otras cosas maravillosas de la mesma tierra.* 7 vols. Ed. M. León-Portilla. Mexico City: Universidad Nacional Autónoma de Mexico, 1975–1983.

Torre, T. de la. "Diario del viaje de Salamanca a Ciudad Real, Chiapas, (1544–1545)." In *Pasajeros de Indias: viajes transatlánticos en el siglo XVI,* comp. J. L. Martínez, 248. Mexico City: Alianza Editorial, 1984.

Torres, A. de. "Relación de cómo una monja de Úbeda se tornó hombre (1617)." In *Relaciones Históricas de los Siglos XVI y XVII,* ed. F. R. Uhagon y Guardamino, Marqués de Laurencin, 335–337. Madrid: La Sociedad de Bibliófilos Espa-]ñoles, 1896.

Torres Fontes, J., and R. Bosque Carceller, eds. *Epistolario del Cardenal Belluga.* Murcia, Spain: Academia Alfonso el Sabio, 1962.

Vázquez de Espinosa, A. *Compendio y descripción de las Indias Occidentales.* Madrid: Ediciones Atlas, 1969.

Vega, G. de la. *Comentarios reales de los Incas.* 3 vols. Lima: Universidad Nacional Mayor de San Marcos, 1960.

Veitia Linaje, J. de. *Norte de la contratación de las Indias occidentales.* Seville: I. F. Blas, 1672.

Vetancurt, A. de. *Teatro mexicano: descripción breve de los svcessos exemplares, históricos, políticos, militares, y religiosos del Nuevo Mundo occidental de las Indias.* Mexico City: Por Doña María de Benavides, viuda de Iuan de Ribera, 1698.

Vitoria, F. de. *De Indis et de ivre belli: relectiones Francisci de Victoria.* Ed. E. Nys. Washington, D.C.: Carnegie Institution of Washington, 1917.

———. "On Dietary Laws, or Self-Restraint," in *Political Writings: Francisco de Vitoria,* ed. A. Pagden and J. Lawrance, 211–227. Cambridge: Cambridge University Press, 1991.

———. "On the American Indians," in *Political Writings: Francisco de Vitoria,* ed. A. Pagden and J. Lawrance, 273–275. Cambridge: Cambridge University Press, 1991.

———. *Relecciones del estado, de los indios, y del derecho de la guerra.* Mexico City: Editorial Porrua, 1974.

Vivés, J. L. *De institutione feminae christianae: la formación de la mujer cristiana.* Trans. J. Beltrán Serra. Valencia: Ajuntament de València, 1994.

Secondary Sources

Adorno, R. *Guaman Poma: Writing and Resistance in Colonial Peru.* Austin: University of Texas Press, 2000.

Adorno, R., and K. J. Andrien, eds. *Transatlantic Encounters: Europeans and Andeans in the Sixteenth Century.* Berkeley and Los Angeles: University of California Press, 1991.

Aguirre Beltrán, G. *Medicina y magia: el proceso de aculturación en la estructura colonial.* Mexico City: SEP/INI, 1973.

Ahmad, A. *In Theory: Classes, Nations, Literatures.* London: Verso Books, 1992.

————. "Postcolonialism: What's in a Name?" In *Late Imperial Culture,* ed. R. de la Campa, E. A. Kaplan, and M. Sprinker, 11–32. London: Verso, 1995.

Alberro, S. *Inquisición y sociedad en México (1571–1700).* Mexico City: Fondo de Cultura Económica, 1993.

————, ed. *El placer de pecar y el afán de normar: ideologías y comportamiento familiares y sexuales en el México colonial.* Mexico City: Planeta, 1986.

Albuquerque, K. de. "On Golliwogs and Flit Pumps: How the Empire Stays with Us in Strange Remembrances." *Jouvert: A Journal of Postcolonial Studies* 2.2 (1998): 1–5. Available at http://152.1.96.5/jouvert/v2i2/confour.htm

Alejandre, J. A. *El veneno de Dios: la Inquisición de Sevilla ante el delito de solicitación en confesión.* Madrid: Siglo XXI, 1994.

Althusser, L. "Contradiction and Overdetermination." In *For Marx,* trans. B. Brewster. London: Verso, 1979.

————. *Essays in Self-criticism.* Trans. G. Lock. London: NLB–Atlantic Highlands, 1976.

Anadón, J. *Garcilaso Inca de la Vega, an American Humanist: A Tribute to Jose Durand.* Notre Dame, Ind.: University of Notre Dame Press, 1998.

Anawalt, P. R. *Indian Clothing before Cortes: Mesoamerican Costumes from the Codices.* Norman: University of Oklahoma Press, 1981.

Anderson, B. *Imagined Communities: Reflections on the Origins and Spread of Nationalism.* London: Verso, 1951.

Ankersmit, F. "Reply to Professor Zagorin." *History and Theory* 29.3 (1990): 96, 277–282.

Anzaldúa, G. *Borderlands–La Frontera: The New Mestiza.* San Francisco: Spinsters/Aunt Lute, 1987.

————. *Interviews-Entrevistas.* Ed. A. L. Keating. New York: Routledge, 2000.

Archetti, E. *Masculinities: Football, Polo, and the Tango in Argentina.* Oxford, UK; New York: Berg, 1999.

Arenal, E., and S. Schlau. *Untold Sisters: Hispanic Nuns in Their Own Words.* Albuquerque: University of New Mexico Press, 1989.

Arjona Castro, A. *La sexualidad en la España musulmana.* Córdoba: Universidad de Córdoba, 1990.

Azoulai, M. *Les Péchés du Nouveau Monde: les manuels pour la confession des Indiens XVIe–XVIIe siècle.* Paris: Éditions Albin Michel, 1993.

Bailey, D. S. *Homosexuality and the Western Christian Tradition*. Hamden: Archon Books, 1975.

Bal, M. *Quoting Caravaggio: Contemporary Art, Preposterous History*. Chicago: University of Chicago Press, 1999.

Balderston, D., and D. J. Guy, eds. *Sex and Sexuality in Latin America*. New York: New York University Press, 1997.

Balibar, E. "Racism as Universalism." *New Political Science* 16.17 (1989): 19.

Bauer, R. "Imperial History, Captivity, and Creole Identity in Francisco Núñez de Pineda y Bascuñán's *Cautiverio feliz*." *Colonial Latin American Review* 7.1 (1998): 59–82.

Beauvoir, S. de. "Must We Burn Sade?" In *Marquis de Sade: The 120 Days of Sodom and Other Writings*, comp. A. Wainhouse and R. Seaver, 3–64. New York: Grove Press, 1966.

Behar, R. "Sexual Witchcraft, Colonialism, and Women's Powers: Views from the Mexican Inquisition." In *Sexuality and Marriage in Colonial Latin America*, ed. A. Lavrín, 178–206. Lincoln: University of Nebraska Press, 1989.

Bem, S. L. *The Lenses of Gender: Transforming the Debate on Sexual Inequality*. New Haven, Conn.: Yale University Press, 1993.

Benítez, F. *Los demonios en el convento: sexo y religión en la Nueva España*. Mexico City: Era, 1992.

Bennassar, B. *L'Homme espagnol: attitudes et mentalités du XVIe au XIXe siècle*. Paris: Hachette, 1975.

———. *Inquisición española: poder político y control social*. Trans. J. Alfaya. Barcelona: Editorial Crítica, 1984.

———. "Le modèle sexuel: l'Inquisition d'Aragon et la répression des pechés abominables." In *L'Inquisition Espagnole (XVe–XIXe siècles)*, ed. B. Bennassar, 339–369. Paris: Hachette, 1979.

Bennett, J. "'Lesbian-Like' and the Social History of Lesbianisms." *Journal of the History of Sexuality* 9.1–2 (January–April 2000): 1–24.

Bergmann, E. L., and P. J. Smith, eds. *¿Entiendes? Queer Readings, Hispanic Writings*. Durham, N.C.: Duke University Press, 1995.

Bermejo Cabrero, J. L. "Justicia penal y teatro barroco." In *Sexo barroco y otras transgresiones premodernas*, ed. F. Tomás y Valiente, B. Clavero, A. M. Hespanha, J. L. Bermejo, E. Gacto, and C. Alvarez Alonso. 91–108. Madrid: Alianza Editorial, 1990.

———. "Tormentos, apremios, cárceles, y patíbulos a finales del antiguo régimen." *Anuario de Historia del Derecho Español* 56 (1986): 683–727.

Betteridge, Tom, ed. *Sodomy in Early Modern Europe*. Manchester, U.K.: Manchester University Press, 2002.

Beylen, J. van. *Zeilvaart Lexicon: Viertaglig Maritiem Woordenboek*. Weesp, Netherlands: De Boer Maritiem, 1985.

Bhabha, H. K. "Of Mimicry and Man: The Ambivalence of Colonial Discourse." *October* 28 (1984): 125–133.

———. "The Other Question: The Stereotype and Colonial Discourse." *Screen* 24.6 (1985): 18–36.

———, ed. *Nation and Narration.* London: Routledge, 1990.

Billinkof, J. *The Avila of Saint Teresa: Religious Reform in a Sixteenth-Century City.* Ithaca, N.Y.: Cornell University Press, 1989.

Blackmore, J. *Manifest Perdition: Shipwreck Narrative and the Disruption of Empire.* Minneapolis: University of Minnesota Press, 2002.

———. "The Poets of Sodom." In *Queer Iberia: Sexualities, Cultures, and Crossings from the Middle Ages to the Renaissance,* ed. J. Blackmore and G. S. Hutcheson, 195–221. Durham, N.C.: Duke University Press, 1999.

Blackmore, J., and G. S. Hutcheson, eds. *Queer Iberia: Sexualities, Cultures, and Crossings from the Middle Ages to the Renaissance.* Durham, N.C.: Duke University Press, 1999.

Bleys, R. *The Geography of Perversion: Male-to-Male Sexual Behaviour outside the West and the Ethnographic Imagination (1750–1918).* London: Cassell, 1996.

Boissonnade, P. *Life and Work in Medieval Europe (Fifth to Fifteenth Centuries).* Trans. E. Power. London: Routledge and Kegan Paul, 1949.

Boswell, J. *Christianity, Social Tolerance, and Homosexuality: Gay People in Western Europe from the Beginning of the Christian Era to the Fourteenth Century.* Chicago: University of Chicago Press, 1980.

Boudriot, A. *The Seventy-Four Gun Ship: A Practical Treatise on the Art of Naval Architecture.* Trans. D. H. Roberts. Ashley Lodge, U.K.: Jean Boudriot Publications, 1986.

Boxer, C. R. *Mary and Misogyny: Women in Iberian Expansion Overseas (1415–1815).* London: Duckworth, 1975.

Brading, D. A. *The First America: The Spanish Monarchy, Creole Patriots, and the Liberal State (1492–1867).* Cambridge: Cambridge University Press, 1991.

Bravo-Villasante, C. *La mujer vestida de hombre en el teatro español (siglos XVI–XVII).* Madrid: Sociedad General Española de Librería, 1976.

Bray, A. *Homosexuality in Renaissance England.* Viborg, Denmark: Gay Men Press, 1988.

Bredbeck, G. W. *Sodomy and Interpretation: Marlowe to Milton.* Ithaca, N.Y.: Cornell University Press, 1991.

Brown, C. "Queer Representation in the *Arçipreste de Talavera,* or the *Maldezir de mugeres* Is a Drag." In *Queer Iberia: Sexualities, Cultures, and Crossings from the Middle Ages to the Renaissance,* ed. J. Blackmore and G. S. Hutcheson, 73–103. Durham, N.C.: Duke University Press, 1999.

Brown, J., and J. H. Elliott. *A Palace for a King: The Buen Retiro and the Court of Philip IV.* New Haven, Conn.: Yale University Press, 1980.

Brown, J. C. *Immodest Acts: The Life of a Lesbian Nun in Renaissance Italy.* New York: Oxford University Press, 1986.

Brown, P. *The Body and Society: Men, Women, and Sexual Renunciation in Early Christianity.* New York: Columbia University Press, 1988.

Bruggeman, M. *Brugge en kant: een historische overzicht.* Bruges: Marc van de Wiele, 1985.

Bullough, V. L., and B. Bullough. *Sin, Sickness, and Sanity: A History of Sexual Attitudes.* New York: New American Library, 1977.

Burg, B. R. *Sodomy and the Pirate Tradition: English Sea Rovers in the Seventeenth-Century Caribbean.* New York: New York University Press, 1984.

Burshatin, I. "Interrogating Hermaphroditism in Sixteenth-Century Spain." In *Hispanisms and Homosexualities,* ed. S. Molloy and R. McKee Irwin, 3–18. Durham, N.C.: Duke University Press, 1998.

———. "Written on the Body: Slave or Hermaphrodite in Sixteenth-Century Spain." In *Queer Iberia: Sexualities, Cultures, and Crossings from the Middle Ages to the Renaissance,* ed. J. Blackmore and G. S. Hutcheson, 420–453. Durham, N.C.: Duke University Press, 1999.

Bustos-Aguilar, P. "Mister Don't Touch the Banana: Notes on the Popularity of the Ethnosexed Body South of the Border." *Critique of Anthropology* 15.2 (1995): 149–170.

Butler, J. *Gender Trouble: Feminism and the Subversion of Identity.* New York: Routledge, 1990.

Buxán Bran, X. M., ed. *Conciencia de un singular deseo: estudios lesbianos y gays en el estado español.* Barcelona: Laertes, 1997.

Cahen, C. *Introduction a l'histoire du monde musulman médiéval (Vlle–XVe siècle).* Paris: Librairie d'Amérique et d'Orient, 1982.

Callahan, M. "Mexican Border Troubles: Social War, Settler Colonialism and the Production of Frontier Discourses, 1848–1880." Ph.D. diss., University of Texas at Austin, 2002.

Camamis, G. *Estudios sobre el cautiverio en el siglo de oro.* Trans. M. Guillén. Madrid: Gredos, 1977.

Caminha, A. *Bom-Crioulo.* Rio de Janeiro: Domingos de Magalhães Editor, 1895.

———. *Bom-Crioulo: una obra maestra de la literatura brasileña del siglo XIX.* Trans. L. Zapata. Mexico City: Editorial Posada, 1987.

Candau Chacón, M. L. *Los delitos y las penas en el mundo eclesiástico sevillano del XVIII.* Seville: Publicaciones Diputación Provincial de Sevilla, 1993.

Canizares-Esguerra, J. *How to Write the History of the New World: Historiographies, Epistemologies, and Identities in the Eighteenth-Century Atlantic World.* Stanford, Calif.: Stanford University Press, 2001.

Cansinos Assens, R., ed. *El Koran: versión literal e íntegra.* Madrid: Aguilar, 1981.

Carrasco, R. "Le châtiment de la sodomie sous l'Inquisition (XVIe et XVIIe siècle)." *Mentalités: histoire des cultures et des sociétés* 3 (1989): 53–69.

———. *Inquisición y represión sexual en Valencia: historia de los sodomitas (1565–1785).* Barcelona: Laertes, 1985.

———. "Les pouvoirs et 'le pervers': éléments pour une histoire de certains minorités à l'époque de Philippe IV." *Imprévue* (1980–1981): 31–52.

———, ed. *La Prostitution en Espagne: de l'époque des Rois Catholiques à la IIe République.* Paris: Annales Littéraires de l'Université de Besançon, Les Belles Lettres, 1994.

Cascardi, A. *The Limits of Illusion: A Critical Study of Calderón.* New York: Cambridge University Press, 1984.

Chao, Manu. *Clandestino.* Virgin France, 1998. Compact disc.

Chatterjee, P. *The Nation and Its Fragments: Colonial and Postcolonial Histories.* Princeton, N.J.: Princeton University Press, 1993.

Chatterjee, P., and G. Pandey, eds. *Subaltern Studies 7: Writings on South Asian History and Society.* New Delhi: Oxford University Press, 1994.

Chaunu, P., and H. Chaunu. *Seville et l'Atlantique.* 6 vols. Paris: A. Colin, 1955–1959.

Clavero, B. "Delito y pecado: noción y escala de transgresiones." In *Sexo barroco y otras transgresiones premodernas,* ed. F. Tomás y Valiente, B. Clavero, A. M. Hespanha, J. L. Bermejo, E. Gacto, and C. Alvarez Alonso, 57–89. Madrid: Alianza Editorial, 1990.

Clendinnen, I. *Ambivalent Conquests: Maya and Spaniard in Yucatán (1517–1570).* Cambridge: Cambridge University Press, 1987.

———. "The Cost of Courage in Aztec Society." *Past and Present* 107 (1985): 45–89.

———. "Disciplining the Indians: Franciscan Ideology and Missionary Violence in Sixteenth-Century Yucatán." *Past and Present* 94 (1982): 27–59.

Contreras, J. *El Santo Oficio de la Inquisición de Galicia: poder, sociedad, y cultura (1560–1700).* Madrid: Akal Editor, 1982.

Cooper, F., and A. L. Stoler. "Between Metropole and Colony: Rethinking a Research Agenda." In *Tensions of Empire: Colonial Cultures in a Bourgeois World,* ed. F. Cooper and A. L. Stoler, 1–58. Berkeley and Los Angeles: University of California Press, 1997.

Copete, M. L. "Criminalidad y espacio carcelario en una cárcel del antiguo régimen: la cárcel real de Sevilla a finales del siglo XVI." *Historia Social* 6 (1989): 105–125.

Corcuera de Mancera, S. *El fraile, el indio, y el pulque: evangelización y embríaguez en la Nueva España (1523–1548).* Mexico City: Fondo de Cultura Económica, 1991.

The Country Life Book of Nautical Terms under Sail. London: Trewin Copplestone Publishing, 1978.

Creighton, M. S., and L. Norling, eds. *Iron Men, Wooden Women: Gender and Seafaring in the Atlantic World (1700–1920).* Baltimore: Johns Hopkins University Press, 1996.

Crompton, L. "Male Love and Islamic Law in Arab Spain." In *Islamic Homosexualities: Culture, History, and Literature,* ed. S. O. Murray and W. Roscoe, 142–157. New York: New York University Press, 1997.

Cuder Domínguez, P. Introduction to *Exilios femeninos,* ed. P. Cuder Domínguez, 11–12. Huelva, Spain: Universidad de Huelva Publicaciones, 2000.

Cuevas, M. *Historia de la iglesia en México.* 5 vols. Mexico City: Antigua Imprenta de Murguia, 1921.

Davis, N. Z. *The Return of Martin Guerre.* New York: Penguin Books, 1985.

Deans-Smith, S. *Bureaucrats, Planters, and Workers: The Making of the Tobacco Monopoly in Bourbon Mexico.* Austin: University of Texas Press, 1992.

Dekker, R. M., and L. C. van de Pol. *The Tradition of Female Transvestism in Early Modern Europe*. London: Macmillan, 1989.

Deleito y Piñuela, J. *La mala vida de la España de Felipe IV*. Madrid: Alianza Editorial, 1987.

Derrida, J. "The Deconstruction of Actuality." *Radical Philosophy* 68 (1994): 28-41.

————. *Of Grammatology*. Trans. G. C. Spivak. Baltimore: Johns Hopkins University Press, 1977.

Descombes, V. *Modern French Philosophy*. Cambridge: Cambridge University Press, 1979.

Domínguez García, B. "La fantasía como exilio interior femenino en *Three Times Table* de Sara Maitland." In *Exilios femeninos*, ed. P. Cuder Domínguez, 217–226. Huelva, Spain: Universidad de Huelva Publicaciones, 2000.

Domínguez Ortiz, A. *Orto y ocaso de Sevilla: estudio sobre la prosperidad y decadencia de la ciudad durante los siglos XVI y XVII*. Seville: Junta de Patronato de la Seccion de Publicaciones de la Excma. Diputacion Provincial, 1946.

————. *Sociedad y mentalidad en la Sevilla del antiguo regimen*. Seville: Servicio de Publicaciones del Ayuntamiento de Sevilla, 1983.

Drost, G. W. "De Moriscos in de publicaties van Staat en Kerk (1492-1609)." Ph.D. diss., Rijksuniversiteit te Leiden, Netherlands, 1984.

Duberman, M. B., M. Vicinus and G. Chauncey, Jr., eds. *Hidden from History: Reclaiming the Gay and Lesbian Past*. New York: NAL Books, 1989.

Dugaw, D. "Female Sailors Bold: Transvestite Heroines and the Markers of Gender and Class." In *Iron Men, Wooden Women: Gender and Seafaring in the Atlantic World (1700–1920)*, ed. M. S. Creighton and L. Norling, 34–54. Baltimore: Johns Hopkins University Press, 1996.

Dynes, W. R., ed. *Encyclopedia of Homosexuality*. 2 vols. New York: Garland, 1990.

Eisenberg, D. Introduction to *Spanish Writers on Lesbian and Gay Themes: A Bio-Critical Sourcebook*, ed. D. W. Foster, 1–21. Westport, Conn.: Greenwood Press, 1999.

————. "Juan Ruiz's Heterosexual Good Love." In *Queer Iberia: Sexualities, Cultures, and Crossings from the Middle Ages to the Renaissance*, ed. J. Blackmore and G. S. Hutcheson, 250–274. Durham, N.C.: Duke University Press, 1999.

————. "Spain." In *Encyclopedia of Homosexuality*, vol. 2, ed. W. R. Dynes, 1236–1242. New York: Garland, 1990.

Eslava Galán, J. *Historia secreta del sexo en España*. Madrid: Temas de Hoy, 1996.

Espejo Muriel, C. *El deseo negado: aspectos de la problemática homosexual en la vida monástica (siglos III–VI d.c.)*. Granada: Universidad de Granada, 1991.

Fanon, F. "Algeria Unveiled." In *A Dying Colonialism*, trans. H. Chevalier, 21–52. Middlesex, England: Penguin Books, 1970.

Farriss, N. M. *Maya Society under Colonial Rule: The Collective Enterprise of Survival*. Princeton, N.J.: Princeton University Press, 1984.

Fernández del Castillo, F. *Libros y libreros en el siglo XVI*. Mexico City: Tip. Guerrero, 1914.

Feros, A. *Kingship and Favouritism in the Spain of Philip III (1598–1621)*. Cambridge: Cambridge University Press, 2000.

Firpo, A. R. "Los reyes sexuales: ensayo sobre el discurso sexual durante el reinado de Enrique IV Trastamara (1454–1474)." *Mélanges de la Casa Veláquez* 20 (1984): 217–226.

Fletcher, R. *Moorish Spain*. Berkeley and Los Angeles: University of California Press, 1992.

Florescano, E. *Memory, Myth, and Time in Mexico: From the Aztecs to Independence*. Austin: University of Texas Press, 1994.

Foster, D. W. *Gay and Lesbian Themes in Latin American Writing*. Austin: University of Texas Press, 1991.

———. *Sexual Textualities: Essays on Queer/ing Latin American Writing*. Austin: University of Texas Press, 1997.

———, ed. *Spanish Writers on Lesbian and Gay Themes: A Bio-Critical Sourcebook*. Westport, Conn.: Greenwood Press, 1999.

Foucault, M. *The Archaeology of Knowledge*. Trans. A. M. Sheridan Smith. London: Tavistock, 1972.

———. *Discipline and Punish: The Birth of the Prison*. Trans. A. Sheridan. New York: Vintage Books, 1979.

———. *Historia de la locura en la época clásica*. Trans. J. J. Utrilla. Mexico City: Fondo de Cultura Económica, 1976.

———. *The History of Sexuality*. 3 vols. Trans. R. Hurley. New York: Vintage Books, 1978, 1985, 1986.

Fradenburg, L., and C. Freccero, eds. *Premodern Sexualities*. New York: Routledge, 1996.

Franco, J. "Beyond Ethnocentrism: Gender, Power, and the Third-World Intelligentsia." In *Marxism and the Interpretation of Culture*, ed. C. Nelson and L. Grossberg, 503–515. London: Macmillan Education, 1988.

Garber, M. B. "The Occidental Tourist: *M. Butterfly* and the Scandal of Transvestism." In *Nationalisms and Sexualities*, ed. A. Parker, M. Russo, D. Sommer and P. Yaeger 121–146. New York: Routledge, 1992.

———. *Vested Interests: Cross-dressing and Cultural Anxiety*. New York, Routledge, 1992.

García Carcel, R. *Herejía y sociedad en el siglo XVI: la Inquisición en Valencia (1530–1609)*. Barcelona: Península, 1980.

García Valdés, A. *Historia y presente de la homosexualidad: análisis crítico de un fenómeno conflictivo*. Madrid: Akal Editor, 1981.

Garza Carvajal, F. *The Little Canes: Male Fantasies of Carnal Copulation between Inés and Catalina, Two Dykes Roaming the Early Modern Castillian Countryside*. Forthcoming, 2003.

———. *Quemando mariposas: sodomía e imperio en España y México (siglos XVI–XVII)*. Barcelona: Laertes, 2002.

———. "Silk Laced Ruffs and Cuffs: An Inherent Link between *Sodomie* and Notions of Effeminacy in Andalucía and México (1561–1699)." *Thamyris: Myth-making from Past to Present* 7.1–2 (2000): 7–39.

———. "Tattoos, Demons, and the Spectacle of It All. The Second Inquisitorial Trial of Francisco Hernández: 1602–1603." Amsterdam: Bibliotheek CEDLA, 1994. Unpubl. manuscript.

———. *Vir: Perceptions of Manliness in Andalucía and México (1561–1699)*. Amsterdam: Amsterdamse Historische Reeks, 2000.

Geertz, C. *The Interpretation of Cultures.* New York: Basic Books, 1973.

Gibson, C. *The Aztecs under Spanish Rule: A History of Indians of the Valley of Mexico (1519–1810).* Stanford, Calif.: Stanford University Press, 1964.

Ginzburg, C. *The Cheese and the Worms: The Cosmos of a Sixteenth-Century Miller.* Trans. John and Anne Tedeschi. London: Penguin Books, 1992.

———. "Morelli, Freud, and Sherlock Holmes: Clues and Scientific Method." *History Workshop Journal* 9 (1980): 5–36.

Goldberg, J. *Sodometries: Renaissance Texts, Modern Sexualities.* Stanford, Calif.: Stanford University Press, 1992.

———, ed. *Queering the Renaissance.* Durham, N.C.: Duke University Press, 1994.

———. *Reclaiming Sodom.* New York: Routledge, 1994.

Góngora, M. *El estado en el derecho Indiano: época de fundación (1492–1570).* Santiago de Chile: Instituto de Investigaciones Histórico-Culturales, 1951.

González-Casanovas, R. J. "Male Bonding as Cultural Construction in Alfonso X, Ramon Llull, and Juan Manuel: Homosocial Friendship in Medieval Iberia." In *Queer Iberia: Sexualities, Cultures, and Crossings from the Middle Ages to the Renaissance*, ed. J. Blackmore and G. S. Hutcheson, 157–192. Durham, N.C.: Duke University Press, 1999.

Gramsci, A. *Selections from the Prison Notebooks of Antonio Gramsci.* London: Lawrence and Wishart, 1971.

Green, J. N. *Beyond Carnival: Male Homosexuality in Twentieth-Century Brazil.* Chicago: University of Chicago Press, 1999.

Gruzinski, S. "Las cenizas del deseo: homosexuales novohispanos a mediados del siglo XVII." In *De la santidad a la perversión o de por qué no se cumplía la ley de Dios en la sociedad novohispana*, ed. S. Ortega, 255–281. Mexico City: Editorial Grijalbo, 1985.

———. *The Conquest of Mexico: The Incorporation of Indian Societies into the Western World (16th–18th Centuries).* Trans. E. Corrigan. Cambridge, U.K.: Polity Press, 1993.

———. *Les Hommes-Dieux du Mexique: pouvoir indigène et société coloniale, XVIe–XVIIIe siècles.* Paris: Archives Contemporaines, 1985.

———. *Man-Gods in the Mexican Highlands, Sixteenth–Eighteenth Centuries.* Stanford, Calif.: Stanford University Press, 1989.

Guerra, F. *The Pre-Columbian Mind: A Study into the Aberrant Nature of Sexual Drives, Drugs Affecting Behaviour and the Attitude Towards Life and Death, with a Survey of Psychotherapy in Pre-Columbian America.* London: Seminar Press, 1971.

Guerra Manzo, E. "El problema del poder en la obra de Michel Foucault y Norbert Elias." *Estudios Sociológicos* 17.49 (January–April 1999): 95–120.

Gutiérrez, R. A. *When Jesus Came, the Corn Mothers Went Away: Marriage, Sexuality, and Power in New Mexico (1500–1846)*. Stanford, Calif.: Stanford University Press, 1991.

Haliczer, S. *Inquisition and Society in the Kingdom of Valencia (1478–1834)*. Berkeley and Los Angeles: University of California Press, 1990.

Halperin, D. M. *One Hundred Years of Homosexuality and Other Essays on Greek Love*. London: Routledge, 1990.

Halpern, R. *Shakespeare's Perfume: Sodomy and Sublimity in the Sonnets, Wilde, Freud, and Lacan*. Philadelphia: University of Pennsylvania Press, 2002.

Hanke, L., ed. *Los Virreyes españoles en America durante el gobierno de la Casa de Austria*. 4 vols. Madrid: Atlas, 1976–1978.

Harrison, R. *Signs, Songs, and Memory in the Andes: Translating Quechua Language and Culture*. Austin: University of Texas Press, 1989.

Harten, M. van. *Instruments of Torture: From the Middle Ages to the Age of Enlightenment*. Amsterdam: Inter-Expo, 1991.

Harvey, L. P. *Islamic Spain (1250–1500)*. Chicago: University of Chicago Press, 1990.

Heise, U. K. "Transvestism and the Stage Controversy in Spain and England (1580–1680)." *Theatre Journal* 44 (1992): 357–374.

Hekma, G. "A Female Soul in a Male Body: Sexual Inversion as Gender Inversion in Nineteenth-Century Sexology." In *Third Sex, Third Gender: Beyond Sexual Dimorphism in Culture and History*, ed. G. Herdt, 213–240. New York: Zone Books, 1994.

Hemker, M. "Oppervlakkige openheid is te prefereren boven oppervlakkige koelheid: Jonathan Katz wil homoseksualiteit weer politiek maken." *Folia: Weekblad voor de Universiteit van Amsterdam* 38 (18 June 1999): 11.

Hennessy, R. *Materialist Feminism and the Politics of Discourse*. New York: Routledge, 1993.

Hennessy, R., and C. T. Mohanty. "The Construction of Woman in Three Popular Texts of Empire: Toward a Critique of Materialist Feminism." *Textual Practice* 3.3 (1989): 323–359.

Herrera Puga, P. *Sociedad y delincuencia en el Siglo de Oro*. Madrid: Católica, 1974.

Higgs, D., ed. *Queer Sites: Gay Urban Histories since 1600*. London: Routledge, 1999.

Howes, R. "Race and Transgressive Sexuality in Adolfo Caminha's *Bom-Crioulo*." *Luso-Brazilian Review* 38.1 (2001): 41–62.

Huerga, A. *Los Alumbrados de la alta Andalucía (1575–1590)*. Vol. 2. Madrid: Fundación Universitaria Española, 1978.

———. *Historia de los Alumbrados*. Vol. 1. Madrid: Fundación Universitaria Española, 1978.

Hunt, L. A. "Introduction: History, Culture, and the Text" In *The New Cultural History: Essays (Studies on the History of Society and Culture)*, ed. L. A. Hunt, 1–24. Berkeley and Los Angeles: University of California Press, 1989.

————, ed. *The Invention of Pornography: Obscenity and the Origins of Modernity (1500–1800)*. New York: Zone Books, 1993.

Hurteau, P. "Catholic moral discourse on male sodomy and masturbation in the seventeenth and eighteenth centuries." *Journal of the History of Sexuality* 4.1 (1993): 1–32.

Hutcheson, G. S. "Desperately Seeking Sodom: Queerness in the Chronicles of Alvaro de Luna." In *Queer Iberia: Sexualities, Cultures, and Crossings from the Middle Ages to the Renaissance*, ed. J. Blackmore and G. S. Hutcheson, 222–249. Durham, N.C.: Duke University Press, 1999.

Hutcheson, G. S., and J. Blackmore. Introduction to *Queer Iberia: Sexualities, Cultures, and Crossings from the Middle Ages to the Renaissance*, ed. J. Blackmore and G. S. Hutcheson, 1–19. Durham, N.C.: Duke University Press, 1999.

Israel, J. I. *Race, Class, and Politics in Colonial Mexico, (1610–1670)*. London: Oxford University Press, 1975.

Jacobs, A. P. "Migraciones laborales entre España y América: la procedencia de marineros en la carrera de Indias (1598–1610)." *Revista de Indias* 193 (1991): 523–543.

————. *Los movimientos migratorios entre Castilla e Hispanoamérica durante el reinado de Felipe III (1598–1621)*. Amsterdam: Rodopi, 1995.

Jenkins, K. *Why History? Ethics and Postmodernity*. London: Routledge, 1999.

Johnson, L. L., and S. Lipsett-Rivera, eds. *The Faces of Honor: Sex, Shame, and Violence in Colonial Latin America*. Albuquerque: University of New Mexico Press, 1998.

Jordan, M. *The Invention of Sodomy in Christian Theology*. Chicago: University of Chicago Press, 1997.

Kagan, R., and G. Parker, eds. *Spain, Europe, and the Atlantic World: Essays in Honour of John H. Elliott*. Cambridge: Cambridge University Press, 1995.

Kagan, R. L. *Inquisitorial Inquiries: The Brief Lives of Secret Jews and Other Heretics*. Forthcoming.

————. *Lucrecia's Dreams: Politics and Prophecy in Sixteenth-Century Spain*. Berkeley and Los Angeles: University of California Press, 1990.

Kamen, H. *Spain: A Society of Conflict (1469–1714)*. New York: Longman, 1983.

Kamer, H. N. *Het VOC Retourschip: een panorama van de 17de- en 18de-eeuwe Nederlandse Scheepsbouw*. Amsterdam: De Bataafsche Leeuw, 1995.

Keen, M. *Chivalry*. New Haven, Conn.: Yale University Press, 1984.

Kellogg, S. *Law and the Transformation of Aztec Culture (1500–1700)*. Norman: University of Oklahoma Press, 1995.

Kimball, G. "Aztec Homosexuality: The Textual Evidence." *Journal of Homosexuality* 26.1 (1993): 7–24.

Klor de Alva, J. J., H. B. Nicholson, and E. Quiñones Keber, eds. *The Works of Bernardino de Sahagún: Pioneer Ethnographer of Sixteenth-Century Aztec Mexico*. Austin: University of Texas Press, 1988.

Kramer, L. "Historical Narratives and the Meaning of Nationalism." *Journal of the History of Ideas* 58.3 (July 1997): 525–545.

Kulick, D. *Travesti: Sex, Gender, and Culture among Brazilian Transgendered Prostitutes.* Chicago: University of Chicago Press, 1998.

Kuznesof, E. A. "Ethnic and Gender Influences on 'Spanish' Creole Society in Colonial Spanish America." *Colonial Latin American Review* 4.1 (1995): 153–175.

Lacarra, M. E. "La evolución de la prostitución en la Castilla del siglo XV y la mancebía de Salamanca en tiempos de Fernando de Rojas." In *Fernando de Rojas and "Celestina": Approaching the Fifth Centenary*, ed. I. A. Corfis and J. T. Snow, 33–58. Madison, Wisc.: Hispanic Seminary of Medieval Studies, 1993.

———. "Parámetros de la representación de la sexualidad femenina en la literatura medieval castellana." In *La mujer en la literatura hispánica de la Edad Media y el Siglo de Oro*, ed. R. Walthaus, 23–43. Amsterdam: Rodopi, 1993.

Ladero Quesada, M. A. *Andalucia en torno a 1492: estructuras, valores, sucesos.* Madrid: Editorial MAPFRE, 1992.

La Nef. *Musique pour Jeanne la Folle, Spain 1479–1555.* Troy, N.Y.: Dorian Discovery, 1995. Compact disc.

Laqueur, T. W. *Making Sex: Body and Gender from the Greeks to Freud.* Cambridge: Harvard University Press, 1990.

Lavrín, A. "Sexuality in Colonial Mexico." In *Sexuality and Marriage in Colonial Latin America*, ed. A. Lavrín, 47–95. Lincoln: University of Nebraska Press, 1989.

Lea, H. C. *A History of the Inquisition of Spain.* 4 vols. New York: Macmillan, 1906–1907.

Leiva, J., and N. Montoya. *La caña rota: la confesión de un confesor del siglo XVIII.* Berriozar, Spain: Editorial Azagaya, 1995.

Levey, S. *Lace: A History.* London: Victoria and Albert Museum, 1983.

Lipton, S. "*Tanquam effeminatum:* Pedro II of Aragon and the Gendering of Heresy in the Albigensian Crusade." In *Queer Iberia: Sexualities, Cultures, and Crossings from the Middle Ages to the Renaissance*, ed. J. Blackmore and G. S. Hutcheson, 107–129. Durham, N.C.: Duke University Press, 1999.

López Austin, A. *Cuerpo humano e ideología: las concepciones de los antiguos nahuas.* 2 vols. Mexico City: Universidad Nacional Autónoma de México, Instituto de Investigaciones Antropológicas, 1980.

———. *Historia vieja de la mierda.* Mexico City: Ediciones Toledo, 1988.

Lorenzo Pinar, F. J. *Beatas y mancebas.* Zamora, Spain: Semuret, 1995.

Lucena Salmoral, M. *America 1492: Portrait of a Continent Five Hundred Years Ago.* Milan: Anaya Editoriale, 1990.

Lucio Pérez, J. I. "Notas" and *Portarretrato Azul y Ocre 2/2.* Letter and painting to Garza Carvajal, 22 April 1999.

Lumsden, I. *Machos, Maricones, and Gays: Cuba and Homosexuality.* Philadelphia: Temple University Press, 1996.

Lynch, J. *Spain 1516–1598: From Nation to World Empire.* Oxford: Oxford University Press, 1991.

Lyotard, J. F. *Toward the Postmodern.* New York: Humanity Books, 1998.

MacKenzie, J. M. *Orientalism: History, Theory, and the Arts.* Manchester, U.K.: Manchester University Press, 1995.

Mak, G. "Opgehangen aan woorden: de tweeslachtige memoires van Herculine Barbin." *Lover* 2 (1995): 10–17.

Mantecón, T. A. "Meaning and Social Context of Crime in Preindustrial Times: Rural Society in the North of Spain, Seventeenth and Eighteenth Centuries." *Crime, History, and Society* 1.2 (1998): 49–73.

Marías, J. "My Fair Arzallus." *El País Semanal* (19 May 2002): 8.

Mas, A. *Les turcs dans la littérature espagnole du Siècle d'Or: recherches sur l'evolution d'un thème littéraire.* Paris: Centre de Recherches Hispaniques, Institut d'Etudes Hispanique, 1967.

Mason, P. "Reply to Trexler." *Anthropos* 94 (1999): 315.

———. "Sex and Conquest. A Redundant Copula?" *Anthropos* 92 (1997): 577–581.

McIntosh, M. "The Homosexual Role." *Social Problems* 16.2 (1968): 182–192.

Meer, T. van der. "The Prosecution of Sodomites in Eighteenth-Century Amsterdam: Changing Perceptions of Sodomy." In *The Pursuit of Sodomy: Male Homosexuality in Renaissance and Enlightenment Europe,* ed. K. Gerard and G. Hekma, 263–310. New York: Harrington Park Press, 1989.

———. *Sodoms zaad in Nederland: het ontstaan van homoseksualiteit in de vroegmoderne tijd.* Nijmegen, Netherlands: Sun, 1995.

———. "Sodomy and the Pursuit of a Third Sex in the Early Modern Period." In *Third Sex, Third Gender: Beyond Sexual Dimorphism in Culture and History,* ed. G. Herdt, 137–212. New York: Zone Books, 1994.

Melquiadez, A. "La teología en el siglo XVI (1470–1580): el ideal de hombre nuevo en nuestros místicos." In *Historia de la teología española: desde fines del siglo XVI hasta la actualidad,* vol. 1, ed. B. Parera, 693–695. Madrid: Fundación Universitaria Española, 1983.

Menéndez Pidal, R. *El padre las Casas, su doble personalidad.* Madrid: Espasa-Calpe, 1963.

Merrick, J., and B. Ragan, eds. *Homosexuality in Early Modern France: A Documentary Collection.* New York: Oxford University Press, 2001.

Merrick, J., and M. Sibalis, eds. *Homosexuality in French History and Culture.* New York: Haworth Press, 2002.

Mignolo, W. D. *The Darker Side of the Renaissance: Literacy, Territoriality, and Colonization.* Ann Arbor: University of Michigan Press, 1994.

Mirabet y Mullol, A. *Homosexualidad hoy: ¿aceptada o todavía condenada?* Barcelona: Herder, 1985.

Mirrer, L. "Representing 'Other' Men: Muslims, Jews, and Masculine Ideals in Medieval Castilian Epic and Ballad." In *Medieval Masculinities,* ed. C. Lees, 169–186. Minneapolis: University of Minnesota Press, 1994.

Mohanty, C. T. "Cartographies of Struggle." In *Third World Women and the Politics of Feminism,* ed. C. T. Mohanty, A. Russo, and L. Torres, 14–15. Bloomington: Indiana University Press, 1991.

———. "Under Western Eyes: Feminist Scholarship and Colonial Discourses." In *Colonial Discourse and Post-colonial Theory,* ed. P. Williams and L. Chrisman, 196–220. New York: Columbia University Press, 1994.

Molloy, S., and R. McKee Irwin (eds.) *Hispanisms and Homosexualities*. Durham, N.C.: Duke University Press, 1998.

Monick, E. *Phallos: Sacred Image of the Masculine*. Toronto: Inner City Books, 1987.

Monsiváis, C. *Amor perdido*. Mexico City: Biblioteca Era, 1978.

———. "Ortodoxia y heterodoxia en las alcobas." *Debate feminista* 6.11 (April 1995): 183–212.

Montejano, D. *Anglos and Mexicans in the Making of Texas (1836–1986)*. Austin: University of Texas Press, 1987.

Monter, E. W. "Sodomy: The Fateful Accident." In *History of Homosexuality in Europe and America*, vol. 5, ed. W. Dynes and S. Donaldson. New York: Garland, 1992. 276–299.

Moore-Gilbert, B. *Postcolonial Theory: Contexts, Practices, Politics*. London: Verso, 1997.

Moraga, C., and G. Anzaldúa, eds. *This Bridge Called My Back: Writings by Radical Women of Color*. Watertown, Mass.: Persephone Press, 1981.

Morales Padrón, F. *Historia de Sevilla: la ciudad del quinientos*. Sevilla: Editorial Universidad de Sevilla, 1983.

Mosse, G. L. *Nationalism and Sexuality: Middle-Class Morality and Sexual Norms in Modern Europe*. Madison: University of Wisconsin Press, 1985.

Mott, L. R. B. *Homossexuais da Bahia: dicionario biografico (secvlos XVI–XIX)*. Salvador: Editora Grupo Gay da Bahia, 1999.

———. *O sexo proibido: virgens, gays, e escravos nas garras da Inquisicao*. Campinas, Brazil: Papirus Editora, 1988.

Murray, S. O., ed. *Latin American Male Homosexualities*. Albuquerque: University of New Mexico Press, 1994.

———. *North American Homosexualities*. Forthcoming.

———. *Oceanic Homosexualities*. New York: Garland, 1992.

Murray, S. O., and W. Roscoe, eds. *Islamic Homosexualities*. New York: New York University Press, 1997.

Nandy, A. *Intimate Enemy: Loss and Recovery of Self under Colonialism*. New Delhi: Oxford University Press, 1983.

Naranjo, M. *Palabra de mujer*. Spain: Sony, 1997. Compact disc.

Nesvig, M. A. "The Complicated Terrain of Latin American Homosexuality." *Hispanic American Historical Review* 81.3–4 (August–November 2001): 689–729.

Nietzsche, F. W. *The Birth of Tragedy and Other Writings*. Ed. R. Geuss and ed./trans. R. Speirs. Cambridge: Cambridge University Press, 1999.

Nirenberg, D. *Communities of Violence: Persecution of Minorities in the Middle Ages*. Princeton, N.J.: Princeton University Press, 1996.

Noordam, D. J. "Sodomy in the Dutch Republic, 1600–1725." In *The Pursuit of Sodomy: Male Homosexuality in Renaissance and Enlightenment Europe*, ed. K. Gerard and G. Hekma, 207–228. New York: Harrington Park Press, 1989.

Noordegraaf, L. "Overmoed uit onbehagen." In *Ideeën en ideologieën: studies over economische en sociale geschiedschrijving in Nederland (1894–1991)*, ed. L. Noordegraaf, vol. 2, 665–688. Amsterdam: Amsterdamse Historische Reeks, 1991.

―――. "Tot lering en vermaak." In *Ideeën en ideologieën: studies over economische en sociale geschiedschrijving in Nederland (1894–1991),* ed. L. Noordegraaf, vol. 1, 11–14. Amsterdam: Amsterdamse Historische Reeks, 1991.

Novo, S. *Las locas, el sexo, y los burdeles.* Mexico City: Diana, 1979.

Núñez Roldán, F. *El pecado nefando del Obispo de Salamina; un hombre sin concierto en la corte de Felipe II.* Seville: Universidad de Sevilla, 2002.

O'Gorman, E. *La invención de América: el universalismo de la cultura de Occidente.* Mexico City: Fondo de Cultura Económica, 1958.

Olivier, G. "Conquérants et missionnaires face au 'péché abominable,' essai sur l'homosexualité en Mésoameriqué au moment de la conquête espagnole." *Cahiers du Monde Hispanique et Luso-Brésilen* 55 (1990): 19–51.

Ortega Noriega, S. "El discurso teológico de Santo Tomás de Aquino sobre el matrimonio, la familia, y los comportamientos sexuales." In *El placer de pecar y el afán de normar: ideologías y comportamiento familiares y sexuales en el México colonial,* ed. S. Alberro, 17–75. Mexico City: Planeta, 1986.

Ots Capdequí, J. M. *El estado español en las Indias.* Mexico City: Gráf. Panamericana, 1941.

Ouweneel, A. *De vergeten stemmen van Mexico: een reeks ontmoetingen in de acttiende eeuw.* Amsterdam: Amsterdam University Press, 1996.

―――. "Platgetreden paden: over het erfgoed van de Indianen." *Cuadernos del CEDLA* 4.6 (January 2000): 1–24.

―――. *Shadows over Anáhuac: An Ecological Interpretation of Crisis and Development in Central Mexico, 1730–1800.* Albuquerque: University of New Mexico Press, 1996.

Pagden, A. *Spanish Imperialism and the Political Imagination.* New Haven, Conn.: Yale University Press, 1990.

Pagden, A., and J. Lawrance, eds. *Political Writings: Francisco de Vitoria.* Cambridge: Cambridge University Press, 1991.

Parera, B. "La Escuela Tomista española en el siglo XVII." In *Historia de la teología española: desde fines del siglo XVI hasta la actualidad, vol. 1,* ed. B. Parera, 9–38. Madrid: Fundación Universitaria Española, 1983.

―――. "Los Inicios de la Escolástica Barroca." In *Historia de la teología cristiana: prereforma, reformas, contrareforma, vol. 2, ed.* B. Parera, 596–644. Barcelona: Herder, 1989.

Parker, A., M. Russo, D. Sommer, and P. Yaeger. Introduction to *Nationalisms and Sexualities,* ed. A. Parker, M. Russo, D. Sommer, and P. Yaeger, 1–18. New York: Routledge, 1992.

―――, eds. *Nationalisms and Sexualities.* New York: Routledge, 1992.

Parker, R. *Beneath the Equator: Cultures of Desire, Male Homosexuality, and Emerging Gay Communities in Brazil.* London: Routledge, 1999.

Penyak, M. L. "Criminal Sexuality in Central Mexico, 1750–1850." Ph.D. diss., University of Connecticut, Storrs, 1993.

Pérez Escohotado, J. *Sexo e inquisición en España: historia de la España sorprendente.* Madrid: Temas de Hoy, 1992.

Pérez-Mallaína, P. E. *Los Hombres del Océano.* Seville: Diputación Provincial de Sevilla, 1992.

————. *Spain's Men of the Sea: Daily Life on the Indies Fleets in the Sixteenth Century*, Trans. C. R. Phillips. Baltimore: Johns Hopkins University Press, 1998.

Perry, M. E. *Crime and Society in Early Modern Seville.* Hanover, N.H.: University Press of New England, 1989.

————. "From Convent to Battlefield." In *Queer Iberia: Sexualities, Cultures, and Crossings from the Middle Ages to the Renaissance*, ed. J. Blackmore and G. S. Hutcheson, 394–419. Durham, N.C.: Duke University Press, 1999.

————. *Gender and Disorder in Early Modern Seville.* Princeton, N.J.: Princeton University Press, 1990.

————. "The Manly Woman: A Historical Case Study." *American Behavioral Scientist* 31.1 (1987): 86–100.

Perry, M. E., and A. J. Cruz. *Cultural Encounters: The Impact of the Inquisition in Spain and the New World.* Berkeley and Los Angeles: University of California Press, 1991.

Phelan, J. L. *The Millennial Kingdom of the Franciscans in the New World.* Berkeley and Los Angeles: University of California Press, 1970.

Phillips, C. R. *Six Galleons for the King of Spain: Imperial Defense in the Early Seventeenth Century.* Baltimore: Johns Hopkins University Press, 1986.

Phillips, L. "Lost in Space: Siting/Citing the In-between of Homi Bhabha's *The Location of Culture.*" *Jouvert: A Journal of Postcolonial Studies* 2.2 (1998): 1–14. Available at http://152.1.96.5/jouvert/v2i2/confour.htm

Port, M. van de. *Gypsies, Wars, and Other Instances of the Wild: Civilisation and Its Discontents in a Serbian Town.* Amsterdam: Amsterdam University Press, 1998.

Prieur, A. *Mema's House, Mexico City: On Transvestites, Queens, and Machos.* Chicago: University of Chicago Press, 1998.

Pym, R. J. "The Subject in Spain's Seventeenth-Century Comedia." *Bulletin of Hispanic Studies* 75 (1998): 290–292.

Quesada, N. "Erotismo en la religión azteca." *Revista de la Universidad de México* 28.2 (1974): 6–19.

Quiroga, J. *Tropics of Desire: Interventions from Queer Latino America.* New York: New York University Press, 2000.

Radding, C. *Wandering Peoples: Colonialism, Ethnic Spaces, and Ecological Frontiers in Northwestern Mexico (1700–1850).* Durham, N.C.: Duke University Press, 1997.

Radhakrishnan, R. *Diasporic Mediations: Between Home and Location.* Minneapolis: University of Minnesota Press, 1996.

Reade, B. *Het Spaanse costuum.* Amsterdam: n.p., 1951.

Rediker, M. B. *Between the Devil and the Deep Blue Sea: Merchant Seamen, Pirates, and the Anglo-American Maritime World (1700–1750).* New York: Cambridge University Press, 1987.

————. "Liberty beneath the Jolly Roger: The Lives of Anne Bonny and Mary Read, Pirates." In *Iron Men, Wooden Women: Gender and Seafaring in the Atlantic*

World (1700–1920), ed. M. S. Creighton and L. Norling, 1–33. Baltimore: Johns Hopkins University Press, 1996.

Redondo, A., ed. *Amours légitimes et amours illégitimes en Espagne (XVIe–XVIIe siècles)*. Paris: Publications de la Sobornne Nouvelle, 1985.

———. *Relations entre hommes et femmes en Espagne aux XVIe et XVIIe siècles*. Paris: Publications de la Sorbonne Nouvelle, 1995.

Rey, M. "Police et sodomie a Paris au XVIIIe siècle: du péche au desordre." *Revue d'Histoire Moderne et Contemporaine* 29 (1982): 113–124.

Rhodes, E. "Skirting the Men: Gender Roles in Sixteenth-Century Pastoral Books." *Journal of Hispanic Philology* 11.2 (winter 1987): 131–149.

Richards, J. *Sex, Dissidence, and Damnation: Minority Groups in the Middle Ages*. London: Routledge, 1990.

Rodríguez, P. *La vida sexual del clero*. Barcelona: Ediciones B, 1995.

Roscoe, W., and S. O. Murray. Introduction to *Islamic Homosexualities*, ed. S. O. Murray and W. Roscoe, 1–13. New York: New York University Press, 1997.

Rosselló i Vaquer R., and J. Bover Pujol. *El sexe a Mallorca: notes historiques*. Palma de Mallorca: Miquel Font, 1992.

Rousseau, G. "No Sex Please, We're American: Erotophobia, Liberation, and Cultural History." *Arcadia: Zeitschrift für Allgemeine und Vergleichende Literatuurwissenschaft* 33 (1988): 12–45.

Rubin, G. "The Traffic in Women: Notes on the Political Economy of Sex." In *Toward an Anthropology of Women*, ed. R. R. Reiter, 157–210. New York: Monthly Review Press, 1976.

Rubio Vela, A. *Epistolari de la Valencia medieval*. Valencia: Institut Interuniversitari de Filologia, 1985.

———. *Peste negra, crisis, y comportamientos sociales en la España del siglo XIV: la ciudad de Valencia, 1348–1401*. Granada: Universidad Secretariado de Publicaciones, 1979.

Ruggiero, G. *The Boundaries of Eros: Sex, Crime, and Sexuality in Renaissance Venice*. New York: Oxford University Press, 1985.

Ruiz, T. F. *Spanish Society (1400–1600)*. Harlow, U.K.: Longman, 2001.

Sacher-Masoch, L. von. "Venus in Furs." In *Masochism*, comp. G. Deleuze, 143–293. New York: Zone Books, 1989.

Sahuquillo, A. *Federico García Lorca y la cultura de la homosexualidad: Lorca, Dali, Cernuda, Gil-Albert, Prados, y la voz silenciada del amor homosexual*. Stockholm: Romanska Institutionen, Stockholms Universitet, 1986.

Said, E. *Culture and Imperialism*. London: Chatto and Windus, 1993.

———. *Orientalism*. New York: Vintage Books, 1979.

Saint-Saëns, A., ed. *Religion, Body, and Gender in Early Modern Spain*. San Francisco: Mellen Research University Press, 1991.

———. *Sex and Love in Golden Age Spain*. New Orleans: University Press of the South, 1996.

Sánchez-Albornoz, C. *De la Andalucía islámica a la de hoy*. Madrid: RIALP Editorial, 1983.

Sánchez Ortega, M. H. "Costumbres y actitudes eróticas en la España de los Austrias." *Historia 16* 124 (1986): 48–58.

———. *La mujer y la sexualidad en el antiguo régimen: la perspectiva inquisitorial*. Torrejón de Ardoz, Spain: Akal, 1992.

Sangari, K., and S. Vaid, eds. *Recasting Women: Essays in Indian Colonial History*. New Brunswick, N.J.: Rutgers University Press, 1990.

Santiago, S. "The Post-Modern Narrator." In *The Space In-Between: Essays on Latin American Culture*, ed. A. L. Gazzola, 133–146. Durham, N.C.: Duke University Press, 2001.

———. "The Rhetoric of Verisimilitude." In *The Space In-Between: Essays on Latin American Culture*, ed. A. L. Gazzola, 64–78. Durham, N.C.: Duke University Press, 2001.

———. "Why and for What Purpose Does the European Travel?" In *The Space In-Between: Essays on Latin American Culture*, ed. A. L. Gazzola, 9–24. Durham, N.C.: Duke University Press, 2001.

Sarkar, T. "The Hindu Wife and the Hindu Nation: Domesticity and Nationalism in Nineteenth-Century Bengal." *Studies in History* 8.2 (1992): 219–220.

Sarrión Mora, A. *Sexualidad y confesión: la solicitación ante el Tribunal del Santo Oficio (siglos XVI–XIX)*. Madrid: Alianza Editorial, 1994.

Schafer, E. *El Consejo Real y Supremo de las Indias: su historia, organización, y labor administrativa hasta la terminación de la casa de Austria*. Seville: Imprenta M. Carmona, 1935.

Scholes, F. V., and E. B. Adams, eds. *Documentos para la historia del México colonial*. Mexico City: José Porrua e Hijos, 1955.

Schwartz, S. B., ed. *Victors and Vanquished: Spanish and Nahua Views of the Conquest of Mexico*. Boston: Bedford/St. Martin's, 2000.

Scott, J. W. "Gender: A Useful Category of Historical Analysis." *American Historical Review* 91 (1986): 1053–1075.

Sedgwick, E. K. *Epistemology of the Closet*. New York: Harvester Wheatsheaf, 1991.

———. "Nationalisms and Sexualities in the Age of Wilde." In *Nationalisms and Sexualities*, ed. A. Parker, M. Russo, D. Sommer, and P. Yaeger, 235–245. New York: Routledge, 1992.

Seed, P. "Social Dimensions of Race: Mexico City (1753)." *Hispanic American Historical Review* 62.4 (1982): 569–606.

———. *To Love, Honor, and Obey in Colonial Mexico: Conflicts over Marriage Choice (1574–1821)*. Stanford, Calif.: Stanford University Press, 1988.

Seth, S., L. Gandhi, and M. Dutton. "Postcolonial Studies: A Beginning. . . ," *Postcolonial Studies* 1.1 (1998): 7–11.

Siegel, R. "La autobiografía colonial: un intento de teorización y un estudio de escritos autobiográficos femeninos Novohispanos." Ph.D. diss., University of Texas at Austin, 1997.

Sigal, P. H. *From Moon Goddesses to Virgins: The Colonization of Yucatecan Maya Sexual Desire.* Austin: University of Texas Press, 2000.

———. *Infamous Desire.* Chicago: University of Chicago Press, 2003.

Silverblatt, I. M. *Moon, Sun, and Witches: Gender Ideologies and Class in Inca and Colonial Peru.* Princeton, N.J.: Princeton University Press, 1987.

Sinha, M. *Colonial Masculinity: The "Manly Englishman" and the "Effeminate Bengali" in the Late Nineteenth Century.* Manchester, U.K.: Manchester University Press, 1995.

Socolow, S. M. *The Women of Colonial Latin America: New Approaches to the Americas.* Cambridge: Cambridge University Press, 2000.

Spivak, G. C. "Can the Subaltern Speak?" In *Colonial Discourse and Post-colonial Theory,* ed. P. Williams and L. Chrisman, 66–111. New York: Columbia University Press, 1994.

———. "Can the Subaltern Speak?" In *Marxism and the Interpretation of Culture,* ed. C. Nelson and L. Grossberg, 271–313. London: Macmillan Education, 1988.

———. "Criticism, Feminism, and the Institution." In *The Post-Colonial Critic: Interviews, Strategies, Dialogues,* ed. S. Harasym, 17–58. New York: Routledge, 1990.

———. "A Literary Representation of the Subaltern: A Woman's Text from the Third World." In *In Other Worlds: Essays in Cultural Politics,* ed. G. C. Spivak, 241–268. New York: Routledge, 1988.

———. "Reading the Satanic Verses." *Public Culture* 2.1 (1989): 94.

Spurling, G. "Honor, Sexuality, and the Colonial Church." In *The Faces of Honor: Sex, Shame, and Violence in Colonial Latin America,* ed. L. L. Johnson and S. Lipsett-Rivera, 45–67. Albuquerque: University of New Mexico Press, 1998.

Stepto, M., and G. Stepto, trans. *Lieutenant Nun: Memoir of a Basque Transvestite in the New World/Catalina de Erauso.* Boston: Beacon Press, 1996.

Stern, S. J. *The Secret History of Gender: Women, Men, and Power in Late Colonial Mexico.* Chapel Hill: University of North Carolina Press, 1995.

Stewart, A. *Close Readers: Humanism and Sodomy in Early Modern England.* Princeton, N.J.: Princeton University Press, 1997.

Stoler, A. L. "Carnal Knowledge and Imperial Power: Gender, Race, and Morality in Colonial Asia." In *The Gender/Sexuality Reader: Culture, History, Political Economy,* ed. R. N. Lancaster and M. Di Leonardo, 13–36. New York: Routledge, 1997.

———. *Carnal Knowledge and Imperial Power: Race and the Intimate in Colonial Rule.* Berkeley and Los Angeles: University of California Press, 2002.

———. "Making Empire Respectable: The Politics of Race and Sexuality in Twentieth Century Colonial Cultures." *American Ethnologist* 16.4 (1989): 634–660.

———. "Rethinking Colonial Categories: European Communities and the Boundaries of Rule." *Comparative Studies in Society and History* 31.1 (1989): 134–201.

Tarragó, R. E. *The Pageant of Ibero-American Civilization: An Introduction to Its Cultural History.* New York: University Press of America, 1995.

Taylor, C. L. "Legends, Syncretism, and Continuing Echoes of Homosexuality from

Pre-Columbian and Colonial México." In *Latin American Male Homosexualities*, ed. S. O. Murray, 80–89. Albuquerque: University of New Mexico Press, 1995.

Taylor, W. B. *Drinking, Homicide, and Rebellion in Colonial Mexican Villages.* Stanford, Calif.: Stanford University Press, 1979.

———. *Magistrates of the Sacred: Priests and Parishioners in Eighteenth-Century Mexico.* Stanford, Calif.: Stanford University Press, 1996.

Temprano, E. *El árbol de las pasiones: deseo, pecado, y vidas repetidas.* Barcelona: Ariel, 1994.

Todorov, T. *La conquista de América: el problema del otro.* Trans. F. B. Burla. Mexico City: Siglo Veintiuno Editores, 1987.

Tomás y Valiente, F. "El crimen y pecado contra natura." In *Sexo barroco y otras transgresiones premodernas*, ed. F. Tomás y Valiente, B. Clavero, A. M. Hespanha, J. L. Bermejo, E. Gacto, and C. Alvarez Alonso, 33–56. Madrid: Alianza Editorial, 1990.

———. "Delincuentes y pecadores." In *Sexo barroco y otras transgresiones premodernas*, ed. F. Tomás y Valiente, B. Clavero, A. M. Hespanha, J. L. Bermejo, E. Gacto, and C. Alvarez Alonso, 11–31. Madrid: Alianza Editorial, 1990.

———. *El Derecho penal de la monarquía absoluta (siglos XVI, XVII, XVIII).* Madrid: Tecnos, 1992.

———. *Manual de Historia del Derecho español.* Madrid: Tecnos, 1995.

———. *La tortura en España: estudios históricos.* Barcelona: Ariel, 1973.

Tomizza, F. *Heavenly Supper: The Story of Maria Janis.* Trans. A. J. Schutte. Chicago: University of Chicago Press, 1991.

Toribio Medina, J. *Historia del Tribunal del Santo Oficio de la Inquisición en México.* Mexico City: Ediciones Fuente Cultural, 1952.

Torrente Ballester, G. *Filomeno, a mi pesar: memorias de un senorito descolocado.* Barcelona: Planeta, 1988.

Tovar de Teresa, G. *Pegaso o el mundo barroco novohispano en el siglo XVII.* Mexico City: Editorial Vuelta, 1993.

Traslosheros H., J. E. "Los motivos de una monja: Sor Feliciana de San Francisco, Valladolid de Michoacán (1632–1655)." *Historia Mexicana* 67.4 (1998): 735–763.

Traub, V. *The Renaissance of Lesbianism in Early Modern England.* Cambridge: Cambridge University Press, 2002.

Trexler, R. C. "Rejoinder to Mason." *Anthropos* 93 (1998): 655–656.

———. "Rejoinder to Mason." *Anthropos* 94 (1999): 315–316.

———. *Sex and Conquest: Gendered Violence, Political Order, and the European Conquest of the Americas.* Cambridge, U.K.: Polity Press, 1995.

Trumbach, R. "Gender and the Homosexual Role in Modern Western Culture: The Eighteenth and Nineteenth Centuries Compared." In *Homosexuality, Which Homosexuality?* ed. D. Altman, C. Vance, M. Vicinus, and J. Weeks, 151–153. Amsterdam: Uitgeverij An Dekker/Schorer, 1989.

———. "London's Sapphists: From Three Sexes to Four Genders in the Making of Modern Culture." In *Third Sex, Third Gender: Beyond Sexual Dimorphism in Culture and History*, ed. G. Herdt, 111–136. New York: Zone Books, 1994.

———. "Sodomite Subcultures, Sodomitical Roles, and the Gender Revolution of the Eighteenth Century: The Recent Historiography." In *Unauthorized Sexual Behavior during the Enlightenment*, ed. R. P. Maccubbin, 114–117. *Eighteenth-Century Life* 9.3 (1985).

Turley, H. *Rum, Sodomy, and the Lash: Piracy, Sexuality, and Masculine Identity*. New York: New York University Press, 1999.

Turner, J. G., ed. *Sexuality and Gender in Early Modern Europe*. Cambridge: Cambridge University Press, 1993.

Twinam, A. *Public Lives, Private Secrets: Gender, Honor, Sexuality, and Illegitimacy in Colonial Spanish America*. Stanford, Calif.: Stanford University Press, 1999.

Vainfas, R. *Tropico dos pecados: moral, sexualidade, e Inquisicao no Brasil*. Rio de Janeiro: Editora Campus, 1989.

de Vallbona, R., ed. *Vida i sucesos de la Monja Alférez: autobiografía atribuida a Doña Catalina de Erauso*. Tempe: Arizona State University Press, 1992.

Vasvári, L. "The Semiotics of Phallic Agression and Anal Penetration as Male Agonistic Ritual in the *Libro de buen amor*." In *Queer Iberia: Sexualities, Cultures, and Crossings from the Middle Ages to the Renaissance*, ed. J. Blackmore and G. S. Hutcheson, 130–156. Durham, N.C.: Duke University Press, 1999.

Vázquez, F. *Mal menor: políticas y representaciones de la prostitución (siglos XVI–XIV)*. Cádiz: Universidad de Cádiz, 1998.

Vázquez García, F., and A. Moreno Mengíbar. *Sexo y razón: una genealogía de la moral sexual en España (siglos XVI–XX)*. Madrid: Ediciones Akal, 1997.

Velasco, S. *The Lieutenant Nun Transgenderism, Lesbian Desire, and Catalina de Erauso*. Austin: University of Texas Press, 2001.

Villegas López, S. "Santidad y exilio: la leyenda dorada de Michèle Roberts." In *Exilios femeninos*, ed. P. Cuder Domínguez, 235–244. Huelva, Spain: Universidad de Huelva Publicaciones, 2000.

Vincent, B., and R. Carrasco. "Amor y matrimonio entre los moriscos." In *Minorías y marginados en la España del siglo XVI*, ed. B. Vincent, 47–71. Granada: Diputación Provincial, 1987.

Viswanathan, G. "Raymond Williams and British Colonialism." *Yale Journal of Criticism* 4.2 (1991): 47–66.

Voekel, P. *Alone before God: The Religious Origins of Modernity in Mexico*. Durham, N.C.: Duke University Press, 2002.

———. "Scent and Sensibility: Pungency and Piety in the Making of the Gente Sensata, Mexico, 1640–1850." Ph.D. diss., University of Texas at Austin, 1997.

Wagenaar, W. A., P. J. van Koppen, and H. F. M. Crombag. *Anchored Narratives: The Psychology of Criminal Evidence*. Hertfordshire, U.K.: Harvester Wheatsheaf, 1993.

Weeks, J. "Against Nature." In *Homosexuality, Which Homosexuality?* ed. D. Altman,

C. Vance, M. Vicinus, and J. Weeks, 199–213. Amsterdam: Uitgeverij An Dekker/Schorer, 1989.

————. *Against Nature: Essays on History, Sexuality, and Identity.* London: Rivers Oram, 1991.

————. *Sex, Politics, and Society: The Regulation of Sexuality since 1800.* London: Longman, 1981.

Weismantel, M. *Cholas and Pishtacos: Stories of Race and Sex in the Andes.* Chicago: University of Chicago Press, 2001.

Weissberger, B. "¡A tierra, puto! Alfonso de Palencia's Discourse of Effeminacy." In *Queer Iberia: Sexualities, Cultures, and Crossings from the Middle Ages to the Renaissance,* ed. J. Blackmore and G. S. Hutcheson, 291–319. Durham, N.C.: Duke University Press, 1999.

White, H. "Historical Emplotment and the Problem of Truth." In *The Postmodern History Reader,* ed. K. Jenkins, 392–396. London: Routledge, 1990.

————. *Tropics of Discourse.* Baltimore: Johns Hopkins University Press, 1978.

Whitehead, S. M. *Men and Masculinities: Key Themes and New Directions.* Cambridge, U.K.: Polity, 2002.

Zavala, I., ed. *Discursos sobre la "invención" de América.* Amsterdam: Rodopi, 1992.

Zavala, S. A. *La filosofía política en la conquista de América.* Mexico City: Fondo de Cultura Económica, 1947.

INDEX

Printed and bound by CPI Group (UK) Ltd, Croydon, CR0 4YY

09/06/2025

14685839-0004